COMMUNICATION RESEARCH

McGraw-Hill Series in Mass Communication

CONSULTING EDITOR

Alan Wurtzel

Anderson: Communication Research: Issues and Methods
Dordick: Understanding Modern Telecommunications
Gamble and Gamble: Introducing Mass Communication
Sherman: Telecommunications Management: The Broadcast and Cable Industries
Wurtzel: Television Production

COMMUNICATION RESEARCH

ISSUES AND METHODS

JAMES A. ANDERSON

University of Utah

McGraw-Hill Publishing Company

New York   St. Louis   San Francisco   Auckland   Bogotá   Caracas
Hamburg   Lisbon   London   Madrid   Mexico   Milan
Montreal   New Delhi   Oklahoma City   Paris   San Juan
São Paulo   Singapore   Sydney   Tokyo   Toronto

**First to Carol
and then to Sam**

This book was set in Times Roman by Black Dot, Inc. (ECU).
The editor was Barbara Raab;
the production supervisors were Denise L. Puryear and Marietta
Breitwieser; the cover was designed by Joseph Gillians.
Project supervision was done by The Total Book.
R. R. Donnelley & Sons Company was printer and binder.

COMMUNICATION RESEARCH

Issues and Methods

3 4 5 6 7 8 9 0   DOCDOC   9 7 6 5 4 3 2 1 0

ISBN 0-07-001651-8

Library of Congress Cataloging-in-Publication Data

Anderson, James A. (James Arthur), 1939-
   Communication research.

   Includes bibliographical references and index.
   1. Communication—Methodology. 2. Communication—Research. I. Title.
P91.A54 1987   001.51'072   86-10490
ISBN 0-07-001651-8

CONTENTS

PREFACE

No single text can present even an introduction to all there is to know concerning the rational justifications and conventional practices of research. The best we can hope to accomplish is a working overview. This book is designed to get you started in a multilevel approach to learning the discipline of science as practiced within the field of communication.

All research texts have to deal with the balance between reasons and methods. This book tips the scale toward the reasons that justify the methods that we use. In considering these reasons, I have not been reluctant to consider both the logical and the ideological. In this text, research is not a sacred activity; it is everyday work with its own anomalies and contradictions which in no way diminish it.

Had this book been written 10, even 5 years ago, it would have been remarkably different. In that time, we have moved to a radically new understanding of research in the human sciences. We have moved from a single majority to revolutionary debate to more open dialogue about the appropriate ideology, functions, and methods of the human sciences. To present the import of that dialogue, I have taken a pragmatic approach based on what we actually do and the way we actually argue rather than a reconstructed approach which would present an idealized form of practice. As you might suspect, this manner of presentation is inherently controversial. In fact, it dwells on the controversies of the field and limits the space given to recipes. Consequently this text will read differently from the typical textbook. You will not find answers to the controversies raised—no presentation of competing positions should be read as such; they must be resolved by each of us. The text is designed to force you to make choices before you take action.

Throughout this text, I have limited myself to a discussion of the research methods of *empirical science*. I do not privilege science, but I do distinguish it from other forms of inquiry. Science cannot accomplish the scholarship of critical theory or social commentary, but neither of them can accomplish the scholarship of science. Empirical science itself is composed of many communities. This text focuses on two central locations of quantitative and qualitative research. There are many variants of both of these which will have to await your advanced study.

Advice to the Reader

I have organized this book into three major sections and an epilogue. The first section (1) establishes the distinguishing characteristics of the practice of empirical science, (2) considers that practice within the discipline of communication, and (3) examines the underlying, enabling beliefs which direct its performance. The second section examines quantitative research starting with an overview and then moves through the topics of measurement, sampling, and analysis. The third section parallels the second but for qualitative research, studying issues of design and strategies of execution. It also includes the epilogue, which harvests the comments on ethics, on unity of perspectives, and on the future of research in communication, which were sown through the preceding chapters. In this gathering place, we try to examine the sum of these issues.

Throughout this text I have followed the old public speaking rubric of "Tell them what you're going to tell them; tell them; and then tell them what you told them." Each chapter begins with a summarizing overview to give an idea of the ground to be covered. Each major section in a chapter ends with an analytic summary which both reviews what was presented and draws specific conclusions about its import. And finally, each chapter ends with a summary of the whole. The chapter overviews, and section and chapter summaries provide a good review of the content.

Each major section of every chapter is followed by exercise questions. The questions are designed to help the reader engage the content in some furthering use. That is, the questions are generally not review questions but problems which require applications of what has been learned, which explore the significance of practices in the field, or which call for the reader to take a position on some issue. They have shown good success when used as discussion items. I certainly recommend that readers test their understanding of the content by working through an answer or two for each set.

A Cautionary Note

This text may present some difficulties for the beginning student. First, because it presents complex issues and not simple answers, and second because it is written on a professional level—that is, I assume some prior contact with both a body of theory in communication and with some research literature based on that theory. Although I have provided extended examples with the text, if you are that novice I would make two suggestions: The best, I think, is to plan some parallel reading in the literature. A readily available source that provides a broad view (but not without its limitations) is the multivolume *Communication Yearbook*. Supplement that with readings of your choice from such journals as *Journalism Quarterly, Critical Studies in Mass Communication, Human Communication Research,* and *Journal of Communication*. The importance of this reading is to get a sense of the activity—not to master it. A lesser solution is to read through Chapters 4 and 9 before tackling Chapter 3. In general, the novice can expect that a better understanding of the first section will emerge as the rest of the book is worked through. Be patient; one needs both the background of the first section and the specific practices presented in the other two sections to achieve a full understanding.

Finally, the reader should be aware that science is a practice—not a scripture. Science is what those of us who claim to be and are accepted as scientists do. When one captures its activities in a text such as this, one provides a snapshot of part of the action with a perspective fixed in time.

A Word of Thanks

Whatever its limitations, this text has benefited greatly from many who have shared their time and talents. First, my thanks go to those colleagues—academic, industrial, and consultant scientists—who participated in the extensive interviews that permitted the pragmatic approach of this text. Those interviews took over a year to complete. They are a treasured resource. Next, to my reviewers whose patient efforts saved me from more than one error; in particular to, Susan Tyler Eastman, Michael Pacanowsky, Mary S. Strine, Angela Anderson Brown, Mary Anne Fitzpatrick, Timothy P. Meyer, Bryon Reeves, Randall Stutman, Stuart Surlin, University of Windsor; Paul J. Traudt, Ellen Wartella, and Alan Wurtzel. Finally, The Department of Communication at Utah offers a unique environment to a writer. The staff is not only competent; it is helpful. My colleagues represent a mastery of the field which they unselfishly share. I learn from them everyday.

James A. Anderson

COMMUNICATION RESEARCH

SECTION **ONE**

THE SCIENTIFIC STUDY OF COMMUNICATION

It should be an interesting book, if these are the kinds of things you are going to be dealing with. These are the things that are said only to spouses and colleagues in the privacy of the home or behind office doors.[1]

The human mind has found a number of ways to come to understand itself and the world. The creative arts, analytical criticism, and empirical science, among others, are routes to understanding available to each of us. We are concerned with the route provided by empirical science. Science as a set of epistemological methods—methods for generating human knowledge—has certain characteristics which distinguish it, regardless of the subject matter of its application. Science also has particular characteristics which appear as it is practiced within a discipline. In this section of three chapters we will consider, first of all, the characteristics of science and scientists; then, the field of communication as a context for the practice of science; and finally, the practice of the scientific study of communication.

---

[1]Headline quotations and the character sketches that follow are from respondents to a survey conducted by the author of established communication scientists from academia and business. No respondent requested anonymity; the unattributed use of the quotations was a decision by the author. The quotations are intended to give the reader a feel for the humanity of research in communication, not to espouse the opinions expressed (even if they are true as in this case).

1

SCIENCE AND SCIENTISTS

SCIENCE

The nature of science is not determinate, fixed in time for all cultures. It is, rather, a practice that shows regular and sometimes spectacular change. The popular image of science is that of European, Galilean science with its emphasis on material experimentalism in search of universal, physical laws. Nevertheless, there is much more which claims to be science, even within our own field of communication.

This rumination about science will not attempt a formalist, reconstructed definition of science. Such is the province of the philosophers of science. Instead, it will comment on those characteristics which are empirically evidenced in its performance.

Characteristics of Science

Science is a human enterprise conducted within a community of practitioners; its goal is to make sense out of human experience within authoritative, empirically grounded explanation to serve some human purpose (adapted from Leahey, 1980). We will consider each of these characteristics in its turn:

A Human Enterprise   That science is a human enterprise means that it is open to the processes and influences that beset any human activity. Science is an element of the larger social community. It is part of the social world that it studies. It is moored in space and time. As with all elements it is defined by and in turn helps define the culture in which it appears. It is political, defending its

3

CHARACTER SKETCH: THE DOUBTING SCIENTIST

You asked me if I got caught up in the scholarly life in graduate school. I don't think so. Maybe I did and don't know it. But I remember then—and I still have these thoughts— thinking, "What are these people saying?" Even today we have guest lecturers come to visit us and everybody is sitting around with furrowed brows and thinking "Oh, this is heavy stuff." And I'm sitting there thinking "I don't know what the hell is happening but I can't show it. I have to act like I'm really interested in this stuff." Well, I fake it a lot less now, but I still think the same things. I'm an academic in the sense that I like the search for new things. I like to find out things I didn't know. I'm always curious. But I'm not the kind of person who sits back in the office and muses about the state of cognition in the universe. I'm much more likely to redefine the problem into something I can get my hands on and proceed from there. I guess I do have those thoughts about the universe, but I have them in the dark hours. I don't have them at work.

The goal of science? You mean aside from the textbook explanations about prediction and explanation and all? Well, one thing it does, it gives you something to do. Although that's funny from a philosophical standpoint, I don't want to be perceived as facetious. In the bigger view of things, science is just one more activity that human beings do. That's not to say that I don't make value judgments about the fact that I don't want to be a street sweeper or something like that. But I do think that both the street sweeper and the scientist have something in common. They put in their time for a particular goal. That's nothing to be sneezed at.

By now in this interview you've expanded my mind to the point where I can't give you a full-pitched answer because too many things are running through my mind. I don't know how this is going to come out but, science should provide people at a given point in historical time with an adequate, usable, understandable interpretation of reality. I sure don't believe that it can or does provide any kind of lasting truths although some of it persists. It provides a view that is compatible with certain people at a certain time. Just look at what used to be "true" in our own field. I think that it is a job in which you try as hard as you can to help people understand things and to bring usable knowledge to people. On the other hand, you shouldn't have any illusions that somehow or another you're not just as much on a treadmill as everybody else. You're not special.

rights and privileges, repulsing criticism, managing demands, seeking influence, being influenced, competing for finite resources, and winning and losing.

Conducted within a Community of Practitioners   The practice of science is institutionalized within a community of individuals who both aspire to membership and are recognized as members. The **scientific community** functions in the same manner as any community. It has its membership requirements, its hierarchy, its codes of conduct, its encultured truths.

It is not science unless done by a scientist, and one is not a scientist unless recognized as such. As a rule, science refuses standing to those who are not members. It will not accept as legitimate the claims and arguments of these non-members.

The community establishes the criteria of success and bestows recognition on those that meet them. It confers status and power in hierarchical rankings both between disciplines and within a discipline. Some scientists are certainly more equal than others.[2]

The community serves as a repository of the conventional wisdom of science—what it is, how it is to be practiced, what its truths are. It is this community which specifies the acceptable methods that we should use as scientists. These norms are enforced in the myriad of everyday decisions within the community: What research is deserving of support; what findings will have a public presentation; what individuals will be recognized. That the methods of science are validated by the scientific community means that they are subject to the same processes of negotiation as any community norm. They are subject to change, rejection, revival.

The scientific community also has its anomalies and contradictions. For example, the community espouses a doctrine of mutual support, but its members are often intensely competitive.

There is growing evidence that the scientific community is no longer singular (if it ever was). There may be, in fact, several communities which lay claim to the title of science. Perhaps the most important, for our purposes, is the claim that there are separate communities for the **physical** and **human sciences**.

The significance of the separation is substantial. If separate, the members of the human sciences would no longer need to look to the norms of the physical sciences to legitimize their research practices. The human sciences would no longer be bound by the same systems of logic, need use the same methods nor accept the same "facts" as evidence.

The basis for the claim of separate communities is the argument that the requirements for a scientific explanation are different within the physical and human sciences. The human sciences must explain not only the characteristics and acts of the individual but also the meaning that those characteristics and acts have for the individual. In short, the human sciences must take account of the facts that human beings interpret both themselves and the science which intends to explain them; stones don't do that (at least, not in a manner that we recognize). The argument for separate communities is long from over, but it has its effect. For some it is heresy, for others reformation.

Making Sense of Human Experience The epistemological underpinnings of modern science reject the notion that what we experience is directly understandable. Sensations are considered chaotic until we learn to interpret them as things, events, actions. The purpose of science is to provide a perspective of right interpretations—the right stuff, if you will, of **sense-making**.

---

[2]The hierarchy of the physical sciences usually begins with physics and moves through to the biological. The human sciences are less clearly structured with psychology or sociology vying for the top spot. (Of course, we know that it's all communication.)

The main community of science makes sense of the world in three forms of **explanation: prediction, control,** and **understanding.** Prediction is the least complex of the three. Prediction is a type of explanation in which one set of observables is associated with another set in some time frame. Prediction as a form of explanation is well-known. A simple example would read: When X appears, Y will follow.

Prediction requires the careful description of the conditions surrounding the appearance of a **phenomenon.** When there are **regularities** in those conditions, then prediction is possible. Prediction requires no understanding of the mechanisms by which something occurs. It requires only the regular occurrence of an **index** of another phenomenon's appearance.

For example, I can quite competently predict the level of traffic on the thoroughfares by my watch. I know that traffic on the roads that I travel will be at its peak between 7 and 8 in the morning and again between 4:30 and 5:30 in the afternoon. While this knowledge of a predictable characteristic of traffic is very useful, it contains no understanding of how the increase occurs nor of the mechanisms which can control the increase. In short, I can predict the traffic level, but I cannot tell you how or why it occurs.

Explanation that leads to control, on the other hand, requires knowledge of the mechanism which connects some **antecedent condition** and its **consequent.** Adjusting the time on my watch will not change the level of traffic. The time of day as shown on my watch is not part of the mechanism which regulates the level of traffic flow. While my watch is a reliable indicator of traffic flow, it is neither necessary nor sufficient for the traffic flow to occur. On the other hand, one may claim that the institutionalization of the work day is part of that mechanism. Consequently explanations which would seek to control that traffic would involve those forces which define the "9 to 5" pattern of work.

Control as an explanation makes two assumptions about the world not required for prediction. Control assumes that the relationship between an index of a future state and that predicted state is not happenstance but is the result of a causal chain. There is, indeed, an observable connection between the two. It also assumes that that connection can be manipulated and, therefore, the outcome controlled. These assumptions are seen as describing a material unity of reality and the ultimate power of human knowledge.

The level of explanation called understanding details the underlying structures and mechanisms in which the phenomena appear. These structures and mechanisms are conceptual not **empirical.** They interpret the observable phenomena as *meaningful* occurrences. If you will allow me the use of a cultural notion, they tell the story of the phenomena.

Understanding does not necessarily imply prediction or control. We can posit an understanding of phenomena which have appeared in the past (the extinction of the dinosaurs) or will appear in the distant future and are, therefore, not predictable. We can understand a system of causes and consequences without the ability to manipulate them to achieve control.

For some interpreters of science, these purposes are ordered with understanding being at the highest level of scientific explanation and prediction the lowest. Others would reject understanding as a scientific explanation. They would claim that understanding has a tenuous link with its empirical evidence and can rarely be validated. Explanations with demonstrable prediction and control, however, are firmly planted in their empirical evidence and are, therefore, often considered the particular purview of science.

Much of the practice of the human sciences rejects this strict **empiricist** position. Most of the scientific explanation that we read contains such unobservable concepts as consciousness, motivations, purposes. These concepts are used to construct an explanation which leads to an understanding of the connections among the phenomena observed.

The field of communication shows little integration within its explanatory discourse. Its statements about communication are fragmentary and are characterized by weak association and low levels of prediction. Control is absent. Understanding which is dependent on the synthesis of powerful observations is not yet possible. There is plenty of work to be done.

As a final comment, let me note that science is not the only human endeavor that attempts an interpretation of the world. Other forms of inquiry also seek to interpret the world we live in. Scientists sometimes fall into the doctrine of **scientism**, which holds that science is the only form of inquiry which in the long run will be successful. Scientism will be more fully discussed in a later section of this chapter.

Authoritative, Empirically Grounded Explanation   Scientific explanation is directed towards the description of the (a) **characteristics**, (b) **methods and practices**, and (c) **causes and consequences** of phenomena—what a thing is; how it functions; and why. These descriptions are the explanations of **ontology** (characteristics, what a thing is), **praxiology** (methods and practices, how it functions) and **epistemology** (its causes and consequences, the why of it). We will visit with each of these three and then consider the purposes for these descriptions.

Characteristics   In logic, **quantification theory** would hold that an entity is the sum of its characteristics. A characteristic, then, is a property of an individual or object—a trait, an **attribute**, or a quality. Thinking of people, a characteristic is something which identifies an individual as that individual. I like to think of it as a meaningful observation about an individual. It is a way that I identify and distinguish that individual person, thing, event, or process. It is an observation because it is something that I can see, hear, feel, etc., either directly or through instruments. It is meaningful because I make sense out of what is observed by giving it an identity as a characteristic. By ascribing the elements of a particular observation to the notion of a characteristic, I organize those elements into a meaningful unit.

For example, we might say that Joe has an authoritarian personality trait. We mean that Joe's behavior is observed as regular patterns (which may be responses to a personality inventory—an instrument to measure behavior) which

---

CHARACTER SKETCH: A CHANGE OF PERSPECTIVE

Well, I think I find myself with a growing affinity toward the interpretive methods in science. But I really can't quite please my dear friends who are ethnomethodologists. I get along with them very well and like them very much, but I can't abandon some of my quantitative training. We all laugh about it. They'll say, "You know you still have some of that deductive bias." And I'll say, "I know I just can't seem to get away from it." I think that I still prefer an extremely systematic method which may not lead to the kind of creative discoveries that I see with my ethnomethodological friends. On the other hand, I find that the traditional linear methods of input predicting output simply aren't useful in describing what actually goes on in group processes. When we look at negotiation sessions, we find that the process involves an interpretive creation of issues and positions. If you're not inside that process, you'd never see it.

---

can be made meaningful by ascribing them to the concept of authority. Joe's personality trait is a merger of his consistent behavior and our interpretation of it. Characteristics, then, are meaningful interpretations of observable regularities. And yes, even characteristics like height and weight are interpretations.[3]

The examination of characteristics takes many forms: Intelligence tests, personality inventories, attitude scales, measurements of aptitudes, skills, interests and surveys of most every kind are all part of the effort to describe the characteristics of phenomena. **Content analysis** investigates the attributes of what we read, watch and listen to. Mass media research which corresponds to the theory of **uses and gratifications** considers the characteristic purposes individuals have for attending the media and other activities. Finally, research which deals with characteristics makes a common appearance in the popular press. Public opinion polls, election surveys, readership studies, and broadcast ratings are all studies of characteristics.

Methods and Practices The description of methods and practices starts from the assumption that the way we have of doing things is also the way in which we make our material reality meaningful. These methods and practices are used to construct the social realities in which we live. The explanation given by methods and practices is the particular contribution of an intellectual tradition beginning with German **phenomenological sociology** and incorporating the lines of thought provided by **symbolic interactionism** and **ethnomethodology**.

The fact that we call what we scientists do **"the scientific method"** can be used as an example of this type of explanation. The scientific method is a collection of activities, held in common by the community of scientists, that validates the

---

[3]How is height an interpretation? (I will leave weight for you to answer in the exercises.) Height is the perpendicular distance between two parallel lines. In order to observe height, I must first understand the parallel lines. None of this implies that there isn't something out there to be interpreted, however.

explanation produced as scientific. Science, as we know it, is created in those methods. Understanding what scientists actually do helps us to understand the characteristics, and their sources, of scientific explanation.

To use another example, understanding the methods and practices which bind together the working organization of a newspaper helps us to understand what a newspaper is and why, because we become privy to the reality in which a newspaper gets produced. The study of methods and practices makes explicit the **reality constructs** under which the practitioners operate and take for granted. It is the description of these reality concepts that is the contribution contained in the study of methods and practices.

The explanatory responsibility for methods and practices, or **ethnological** studies as they are known, is a relatively recent addition to the enterprise of science. It represents a move away from a stance of **material determinism** which seeks to explain the causes of human behavior as nonthinking conditions and forces. Ethnological studies argue that much of an individual's response to our common material reality comes from cognitively held social realities.

Ethnological studies may appear to be unique to the human sciences, but they have found their place in the examination of animal and plant behavior also. The work of Jane Goodall with the social behavior of chimpanzees has been widely publicized. Ethnological studies are not accepted as scientific by all scientists either in the human or physical sciences. Such studies do represent, however, an increasing part of the activity of the scientific community.

Causes and Consequences   When a researcher begins to consider why something happens, that analyst is considering the causes and consequences of phenomena. Causes and consequences concentrate on the relationships between phenomena—how one phenomenon affects another. The description of causes and consequences is at the very heart of modern science. The true nature of the scientific revolution of the 1600s was not the invention of new knowledge, but the general acceptance by the scientific community of a new way of understanding the world. No longer were phenomena seen as the portents of a capricious intellect; they were now seen as elements within stable and predictable relationships—a unified material reality. So successful was this new understanding in directing the study of the physical world that it swept away the older forms of explanation.

The most powerful aspect of this new understanding was that the world around us was the result of observable, material conditions which were interrelated in causal connections. In one form or another, then, causal relationships represent the most common scientific **argument** advanced. Because of their importance, we will spend the next few pages considering them.

As it is traditionally formulated, a **cause** is an antecedent condition which results in a consequent condition. Causes have two characteristics, necessity and sufficiency. A cause is considered necessary if the antecedent condition must be present for the consequent to occur. A cause is sufficient if no other condition is needed for the consequent to occur. The quality of classical causal explanation is simple: Given A then B. But it is also unforgiving because necessity requires that there be no appearance of B without A, and sufficiency requires that B must appear given A. If there is deviation from these requirements, it indicates that the explanation offered is somehow in error.

Efforts in the human sciences to develop explanation which meets these requirements have generally been frustrated. There seem to be few circumstances in the performance of human behavior which meet these standards. Consequently, most explanation in the human sciences eschews the classical arguments of cause and makes use of statistical notions of association. In this form of explanation, antecedent conditions are associated with subsequent conditions according to some probability. That is, the appearance of A is related to the appearance of B in time (before, after, or cotemporaneously) with some degree of regularity. In this **stochastic** explanation, the relationship between A and B now reads: Given A, B is likely.

Stochastic explanations give up the burden of always having to be right. That is, causal explanations *require* the appearance of B in the presence of A for their validity; stochastic explanations permit B to be sometimes absent. Valid causal explanations are perfect predictors of B; stochastic explanations will have a given rate of error in predicting B.

While loosening the relationship between A and B, stochastic explanations, as they are typically constructed, do not abandon the idea of a controlling **dependency** between A and B (as compared with a simple predictive association —a common appearance in time). The character of this dependency can take a number of forms. The language which seems most near to causality describes the relationship as a pathway. E.g., phenomenon A leads to phenomenon B. Frustration leads to aggression; strategy X leads to compliance gaining; good information leads to good decisions. This relationship is called a **conditional relationship** because the appearance of B is considered conditional upon the appearance of A. That is, B is the result of A.

Claims of conditional relationships appear in any argument where one phenomenon is considered a consequent of another. These explanations are the modern day equivalent of classic causality and while B will not always follow from A, B is *unlikely* in the absence of A. Such claims are made when the researcher has a high degree of confidence in the strength of the relationship.

Other, less demanding, forms of dependency relationships appear in the research literature. Two common ones are **facilitation** and **indexing**. In a facilitation explanation, A facilitates the appearance of B. B is probable without A (which distinguishes this argument from a conditional relationship), but more readily appears with A. Facilitation implies some idea of efficiency or goodness of fit. It's easier to drive a nail with a hammer than a screwdriver though the job can be done with either. Good leadership facilitates group accomplishments.

Indexing is, perhaps, the weakest of the explicit dependency relationships. An index variable (phenomenon) is reliably associated with some other variable. The relationship is more than simple prediction because the index works within some theoretical system which links the two variables in a construct other than time. The presence of violence in the media as an index of the level of aggression in society is this sort of claim.

CHARACTER SKETCH: BECOMING A SCHOLAR

Oh, I think I was probably drifting through much of my undergraduate period. I didn't have a specific goal in mind, at that time. I was interested in foreign languages. My major was German. I spent a good bit of my time as an undergraduate doing intercollegiate debate. Debate was something I enjoyed doing. It led me to think a little bit about working in foreign service, but I ended up doing something completely different. Actually it was by accident that I got interested in what later became my career interests. I graduated from college in 1970. If you recall, that was the year of all of the bad college riots. My university was likewise affected. We had a serious riot problem, and toward the end of the year, we closed down about a month before classes were over. I had spent that whole year getting ready for the college national. I thought that when it was over I would devote the time to figuring my future. When the tournament was over, the school closed. I had no time at all to plan my future. Fortunately I got an unusual opportunity when a friend of mine who was working on a political campaign in Texas asked me if I would be interested in working on the campaign. The issues in the campaign were the same that we had debated. With no other plans, I accepted. I really enjoyed the work and became interested in political communication. As a result, I decided to go back to graduate school and work on a masters and Ph.D. in political communication. And that's the real life story.

Before leaving dependency relationships, it should be noted that prediction when considered an incomplete explanation is an argument for an implicit dependent relationship. Prediction as a form of explanation, presumably, contains no concept of dependency as the only link between variables is their closeness in time. But prediction can be used as an argument for a dependent relation when the success of the prediction is held to imply an underlying mechanism yet to be discovered.

The move to an argument of dependency from evidence of association is a bit tricky as the evidence for an association, as we shall see, is not the evidence for a dependent relationship. Evidentiary weakness does not prevent the claim, however, as such arguments as "smoking tends to cause cancer" or "violence on television leads to aggression" testify.[4]

The word "cause" has a special standing in the lexicon of science. Its classical form is often considered the ultimate in scientific explanation. All of science, however, makes use of probabilistic statements of cause not classical statements of cause. (Even the "laws" of physics have a rate of error.) Our understanding of cause, in the logic-in-use of actual scientific arguments, has been enlarged to see antecedent conditions as evocative, facilitative or indicative of a consequent. The explanatory power of "causal arguments," then, has to be considered according to the specific character of the relationship between the antecedent and the consequent.

---

[4]I do not suggest that either of these claims are false. Just that the evidence is of one sort and the argument of another.

In the absence of causal arguments, the idea of consequences becomes somewhat muddled because, in a strict sense, a consequence is the result of some cause. Nevertheless, in practice, a consequence is that which is dependent in some manner, predicted by, or simply follows what preceded. Therefore, consequences can be considered as the states, events, or conditions that are causally, dependently, or temporally related to some previous state, event, or condition. Only in a causal argument, however, is a consequence an effect. In the various forms of dependency arguments, a consequence is an **effect** or an **outcome**; in prediction and other time-based relationships, it is a **subsequent**. Whether in causation, dependency, or time, a consequence, like its antecedent condition, is an element of a relationship. An adequate description of that relationship informs us of the properties of the phenomena which are cause and consequence.

Empirically Grounded   Modern scientific explanation is empirically ground-ed. For some that means that scientific explanation is the simple description of phenomena and their regularities which are available for all to see. For others, including myself, it means that scientific explanation is an argument the claims of which are supported by empirical evidence.

The notions contained in the words **empiricism** and **empirical** have an interesting history. Empiricism is a belief that all human knowledge rests on sensory experience. The first empirics, a group of Greek physicians, were considered charlatans. In fact the definition of an empiric, given by dictionaries less than 30 years old, is of one "who is ignorant of scientific principles" (Webster's, 1960, p. 476). How have we come from those beliefs of empiricism as a false doctrine to the position that empirical evidence is the central evidence of science?

The movement begins in the fifteenth century when the purpose of Western thought began to shift from the celebration of God to the explanation of a material reality. By the end of the nineteenth century, science was deliberately godless, and the final principles of explanation rested on what we could see, hear, touch, smell, and taste. Philosophers of science reconstructed this practice into an empiricist doctrine which purported to approximate the true model of scientific reasoning.

But the strict empiricist foundation and its reconstruction in philosophy are no longer generally accepted because there is simply too much of what we claim as reality which cannot be directly, or even in moderate indirection, achieved through sensory experience.

Nevertheless, science remains empirical in that its justification is in the interpretation of the material reality in which we function. In short, science makes sense of what we see, hear, and touch even though its explanation may incorporate much beyond that. One aspect of my job as a communication scientist is to explain the material communication behaviors I observe. But I may well use metaphysical concepts such as socially held meanings which have no material reality to accomplish that explanation.

The empirical character of science makes it a public way of acquiring knowledge. Its object of study begins with events which are observable by any of us. Its arguments are based on evidence which must pass the test of **intersubjective agreement**. That is, the evidence must be reproducible by others. Its knowledge is egalitarian not based on personal revelation, intuition, authority, or beliefs. It is not, therefore, given to certain persons by virtue of some elite quality or position; it is a way of acquiring knowledge available to all.

The explanations that make up the body of scientific knowledge within a discipline, while often attributed to a single individual, are actually the product of a public process of review and acceptance. Both the scientific community and the society at large participate in this process. The benefit to both is an orderly growth of knowledge and the reduction of idiosyncratic error.[5]

With publication, a particular article has completed only a part of this process. While the text has passed the first level of review, its claims have yet to become part of science. That process requires community adoption as shown by citations in other works and the formulation of other research based on these claims. This process is not simply the "test of time" but is often seen as a process of distillation. In it, the particulars of time and place are slowly removed until what remains is the persistent contribution. Much of what we read is bound in the here and now. The reader in addressing any particular work needs to assess its place in the larger body of discourse. Much of what's published never makes it into that larger body.

Authoritative   The remaining characteristic of scientific explanation is that it is **authoritative**. Authoritative implies that there is a single explanation which will best accommodate a phenomenon. Multiple explanations for the same phenomena are simply not the hallmark of a mature understanding of those phenomena. Multiple explanations certainly exist, especially in the human sciences, but it is assumed that better inquiry will lead us to the best of the lot. The authoritative criterion of scientific explanation is in part derived from the logical traditions of scientific inquiry and its conceptualization as a discoverer of truth. Not all scientists hold to those traditions of Aristotelian logic nor see science as truth. Nevertheless, the practice of science is to hold multiple explanations of the same phenomena as competitive and not as either complementary or independent.

To Serve Some Human Purpose   The activity of science is not self-righteous, but must be done within a structure and in a manner and form which benefit the society of which it is a part. Science has to serve its societal purposes, and those purposes certainly affect the nature of science. These purposes direct the questions that are asked and imprint on the methods considered legitimate. An

---

[5]Those of us around in the 1960s when Marshall McLuhan exploded on the communication scene remember when this process was subverted by the media. The change in knowledge claims was neither orderly nor necessarily growth.

excellent example in our field has been the influence and power of government interests in directing the agenda of media effects research. Our current literature in this area is a legacy of past funding programs.[6]

In a more microanalysis, what the individual scientist pursues has to serve his or her purposes also. The moviedom vision of the altruistic scientist driven to arcane studies strips the scientist of his or her humanity. All of the motivations which function for others function for scientists, too. When the story of the great discovery is retold, it is not unusual to neglect all but the finest of motives. Most of science is not the great discovery. Being a scientist is everyday labor. It gets done for the same reasons as all labor.

EXERCISES

1 What is one major difference between a "crackpot" theory and a scientific theory?
2 How can science and art both be interpretations of life?
3 What happens to the characteristic of weight in space travel?
4 Sarah consistently drove 15 miles over the speed limit. As she swerved in and out of traffic, she muttered about the incompetence of the other drivers. "Can't even drive decently; always in my way." How do Sarah's driving practices create her reality of the incompetence of others?
5 The following set of questions explore the requirements of sufficiency and necessity in causal and conditional relationships:
   a How would we describe the relationship between A and B if, when A appears, B always follows, and B never appears without A?
   b How would we describe the relationship between A and B if, when A is present, B always follows, but B sometimes appears without A?
   c How would we describe the relationship between A and B if, when A appears, B sometimes follows, but B never appears without A?
   d How would we describe the relationship between A and B if, when A appears, B usually follows, and B rarely appears without A?
6 Thinking about what happens when you watch television, which, if any, of the previous four relationships describes the relationship between your viewing of violence on television and the appearance of aggressive behavior in you?·
7 Pre-Copernican astronomers could predict the sunrise with good accuracy, but their understanding of the occurrence was wrong. How is this an example of the independence between forms of explanation?
8 What must one be able to do in order to control phenomena?
9 What must one know about those phenomena in order to understand how the control works?
10 How is persuasion theory an example of a control type explanation?
11 What is the value, if any, of understanding without prediction or control?
12 What does it mean that a scientific explanation is essentially an argument supported by empirical evidence?
13 What is the importance of the history of a research claim?
14 How does society set the agenda for science?

---

[6]For an interesting discussion of this legacy, see Rowland's *The Politics of TV Violence* (1983).

SCIENTISM

Scientism is the doctrine of science as complete knowledge. It establishes a hierarchy of human endeavor with science at the top. The image of science embodied in scientism is usually Newtonian physics or some other reconstructed image of how science ought to be rather than how it is actually practiced. I object to scientism because it wrongly lessens the value of the contributions of other intellectual inquiry, can blind us to the obvious failings in scientific practice, and encourage a false sense of pride.

Scientism attributes to science other characteristics which are quite attractive but no less problematic. We will consider three: science as truth, science as progressive, and the ideology of a purifying method. In this consideration we will not resolve the problematic nature of the issues but rather touch on the main lines of the arguments.

Science as Truth

The position that the product of good science is truth derives from the search for the universal generalizations—the laws of nature—which describe the order of phenomena. The discovery of these generalizations is often considered the singular purpose of science. Obviously if science provides an adequate description of the underlying order of phenomena that description must be true. This position clearly assumes that there is an underlying order, that it is unitary, stable, and knowable and that it will, therefore, provide validation of the truth of scientific description.

Instrumentalism   There are, at least, two alternative positions which scientists take. They are called **instrumentalism** and **cultural relativism**. For instrumentalists, it is enough that the propositions of science work. That is, that they are good enough to permit us to get on with what it is that we humans wish to do. This position is more parsimonious than that of science as truth. It needs no assumption of an underlying order to validate the work of science. Science need not be true to some presumed reality but it must be useful. As new propositions are formed, old ones do not lose their truth value but simply their utility for some end.

Cultural Relativism   A more radical position is that the propositions of science are conventional. That is, they are part of the wisdom held by a culture at a particular point in time. The valid scientific propositions of one culture may be false in another. They may have no truth-value beyond being part of a conventional wisdom. And there is no necessity that they survive in future cultural stances.

COMMENTARY:

I have presented three choices in the conceptualization of the value of scientific explanation —scientism, instrumentalism, and cultural relativism. Are these just "head games" with no impact on methodology? Perhaps, but I think not. They certainly matter in the way scientists perceive themselves. For myself, the burden of truth is too much. Claiming that we carry it elevates science beyond what is ordinarily human. The truth myths and mythic heroes that we teach in our courses are precisely that—myths and mythic heroes. On the other hand, I am not willing to let go of an underlying material reality to the extent that cultural relativism appears to require.

Science as Progressive

George Gale in his text, *Theory of Science* (1979) writes:

> In our own times we are completely adjusted to the fact that scientific progress usually means change in our style of life. In fact, it is a commonplace view that the main role of science in society is to make human life richer and easier. (pp. 62–63)

It is certainly true that many of the products of scientific discoveries have made life easier for some. These applications, however, are not the consequence of science but of other societal institutions. Science itself would appear to have no basis for determining what is richer, easier, better. These are questions of value which are certainly addressed by scientists but not by science.

There is another sense in which science can be considered as progressive: The idea that over time our science becomes better. That is, our propositions are better approximations of reality, have greater utility, are less error prone. In the winnowing process of time we sort out the fruitful from the empty husks. Now that is a comforting idea.

COMMENTARY:

If you make science the benefactor of those improvements in the quality of life, you must also make it responsible for the degredations. The applications of science, in my lifetime, have increased the average lifespan by some twenty years and developed the capability of destroying the earth in an atomic flash.

The Ideology of Method

One of the consequences of scientism has been the transformation of method into ideology. For example, we often read of the scientific method as if there were a single method or set of methods which distinguished science. There are, of course, any number of methods which can be used by science to accomplish some purpose. The proof of the method is its utility in solving the problem. In the ordinary practice of science, however, certain methods become typical. These typical methods vary across disciplines and within disciplines as the questions pursued by the members vary. Clinical disciplines such as social work which approach questions of individual behavior, will use case study methods; sociology which focuses on aggregate behavior, however, will use survey methods. In a diverse field such as communication, one will find subdivisions which support several different methods.

Method becomes ideology when the community of the field of study (say, communication) determines that only certain questions are legitimate and only certain methods provide valid answers. Other questions and other methods are rejected at the ideological level—the level of belief and value. At that point it is the method which defines the work as scientific and not its explanatory content or its utility.

COMMENTARY:

Method becomes ideology because it is useful to control membership (you cannot be one of us unless you know our methods); to distinguish nonmembers (you cannot be one of us because you do not use our methods); and to distribute power and resources (you must use our methods to eat at our table).

__Methodological ideology__ is a characteristic of actual science (and is one reason why I doubt that science is necessarily progressive). It is an application of Kaplan's (1964) law of the hammer—given a hammer there are, suddenly, a lot of things that have to be hit. Nevertheless, the question of methods is not trivial. The right choice is a hallmark of good science. The right choice is made by matching the method with the question to be answered with the resources at hand. To debate method requires us to debate the nature of the question to be investigated and the utility of the answer which can be gained.

SCIENTISTS

The practice of science within a subject matter discipline forms a work community. The members of this community are the individuals who participate in the development of scientific explanation (the actual product of science) within the content area. The field of communication has its community of scientists. This section explores that community, investigating the roles of science and the people who fill them.

The Roles of Science

As we have seen, scientific explanation which promotes understanding, prediction, or control is a description of phenomena and their relationships. This explanation is based upon careful observation of our sensate world and the interpretation of those observations in the creative act of discovery. This two-step process gives rise to two major categories of research activity—that connected with the observations of phenomena and that connected with the discovery and description of relationships. Let me pause here to clarify this distinction.

The phrase, "He extended his hand in friendship," contains both an empirical element and an element of discovery. The empirical element is the extended hand. That is what I can see. The element of discovery is the act of friendship. Friendship cannot be seen; it is a conceptualization of a relationship. As a concept it has to be created. Someone has to be clever enough to recognize the relationship among the acts that can be seen. One more example: presume that you observed a driver stop at a red light. In fact every time this driver came to a traffic signal that was red in his direction he stopped. You might be tempted to conclude that the red light caused him to stop. But what did you see? You saw the red light and the action of the car stopping. You saw the antecedent condition (red light) and the consequent action (stopping) and in those observations you *discovered* the cause, but you didn't *observe* the cause. The relationship and its causal nature was something that you created as an explanation of why when the traffic light was red, the car stopped.

Now in this explanation, to bring us back to center of this section, there are two major activities—the observation of the traffic signals and the driver and the act of discovery of the relationship between them. Someone has to do both of these things for there to be scientific understanding of these phenomena and their relationship. It does not, however, have to be the same someone.

The Roles of Observation

The roles of observation are filled by those individuals that Mitroff and Kilmann (1982) would call analytical scientists. They are the surveyists, experimentalists, anthropological field observers, statisticians, and those concerned with instrumentation—the methods of observation. A surveyist makes observations of, usually, large groups of respondents, who are in otherwise ordinary settings, using some instrumentation such as a questionnaire. An experimentalist collects information (observations) from respondents in controlled or manipulated environments. A field worker records (orally, visually, and/or verbally) the actions of respondents in naturalistic settings. A statistician makes observations on fields of numbers. A **methodologist**, concerned with instrumentation, works to develop the surveyist's questionnaires, the experimentalist's measures, and the field worker's recording techniques. One person might do all of these things, but typically we show affinities for one activity over another. Further, working with a particular focus develops a technical competence and an expertise. Success in one area is demanding enough.

Disciplines and subareas within disciplines, too, can come to be characterized

CHARACTER SKETCH: INVENTION AND THE COMMUNITY OF SCHOLARS

I'm not a methodologist. I think everyone who knows me realizes that. I don't deny my antipathy—no, it's not antipathy; it's apathy—toward method and techniques. I prefer to leave that to others. If I like to do anything, it's more in the area of innovation, invention, creation. That's the area—developing the research question. How you go about answering it, I would probably leave to someone else. Not that I go looking for somebody to do that. I haven't coauthored that often, in the sense that working on a joint product with somebody else. To me, the community of scholars occurs in that invention process. It's a lot of talking, much, perhaps, when the other person doesn't even know that we've been talking about something that I got an idea about. I'll then develop it later on in conversation with somebody else. In any case, the community of scholars has worked very well for me. I don't seek out people to comment on material that I've written. I work with people at the inventional stage, the creative stage. When it's written, I figure it's got to stay and fall on me. I cast the pearls, and if those swine don't like that sucker, . . . but, I do wonder if some piece has had impact. I can remember finding some textbook and seeing my name in there and getting a warm glow inside. Son of a gun, somebody else found value in this.

by styles of research. Research into mediated communication (radio, television, newspapers, etc.) has shown a lot of survey, some experimental, but little field observation. Many critics find a lack of balance in the observational data of an area to be problematic as the area becomes caught in the biases of a single method.

The Roles of Discovery

As scientific explanation is the description of what's there, it is easy to think of the process of scientific discovery as akin to turning over a rock. There is certainly some of that, but scientific discovery is also a creative act. We have seen that the empirical evidence is relationship free. The description of the relationship is left to the interpretive powers of the scientist. Note that I am not arguing that the relationship doesn't exist, just that its description can't be found but must be created to fit the empirical evidence. Freud never saw a superego, but his description of the relationships within an individual's behavior are made meaningful by that creation. The scientific descriptions of relationships are indeed creations, but creations that are bound to the empirical evidence of careful observation. The better our observations the more error can be excluded from the explanation of those observations. Nevertheless, explanation, even useful explanation, can always be erroneous. In the long run, it is argued, relational explanations, which are not supported by observations, will be discarded.

The act of creation in scientific explanation occurs at many points in the process. It occurs in the development of hypotheses for deductive study and in

---

CHARACTER SKETCH: THE WORK OF CORPORATE RESEARCH

You get so many things that you'd like to do. You have to look at them on a priority standpoint. You should understand that in a company like this one, as well as a small one, what makes these things go is profit. So, you have to work very carefully with budget and look after your financial and other kinds of resources. Some of those constraints are just the time and energy that I have in my staff to make those things go. What happens, after a while, is that you develop your plans and objectives within those resources. Yet, every once in a while, there's a concept that comes up that you want. Then, there's a lot of selling that has to be done. You have to sell it to management. You have to develop your presentation. The proposal has to be strong enough to be the very reason to approach it. You have to take care of the objections. You know, that's mostly what I do. Now, that you've made me talk about it; it's interesting to see that that's the thing I do. That work is just a matter of fact during a day around here. I guess we take so much for granted.

Is it science? I guess I never really looked at it as within the mosaic of science as much as I look at it as in the mosaic of marketing. We play a very, very important role. You take a manufacturing company out there. You take a look at their strategic planning, their goals, their marketing plans, their communication plans, and if all those elements are tied into good information for decision making where research plays a role, then that company is really growing. We can help and we can assist. We truly can make a contribution to the market and to the field and to research development.

---

the inductive extraction of unifying concepts. It is the heart of the development of theory and of any meaningful interpretation of events. The interpretation of survey data, the design and interpretation of experimental protocols, the extended descriptions of cultural analysis, the integrated explanations of theory, all involve acts of creation through which relationships are discovered. Individuals who synthesize their own observations or the observations of others into coherent description, who develop **research protocols**, who devise research hypotheses, who extend claims in theory are all involved in the roles of discovery. These are all scientists even though they may conduct no observations of their own.

The combination of the roles of observation and discovery rarely occurs with equal weight either with a single individual or within a discipline. Areas within the field of communication such as journalism appear to be generating much empirical evidence but little explanation. Whereas other areas such as conversational analysis seem to provide provocative explanation with little evidence. This imbalance appears to rectify itself, over time, in palace revolutions as practitioners become frustrated by the lack of progress which is a consequence of this imbalance. Science needs both observation and discovery to fuel its engine.

Supporting Roles

There are important members of the scientific community who might neither observe nor discover. And while I list them under the heading of supporting roles, they often have more impact on a field than either of the former. These are first, the editors, critics, members of review panels, teachers, administrators, and association leaders who control the resources and public performances of science and second, the consumers of research—the critical reader.

Governance Roles   As Ziman (1968) and more recently Miller (1983) have pointed out, science is public knowledge. Explanation requires an acceptance within public presentation to the community of science before it becomes scientific. An idea which does not pass the gauntlet of review does not become part of the body of scientific knowledge. This review is a double-edged sword, of course. Not only does it keep out the spurious, but also that which is merely poorly written or in the wrong form or, perhaps, contrary to the reviewer's beliefs. We can comfort ourselves with the examples of ideas which finally made it past thick-headed gatekeepers, but we must also wonder at the unknown ideas irrevocably lost. I've mourned more than one paper myself.

Nevertheless, these same thick-headed individuals have often exerted the leadership to direct the field away from futile practices, expose the weaknesses of common claims, argue for the acceptance of more heuristic approaches. In short, they fill the roles of governance within the scientific community. They reflect the successes and shortcomings of all governments.

The Critical Reader   The **critical reader** is a role mentioned often in this text. The critical reader is each of us who in any way is a consumer of research. The reader is the community for whom the research is written. The progress of science depends on the quality of the reader. If the reader is uninformed, noncritical, then the practice of science will be parochial and can quickly fall into error. It is likely that many of you will not go into the practice of research. All of you, however, will be consumers of research. Those of us who conduct research need your good sense.

Scientists in Society

Scientists find their way in society in a variety of professions, but three provide a major entree: the academic scientist, the industrial scientist, and the consultant. The published product—and here I again distinguish individual publications from community-adopted scientific explanation—of these professions has certain characteristics as a consequence of the particular forces at work within them. I comment briefly on each.

The Academic Scientist   Lee Thayer (1983) in a roundelay critical of the practices of communication science offers this comment on academic research:

> It would be comforting to buy into the grand pretenses that are given in university catalogues, in the philosophies of academic journals, and in research grant proposals: here one does not do research merely because one "wants" to do it, but to produce what "needs" to be known, thus providing yet one more cornerstone in the temple of

"scientific knowledge." Long socialization into the academic-research establishment teaches how to profess one thing while doing another. (p. 82)

Indeed, as is the point of Thayer's comment, academic scientists perform research for the same mixed bag of human motives as characterize any other human enterprise. It has no higher standing on an altruism scale and is subject to its own particular set of biases.

Because of the nature of the system in academia, professorial research tends to lack a programmatic focus, resulting in short, fragmented activity. That activity proceeds in main lines of research where contributions are small, and methods and claims are repetitious. Daring is not a characteristic of academic research.

On the other hand, academic research appears to be free of an institutional bias. That is, while individuals and usually departments have points of view, universities usually do not. The university system does not impose a perspective, choice of subject matter, or method on the individual. One can find all manners of research in academia.

The Industrial Scientist   The industrial scientist (I use the term "industrial" for any profit-making organization) is not quite so free. With notable exceptions, the main body of industrial research has its agenda and methods set by the institution. Its ends are not the narcissistic addition to a vita or a contribution to the corpus scientiae, but the goals of the institution. There is a point of view being expressed. In the United States it is, typically, capitalist, managerial, and assumes a progressive technology. This is not to say that the research is dishonest, but that it has a characteristic metaphysics. Finally, industrial research is always proprietary. It is edited for the good of the institution which supports it. Findings which are competitively useful are not disclosed.

The Consultant   The consultant is the least likely scientist of the three. Consultant research, too, has as its goals those of the sponsoring institution. It carries the further difficulty of being directed toward a particular problem within a particular setting. Whether its findings can generalize to that class of problems in other settings is always at issue. Generally the consultant is not acting as a scientist to produce explanation, but as a technician using technical methods to effect a particular solution.

For example, in a recent consultant effort of my own, I used the technical methods of surveys and field experimentation to devise a solution to faulty work practices within a media production house. The solution proposed was particular to the individuals involved and would not even be sensible to someone outside the organization.

Consultants are readily found in communication. They are the advisers to campaigns, the advocates of communication policy, the shapers of television news programs, the analysts of managerial practices. We do nothing to lessen their status by not conferring the title of scientist; we only distinguish the

CHARACTER SKETCH: THE CONSULTANT LIFE FOR ME

I don't think I'm a scientist in an ivory tower sense. I have to be in the world working with the issues that people have to face and solve everyday. I find myself very oriented to finding solutions. I think that's why I work as a [consultant]. There's a real thrill at facing a new situation. Discovering that once again your technical competence can uncover structures and patterns that were hidden from the very folks that were involved in them. Don't get me wrong. I don't think that reflects on me so much as it is a celebration of the analytical method. The method works.

characteristics of their research. The significance of the title of "scientist" is not that it identifies a job title but that it identifies a manner of work directed toward public knowledge. If the manner of work is not that accepted by the scientific community and if the outcome does not enter into public discourse, then the effort is not part of science, although it may be technically demanding and even true.

Characteristics of the Community of Human Science

The community of the human sciences is not homogeneous. Loud arguments are heard over the propriety of different methods of study, the character of knowledge claims, the worth of those claims, who holds rightful membership and so on. It is indeed a human community. And as is typical of human communities individuals surround themselves with others of like mind and resist the intrusion of outsiders. Disciplines, institutions, departments, and journals show different perspectives and methods as science. Science as a reflection of its community is also not unidimensional. Science gets practiced within a context. In many ways, it varies as the context varies. Its variations within the context of the discipline of communication concerns the next chapter.

EXERCISES

1 What is the cultural value of scientism to scientists?
2 How can methodological ideology stem progressive growth in science?
3 What is the importance of observation in science?
4 How is understanding an act of discovery?
5 What is the importance of publication in defining a scientist?
6 How does the absence of publication generally deny the title of scientist to the consultant?

SUMMARY

In this chapter science was seen as a human enterprise conducted within a community of practitioners; the goal of which is to make sense out of human experience within authoritative, empirically grounded explanation to serve some human purpose.

As a human enterprise it is subject to all of the influences of any human activity. Its community has its own rules of membership and norms of behavior. Its explanation aims at the best description of characteristics, methods and practices, and causes and consequences of phenomena for the purposes of prediction, control, and understanding. This explanation is based on empirical observation and is a public way of knowledge. Science is within the reality it studies and serves the purposes of the cultural milieu in which it functions.

Scientism is a doctrine which holds that science is the most effective way to truth. Its tenets are that scientific explanation is ultimately true, its history is progressive, and its methods singular. Alternatives to scientism are instrumentalism and cultural relativism.

Scientists are those individuals in the roles of observation and discovery who add to the public discourse about phenomena and their relationships.

RELATED READINGS

Gale, G. *Theory of science.* New York: McGraw-Hill Book Company, 1979.

Kaplan, A. *The conduct of inquiry.* San Francisco: Chandler Publishing Co., 1964.

Mitroff, I. I. and Kilmann, R. H. *Methodological approaches to social science.* San Francisco: Jossey-Bass Publishers, 1982.

Ziman, J. M. *Public Knowledge.* Cambridge (U.K.): Cambridge University Press, 1968.

COMMUNICATION AS A FIELD OF RESEARCH

"We may be growing up. We used to say, 'We don't talk to those people in journalism or speech or whatever was different from us because they really don't have anything to say.' Well, we still don't talk to them very much, but now we say, 'You know we really ought to.' "

SYNOPSIS

In the previous chapter we learned that science is an activity that is bound in the context of a discipline and practiced within a community of scholars. This chapter explores the nature of the discipline of communication and illustrates the character of our field.

Communication is a delightfully diverse discipline. Old in traditional studies, yet young as a science, it is vigorous and full of discovery. Like age and youth can sometimes be, it is also fractious, contentious and irritatingly naive. It cannot agree on its proper object of study nor the methods to use, which is not to say that individual communication scholars do not hold strong opinions on these issues. What communication presents is a melange of interests that can be pursued in a variety of ways. As a result, the study of communication requires the scholar to make decisions. In our case they are substantive decisions indeed. We will find ourselves addressing the nature of reality, knowledge, human behavior, evidence, and arguments, among other issues, not for the purpose of providing answers but to come to know the alternatives for reasoned choice.

This chapter begins with a brief historical view within American scholarship of the two initiating forces in the academic discipline of communication—speech and journalism. The major part of this chapter will be concerned with dissecting the field of communication to show the separate parts as choices that can be made. In the last section we will try to pick up the common threads.

A BRIEF AMERICAN HISTORY OF THE FIELD OF COMMUNICATION

Academic disciplines are relatively new in the history of universities. They developed from the Germanic tradition of higher education which placed an emphasis on specialization rather than the broad liberal traditions common to British universities. The American institutions have displayed a true affinity for specialization, dividing the academic world into finer and finer distinctions. No small part of that effort of division is the axis of academy and marketplace. When communication seeks its practical outlet and identifies itself with a particular industry, distinctions among journalism, radio-television, film, organizational, and interpersonal communication naturally form. The result is that it is rare to find the interests of communication listed under a single academic heading.

The administrative convenience of separate academic homes also has an impact on the practice of science in a field of knowledge. The maintenance of separate administrative bureaus requires the justification of a separate discipline. Consequently, separate professional associations, publication organs, and even theory and methods arise to support that claim. These comments are meant to be descriptions of the practical realities of academia, not ills to be cured. A problem arises only if we consider these political distinctions to be part of our understanding of communication per se.

This process of division which loosed both the forces which would define communication as a field and the forces which would keep splintering it apart began in the mid-1800s. University learning in the United States had been traditionally organized around classical texts and courses of instruction, professorial chairs, and individual lecturers. The university was a department of the whole. The nineteenth century, however, witnessed an explosive growth in knowledge. With the expansion in enrollments following the Civil War, reorganization of higher learning appeared inevitable. By the late nineteenth century the department was a fact of academic life and with it the accompanying disputes of territory.

The communication combatants in that dispute were speech, literature, and journalism. In the early going, literature was the central focus as departments of English gained the political high ground. These departments subsumed the study of rhetoric, oral performance, and journalism in apparently unhappy ways. Before the first two decades of the twentieth century were over, speech and journalism had declared their independence. In doing so, these two "essentially practical enterprises" began a continuing effort to find "academic legitimation" (Carey, 1979, p. 283). In speech, part of this effort would be the use of science as an epistemology to justify the separation. In journalism, there would develop a strong professional component. Literature, of course, was neither scientific nor professional, hence the effectiveness of these strategies.

HISTORICAL INSIGHTS INTO THE FIELD OF SPEECH

Modern-day departments and schools of communication (as opposed to mass communication) are most likely to find their origins in early departments of speech which may have split more than once before gathering again in some reorganization. Spirited independence is a treasured description applied by speech scholars to their history of separatism. It didn't begin there but certainly reached a high point when a committee of 17 met in Chicago on November 28, 1914, to found the National Association of Academic Teachers of Public Speaking. The association served two purposes: It identified what was to become speech as a separate discipline from English with all rights thereof, and it moved to distance its members from the itinerant teachers of elocution by calling itself "academic."

As to the first, Woolbert (1916) wrote:

It is my contention that there should be separate departments for these two lines of study, because *they are essentially different disciplines.* In the first place, they differ in their field of operations. English is given up specifically to thought that is written, speech science to thought that is spoken. Speech science . . . must be built on a basis of oral expression and can lead to academic honors and dignities only by studies and investigations into speech and its kindred oral sciences and arts.

English is concerned with the past more than with the present, while speech science must occupy itself more with the present than with the past. [T]he man who is rightly trained to teach speech science finds his greatest inspiration in giving the world something for the present, in helping men and women to make speeches, to interpret literature, and to present the drama for the profit and delight of others. (pp. 65–66)

And as to the second, O'Neill (1916), the first president of the association, wrote:

As the result of the experience which I have had in connection with my own work, and more especially with the affairs of this Association since a year ago, I have been forced to the conclusion that there is one type of English teacher who is a distinct menace to the discovery and dissemination of scientific truths in this field, and to the proper methods of administering, in classroom and clinic, to the needs of the young people in the schools of this country. The type of English teacher toward whom we must individually and collectively be on our guard is found among those teachers who profess a deep interest in public speaking in all its phases, who perhaps say that it is the coming thing, a great discovery, a wonderful labor-saving device. This type of instructor usually has a few very definite and very forceful principles which constitute his working knowledge and professional code. Such statements as "Open your mouth," "Throw back your shoulders," "Stand on two feet," "Have something to say," "Never use notes," "Don't shout," "Be clear," "Talk out loud," "Don't make gestures," and similar puerile, if not erroneous banalities, constitute their stock in trade. (pp. 53–54)

As you might suspect, not everyone leapt to the standard Woolbert and O'Neill were carrying. Departments of English held a plurality in speech offerings until midcentury, and elocution, in its modern forms, still lays claim to a rightful place in the academy.

The Content of Speech

What these and other early writers were attempting to do was to establish the legitimate, academic content of the new discipline—what it is that speech scholars would be responsible for and could do better than any other. Self-defining legitimation is a process which continues today (not only in communication). Speech's emphasis on performance and on communication in the ongoing present has forced changes in its subject matter in response to changes in technology and society. Speech began with an emphasis on the content and platform arts of public address and drama. In succeeding years, it added film, radio, discussion methods, group communication, television, and organizational communication among others. It also, for the most part, lost its component of drama and theater arts—such scholars exercising their own independent streak, and the emphasis on the performance of public speaking continues to fade.

The additions to speech contained the forces which initiated the fracture, in subsequent years, of many a department. Broadcasting, radio-television-film, and telecommunication are departmental names familiar to us all. In many cases, these departments began in speech and broke away when their interests could be better served by separate administration. One can trace the process by looking at the string of publication as broadcasting begins to enter speech. Initially radio and in its turn television are introduced as performance media. The writers see speech's initial responsibility as performance training.

Scholars in broadcasting began enlarging the scope of interest to include the industry—its management, structure, conduct, performance, and economics; the place of media in society—the effects, functions, uses, and gratifications; the audience and ever so much more. The result was a group of scholars whose interests were quite different from those belonging to the parent department. From that point, divestiture was simply a question of how the political interests of that community would be served.

Departments of speech/communication are witnessing a new set of pressures as the field of organizational communication gains adherents. While origins are always debatable, certainly one of the major streams in organizational communication begins in the late 1950s with the work of Charles Redding at Purdue University. In the quarter-century since, this specialty has become the tail that wags the dog in many departments.

The process of specializing, fracturing, and redefining of speech/communication is sure to continue. Changes in communication technology alone will provide all that is necessary. These are, nevertheless, essentially political processes. They do not represent necessary differences in the structure and process of communication itself.

The Early Emphasis on Social Science

I hold that by the scholarship which is the product of research the standing of our work in the academic world will be improved. It will make us orthodox. Research is the standard way into the sheepfold. (Winans, 1915, p. 17)

From the beginning, research of every kind was considered a tool by which the young discipline could build its own house. But the sciences held a special attraction because they, indeed, represented a difference from the research of those toward whom "we bristle with defiance."

Speech (in contrast to journalism), with its primary concern on the individual performer, tended toward a psychological rather than a sociological focus. That is, its level of attack tended to be at the individual's relationship to content as performer and receiver. Whether by this subject matter affinity or personal training, the early writers reported on the psychology rather than the sociology of speech. Woolbert (1917), whom we've already met, was a persistent preacher on the psychological science of speech. In the second annual convention, he laid out a methodological primer:

Just to show that some of these problems are not out of the range of possibility for many of us, here are a few methods that can be employed by the man who wills to use them. Let him engage the services of from three to—as many subjects as he can get. He can secure them from among members of his staff, from students who have a peculiar interest in his work or in him, or from certain classes. Set hours of meeting, and keep them as punctiliously as classes. Use your subjects as readers, reciters, speakers, and listeners. Work out blank forms for recording your data. (There is no patent rule for this; it is always a matter of cut and try.) Find out by frequent trial and error, the system that minimizes waste and yet preserves accuracy and control. Use one method until it fails or else develops into something better. Then go at it with patience and with a light heart. (p. 24)

In those beginning conferences, Winans noted that speech was without a research literature and Woolbert said it was without a research method. Thirty-four years later Simon (1951) ranked speech as a science on the order of sociology, psychology, biology, chemistry, and even physics. A dizzying ascension. It did have something of a literature by then, the decade of the 1930s had been an active one. It was still struggling to find its method. Simon argued against the prevailing practice of mimicking psychology:

No student solves his own problems by laboring in his neighbor's vineyard or using his neighbor's tools.

Speech science, in short, is not a subject-matter concept nor transplanted data or methods. Rather it is a type of knowledge and a method of obtaining knowledge by observation and generalization on the communicative level. (p. 289)

The Historical Legacy

It is certainly true that we live our history. It is also true that we can take most any interpretation from that history and apply it to the present condition. With care, then, not to overcharacterize, what is the historical legacy of speech as a context for research? From the beginning speech has been embroiled in a battle to free itself, to define itself, and to find its rightful place in the academy. It has claimed oral performance as its mainstay and science as one of its methods. It has had to withstand attack from without. There are still those who would redistribute the parts of speech into psychology, English, and sociology. The enrollment crunch of the 1970s saw a few departments lose that political battle. It has had to withstand attack from within. Mass communication, the dramatic arts, organizational communication, and, perhaps, one day, new technology have coalesced as powerful interest groups and split departments.

At the same time, speech has led the communication movement—the principal notion of which is that communication research and theory is itself indivisible. Theory and research in mass communication, for instance, must be accountable to that in interpersonal, organizational, and all other divisions of convenience.

Lastly, speech has used science as a strategy in the effort of self-justification. It was a means of separating from English. Members criticized members for continuing with "their" methods of rhetorical analysis. It was also a means of showing one's own worth by out "sciencing" even the "basic sciences" of psychology and sociology. There continues a strong avant-garde desire to have the newest and the best (often used synonymously) in science. The current interest in naturalistic methods may even be a part of that.

The importance of this history is primarily for the reader, but also for the practitioner in reflective moments. Any piece of research literature has to be understood within its own context. An article is accomplishing more than the examination of its hypothesis. It reflects the personal history of the author and the field and, generally, seeks the advancement of both. Looking back in time, these other arguments jump out at the reader as anomalous addenda such as Simon's vineyard analogy. Present-day research contains the same kind of arguments, and they will appear odd to those following.

Such arguments can be difficult for practitioners to see because this type of argument is the method by which we maintain what we know to be true. In reflective moments, however, even practitioners can see the self-serving components of arguments for reliability, representativeness, validity, membership, perspective of the other, and the like. These are forms of argument which I have yet to present in this text. Suffice it to say at this point, they all hang on the willingness of the reader to accept the current mode of research as evidence. They are arguments from method, and method is bound in history.

New research generally considers old questions with new methods. A final visit with Woolbert (1917) demonstrates the case:

> I could get great fun out of investigating the relation of campaign oratory, to various political campaigns. There is no end of the field in which one could work; national, state, and local elections in America, and similar campaigns in the countries of Europe. (p. 17)

For one with a desk piled high with data from the last campaign, there is certainly no end, but the "fun" I'm not sure of.

HISTORICAL INSIGHTS IN THE STUDY OF JOURNALISM

American schools and departments of journalism began their organized history a bit earlier than speech. The University of Wisconsin had a four-year course of study under Willard G. Beyer by 1906; the University of Missouri School of Journalism appeared in 1908; and Columbia University received a $2 million endowment for the Pulitzer School of Journalism which opened in 1912. The American Association of Teachers of Journalism was organized that same year, coincidentally, in Chicago in late November.

In reading the establishment literature of journalism education, one is struck by three recurring themes: the search for legitimation, the emphasis on training for a professional craft, and the relationship between journalism and the social sciences.

The Search for Legitimation

Journalism sought legitimation from two sources: the academy and the profession. In the academy this search played the same theme we heard in the section on speech. Grant Hyde (1929) sounds its major chord in a stock-taking review:

> All of us "old-timers" can look back at the years when the journalism teacher was regarded with a good deal of amusement by his academic colleagues. We consoled ourselves by saying that all academic subjects were new once upon a time and all went through a similar period of suspicion, if not scorn. On many campuses, we have established ourselves, by doing good work, by holding up high standards among our students, and by letting it be known that we stood for the highest type of college education. Is the battle won—or is further campaigning necessary? (p. 11)

Hyde's query gets repeated regularly in the decades that follow.

In the industry, journalism sought to have its professional course of study taken seriously and its research applied. In discussing these efforts a colleague wrote to me:

> It is not surprising that editors who have no training or awareness of research should have been (many still are) reluctant to cooperate with scholars in journalism schools. This distaste is compounded by a feeling among many in the newspaper business that the typical master's thesis is useless. I recall one editor's disgust with the flood of questionnaires he got from journalism students, which led him to say, "I don't want you to ask me but to tell me."
>
> The same kind of half-acceptance of journalism education has been and still is exhibited by professionals. Those with a "liberal" education tend to insist on a liberal education in preference to a professional one. Alfred Friendly, the late managing editor of *The Washington Post,* for example, once urged that . . . professional courses be reduced to zero. That this attitude is still with us is evidenced as recently as about three months ago in the American Society of Newspaper Editors Bulletin [November, 1984], an issue devoted to the question, "Do we need journalism schools?" I judge that many in the newsgathering arena regard the questions of media behavior and what mass media do for and to different people as still the legitimate bailiwick of psychology and the other long-established behavioral sciences. (Hollstein, 1985, pp. 1–2)

As we shall see, the search for legitimation from those in the marketplace has distinctly, but not surprisingly, flavored the development of journalism education and its research.

Professional Education

Journalism prior to the end of World War II was almost entirely an undergraduate program of professional education. It likened itself to the fields of law and
medicine. It prepared its undergraduates for the world of work in press and
public relations. As noted, it sought recognition from the industry and worried if
that recognition was not as fulsome as desired. So widespread was this concern
that it prompted one critic to comment:

> What is so sacred about the newspaper industry? Certainly its production methods are
> not. Certainly its editorial techniques are not. Certainly its record of service is not.
> (Smart, 1955, p. 349)

The emphasis on the journalistic profession—the craft itself—gave a definite
character to the research which appeared prior to the 1950s. The research
coming from the schools of journalism of that early era was primarily concerned
with the history, conduct, and performance of publications. The societal
questions of public opinion formation, the role of journalism in campaigns, the
effects of content, and the like were being asked primarily (but not exclusively)
in the research of political science and sociology, not journalism.

In the 1950s three movements combined to radically change the character of
journalism research: The explosive growth in college enrollments, the establishment, at the University of Minnesota, of the first Ph.D. program in journalism
(1950), and the development of a research literature in mass communication.

The returning GI's had a profound effect on all of higher education. Their
sheer numbers provided the critical mass necessary to establish a graduate
curriculum in areas which could previously justify only a few courses. Their
arrival can be seen as the final push in the development of a complete graduate
program in journalism.

For the most part, the early master's degree programs in journalism were an
extension of the professional focus of the undergraduate program. Beyer, at
Wisconsin, developed the first Ph.D. minor in journalism and located it within
the programs of political science and sociology. Graduates from this program
influenced the development of the journalism Ph.D. programs that followed.
The Ph.D. is generally a degree of the academic community. Its professional
expectation is the performance of research and teaching. The profile of
instructors in journalism education, then, begins to show a subtle change: The
practitioners-turned-academicians were being joined by the young scholars
whose training and socialization made them better competitors within the
academic community.

The research efforts of this latter group meshing with a wartime interest in
propaganda and the press began to develop a new literature in journalism—a
literature of mass communication theory. This theory became part of the
content of journalism education. No longer was the theory of journalism in
society the purview of sociology or political science. It was now claimed by
journalism itself. The vigorous pursuit of this claim has seen a lessening of the
emphasis on professional education and on industry research, although both are
still clearly characteristic of journalism.

Journalism's Relationship with the Social Sciences

The early scholars in journalism appeared to approach journalism's role in the social sciences in a manner different from that taken by those in speech. From the beginning, speech, as we saw, claimed itself as a science of the same status as psychology and sociology. Journalism claimed for itself a unique role. It was a profession and a practice which both supported and was supported by the basic sciences. Two analogies are used to describe the relationship. The first is to mathematics:

> Journalism is an academic subject of the highest order because it is to the social sciences what mathematics is to the physical sciences. Without journalism we could not have the social sciences.
>
> Frequent attempts have been made to classify journalism as a social science, but it refuses to be so classified, just as it is impossible to classify mathematics as a physical science. None the less, both are sciences. (Johnson, 1930, p. 32)

The author, then president of the association, goes on to show how political science, economics, sociology, social work, and history are all dependent on the activity of journalism to provide the content of their disciplines in the same way that mathematics provides the structural undergirding for the physical sciences.

This argument does two things: First, it legitimizes journalism by comparing it to an academic holy of holies, mathematics; second, it suggests that journalism is not merely an equal to other social sciences but is transcendent of all of them. The social sciences should come to know the truths of journalism to better understand their own analysis.

A somewhat less ambitious claim is made in the analogy between medicine and journalism. Schramm, then director of the University of Iowa School of Journalism, provided the allusion:

> As medicine is applied natural science, so journalism has been conceived in many schools as applied social science. (Schramm, 1947, p. 10)

Schramm goes on to argue for the symbiotic relationship between the practice of journalism and the social sciences. Science and its application support one another. Science without application is mere theorizing; the application without science is only a craft, not a profession.

This analogy appears to be the more popular of the two, but both tend to have the same effect on the conduct of research: It narrows the focus of research to the internal workings of the journalistic system. The role of journalism in society is a question given to the sociologists and political scientists. Johnson once again comments:

> Almost every vital interest of journalism is closely associated with some other field of knowledge. Rather than seek independent funds and endowments by which to conduct studies let us secure representation on survey and research groups working on problems that have a journalistic significance. (p. 38)

Not everyone agreed that the larger questions should be entrusted to others.

Allen, writing at the same time as Johnson, points out at least one of the dangers:

> We have all had the experience of inspecting the best work of sociologists in this field and feeling that there is something vaguely wrong about it, a subtle poison of half-truths, a cynicism and underlying hostility to the newspaper processes that is only concealed by an effort to be fair. Yet we have no right to criticize the able and earnest efforts of others in this field until we ourselves are able to prove how much better this matter can be studied by one who understands, and has a fellow-feeling for, the professional processes. (1930, p. 43)

The attitude toward journalism as an applied social science is strong. It appears not only in writing about the role of research in the discipline, but also, in curricular design which shows repeated calls for a firm grounding in sociology, psychology, political science, and the like.

The attitude toward journalism as transcendent of science also continues. In contemporary times, Ziff has written (1973):

> The journalist finds himself in the same position as the scientist, the artist and the historian: His body of knowledge is potentially infinite, and like Agassiz, James, or Bloch, he attempts to set guideposts in the flux, to indicate with humility and pride that this much of the infinity is known. (p. 74)

As we shall see, there is yet another opinion. Following the end of World War II, journalism began to adopt an independent role in the development of social theory with the rise of mass communication studies. Carey (1979) points out that between 1944 with the publication of *The People's Choice* and 1954 with the third in the list of Schramm's edited works, *The Process and Effects of Mass Communication,* there was an outpouring of research literature in mass communication. This research literature came primarily from social psychology, political science, and sociology. It found a loving home in journalism. It also became the new model for research in journalism and rapidly replaced interpretive history as the front runner.

During the same period, television was gaining rapid acceptance in society. With the lifting of the freeze in 1952, television's advance was overwhelming. This social phenomenon provided a significant subject matter that could be pursued without precedent. Journalism's research literature of the 1950s and 1960s is greatly the literature of television and its effects.

Between 1950 and 1980, then, journalism demonstrated a new solution to its problem of its relationship to the social sciences. It adopted mass communication theory as initially posited by the sociologists and political scientists as its scientific body of knowledge and quantification as its method. This predominance was, of course, not absolute. Historical, content, and industry studies continued to hold positions of visibility though mass communication appeared to have center stage.

The Legacy for Today's Research in Journalism

While realizing that exceptions abound, we can, nevertheless, characterize scientific research (read as a type not as a value judgment) in journalism as coming out of either sociological or economic theory and directing its attention to questions concerning journalism in society or toward the structure, conduct, and performance of its industry.

The sociological character of journalism is seen in its concern for audiences rather than individuals, its focus on journalistic functions in governance, opinion formation, information diffusion and the like, and its interest in defining the role of journalism in a modern society.

The economic character of journalism research is seen in studies of the product itself, the viability of industry practices, the consequences of different structures, and the like. These two sets of concerns, sociological and economic, are often combined to consider questions relating structures and functions, practices and effects, and performance and worth.

The individual, rather than audiences or society, makes a lesser appearance in journalism research. Nevertheless, the individual does appear in studies in uses and gratifications—that notion of purposeful attendance—and those which look at the effects of content. The individual in these studies is objectified as an entity which could stand for any one of us. My personal search could find no example of the **situated individual** appearing in the periodicals cited by journalism scholars. (Studies which concern the situated individual relate the performance of an actual person.) Although the examination of the situated individual is a thrust of New Journalism, it apparently has yet to become a force in journalism research.

EXERCISES

1 Examine the course catalogue at your university. What departments offer courses which study communication?
2 What communication journals are available in your library? Would you consider the *Journal of Marriage and the Family* a communication journal?
3 Considering the history of communication where do you think the study of New Technology will be located?
4 What is the importance of the separate histories of speech and journalism for attempts to bring them together?

IMPLICATIONS FOR COMMUNICATION

"There is no such thing as mass communication theory, interpersonal theory, organizational theory. There is only communication theory."

"In our university the department included broadcasting and had close ties with the school of journalism. A whole lot of things were loosely coupled in that department. It was a big, sprawling, interesting department. You could see that broadcasting, speech and

journalism were always going to be around. What we were beginning to figure out was that the thing uniting us was communication."

The study of the characteristics, methods and practices, and causes and consequences of communication is presently segmented into the separate territories of a number of interest groups. The history of speech and journalism clearly tells us why. The loosely melded constituencies of communication have different heritages, academic training, are attached to different industries, and are themselves concerned for their own legitimation. We can conclude that there is yet no study of communication per se, but rather, there are communication studies. The significance of this distinction is that no one is charged with the grand design. We find ourselves divided by the sociological level of our questions, the communication elements we emphasize, the theoretical constructs that we use to define our interests, our research traditions and the perspective we take on the world about us. The sections that follow in this chapter detail the effects of these differences.

THE SOCIOLOGY OF COMMUNICATION

"The study of the effects of mass communication is only meaningful when studied in the aggregate of mass audiences. The information you get from an individual about himself is unreliable."

The discipline of communication can first be organized on sociological grounds beginning with the smallest **sociological units** in interpersonal communication and moving to the larger settings of organizational communication through journalism and mass communication to intercultural communication.

The sociological scope of a researcher's interests has substantive implications for his or her methods. Clearly societal events that occur only within large aggregates cannot be studied through individual observation. But the consequence is more than using the right tool for the task at hand; research at these differing sociological levels has developed different models of the reality it studies. As a result, the characteristic explanations that one would use to, say, describe the behavior of dyads would not appear in a study of social institutions.

Just to give one small example: In his study of friendship, Rawlins (1983) was very concerned about the separate motives that the members of the friendship pairs expressed for continuing their relationship. In their study of the choice of candidates by the voting public, Hofstetter and Strand (1983) could not be concerned about the motives of an individual voter, but rather sought explanations that would cover all voters regardless of their individual motives. For Rawlins, then, friendship is an individual negotiation. For Hofstetter and Strand, voting is not an individual decision, but the result of forces in society.

Of course, friendship could be studied on a different sociological level. Friendship is, after all, a cultural practice. One could examine friendship from the standpoint of cultural rules and norms and never involve the individual. Similarly, voting can be examined as the consequence of an individual's decision making without reference to societal functions. The sociological level of the study is a choice that the researcher makes. It affects not only what one does, but also what one sees as important, and the explanations that will be appropriate.

There is some evidence that the traditional sociological boundaries within the content areas of the field of communication have begun to decay. It can no longer be assumed that, say, a mass communication scholar will necessarily be interested in mass audience behavior rather than the activity of a single individual or that someone in interpersonal communication will not seek to explain the enculturated structures of family communication. This blurring of boundaries means that the literature in any content area will show a distribution over sociological levels. The task that this distribution implies is one of integration. The benefit which could be derived is a lessening of the biases that any one level of attack carries.

THE ELEMENTS OF COMMUNICATION

"Content doesn't do it for me. The same thing with participants and media. For me communication is a micromoment event responsive to situational conditions. It is not rigidly attached to content, participants, or media."

Communication can also be organized by the elements in the process. Traditionally those elements have been content, participants, medium and setting of presentation, outcomes, and the process itself. Particular researchers generally show an affinity for one of these elements over the others. Researchers may direct their attention to content, its characteristics, or methods of production. Others may emphasize the cultural, economic, or sociological institutions of the modes of presentation. Another may be concerned with the **communicants** themselves, the speakers, listeners, actors, audiences and their intentions, motives, purposes, and gratifications. Others may focus on outcomes in individual behavior, audiences, government, economic systems, and societies. Yet others may be concerned with the process itself, the interactant systems and structures by which communication is supported. All of this subject matter and much more is seen in studies which claim membership in the field of communication.

How the Choice of Elements Affects Research

To a large extent, communication scientists make choices from within these divisions at a particular sociological level to put together the structure of their research. For example, one may, for whatever reasons, be interested in the public performances of speakers and feel that the best explanations for the effectiveness of these performances comes from an understanding of what was said. The focus of such a study will be on the content, its intentions, structures, meanings, and the like. Pursuing this interest, one may manipulate the order of arguments to discover which are remembered better or manipulate the structure to provide, say, multisided arguments to test their persuasive effects. Daniels and Whitman (1981) provide us with a good example. Their study concerns the effect of the structure of the introduction of a presentation on the listener's comprehension of the message. It is clear that content is the active element; all the other elements are presumed to be held constant as content is manipulated.

Another researcher may look at this same concern—the public performances of speakers—and decide that it is the setting of the performance that is more important. It is more interesting for this researcher that the same speech given in a classroom, at a political rally, or from the pulpit has greatly different outcomes with the very same words on the very same individuals.

And to complete this example a third scientist may say: "Look, you two are concerned about the effects of content on audiences (persuasion and retention occur in audiences). Audiences come and go, what's really important is the effect on the speaker." This researcher may look at the effect of switch-side debating on the value formations of the debaters.

In the next four sections, we will consider how the character of research varies as different elements of communication come to the fore.

Content Communication has had a traditional affinity for the study of content. Given the historical legacy of literature in speech and the content focus of journalism, the critical and scientific analysis of content is a major segment of our literature. In interpersonal studies, scholars interested in persuasion—now called compliance gaining—have concerned themselves with the construction of arguments and appeals to determine effective images, structures, and forms.

The focus on content has dominated media studies. The concern about violence on TV is a content focus. Fedler, Counts, and Hightower (1982) show a content focus in their study on the offensiveness of newspaper photographs of human suffering. Again, the assumption of these studies is that it is the character of the content that evokes the consequences in the audiences.

Participants The study of particular audiences (see Anderson, Meyer, and Hexamer [1982]) also appears very early in our literature. Children, the aged, the urban poor, women, and racial and other minorities have all been selected for study. In many studies, the particular audiences are the constituency of policy concerns and are selected because of those concerns. Most of the children and violence studies show this characteristic. In other studies, the audiences are considered to have unique characteristics which modify the communication process. Most studies based on developmental state are of this type.

In the last decade or so, there has been a gradual rise of the uses and gratifications model. This model adopts the purposes of the audience as the central issue. Content is no longer considered as having a unidimensional effect across all audience members. Rather it is assumed that the different purposes held by various audience members or audience segments change the ultimate outcome. Violence on TV may be a concern, but not for those who watch it as a healthy outlet for their aggressive tensions. If the object is to control violence in society, one needs to identify those who use televised (or any mediated) violence to heighten their aggressive feelings or perfect their aggressive techniques. Note that here content is the given and what is studied is the nature of the audience.

The concern for the audience is not, of course, limited to studies in mediated communication. Audiences for any event can be examined from the viewpoint of the motives for attendance, relevant cognitive schema, the context of reception and the like. What unifies these studies is the attention to the character of the "receiver."

Ethnological studies, which are just beginning to appear, have a "natural" focus on the participants. These studies hold that reality emerges in the social action among the participants. Therefore, the particular individuals studied are the source of the social action.

Effects and Outcomes   There is a growing distinction in the field between the notions of outcomes and effects. **Effects** studies can actually be seen as content studies. The causal agent is seen as some unit of content and the effect as a result of exposure to the content. Consequently, the ultimate explanatory value of these studies concerns characteristics of content, not behavioral outcomes.

Outcomes studies, on the other hand, investigate the accommodation of communication within the ordinary activities of everyday life. Their explanatory value is detailing how the performance of these activities is accomplished given the available resources. James and McCain (1982), for example, described how references to media characters were used in the everyday play of preschool children. Using an outcomes model, these researchers did not argue that the style of play was the result of exposure to television content. Their explanation showed how the available content was used in play that would have happened regardless. The play made use of television content but was not the effect of that content.

There have been relatively few studies that have focused primarily on outcomes. It is likely that the focus on outcomes will have to await the development of research protocols from theoretical positions that are just beginning to emerge. As they say on the tube, "Stay tuned."

Process   That communication is **process** has been one of the central beliefs of the discipline long before its articulation some 30 years ago. Research directed toward process is relatively recent, however. Not the least reason for this neglect is that the research protocols popular in the 1950s and 1960s made it difficult to examine process. Now we see anthropological protocols, for example, being applied to study organizations as a culture. Organizations such as a university are seen as a total system, albeit with limits, which has values, social norms, mores, social contracts, and interlocking institutions in a manner analogous to any culture. To understand any element, such as the learning outcomes in students, it is necessary to understand the process which maintains the system.

Process is studied not only with institutions but also with individuals. For instance, the investigation of the use of mediated communication as a tool for the development and support of the relationship among sibling dyads (pairs of brothers, sisters, or sister and brother) examines the process invoked by sibling dyads to accommodate mediated communication within the relationship of that dyad. The interest is not in the content, the medium of presentation, the setting of reception or even the individual siblings but in the relationship mutually held between the individuals. An interesting little fillip in this example, which, as all the examples herein, is based on actual research, is that although it is a mass communication study (the effects of television on sibling relationships), its data are the actions and talk of the siblings directed toward one another. The television set is irrelevant. Clearly an interpersonal study, no?

Interpersonal studies are beginning to emphasize the "emergent" character of communication. This notion presents the strong case for process. Its proponents argue that the characteristics and outcomes of any communicative act cannot be predicted with much utility. Instead, these properties will emerge in the course of the interaction between communicants. What can be most usefully explained is how it was done—the process in which those properties appeared.

The examination of process is generating changes in the way communication is studied. Older protocols are being criticized for being static; newer ones for being snapshot research. There is still considerable confusion as to what process is and how it should be studied. We continue to find ways to show our differences.

VARIABLES WITHIN LEVELS AND ELEMENTS

"I want to understand control, identification, and alienation and how these affect and are affected by individual decision makers within organizations."

To fully understand the diversity of the content of the discipline, we must note that each of the elements in communication gets further distinguished by the variables that reside within them. For example, the concerns of health communication with doctor-patient-communication-accuracy can be seen as interpersonal communication exercised in health settings focusing on the content effects for the participants. The sociological level is the dyad, the focus element is content, the delimiting variables are communication accuracy and health settings. The action of these delimiting variables is to set the relevance of the findings for other research and for distribution within the community of readers. This relevance is very specifically drawn by the variables used. If another researcher was interested in the communication accuracy between teacher and pupil—same sociological level, same focus element, and one of two variables the same—the health study would be seen, at best, as marginally relevant. The health article could appear in a publication not usually read by the researcher in instructional communication. It might even be indexed in a reference not seen as appropriate. Consequently, our instructional researcher might not even come into contact with the work.

To get an idea of the scope of this effect, we can list some of the variables which further define the elements of communication. Participants can vary from an individual to dyads, families, friendships, marriage partners, groups, organizations, institutions, and cultures. Further, they can be seen as competent or apprehensive; members of social, racial, or economic classes; purposeful or passive; or developing as individuals, task groups, or institutions. Research has described content as relational, task-defining, entertaining, informing, persuasive, instructional, and political. Media can be radio, television, film, recordings, computers, the telephone; settings can be living rooms, churches, offices, classroom, bars. Outcomes can be defined as concept building, value forming, skill acquiring, decision making, income producing, cost raising, class defining, and reality constructing for individuals, audiences, and institutions. Finally, the process may be seen as the interactions between individuals, groups, organizations, institutions, societies; it may be seen as open, progressive, or regressive; it may consider crucial, the distinctions of class, gender, economic status, or politics.

LEVELS, ELEMENTS, AND VARIABLES: THE INTEREST GROUPS OF THE FIELD

"I'm trying to develop a materialist theory of conversation that I can use to objectively, empirically, quantitatively examine families as an institution to try to come to some coherent theoretical understanding of what's going on with that institution in contemporary, white, middle class society."

The study of communication, then, is distributed among sociological levels, the elements of communication itself, and specific delimiting variables. The combination of these categorizing forces is a discipline that can be viewed as composed of overlapping circles of interest. Some of these circles are near the center and touch upon many others. And there are some on the edges that may have a very tenuous connection with the central core.

We can draw such a figure (see Figure 2-1) and easily decide on major components such as interpersonal, journalism, and mass and organizational communication. But the total figure is unknown. How many circles should we draw? What should be put in, and what left out? In essence, we each must draw our own final figure.

No researcher can travel equally well within and between these circles. Consequently, as we have seen, separate interest groups, associations, and administrative structures to support activity within these circles have developed. For example, there are a number of scholarly organizations supported by the discipline. The three largest are the International Communication Association, the Speech Communication Association, and the Association for Education in Journalism and Mass Communication. These associations are themselves divided into several interest groups as scholars seek to form communities with common pursuits. We can also find a variety of academic departments with different names but committed to the study of some form of communication.

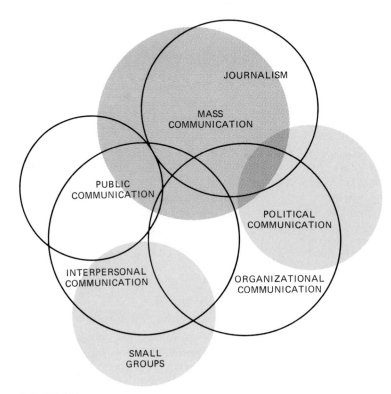

FIGURE 2-1
A partial representation of the interest groups of communication.

These departments have more administrative than explanatory utility, but their existence supports the reality of a fractionated discipline.

PERSPECTIVES IN COMMUNICATION RESEARCH

"The study of mass communication·has been dominated by people who want to control television. People who want to be policy makers rather than scientists. After all the number of commercials a kid watches in a year is not a central issue in theory development."

We are not yet finished with the concepts that divide and distinguish communication. The **perspective of the research** provides an additional division. Organizational research is routinely done with the manager rather than the worker as the intended consumer of its findings. With this intended consumer, the research itself becomes directed toward implicit and explicit managerial goals—perhaps goals of increased productivity, efficiency, and cost control. The function and outcomes of some organizational action is explained in those terms rather than in, say, terms of alienation. O'Reilly and Anderson (1980) provide us with an example in their study of the relationship between various aspects of feedback from managers and the performance and job satisfaction of workers. We would say that this research has a managerial perspective and that one of its outcomes, whether intended or not, would be to advance traditional managerial claims.

Would the nature of the research change if one were to study the same action from the perspective of the worker? Most likely the things that one would measure and the explanations one would apply would change radically.

Research in journalism regularly directs itself to the assumed role of journalists—the development of an informed citizenry—and examines neutrality, clarity and informational value of content. In a perfect example, Weber and Fleming (1983) introduce their study on students' knowledge of current events with the broadside: "An informed citizenry is essential for the maintenance of a democratic society!" (p. 356)

Other research characterizes journalism as the gadfly of government and society and evaluates the effectiveness of journalism as to its success in serving that purpose. When one adopts the opposite assumption that journalism serves to support the status quo in government and society, however, the apparent adversarial relationship disappears and journalism suddenly becomes a tool to bind people to the current system of ideological hegemony.

Actually, the importance of perspective is not limited to these radical examples. Perspective develops because research is not a bloodless activity. Researchers function in the social world that they study. They believe in certain values; they have certain affinities; they serve certain purposes; they are responsible to certain constituencies. Most research on the effects of violence on television moves from the assumptions that violence in society is bad and that government should exercise control over the influences of violence. I am not suggesting that we should argue with those assumptions, only that these assumptions affect the very structure of the research and that different assumptions would lead to different procedures and explanations. You can easily demonstrate the effect of perspective by comparing the design of research seeking to determine the deceptive consequences of advertising content with the design of research seeking to illuminate the effective purchase decision practices of consumers. Both may well examine actual purchases, but the one will do so to show that the purchase was based on faulty information and the other that that information served the purpose of the consumer even when viewed as from an unreliable source.

There are a number of common perspectives within the field of communication. We have already examined the managerial and journalist perspective. Two others are the social activist and the technology perspectives. Social activist research is generally conducted in support of some policy issue usually the proscription of certain content in the mass media, but there are also strong appearances in interpersonal, intercultural, and organizational communication where the values of certain characteristics such as openness, honesty, nonaggressiveness, and accuracy are adopted. Fitzpatrick and Indvik (1982) clearly state the characteristics they value in marital communication when they repeat Balswick and Peek's (1971) description of the inexpressive male as the "tragedy of American society" (p. 210).

The value of technology is an implicit assumption in much communication research. It generally holds that technological advancements are progressive or at least inevitable and therefore deserving of study. Bolton (1983) justifies his research on the adoption of videotext technology by its potential for "dramatically changing consumer behavior" (p. 152).

There is both an industry and anti-industry perspective in those areas which have a professional practice attached to them—public relations, advertising, news reporting, and the like. The industry perspective tends to accept the value of the profession as a given (although it could do better), whereas the anti-industry position assumes the profession is inherently flawed.

There is nothing nefarious here; all research is done from some perspective. The lively debate within the scientific community among competing points of view lets us sort these conflicting positions out. But it is important for us as we examine any particular research study to attempt to make explicit the assumptions that are made within the research. There clearly will be these assumptions —a perspective if you will—that will motivate and justify the research activity. Most researchers aggressively support their points of view and seek counsel from those of a like mind. The final product of research, the published report, is essentially an argument for a particular explanation of the empirical evidence. Again, the good practice of research supports this approach. Self-doubts do not create good arguments. The researcher depends on the informed, skeptical reader to provide the critical review of his or her position.

TRADITIONS IN COMMUNICATION RESEARCH

"As we become part of the science of communication, I hope we try to maintain a sense of our history and to keep people around who understand the history of what communication rhetoric has been over the centuries. I feel sorry for those relatively new academic fields such as sociology that have been around only a hundred years or so."

"I think we're still pretty immature. You can argue that we're really just beginning to study communication. That we are now just organized to legitimize our focus on communication. Even when I was going to graduate school, the faculty members that I learned from, for the most part, were getting their legitimacy from social psychology."

Each of the major communities in communication carries with them their mainline traditions. These traditions appear in texts, papers, lectures, and hallway discussions. They are the unspoken acceptance of one research protocol over another. The choice of entries on a reading list. The researchers deemed heroes of the field. The classic studies. One community may find its roots in sociological functionalism; another in the more individualistic social psychology; still another in rhetorical criticism.

Further, individual schools develop their own local traditions. In the year of this writing, research as practiced in the intermountain west is quite different from research as practiced in schools of the midwest, which themselves show great diversity. Over and over, scholars comment that learning research is much more a process of socialization than it is a learning of content or method. What makes research "sensible" are the assumptions we make about reality, the nature of human behavior, the value of certain kinds of evidence, and the like. For example, if one does not accept that content has a common core of meaning for all who attend to it, then it does not make sense to develop experimental paradigms which vary the characteristics of content to test their effects on audiences. These experimental paradigms do not, of course, test the notion that content has common meaning but rather accept that as a necessary postulate. All research begins with some set of assumptions which themselves are untested but believed.

These assumptions and values are necessary for any method to make sense, and they are transmitted to us in the education process. If one trains at a school where experimentalism is seen as too narrow or where ethnomethodology is seen as a fool's game, one tends to "grow up" discounting those methods.

COMMENTARY:

An honest question remains: What is our freedom of choice within value systems? Can we adopt one rubric of beliefs which justifies the use of a method to approach a particular problem in a certain way for one study and then switch to an opposing view for another? For instance, can I be part of the process by which society upholds the right of managers to exploit workers (to deliberately use pejorative language) in one study and then examine worker self-fulfillment in another? Can we manipulate our traditions in a dilettante fashion? It may be true that science is value-free, but scientists are not. Are we simply hired guns applying a technical method?

Judging from some practices of the field, the answer is yes. Certainly we need to evaluate the beliefs that justify our research and to choose them explicitly. But I am personally uncertain that a value of "anything goes" is useful to science, to society, and to me.

PARADIGMS IN EMPIRICAL SCIENCE

Contemporary practice in the study of communication is composed of several separate paradigms of research. A **paradigm** is a term with many meanings. In the terms that I have been using, a paradigm is the ideology and practices of a community of scholars who hold to a common view of reality, have a common set of criteria for evaluating research activities, and use similar methods.

Empirical science is itself a paradigm of research, but its practice in communication is not unified. For simplicity, we can see empirical science as being practiced by communication scholars in two separate communities (which themselves have many sub groups). The two paradigms have been given a variety of names. Most commonly they are identified as **quantitative** and **qualitative**, but they are also known as deductive/inductive, objective/subjective and materialist/interpretive among others. Unfortunately *none of these names* fits quite right—which is why there are so many of them.

By far, the more dominant of the two is the quantitative/deductive/objective/ materialist paradigm. This paradigm presupposes a material, **objective reality**, that is independent of our understanding of it. This perspective focuses on the objectified attribute as its unit of analysis. It seeks **covering laws** or statements of high generality as its characteristic explanation. The structure of argument within this perspective is ordinarily deductive. The paradigm is empirical, as is the qualitative paradigm, in that it grounds its argument in the evidence of observation. It is called quantitative because its practitioners express their observations in quantified values to use the methods of mathematical analysis. But more than that, there is an underlying assumption that the world is ordered in accordance with the rules of mathematics.

The name I prefer for this paradigm is the one given to it by Guba and Lincoln (1982) who call it **rationalistic**. The paradigm views human behavior atomistically, as divisible into many independent parts each of which performs in reliably systematic rather than random or capricious ways. Human behavior is organized in response to an ordered, external reality. Human behavior is, in short, fundamentally rational[1] (systematized, coherent, consistent) and can be understood through the powers of ratiocination.

Quantitative research (in spite of my preference, I won't proliferate terms) is present-day normal science. It is what embodies scientific study for most and what characterizes the more common derivatives of science—public opinion polls, precision journalism, broadcast ratings, readership studies, advertising effectiveness ratings, campaign analyses, and public policy research. If you are going to be doing science or any of its derivatives today, you are most likely going to be doing quantitative research.

The qualitative/inductive/subjective/interpretive paradigm has as its focus the situated individual, organization, institution, society, or culture. The individual is not best understood attribute by attribute but holistically, and behavior is not best understood act by act but as in process. The paradigm assumes a variable, socially constructed understanding of the things external to us and that we act toward those things in response to that understanding. It holds to the in situ **construction of meaning** and the contextual interpretation of behavior. Here, explanation is directed toward the individual, organization, institution etc., as embedded in a context of particulars. Its goal is a **contingent understanding** of the ordinary, everyday, mundane methods and practices which construct the environment in which human behavior appears.

My preference for the name of this paradigm is **naturalistic**, which identifies the centrality of naturally occurring behavior in natural settings. This paradigm views human behavior as an ongoing performance, the characterization of which is dependent upon the social reality context of its appearance. While behavior is neither random nor capricious, it also is not coherent across contexts and its consistency within a context is subject to the choices made by the individual

---

[1]Not to be confused with the opposite of emotional. In this paradigm, emotions are rational— orderly in their characteristics, causes, and consequences.

actors. Human behavior is, in short, essentially in process and must be understood within the operation of that process. That process is not necessarily rational (orderly, coherent, systematic).

The communication paradigm of qualitative research is very much in development. Its history in our discipline is short although its intellectual traditions reach back to the scientific revolution. Its appearance in the journals of communication has just begun. Nevertheless, it is not so young or undeveloped as to be likely to disappear. It offers a contribution which does not seem to be available through quantification. Its derivatives in journalism and organization analysis are finding their way in the marketplace.

As you might suspect there is a great deal of ideology built into the strong case for each of these paradigms. The ideologies we find in these two paradigms support contrasting positions on the reality and meaning of human behavior and have led to quite different concepts of science, scientists, human behavior, and the natural human. The pure rationalist holds to an objective reality where meaning is common to all and in which behavior is equivalent. The pure naturalist holds to a **contingent reality** where meaning is in embedded in context, and behavior must be interpreted within it.

For the rationalist, humankind is an opportunistic risk-taker scraping to maximize his rewards through trial and error and a ragtag collection of vestigial behaviors. His behavior is in response to a material reality which determines the form and meaning of that behavior. The job of the scientist is to reduce the risk that individuals take in the daily concourse of their life by discovering, beneath the confusion of the particular, the lawlike relationships which can predict and, therefore, control nature.

For the naturalist, humankind is a competent inductive thinker who extracts the essence of things from the countless experiences in which she participates. Given a knowledge of these essences, her behavior creates and responds to the world in which she lives. The job of the scientist is to make publicly explicit what it is that we already intuitively and individually know. The professional scientist can be only a reflection of the individual as a natural scientist.

COMMENTARY:

Paradigms compete for limited resources, adherents, and status. While the endpoints of these paradigms are clearly incompatable in their understanding of the world, there does appear to be a middle ground, a synthesis of these positions which is beginning to develop. At the present, this synthesis is possible only from a instrumentalist point of view. That is, different purposes would direct the choice of different paradigms. A singular view of knowledge would make it impossible to hold both of these paradigms as coherent explanations.

Though our present understanding does not account for how both of these explanatory paradigms could be true, it does not follow that such will always be the case. I find the **criterion of utility** *mighty convincing. The fundamental problems of communication, and the human sciences in general, remain unsolved. Now would not appear to be the time for* *the field to be selecting one approach over another, although each of us surely will. This text is based on the assumption that this move toward synthesis will prove to be healthy.*

EXERCISES

1 On what basis does the researcher choose the sociological level of attack?
2 Classify the following titles according to their likely focus within the elements of communication:
   a "The Effects of Explicit Conclusions within Persuasive Messages."
   b "Three Forms of Communication Apprehension."
   c "U.S. Coverage of Third-World News."
   d "Communication Accuracy and Organizational Performance."
   e "Connotative Meanings of Similar Messages Presented in Various Media."
   f "Public Memos versus Private Conversations: Discovering Social Realities in Middle Management."
   g "Cop Talk and Media Use."
3 From your own experience, justify the researcher in classroom communication accuracy deciding that studies in doctor-patient accuracy would be irrelevant.
4 Can you identify the intellectual traditions in your course of study?
5 What do these traditions take for granted about communication?
6 Paradigms are usually seen as being competitive. Other than their usual contentiousness, why would scientists argue over the qualitative/quantitative paradigms?
7 Give a brief note on the differences between these two paradigms on the view of the individual, behavior, and the notion of reality.
8 Ideological images: A scientist of what paradigm would wear a lab coat and why?
9 For advanced study: I have not used the term positivistic to contrast quantitative and qualitative research although it is often used to describe the quantitative paradigm. What is **positivism**? (A brief discussion occurs in Chapter 9.) Why is it *not* a useful contrast?
10 How would you draw Figure 2-1? What interests would you put at the center and what at the edges?
11 It is said that the liberally educated person is one who can see beyond the values learned. Can that notion apply to the intellectual traditions of scientists?

COMMON THREADS

"I think you can make the argument that in the social realm, communication is paramount."

"If the natural sciences are all physics, then the social sciences are all communication."

This section seeks the common threads in the fabric of communication. It will list them as four: the centrality of communication in social action, the focus on meaning, the concept of process, and the concern for context.

Communication Is Central

It is certainly a central thought that communication is pervasive to all human endeavors. Sociobiologists notwithstanding, to study the social actions of humans and their institutions is to concern one's self with communication. This pervasiveness of communication has led to the general acceptance by the field that the study of every act of communication is somehow important for our understanding of all that we humans do. We may, therefore, disagree in concept and method, but one rarely hears arguments that the study of this communication act or that communication act is not necessary.

Meaning

Within our separate interest groups we all struggle with the concept of meaning. Some do so explicitly, others in implicit assumptions. The concept of meaning is problematic for us all. What is it? How does it function? Is it delivered, constructed, or invoked? That meaning exists and has some effect is a given in communication. Its explanation and understanding is a common effort.

Process

Most communication scholars would see communication as process. The concept of process is as yet poorly defined in our research protocols. The notion of process involves, at least, some time dimension which means that the characteristics, causes, and consequences of some communication act are subject to change over the life of the act. The more simple conceptualizations of this process see it as a linear model in which the conditions at time one are predictive of the consequences at time two. A "put the quarter in the slot and the music comes out here" sort of system. More complex models see communication as a system where several different outcomes might occur at each point in time. Put the quarter in the slot and you might get egg rolls instead of music. The characteristics, methods, practices, causes, and consequences of communication are not initiated in time as in the linear model, rather they are emergent in time. The concept of process, in some form, is widely subscribed.

Context

Context, in its strongest expression as a theoretical construct, would hold that the process of communication is contingent upon the time and place of its performance. To understand the communication act, one must see it in all its particulars. This notion of context limits the generality of any study. The understanding that one could gain of one communicative act would not transfer to another. The arguments for this strong case are growing but not generally held. A less demanding position would hold that there are contextual variables which can change the communication process or its outcomes. These changes, however, are seen as predictable over different communication events.

Context as a **holistic** structure rather than a collection of variables is just beginning to enter into communication theory. Nevertheless, the writing in the field seems to indicate an acceptance of context as a construct to be reckoned with.

These common features are few, but they are enough to motivate an emergent discipline. Communication is crucial to the understanding of our social world. Its central concern is the process of meaning—its characteristics, methods, causes, and consequences.

SUMMARY

This chapter has explored the arena in which communication research is practiced. It was found that the discipline of communication is both old in tradition and developing as a social science. It is not unified, but is more like a field of overlapping circles that constitute communities of interests.

These communities are formed in their different histories and in the intersections of the sociological level of study; the focus elements of participants, content, medium and setting of presentation, outcomes and process; and the delimiting variables of each element and level.

These communities are further subdivided by the particular perspective from which the research is conducted. Perspectives were seen as the assumptive social world values that underlay the activity—values such as success, profitability, the vulnerability of children, the equality of gender. Perspective demonstrates that our research is about the social world, and it is also in the social world.

Lastly, we are divided by research traditions that hold certain methods to be more true than others, certain evidence more valuable, and certain purposes more legitimizing.

In all of this diversity, however, we found some powerful unifying beliefs and concerns. The social world is defined by acts of communication which justify their importance for study. Communication seeks to explicate meaning as occurring in a process embedded in a context.

RELATED READINGS

Carey, J. W. Graduate education in mass communication. *Communication Education,* 1979, *28,* 282–293.

Dance, F. E. X. Speech communication as a liberal arts discipline, *Communication Education,* 1980, *29,* 328–331.

Downs, C. W. and Larimer, M. W. The status of organizational communication in speech departments. *The Speech Teacher,* 1974, *23,* 325–329.

Guba, E. G. and Lincoln, Y. S. Epistemological and methodological bases of naturalistic inquiry. *Educational Communication and Technology Journal,* 1982, *30,* 233–252.

Marlier, J. T. What is speech communication, anyway? *Communication Education,* 1980, *29,* 324–327.

Miller, G. R. Taking stock of a discipline. *Journal of Communication,* 1983, *33,* 31–41.

Weaver, D. H. and Grey, R. G. Journalism and mass communication research in the United States. In G. C. Wilhoit and H. de Bock (Eds.) *Mass communication review yearbook,* vol 1. Beverly Hills, CA: Sage Publications, 1980, 124–151.

PRESUPPOSITIONS OF RESEARCH IN COMMUNICATION

Research does not begin from scratch. The particular questions we study and the methods we use are justified and directed by the fundamental assumptions we make about the character of the world and the people in it. Each of us uses some set of **axioms**, an irreducible metaphysics, upon which to base our reasoning activity. These assumptions are the necessary starting point of our understanding. As axioms these propositions are unquestioned by those who use them but are the basis for argument by those who do not. In the practice of the study of communication there are some well-known points of disagreement about these underlying **postulates**. Of course, any presumption can be brought into question. This chapter explores those points of issue that have appeared in our literature.

SYNOPSIS

This chapter considers three major areas in which the assumptions of research are most often called into question: (a) The manner in which we engage the human object of our study, as an individual, in aggregates, or in groups; (b) the nature of meaning of the behavior we observe, the content we study, and the observations that we make; and (c) the character of empirical facts and claims about them in scientific argument.

There are separate ideas on the solution to the problem of how an individual can be both different and the same as any other. Most research considers the individual to be the sum of a set of attributes. Research based on this assumption attempts to explain the attribute rather than the individual.

Assembling aggregates of measures on individuals is a common method of studying the purified attribute. It is assumed that in this aggregate the general components of human behavior will be liberated from the mask of individual differences.

The concept of membership is introduced as the construct used to claim a special character for groups. The concept is shown to have special explanatory capabilities.

Finally, the dyad is considered. It appears to have a mixed review. It is seen as simply two individuals, an imperfect group, and/or a necessary condition for the special relationship of friendship.

In our visitation on meaning we consider the implications of the contrasting notions of objective and subjective meaning for research design, content studies, and the interpretation of behavior. The assumptions about meaning are, perhaps, the most hotly debated. They extend to the basic concept of the meaning of the world around us—that meaning which we call reality.

Science is concerned with the advancement of claims about empirical facts. The product of science moves forward through the presentation of arguments. The nature of facts and the structure of arguments varies according to the ideological foundations and the methods of reasoning used. The warrants of quantitative and qualitative arguments are examined and compared. Finally, we end by considering the forms of valid conclusions typically drawn from these arguments.

THE MANNER OF ENGAGEMENT

A central concern in the discipline of communication is, obviously, human communication: its antecedents, processes, consequences, and artifacts. To exercise this concern, we have to engage in some manner the human object of this study. To accomplish this engagement a generalized notion of the individual is required. There are two such notions which motivate current research: the individual as the sum of a set of attributes, and the situated or embedded individual as a member.

The first of these is by far the more developed and the more popular. This model motivates research on aggregates (collections of noninteracting individuals) and certain types of groups. It is also used in the study of memberships.

The situated individual model motivates research on the enacting individual, on memberships (collections of individuals interacting within constructed semiotic fields), and on group processes.

In this section we will first consider the two models of the individual spending the greatest time with the first and, then, move to study aggregates and memberships.

The Attribute Model of the Individual

The problem that this model has to solve is how is it that each of us is different yet shares a common nature and is, therefore, alike. One solution to that problem comes to us from quantification theory. Quantification theory holds that every entity (including each individual) is the sum of its attributes. Starting with that principle, the model states that for any distinguishable **class** of entities there is a pool of attributes which taken as a whole identifies the class. Translating this statement into terms applicable to the human individual, we have the proposition that there is some set of attributes which taken as a group belongs uniquely to the human species. Each human individual exhibits each of those attributes to some degree.[1] The set of attributes establishes our common nature; the particular values that each individual exhibits contribute to a unique sum. More directly, the individual (I) is the sum of the particular values (X_j) of the set of human attributes (A_j); or:[2]

$$I = A_1X_1 + A_2X_2 + \ldots + A_nX_n$$

As an individual, then, I share some set of physical, cognitive, emotional attributes with you, but the way they add up with me is different from the way they add up with you.

This model clearly solves our problem. It shows how we are both unique as individuals and the same as human beings. It provides some other interesting ideas too.

From this model, the job of the human sciences is to identify the attributes which define the human as human and to determine the particular values held by an individual. Knowing the attribute set and the particular values, one knows all there is to know about the individual in question and, by extension, all there is to know about humans in general.

The model also provides a mode of attack for the study of humans without having to deal with the enormous complexity of the entire individual. By decomposing the individual into a set of independent attributes, the scientist can gain ultimate knowledge of the individual by studying one attribute at a time. For instance, presuming that symbolic reasoning is a human attribute, we can examine its effect by holding all other attributes constant and allowing symbolic reasoning ability to vary. In this manner, one can learn the effect on the nature of the human individual of this one attribute, in its purified form— uncontaminated by the effects of other attributes.

The model can be applied to any class of entities. I can restrict its scope and consider children aged 10 to 12 of white middle-class parents. I can enlarge its scope to consider all primates. Presuming that I have made valid distinctions, the set of attributes will change as the class changes. Indeed, those changes will tell me what it means to be a child aged 10 to 12 of white middle-class parents, or more generally, a primate.

Problems   The model is a powerful one in that it organizes our thinking and provides a direction of analysis. Most of what we see as science has followed this

---

[1]While beyond our scope here, the problem of missing or zero-valued attributes is involved in many policy debates including those of abortion and death.

[2]Such **algorithms** get read as: A_1X_1 is the value of the first attribute for that particular individual; the elipsis means "and so on until" the last attribute A_n is reached.

model. It is not without its critics, however. The model is, certainly, attacked directly by those who support the contrary situated individual model. Holding the contraryists in abeyance for the moment, there are still plenty of arguments among those who accept the basic quantification model.

Four which have a powerful impact on the practice of science are: (a) Whether the nature of the attributes is objective or subjective, (b) whether the significant attributes are material or constructed, (c) whether the set of attributes is fixed and finite or ever expanding, and (d) whether the attributes can be studied in purified form or as expressed by the individual. A word or two on each follows:

Objective versus Subjective Attributes   As with most human arguments there are a variety of positions that have been taken on the issue of objective versus subjective attributes. Let me set a pair of endpoints and then work the middle. The strong objective endpoint is that the attributes exist out there, independent of our knowledge of them. Our understanding of the attributes may be imperfect, which is why our scientific knowledge is imperfect, but the attribute, itself, is not. Because the attributes exist independent of our understanding of them, an empirical system of science is self-correcting. For example, in the objective reality of the human being, there is an attribute called intelligence. The reason there are many definitions of it is that our understanding of it is faulty, but ultimately a single, true definition will emerge.

The strong subjective viewpoint is that the attributes are sense-making constructions which allow us to accomplish intended epistemological goals. The attributes do not exist objectively, but rather, subjectively, in the way that we construct human knowledge. As the character of human knowledge changes, so too, will the attributes of the world that that knowledge intends to explain. That is, the attributes exist because of our understanding of them. Our knowledge of these attributes doesn't get better; it changes to serve different purposes. The attribute of intelligence, here, is a set of social constructions the differences among which serve different purposes. A single construction will emerge only in an ideologically totalitarian environment.

The middle ground is that the attributes are neither solely objective nor subjective. They are, demonstrating the spirit of compromise, composites. Attributes are our subjective understanding of things that exist out there. Consequently, there is an objective attribute called intelligence, the traits of which are always dependent upon the particular perspective taken of it. Those variations in definition, however, will occur around some stable, central core.

The emphasis that one places on the components of this compromise determines positions on the truth value of science, its independence from ideology, and the like. The differences in these positions are reflected in differences in the fundamental goals of science. In the position of objective, independent attributes, science intends a better and better approximation of the world out there. Science maps the empirical world onto a system of symbolic notation. In the subjective position, science is an ideology which permits a particular system of understanding to exist. Establishment science, for example, is necessary for governance by the establishment. The compromise position permits a whole range of arguments about what is objective and what is ideological. Witness the continuing arguments about the cultural components of our understanding and measurement of intelligence.

Material versus Constructed Material attributes are those which have a physical reality; constructed attributes are the result of the processes of socialization and enculturation. Few deny the presence of both kinds of attributes. The debate centers on the relative significance of each in our understanding of human life.

Materialists hold that the foundations of human behavior—the primitive axioms of human behavior on which all understanding must be based—are found in the physical structure of the human itself. **Constructionists**, on the other hand argue that the material attributes are only the arena in which the important actions by which behavior is made meaningful get performed. For instance, it is true that we must all eat, but what one eats—and how, where, when, why, and with whom one eats it—are all constructed properties. If we are looking to understand what it means to eat, the fact that we all do it is only the starting place.

The importance of the distinction here concerns the generality of one's knowledge. If the significant attributes of a class are material, then our understanding of the class generalizes to all members regardless of the time and place in which they appear. If the significant attributes are constructed, then our understanding of a class is limited to those who have been successfully socialized within a given system. Further, with a material attribute, one can assume the presence of the attribute with the normal individual. Successful socialization, however, would appear to be a circumstance which must be demonstrated in each case.

The ordinary practice of present-day science is a curious mixture of these two positions. Most of the attributes which appear in studies—education, religious preference, self-esteem, apprehension, income, personality, competence, and on and on—are defined by the cultural system in which they appear and are, therefore, constructions. These attributes are treated, however, as if they were material. For instance, a $25,000 income is considered the same regardless of where it is earned even though its significance for an individual living in a small town in Indiana is quite different from that for an individual living in Manhattan.

Finite versus Ever Expanding A fixed and finite set of attributes would permit a valid epistemological method to determine those properties over time. A finite set would establish a definitive goal for science and provide a marker for success at any point. An indeterminate and changing set, on the other hand, sets scientific knowledge firmly in time. What is useful today may be of lesser value in the future. The body of knowledge would have a life span.

How could the set of human attributes be indeterminate and changing? There are evolutionary processes to begin with, but more importantly, or, at least more frequently, changes in the processes of socialization and enculturation. For constructionists, the human being of 1986 is not the same as the human being of

1486 or even 1966. Perfect knowledge of these three entities would be different. Knowing one would not necessarily inform you of the other two.

A fixed, finite set of attributes determines that there will be a fixed, finite set of scientific descriptions which will compose our knowledge of the human individual—the primary tenet of **reductionism**. An indeterminant, changing set means that our knowledge would be ever expanding—the contrary proposition of **expansionism**.

Purified versus Individual Expression   The final pair of these dichotomous arguments concerns the manner in which the attributes themselves can be studied, either through a purifying method or in their expression by the individual. A purified attribute is one which has been isolated from its appearance in combination with all other attributes in any one individual. The method of doing this is the method of aggregation. We will spend more time with this method when we discuss aggregates in the next section. At this point, the method of aggregation involves the examination of a large number of individual examples of an attribute to determine the properties which cut across all examples. These properties are considered the core characteristics of the attribute. These core characteristics cannot be seen except in the aggregation.

Aggregation collects and converges the properties of an attribute in order to properly distinguish it from all others. The proponents of the method of aggregation argue that the individual can express only a single value of an attribute. Aggregates are required to gain an understanding of the whole concept. Studying individuals (or any other entity) one at a time leads to the error of seeing different mechanisms when one is seeing only different values of the same attribute. The study of the individual, as one of our respondents stated, is unreliable.

The contrary view is that the so-called core characteristics are actually fictions created by the very method of aggregation. They don't exist in the behavior of individuals and will, therefore, ultimately fail to provide useful explanation. Instead of eliminating individual differences as aggregation does, the scientist needs to study and preserve these differences. Aggregation leads to the error of explanation applicable only to nonexistent entities.

Most research gets conducted somewhere in between these two perspectives. We have come to think of common attributes as modified by individual differences. There is a **common core**, in this thinking, to the structures of intelligence, attitudes, aptitudes, skills, affinities, motivations, and the like which permits us to generalize across individuals. There are also differences in those structures as they appear in individuals which both limit the generality of the claim and suggest that both aggregates and individuals need to be studied.

Implications   The implications of these presuppositions about individuals show themselves clearly in research practices. When the researcher devises a measurement instrument for some physical or cognitive attribute in order to study that attribute across aggregates of individuals, the assumption is made that the structure and character of the attribute is common across the individuals. Its value may change from individual to individual, but those individuals who display the same value of the attribute are essentially the same on this attribute. Individual differences induced by the particular circumstances of that attribute in the given individuals are viewed as difficulties in **measurement** which must be overcome to get to the true value of the attribute. The focus of the explanation is on the objective, generalized attribute not on the performing individual.

Further, attributes are assumed to be orderly. When the value of the attribute is examined over time or performances to determine its stability, if one performance does not predict another, within good limits, the instability is first assigned to error in instrumentation rather than **volatility** in the attribute. If changes in instrumentation do not produce stable measures, the proposed attribute is considered nonexistent.

Variations in the character of attributes with a single individual is a problem within these research explanations. The performance ascribed to certain attributes, particularly cognitive attributes, appears to change substantially from time to time. Typically these variations are explained by the existence of temporary conditions that either inhibit or enhance the performance. Rarely is the suggestion made that the attribute itself is volatile or unstable. Attributes whose character or structure is subject to rapid and irregular change make prediction and control difficult. It is much more attractive to assume that attributes have a consistent structure and that any change is orderly. The difference in explanation is remarkable. In the first case, if one doesn't perform well on an intelligence test, it was because of fatigue or illness, not because one's intelligence was lessened. The value of the attribute of intelligence remains the same only the conditions of performance change. If one can average out or hold constant the conditions of the performance, the true value of the attribute will appear.

In the second case, even if the conditions of performance remain constant, the characteristics of the attribute may change. Its presence, absence, strength, or weakness becomes unpredictable. No claim can be made for a single, true value.

Explanations of human behavior tend to be much closer to the first interpretation than to the second. We tend to interpret the regularities we perceive in individuals as stemming from the same sources and the irregularities as temporary conditions. This interpretation permits us to maintain the objective attribute as the focus of study rather than the subjective performances of individuals. It is, of course, possible that the regularities are the temporary condition and the irregularities the attribute. This interpretation does not readily support prediction and control, however, and is, therefore, less enticing.

These assumptions about attributes are necessary to produce explanation within the rubrics of prediction and control across individuals. That is, if what I learn about the relationship between attributes in one individual is to tell me anything about the relationship between those attributes in other individuals, then the characteristics of behavior by individuals must be subject to the same laws across individuals. That relationship cannot be limited to its particular expression by an individual in a given time and place.

The Situated Individual

The traditional view of science is best supported by the condition of a finite set of objective, material attributes which can be studied in purified form. This view provides the stable, orderly, and connected world that is the presumed model for an epistemology that seeks covering laws of high generality. There are those, however, who argue that human behavior does not fit into this world. Human behavior is best described by an ever-expanding set of subjective, constituted attributes which must be studied in their expression by the individual. The model of the physical sciences, consequently, is inappropriate as a model for the human sciences.

For these analysts, the individual cannot be decomposed into a set of attributes and that to study, say, intelligence or personality independent of its expression in the individual is empty theorizing. This line of reasoning argues for a different model—the model of the situated individual (SI model). This model underlies much of the naturalistic approach, which is the basis of the second half of this book. The model of the situated individual considers the individual as an organismic whole and argues that just as we cannot understand the concept of life by examining the circulatory system, the respiratory system, and such other systems that we may differentiate from the whole, we cannot understand the living individual through decomposition.

The study of the situated individual is quite different from the study of individual attributes. The SI model advances the study of the individual in action embedded within an organic social system. The understanding gained is of the individual as enacted within that system. The individual has to be understood contextually rather than universally. Consequently, it is the living system—the social action—that becomes the object of study; the individual per se becomes submerged and attributes are those recognized within the system. The system itself is not considered a tangible collection of decomposable elements. It is, rather, seen as an operating **semiotic frame**—a continuously enacted field of meaning in which the significance of the material and the metaphysical is determined.

This SI perspective permits one to deal directly with the individual with all the richness (and confusion) of detail that is associated with individuals. It is not necessary to control all the particularities which make individuals individual. The explanatory goal of this perspective is the particular, not the universal. It is a quite different goal from that which has been traditionally associated with science and is derived from phenomenological and **existentialist** intellectual traditions. In this end, the researcher is not responsible for statements which can generalize to individuals outside the study nor even to the same individuals in a different time. In fact, the research findings cannot be applied to different individuals or times. Hence, explanations of prediction and control are inappropriate. On the other hand, the contribution of this research is its addition to our understanding of life as it is lived which its ideologues claim as the only true understanding.

Problems   The overwhelming problem with the SI model is that it has not been conventionalized. That is, there is yet to develop a set of standard arguments which set the boundaries of the model—its scope of explanation and normal methods. It exists in opposition—in opposition to the attribute model. Consequently, we know what it is not better than what it is. The work of conventionalization is, of course, being done. This text, as its latter chapters lay out a set of conventional methods based on the model, may become a part of that process.

Implications   An implication of the SI model not to be missed is that science is not unified. The physical sciences and human sciences must go their separate ways. The conceptualization of material reality, which has stood the physical sciences in good stead, is considered inappropriate to the study of human behavior in social action. That move is revolutionary and considered high treason by many. It also discards a whole set of efficient conceptual tools by which we formulated our explanations—one of which has been mathematics.

Another implication is that scientific explanation of social action is no longer to be reductionistic and universal. Instead, it is to be expansionistic and contingent. There will be no laws of social action.

Finally, the SI model implies new methods of study. The situated individual is in process and must be understood in action rather than as a fixed set of attributes. The difference has been described as akin to the difference between snapshots and motion pictures.

Aggregates and Memberships

The two models of the individual support different approaches to the study of the individual. The attribute model tends to direct the study of the individual in aggregates while the SI model moves toward the study of the individual in memberships. **Aggregates** and **memberships** are both groupings or collections of individuals. The difference between them is that in aggregates, the individuals are independent, not interrelated, while in memberships, the members are defined by their interdependence. (In this text, I will avoid the use of the term **group** as it is used to refer to either aggregates or memberships.)

Of course, both aggregates and memberships are studied from the perspectives of either models. The character of the explanation, however, is quite different. The sections that follow consider the typical approaches first to aggregates and then to memberships. Finally, the special setting of the **dyad** is discussed.

The Study of Aggregates

An aggregate is any set of independent elements. Aggregates are collections in which the elements are not interdependent. The use of aggregates is very common in research. Most experimental studies use aggregates of volunteer subjects. Almost all surveys use independently selected, separate elements (individuals, couples, households, etc.) as the basis of their data collection. Therefore, public-opinion polls, readership studies, broadcast ratings, and much scientific research are based on aggregates. Aggregates are brought together on the basis of some **category** or **classification**. In these **categorical aggregates**, individuals and measurements are collected because they fit within such classifications as male/female, socioeconomic class, voters, the American public, persons watching television, newspaper readers, audience members, college freshmen, and even human beings. For example, a public-opinion poll based on a sample of voters uses a categorical aggregate or a collection of individuals based on the definition of the category—voter.

The use of aggregates is ordinarily based on the proposition that each individual element *partially* represents a characteristic or consequence common to all. In examining all the partial representations within the aggregate, the complete representation emerges. The underlying axiom here considers human behavior to be composed of both particular and general components. The particular components are those influences which arise from the contingent individual—the particular person in time and space. The general components are those which arise from sources which have a common value across individuals. The axiom further states that when we observe the behavior of a particular person, what we see is a mixture of these particular and general components. It is that mixture that makes an individual's behavior seem so unpredictable and indeterminate. When that behavior is aggregated, however, the individual differences fall to the sides, and the predictable pattern of the central core emerges. In this manner, the method of aggregation liberates us from the confusion of individual differences.

The key to understanding aggregates is that the boundaries of the set are established by definition in the research process. That is, they are defined into existence. Elements do not act to form categories; categories are formed to make sense out of the empirical characteristics of elements. Each of us is a potential element in any number of aggregates simply awaiting definition. For example, I am an element of the aggregates of word processor users, textbook writers, and coffee drinkers because I just created those three classes in such a way that they included my behavior. That is, the manner in which I defined those classes determined who belongs and who doesn't, not any action of the elements out there. (What! Word processor users are word processor users, aren't they?)

The Use of Categorical Aggregates   Scientists use categories to reduce the amount of information that must be handled in order to arrive at generalizations which will hold for all elements of the set. It is hardly efficient to deal with each individual if I can make a categorical statement which will hold for all. Categorical statements assume that some portion of the behavior of individuals aggregated in the category can be explained by the fact that each individual meets the requirements of the category. That is, that the category is a useful device for understanding the behavior of the individual.

Let's see how it works. Presume I define a category called "college seniors."

In it I place all individuals currently enrolled in a baccalaureate degree program at an accredited four-year college or university who have earned sufficient credits that the degree program could be completed in 9 months or less with a workload normal for that institution. (And everyone knows that's the definition of college senior.)

My interest in college seniors starts with my assumption that they are different from people who are not college seniors and that that difference is a function of or is indexed by their being college seniors. If they are not different, that is, if nothing of their behavior is explained by the fact that they are college seniors, then there is no motivation for the formation of the category. Nonetheless, acting on my assumption of difference (which often is not verified), I could then proceed to describe the characteristics of college seniors.

Characteristics of Aggregates   What are the characteristics of college seniors? The characteristics of aggregates of any kind are the characteristics of the individuals which compose the aggregation. Aggregate characteristics are the **rates** of occurrence of the traits the individuals display. For example, public-opinion pollsters have shown a continuing interest in the sexual mores of students. In surveying a sample of college seniors, they might report that "60 percent of college seniors agree that the sexual revolution is over." That statement means that the rate of occurrence of individuals agreeing in some way is 60 in 100.

Of course, any category of individuals will have some rate of agreement (even if zero). How does the obtained rate become a characteristic of the aggregate of college seniors? It is a characteristic of the aggregate because we assume that the obtained rate is *associated with* or *explained by* the category under which we aggregated the individuals. We would reject any alternate explanations such as the rate is due to the collection of individuals who just happened to fill out the survey forms or that the rate may be a function of some other category. If any alternate explanation is true, one would err in assigning it to college students.

Granting the assumption, however, that the rates found in the composite of individuals are explained by the aggregate category, infuses the category with new meaning. One now has a better understanding of what it means to be a college senior. Going in the other direction, one can also initiate a string of reasoning in which being a college senior can be shown to control some portion of those rates. Using attitude toward the sexual revolution as an example, a string of reasoning might conclude that, with all else held constant, being a college senior leads one to a more conservative position (or liberal, depending on whether "over" means won or lost) on sex. In this reasoning string, college seniorness, if you will permit me, is considered one of those common influences which affect that set of human behaviors measured by attitude toward sex.

Let me summarize where we have been thus far: Aggregates are formed in sense-making categories defined in the research process. We use these categories in the hopes of controlling the confusion of individual differences and thus, to uncover the features of behavior common to all elements. The categories we use are assumed to make a valid distinction and that the characteristics arising out of the composition of the aggregate are a function of that distinction. That is, we assume that (a) a true characteristic has been discovered and (b) that it is a function of the aggregating category.

Issues are raised with each of these assumptions, beginning with the fundamental claim that there is a general component of human behavior which can be liberated from the contingent individual. Many find the strong statement of this assumption too deterministic and insensitive to social processes.

What **composite characteristics** actually are also comes into question. Critics attack the "function of" explanation commonly used, claiming that such covering explanations require a casual relationship between an artificial category and the action of an individual. That is, the statement "newspaper readership seeks to be informed" implies that belonging to the category of newspaper readership causes one to seek to be informed (or vice versa). The implication is considered faulty because characteristics which are found to be common to the individuals are, at best, of associational value. They are not caused by the classification. They may be predictive of an individual's identification, but their appearance may also have no meaning beyond the collection at hand.

Further, opponents argue the appearance of a characteristic in a majority or even all of the members of an aggregate does not create a unity where one explanation can generalize to all. This reasoning move is identified as a **reification**—making a thing or acting entity—of a construct. This move inhibits the proper analysis of the actual source of the behavior—the individual. It permits an easy gloss, the covering explanation, to mask the potentially varied relationships between the variables of interest. This is a complex criticism which goes deeper than the analysis of aggregates. Its utility at this point can be seen in that it identifies the danger of common statements like: "State taxpayers refused to support increased taxes for education without reforms." Or: "Carter's record swung the election to Reagan." Such statements assume that all individuals are functioning from a common influence, an assumption certainly in need of empirical support.

Finally, the issue is raised that arguments for a common core of behavior can confuse contingent group processes with some notion of the constancy of the nature of humankind. In this argument, the distinction between memberships and aggregates is crucial: The analysis of an aggregate depends on the assumption that each individual is independent of every other. This assumption of independence permits the conclusion that whatever consistent influence is found approaches the quality of an external, material force. If the researcher, instead, has tapped into membership processes which generate a common social reality, then the communality found could be a function of that membership rather than an essential characteristic of the aggregating category. The findings produced by an analysis appropriate to aggregates, then, are a snapshot along the path of membership but ignore the underlying social mechanisms.

Application of the Attribute and SI Models to Aggregates Clearly the attribute model of the individual fits well with the study of aggregates. Each justifies the other. Aggregation is a method for revealing the complete character of an attribute which appears in some part in individual elements. When the individual is considered to be composed of such attributes, the results of aggregation also reveals the nature of the individual.

The SI model also gets applied to the study of aggregations, but with much less success. The SI model depends on the existence of a common semiotic frame in which all individuals under study participate and by which the actions of the individual can be understood. When the SI model is applied to aggregates such as college seniors or word processor users, the mechanism by which a common semiotic frame could develop and be maintained by the individuals in those aggregations is hardly evident. Appeals have to be made to some notion of public knowledge based on an extended string of synthetic reasoning.

There is also somewhat of a middle ground between aggregates and memberships which presents problems for explanation coming from either model. That middle ground is held by aggregations in which interactive processes also function. A simple example is standees in a ticket line. A researcher may be interested in explaining the attribute of, say, territoriality and set about measuring distances, violations, and so on. At the same time within the aggregate there may be several different memberships of individuals who came together. In this situation, neither the assumption of independence nor the assumption of interdependence is met consistently over the collection. Generally, it is a poor choice to begin a study based on either model.

The Notion of Memberships

The study of memberships (groups) is a traditional area of emphasis in communication. A membership is a different object of study and serves different research purposes from an aggregate. The concept of a membership is distinguished from an aggregate in two ways: (a) The boundary of the membership is established by the members rather than the researcher, and (b) the members are bound together in a mutually developed system of social constructs. Memberships coordinate the activities of their members. Memberships have methods and practices. Methods and practices within collections of individuals are the result of shared concepts of reality developed in membership processes. Individuals when acting as members act out of those shared concepts.

The object of study in the membership is the interaction among dependent members; its purpose is to reach an understanding of that interaction. The examination of aggregates, as we saw, concerned the identification of the defining and distinguishing characteristics of the category.

There are at least two contrasting positions in the study of memberships: The more simple considers the membership as a linear progression—the **membership as the sum of its members**. (This definition appears to best fit the common usage of "group.") A more communication oriented position considers the membership as an interactive process. The sum-of-its-members position seeks explanations for the performance of memberships in characteristics and conditions which are external to the membership process. For example, the individual members' prior position on the alternatives involved in some decision task may be used as the predictor of the final choice. The selection of the final choice is seen as a function of the composition of the membership rather than any "process" activity. In this formulation, the difference between a membership and an aggregate lies in the fact that the influences are combined (as in a compound) not simply listed.

Formulations which see the **membership as a process** rather than the sum of its members make a stronger distinction between a membership and an aggregate. Behavior governed by **membership**, as opposed to behavior which is independent of membership (even individual behavior in the company of others), is explained as a function of the interaction of its members. Influences which are external to that interaction have little explanatory power for membership behavior except insofar as they are introduced into that interaction. Therefore, a person's initial position prior to membership participation has utility for explaining membership behavior only if it is presented to the membership as part of the interaction process. The strong membership-as-process position invests the notion of a membership with its own ontology. That is, a membership has its own individual existence with its own characteristics, methods and practices, and causes and consequences. Putting aggregates and memberships on a continuum, as one moves toward the membership end, the collection gains coordination, coherence, cohesiveness, common motives, values, and the like. A well-developed membership shares among its members a view of the world around it and acts from that view.

The presupposed answer to the question of what is a membership is significant. The choice that one makes between the alternative formulations has a variety of consequences for the questions and design of research. The concept of leadership, for example, changes radically within these positions. In the sum-of-its-members, leadership is assigned to the internal qualities of the individual. Leadership can be discovered in or taught to an individual who can then go and exercise it to lead the membership to some end. In membership-as-process, leadership emerges from the membership as the process exerts different demands. No individual remains in leadership throughout the process.

Application of the Attribute and SI Models to Memberships The sum-of-its-members proponents place strong emphasis on the study of the attributes of membership members. They tend to build models which attempt to explain membership performance from the interrelationship among these attributes. Data collections involve personality inventories, attitude scales, and similar individual measures. Their position and approach are extensions of the attribute model of the individual into the notion of memberships.

The membership-as-process proponents focus on the interactions of the members building models which would attempt to explain membership performance from these interactions. Data collections involve the observation of these interactions as they occur in the membership process and their subsequent analysis. It does not follow, though, that the SI model is in place. In most of these studies, an individual membership is considered to have attributes which are comparable across memberships. That is, membership processes are seen as being composed of characteristics which generalize across particular memberships. All memberships have phases of development, the same requirements for organizational solutions, the same need for the creation and maintenance of a social reality. The actual phases, solutions, and realities that appear are considered particular to the membership, but memberships with the same phases, solutions, and realities are considered equivalent. Consequently, the explanation which develops around memberships presumed to have objective qualities is of the same character as that which develops around individuals invested with objective qualities. This again is an expression of the attribute model.

It is only within those studies that argue that any membership is the product of particular individuals engaged in a particular time and place that one finds a clear application of the SI model. These studies represent to my mind the best fit for the SI model. The concept of membership has been formulated on the interdependent meanings that members have for and with one another. According to this formulation, each individual is defined within that meaning frame which is, of course, the SI model. Just as the attribute model and the study of aggregates justify one another, so too, the SI model justifies the concept of memberships.

Studies which investigate memberships represent a particular challenge for the critical reader because of the variety and often inconsistency of theoretical positions taken within them. Many studies require painstaking effort to determine the operating models and explanatory purpose.

Dyads

The concept of the dyad seems to have carved out a special place in the study of communication. It is first of all a convenient respondent grouping. If one is going to study interaction, one needs at least two individuals which are that much easier to find than three. For these research studies, the dyad is simply the smallest (and, therefore, procedurally efficient) collection possible.

But there is, of course, more. The dyad is seen as specially capable of a particular relationship—friendship. It is a presupposition of this research that friendship per se is negotiated between two people and that it is something different from social relationships negotiated with three or more individuals. Friendship appears to be thought of as being a particular relationship possible only with two. The dyad is, therefore, considered by some as something more than a pair. It is also the necessary condition for a unique human relationship.

In an interesting contrast, the dyad is also considered by some as being an imperfect membership. With only two members, a dyadic membership is particularly vulnerable to dissolution—only one member has to resign. Further, membership interactions are seen as of a different sort within a dyad. Within a dyad, any one member never has to interact with more than one other person. It is questioned whether the dyad is a "true" membership which leaves unanswered just what indeed it is.

The dyad, then, is thought of in four different ways within communication research. It can be, simply the smallest aggregate of individuals, an efficient frame for the observation of interaction, a necessary condition for a unique human relationship or the imperfect expression of a membership. In general, the application of individual models in the dyad follows the application for aggregates and memberships. The attribute model of the individual appears in all four uses; the SI model only in studies of intimate memberships.

Summary: The Manner of Engagement

This section presented two opposing models of the individual: One describes the individual as the sum of a set of attributes; the other considers the individual as an expression within a particular social context.

We then considered the study of the individual within aggregates, memberships, and dyads. Aggregates were defined as a collection of individuals or elements assembled by some classification process. The individuals or elements are assumed to be independent of one another. Aggregates, therefore, cannot act or behave or participate in any concept which requires a dependency among the individuals. The study of individuals in aggregates has been proposed as the method by which the complete character of an attribute which is held only in part by any individual can be revealed. Therefore, aggregates are used to reveal the common influences on human behavior from the masking confusion of individual differences. Aggregates have characteristics which show the distribution of behaviors or actions of the individuals who compose the aggregate. These characteristics are assumed to be a function of the category scheme which defined the aggregate.

Criticisms directed at the presumptions of research using aggregates represent a move away from determinist, universal explanations and move toward contingent, "processual" ones. The practice of the field represents a vigorous mix, although the preponderance of activity is certainly true to the central, component axiom supporting the notion of common causal cores in human behavior.

The attribute model and aggregates were seen as mutually justifying. The SI model could approach aggregates only with difficulty, but researchers would be unlikely to make this application.

Memberships were seen as individuals bound together in a mutually developed system of social constructs. Two approaches to the study of memberships were described—the memberships as the sum of its members and the membership as process. The attribute model was seen as supporting both of these approaches; the SI supported the subjective view of the membership as process approach.

Finally, dyads were shown to have four different uses in communication studies—as the smallest aggregate, as a field for the study of interaction, as a necessary condition for certain relationships, and as an imperfect membership. The attribute model appears in all four of these uses; the SI model appears in the study of intimate memberships.

EXERCISES

1 How would the belief in a material set of attributes support the notion of a fixed and finite set of attributes?
2 How does the concept of objective attributes support the use of aggregates in research?
3 Over several administrations, an individual's personality scores have shown considerable variation. How would an objectivist explain the variation? How would a subjectivist?
4 What is the difference between genius and geniuses?
5 How does the difference explained in the answer to question 4 represent the difference between the attribute and the SI models?
6 Humans claim language as their own even criticizing attempts to teach other primates to communicate in human symbols. How can this position and criticism be explained ideologically?
7 Classifications are said to arise out of differences. Where do those differences reside?
8 How does a successful category define and distinguish an aggregate?
9 Write a definition of the class "word processor user." What components (e.g., ownership, frequency of use) did you use to distinguish users from nonusers? How did that selection affect the nature of the class?
10 Write another definition of that same class "word processor user" but use as different a set of defining components as you can. Would your different definitions organize the empirical characteristics in different ways? How would that change the facts of the matter?
11 Observe your classmates. How would you account for the common modes of dress? How would you explain the differences?
12 To what extent has your explanation in question 11 depended on the result of group processes, e.g., communication among the members?
13 Evidence has shown that fewer females than males become scientists. What difference does it make if this difference is a function of social processes or human nature?
14 Distinguish between the purposes one would have in the study of a membership and those in the study of an aggregate.
15 Show how the membership-as-process position fits the SI model.
16 Thinking about your experiences with friendship, is the dyad a necessary condition?

MEANING

There is, perhaps, no more far-reaching set of assumptions than those which concern the nature of meaning. All of our methods are dependent on some fundamental presupposition of the character of meaning. Where does it reside? How is it transmitted? We will concern ourselves with highlighting four areas where the assumptions of meaning manage the conduct of research—the relationship between content and meaning, the interpretation of behavior, the differing perspectives of the actor and the observer, and the controversy between direct participation and indirect observation.

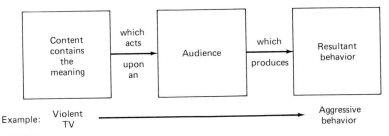

FIGURE 3-1
One view of meaning as delivered.

Content and Meaning

The standard interpretation of the vast literature on media's content effects uses the assumption that content has the same functional meaning for all who received it. It is assumed that content *delivers* its meaning. Therefore, what is violent, sexual, sexist, informative, entertaining, and persuasive for the researcher is considered to be same for each respondent (see Figure 3-1). With this assumption, the performances of respondents which follow exposure to some content can be attributed to the characteristics of that content. To put it more directly, the validity of the explanation that violent content is associated with aggressive behavior is dependent on the content being "violent" for all. If it isn't, if it is instead, boring, revolting, interesting, or childish, respectively, for some respondents, then the explanation fails to properly identify the effective characteristic of the content.

The assumption of the **functional equivalence of meaning** has rarely been questioned in research conducted prior to the 1980s. Now, however, interactionist views are gaining some position. **Interactionist** or constructionist notions of meaning hold that content is only one part in a process of meaning construction. The other parts are the communicants and the contexts in which the communication takes place and in which the subsequent behavior takes place (see Figure 3-2). Content does not deliver its meaning; rather, meaning is constructed from content by the individual operating in some context vis-à-vis that content. Therefore, whether a particular content leads to subsequent aggression depends on the intent of the sender, the cognitive state of the recipient, the context in which the content is received, and the context of the performance which supports the act of aggression. All of these influences have to be of the right value for the relationship between content and aggression to appear. It also suggests that other forms of content might have a relationship to aggression given the right circumstances of reception and performance.

This way of thinking takes a lot of the fun out of content studies because it makes generalized, dependent relations difficult to state. No longer does violent content lead to aggression but (potentially) any content when delivered in a particular manner to an individual of a certain mind set within a given context of reception having the opportunity and support for aggression may be accommo-

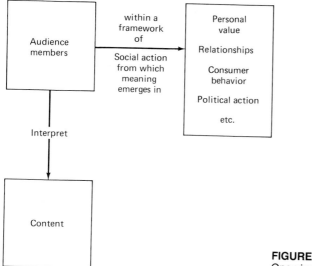

FIGURE 3-2
One view of meaning as constructed.

dated in an aggressive response. While the latter is a much more sophisticated statement, it also precludes effective control of aggression by censoring content.

The growing evidence for the interactionist position also has some disquieting impact on the interpretation of **experimental protocols**. These protocols (a protocol is the entire set of conditions under which an experiment is conducted) set the contexts in which the content is received and the measured behavior performed. Experimentalists argue that their protocols are sterile—have no effect on the relationship between content and respondent behavior. Interactionists respond that such is not possible. Context cannot be absent; the experimental protocol must form the contextual bed. Experimentalists, by ignoring this context, are missing the effect of powerful explanatory variables.

The difference between these positions has a profound effect on our explanation. What we scientists want, of course, are simple, direct relationships. We want "violent content causes aggression." That is, present violent content and aggression must appear. We, obviously, don't get that. We can, however, devise experimental protocols in which aggression tends to appear given violent content. That is, experimental studies have shown that higher rates of aggression occur following exposure to violent content. If the protocols are irrelevant to the relationship, then the stochastic values found in the experiment can generalize to the natural setting. We can legitimately conclude that each violent program results in aggressive behavior at least in a given proportion of the viewers. If the protocols are part of the relationship, however, then the same influences, with functionally equivalent values as present in the experimental conditions, must be present in the natural setting for this conclusion to hold. If we cannot demonstrate that, then the explanation is limited to a statement that a set of conditions have been discovered in which violent content leads to aggression. (In my reading, this is our present state of knowledge.) This statement is useful if one wants to produce aggression, but not useful if one wants to control the presence of aggression in the natural setting.

This extended example has used violence as the content category, but the same arguments apply to any content classification. The rule here is: The power of the characteristics of the content to explain the behavior of respondents is dependent upon the effective meaning of those characteristics being the same across respondents.

One more example: A study in journalism assumes that the content of the newspaper is informative. This classification is based on the stated intent of the publisher and on the characteristics of the content. The researcher conducts a survey and finds that the respondents are not informed as a result of exposure to the content. He gives advice to the publisher on how to improve the informative value of the content. He tests again and finds that the respondents are still, stubbornly, not informed. He concludes that the education establishment has failed to teach Johnny and Jane to read. Meanwhile, his respondents who were enjoying the newspaper for whatever their reasons are now grumbling about how dry and factual the stories have become.[3]

Researchers make the assumption of common meaning at any point where they attempt (a) to explain respondents' behavior as a function of some characteristic content (violent content leads to aggression) or (b) to explain what the effective elements of content are based on respondent behavior (readers didn't learn, the content is at fault). Examples of this assumption can be found in studies of the accuracy, consequences, and/or effectiveness of communication within an organization, the effective qualities of a public speech, the consequences of mediated content, and the like. And, even more fundamental to the research process, every survey questionnaire, personality inventory, and intelligence test is based on the assumption that the items mean the same for all. (This assumption is questioned within claims of systematic bias when test forms are used across social and cultural groups.) The location of meaning—whether in the content, in the intent of the sender, in the receiver, or in the interaction—is a significant assumption in the explanation of the relationship between content and behavior.

The Interpretation of Behavior

[I]n the social sciences we are not dealing with purely physical events, but with events which are interpreted by the actors themselves, by those who are affected by the actions, and by other observers. Thus, we are not content to say that a man is simply waving his arms about, something which could be presumably be described in purely physiological terms. We want to say in addition that the man was signalling to his commanding officer, was waving to his mistress, was doing physical exercise, or was

---

[3]Note that this sentence makes the assumption that all respondents would find the content less acceptable and dry and factual. The assumption of common meaning is very attractive.

reacting to the sting of a wasp. All these activities would look rather similar to an observer and even if some minor physiological differences were to be detected, it would still not alter the fact that we are mainly interested in the . . . actions because they fit into a social framework. (Nicholson, 1983, p. 8)

As Nicholson points out, the meaning of human behavior is not contained in the physical events of that behavior. Meaning is an interpretation from a particular vantage point within a social framework. As social scientists, we are very little concerned with describing the **act**, but very much concerned with describing the **action**.

We so take for granted the meaning of most acts that we often fail to see the interpretation in action. However, the man waved goodbye is a description of an action, and the man's extended fingers of his right hand repeatedly inscribed an arc of 45 degrees with his wrist as the center point is a description of an act. We observe the act; we interpret the action.

The amount of interpretation involved is often disguised by the objective character of quantitative measurement. But consider the amount of interpretation that is involved in a study our campaign research team has conducted for the past three presidential elections. Part of the study involves respondents positioning themselves and the candidates on a common cognitive space described by the issues in the campaign. In the 1984 campaign, the deficit was an issue. One boundary could be described by the following statement: "Deficit spending is a requirement for modern fiscal planning." Respondents were asked to evaluate the degree they were in agreement with this statement and the degree each of the candidates were in agreement with this statement. The research team could then analyze where each respondent was relative to the candidate of choice and to the opposing candidates in the cognitive space defined by the statement.

Of course, what we actually have before us is a check mark on a piece of paper. All the rest of the analysis is an interpretation of the act of that check mark. That is, we assume that the check mark represents the action of a judgment by someone who can competently evaluate his or her own position and the position of others on a common metric. When I pick up the next questionnaire to enter those data, I assume that the check mark on that page represents the same kind of action as the one previous and so on through the entire set. I am sure that you can see several more interpretations that must be applied before those check marks make sense as the position of the voter on campaign issues relative to the position of his or her candidate of choice and the opposing candidates. What justifies that interpretation? The assumptions that (1) a common language and culture produce a common meaning for the instructions and items on the questionnaire; (2) respondents complete the task in a valid manner; and (3) the performance of the data—the check marks—on tests of reliability, validity, and the hypothesis—tests which are themselves interpretations of the characteristics of reliable and valid measures.

In this empirical science we are, in fact, deeply involved in the interpretation of the nonobservables of action. When we read or perform research, we "buy in" to these interpretations and assumptions. The only problem is that the assumptions are so ordinary that they are transparent; we look right through them without noticing, particularly as they are part of the accepted methods of science. We improve science if we make them opaque, make them problematic. What happens to the explanation if the assumptions are not true? What assumptions could be substituted which would account for the data as well? These are always interesting questions that can be applied to any research.

The Differing Perspective of the Actor versus the Observer

In the campaign research example, the act of the check mark is interpreted from the vantage point of the observer. That is, observer (researcher) assigns the meaning of a cognitive judgment to the act of checking the response forms on the page. This is the only valid response. The observer in 'this case is not attempting to explain what the act means to the actor. Could the meanings be different? Of course.

The significance of the difference depends entirely on the purpose of the research. If the study was to describe why people put check marks on paper, the study has failed. But as a matter of fact, once the check marks are on paper, we are no longer concerned about the individuals who produced them. Our concern is with the characteristics of the check marks; whether they can be reliably described and whether they have some explanatory utility in predicting, controlling, or understanding other observable behavior.

In the campaign study, we have found that the distance values between respondent and candidates are connected with voting behavior in a number of different patterns. We describe those patterns by talking about different cognitive mechanisms—different ways people have for ordering their perceptions. Those descriptions explain the recorded behavior of our respondents according to what it means to us, not according to what it means to each of them. Nevertheless, each of them may have separate explanations which would describe the relationship between the distance values and the votes. The combined set of explanations would account for the characteristics of the aggregated data. Still, we do not care.

Our responsibility as scientists is to be true to our observations and to account for them honestly in our explanation. If our explanation accounts for the characteristics of the data, it does not matter that there is another set of explanations that also accounts for the data. In fact, we assume that there are any number of explanations and explanation sets that can account for the data. That is, there are many theories which can be applied to the same data set. What matters to us is whether our explanation works for *our* purpose within the assumptions of our theory.

Aggregate data do not explain the individual but rather an attribute or attribute set of the aggregated individuals. In our example, the attribute, we propose is the cognitive mechanism which associates issue-judgments with voting. We would not claim each individual generated the check marks on the questionnaire through this mechanism. To make that claim would require us to demonstrate that it was the only way those check marks could appear.

We do claim that a cognitive mechanism of this sort accounts for the data we obtained. In short, in our study we have added to the public discourse about human attributes, which was our purpose. We have not explained why each of our respondents behaved the way they did. That explanation would clearly require the analysis of each individual.

Note that our explanation makes use of four presuppositions we have already visited. It assumes (1) the existence of objective attributes which (2) transcend the individual and appear when the masking individual differences are pressed aside. It also assumes that (3) the questionnaire items and the response behaviors have the same functional meanings across all respondents. Finally, it assumes that (4) the behavior of the respondent group is not monolithic but subject to multiple influences. These four presuppositions mark our explanation as seeking at least prediction and probably control, generalized across individuals and yet tentative in scope. You can probably see that without the first three assumptions the procedures used in the study would make little sense. They are fundamental.

The last assumption, however, is not required. The contrary assumption—that the behavior of the respondent group is monolithic—is often made. This assumption does not change the content of our claim, only the extent of its application. Ours is a conservative choice, but one we feel is justified in the light of the limited evidence we have.

In all of this explanation, most of what we have in hard empirical facts are the check marks on separate pieces of paper. From those check marks begins a trail of interpretation, conventional and creative, which gets further and further from those facts. But those facts, those check marks, are not very interesting in themselves. It is that interpretation which makes the contribution.

Direct Participation and Indirect Observation

Our use of questionnaire inventories in the campaign study is a form of indirect observation. Not only do we not see anyone make those marks, the marks themselves are proxies for the behavior we actually want to study. The behavior we want to study is the process involved in making a voting choice, but that behavior is observable only in part (assuming that one accepts cognition as an actual behavior). Even that part is rarely available to the researcher occurring at the inconvenient times and places of everyday life. In order to connect our check marks with voting decisions, we have to create an extended inference. The proof of the inference is when it works to predict actual voting decisions. Our study, as most studies, awaits that proof.

The largely undocumented inference of indirect observation has come under increasing criticism. The experimental protocols, survey questionnaires, and the artificial conditions associated with most research has been scoured as being— well—unnatural. These research techniques, so the claim goes, are used because they are comparatively easy. The researcher wrongly assumes a single reality for us all and appears mostly interested in the quick fix.

But, the argument goes, human behavior is primarily directed by the concepts one holds cognitively—on the inside. The researcher becomes privy to these concepts through direct interaction with people in their everyday settings. Rather than relying primarily on measurement instruments to collect data in artificial settings, the researcher needs to be the prime instrument of observation through participation in natural settings.

The reply is no less acerbic. Although there are examples of poor design and sloppy measurement, if science is to be something more than biography, it must free itself from the individual to seek the general principles of human life. It must function under known conditions with the exercise of control using reliable measurement which is not dependent on the individual using it.

The argument tilts on the fulcrum of reality. Is reality essentially out there for all to see, or is it a social construction in which we behave toward what's out there according to what we believe inside. The more one's position is toward the external reality side, the more acceptable are the assumptions of common influences, the equivalence of meanings and the objectivity of behavior. The more one's position is toward the constructed reality side, the more influences, meanings, and behaviors become contingent on the context of performance.

COMMENTARY:

Ten years ago, the assumption of a common reality would not have been questioned. Today, it is the premise of a lively debate. I find myself somewhere in the middle ground. By carefully defining the conditions of data collection, I apparently tap into a reality, whether external or constructed, that is common enough to generate responses which show systematic relationships useful for certain kinds of explanation as the campaign study demonstrates. On the other hand, I am unwilling to generalize my interpretation of that relationship beyond the particular campaign and conditions of observation despite justification by the common reality assumption. I remain intensely skeptical of claims of a common reaction to research conditions, media content, political campaigns, the behavior of others, and the like. It just doesn't seem likely.

EXERCISES

1 Students sometimes comment that they understood a test item differently from what the instructor intended. How would a constructivist analyze this situation?
2 How would an objectivist (and the instructor) analyze the situation in question 1?
3 What makes an act aggressive?
4 Is your answer to question 3 objectivist or subjectivist?
5 Can a conflict between what an actor claims to be doing and what an observer says the actor is doing be reduced or is this conflict irreducible due to the unique perspective of actor and observer?

6 In the argument of question 5, is there also something that the actor actually did?
7 If the observation of any action involves an interpretation, how can that observation be direct?

ARGUMENTATION IN SCIENCE

Science, as the term is defined here, is concerned with empirical questions—questions of fact. Its arguments are directed toward validating statements of fact and about facts. This all appears rather cut and dried, but, actually, there is considerable uncertainty which surrounds this process. The uncertainty begins with the question of what a fact is and continues in concerns for the proper form of argument for connecting evidence and claim, and the nature of valid conclusions from those arguments. In the short space allotted here, I can do no more than introduce some of the problems which prevent the reduction of this uncertainty.

One comment before proceeding to these three areas: Practitioners do not doubt their claims of fact. That is, when I practice science, I do not doubt the claims that I advance. I do not concern myself with what is a fact or a proper argument. I have available a set of conventional solutions to those problems. These solutions are found in the methods and practices of the scientific community of which I am a practicing member. This section makes those conventional solutions explicit.

Factual Claims

A **fact** is a descriptive statement of what is. For an empiricist, the ontological question which automatically follows, is answered by that which can be experienced. Therefore, a fact is a descriptive statement of what has or can be experienced. The problems are how do I know what I have experienced, how direct must the experience be, and how far can I move from experience before the claim is no longer factual.

As I noted in Chapter 1, most modern-day scientists hold that experience is not directly knowable. Instead, there is an interpretive step by which experience is organized and made sensible. Obviously, the nature of that interpretive step becomes vitally important to our understanding of what knowledge is. If that interpetive step is reliably consistent for the human race, then a single structure for human knowledge is possible. This is the argument advanced by positivists. If this interpretive step is conventional—dependent upon the cultural milieu in which it is made, then human knowledge is relative. This is the argument advanced by the relativists. If this interpretive step is highly idiosyncratic, then an empirical standard, as we understand it, is not possible. This is the position of the existentialists and the **absurdists**.

The conventional solution to this problem is the principle of intersubjective agreement. Intersubjective agreement, as we have seen, is the agreement among common observers. All of science uses this proposition as the solution to the uncertainty of the nature of the interpretation of experience. It is through this principle that private experience moves toward public knowledge. Within science, however, there is considerable disagreement as to when intersubjective agreement has been achieved. For the quantitative researcher these are questions of reliability; for the qualitative researcher these are questions of the degree of membership accomplished by the researcher. No one expects one-to-one correspondence among observers and observations; nevertheless, some agreements must be demonstrated for the argument to be accepted as empirical science. Even the most existential of the interpretivists require that an interpretation be sensible to those interpreted.

We've seen a bit of the argumentation surrounding the question of how direct one's experience must be for it to be admitted into the arena of empirical fact. Directness ranges from the actual participation by the observer to the upper reaches of instrumentation. For those who use measurement devices (questionnaires, surveys, inventories, tests, and the like) it is enough that the event measured could be experienced. For the hardline participant-researchers, measurement devices represent a formidable barrier to an understanding of what is happening.

Finally, we have the question how far from direct experience (a concept we see is problematic on its own) can a statement be formulated and still remain factual? Take the "naturally" factual statement: "I was born on April 6th." I certainly experienced being born (though I have no knowledge of it). But what of April 6th? April 6th has no empirical quality; it is a metaphysical notion—a contrivance of a calendar. Take a more scientific fact-like statement: "Frustration leads to aggression." Both frustration and aggression are concepts which may or may not organize experience, and, of course, the notion of "leads to" is the insightful creation of the author.

The conventional solution to both of these problems is in the acceptable methodology within a community. Scientific methodology is the set of accepted procedures which define both what direct experience is and what is a proper factual statement. Such methodology is specific to the community in which it arises. One cannot, therefore, resolve arguments about such matters across communities. Within a community, it is a different matter depending on the clarity of the standard and the depth of its acceptance.

COMMENTARY:

Few communities practice all that they preach. The beginning researcher is often confused by the appearance of practices that are expressly forbidden or discouraged in the reconstructions presented by methodology texts. Principles of research (as opposed to practices of research) are used primarily to evaluate the product of research rather than to direct its conduct. Methodology texts, including this one, are, at best, only a starting point for an entrance into the practice *of research.*

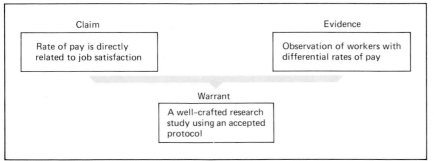

FIGURE 3-3
Claim and evidence are joined according to the rules (warrants) of valid (acceptable) arguments.

Forms of Argument

An argument is a grounded claim supported by warranted evidence (see Rieke and Sillars, 1984). A grounded claim is one which has the potential of acceptance within the audience to which it is addressed. (It cannot be rejected out of hand.) Warranted evidence is composed of statements which are recognized as evidence. In strict rationalist (quantitative) research, the claim is an a priori hypothesis which is connected to (grounded by) some theoretical system, the evidence is presented in statistically analyzed quantified data, and the **warrant** is in the ideological system which contains the accepted practices of that community (see Figure 3-3). In strict naturalist (qualitative) research, the claim is an a posteriori interpretative narrative grounded in membership, the evidence of which is held in field notes and the personal experience of the narrator, and the warrant is the ideological system which contains the accepted practices of that community.

The remainder of this book will explore the claims and evidence given in quantitative and qualitative research. It is to the warrants that we will turn our attention here. The relationship between claim and evidence in empirical science is warranted by the beliefs that are held about the world this science attempts to explain. In the next few paragraphs, I will set out a description of the belief systems which characterize quantitative and qualitative research. These descriptions are reconstructions of widely separated end points; real people fall somewhere in between. I hope that the meaning of these paragraphs will continue to emerge as you become more knowledgeable of the practices which express the ideology described. You may wish to reread this section after reading through the methods chapters.

Quantitative Warrants   The quantitative researcher believes in an ordered, stable universe; a single, unified material reality which includes human behavior in social action and which is "naturally" connected to, yet independent of our knowledge of it. This reality is contained in the sum of independent elements, which can be studied separately.

An ordered, stable universe warrants the search for explanations of prediction and control. By ordered is meant that the phenomena that exist in the universe exist in relation to one another. It is the business of science to discover both the phenomena and their relationships. The assumed stability of these relationships liberates knowledge claims from the decay of time and privileges repeatable methods of generating evidence. That is, scientific knowledge is progressive, giving closer and closer approximations of our universe and reliable methods are by definition better.

A single, unified, **material reality** justifies a single science for its investigation and provides the impetus for objective measurement. The natural connection between reality and our understanding of it means that we can have positive knowledge of that reality. The independence of that reality provides for the notion of validity—defines a true statement—and permits generalization from one environment to another. The **atomistic** nature of the universe means that measurement can be freed from the context of its performance. That is, one can actually measure a concept such as intelligence independently of the intelligent individual.

Qualitative Warrants   For the qualitative researcher, there are multiple realities which incorporate material and subjective components. The central world is a world of meaning; material reality intersects but does not contain the world of meaning. Meaning is the product of social action; humanity is found in society not in the individual. The multiple realities of meaning are not necessarily orderly nor coherent. Further, the order and coherence that is evidenced is bounded in time. Change, even chaotic change, is to be expected. The world is created in our knowledge of it. That is not to say that there is no material existence outside of the human conscious. It is to say that the way we make sense of that material existence is the product of our conscious efforts not of the structure of the universe. Knowledge is always human knowledge—a set of contingent truths.

That material reality is not the whole of the world of meaning motivates the development of a separate science for the study of human behavior in social action. A separate science requires its own methods and practices.

The notion of multiple realities means that evidence is always embedded in the context in which it is formulated. There is no single set of human attributes fixed for all time. Humanity has many expressions. Claims that extend over time and context are suspect.

Obviously in multiple, changeable realities, the criterion of **reliability** has to be carefully applied. It is often irrelevant. Further, the nature of a valid statement changes. **Validity** is set in time and place.

That the multiple realities in which we move are composed in social action of meaning rather than by relationships among material elements requires the researcher to be part of the social action by which a reality is constructed. Objective measurement is rejected; interpretation is valorized.

Finally, the bounded nature of meaning—that meaning arises within a context—validates holistic explanations rather than atomistic fragmentation. Worlds are not to be understood piece by piece but in coherent narratives worthy of their complexity.

COMMENTARY:

In the classroom, after presenting these two positions, I am often asked which one is right. I don't know the answer, but what interests me is that the question is a good example of how our ideology directs our inquiry. The question is a rationalist question.

Nature of Valid Conclusions: Laws, Rules, and Stories
A **law** is a universal generalization. It is a description of a relationship which holds for every case within its scope. A **rule** is a contingent generalization. It is a description of a relationship which holds with a given probability for every case within its scope. A **story** is coherent narrative. It makes sense out of people engaging in social action in everyday life.

In the human sciences, a lawlike statement is the typical goal of those who presuppose a common reality and objective attributes of meaning and behavior. A rule-like statement is the usual goal of those who presuppose a constructed reality and subjective attributes of meaning and behavior. And a story is the valid conclusion for those who hold to a nonfragmentable reality in which the action cannot be understood except in the whole of it.

Laws and Rules   The majority in the practice of the human sciences seek laws or rules as the valid conclusion of their arguments. As rule statements can be seen as modified law statements, it is useful to compare the two kinds. (A following section compares these statements with stories.)

Laws permit no error within the scope of their formulation; a single contrary case calls for a restatement of the law. Rules presume, and sometimes specify, a given rate of error; the number of contrary cases is that rate. A rules perspective rejects the concept of a universal generalization because it presumes that there is insufficient order in the universe of human behavior. Laws which do presume that order are based on hardline assumptions of materialism and causal reasoning; rules incorporate a notion of social constructions in reality and use conditional reasoning.

The consideration of laws and rules can be organized on two dimensions: the strength of dependency implied in the relationship and the extent of the generalization claimed. Conditional reasoning-in-use, as we have seen in Chapter 1, often implies some dependency between the variables in the relationship claimed. We see this dependency in the words used in the hypothesis to describe the relationship. Words such as "leads to," "tends to," "is associated with" represent decreasing levels of dependency. These hypotheses snuggle up to the causal, lawlike end of things. Phrases such as "subsequent to," "appears with," "follows upon," are stochastic interpretations and are closer to the rules end.

Scientists who specify dependent relationships are, indeed, likely to be seeking lawlike statements as their goal and to be using conditional reasoning only as a necessary accommodation for the lack of causal evidence. Analysts who do not add a dependent implication to conditional reasoning are likely to be seeking a rule-like explanation.

The **level of generality** claimed is also a clue as to the explanatory goal of the research. Conclusions which begin with such words as "children," "readers," "consumers," and "audiences" are driving toward lawlike statements about universal classes. Those that begin with "members of this organization," "the family I studied," and "this social group" are not.

Naturally, it seems, practice blurs these fine distinctions. Scientists seeking covering laws have had difficulty in meeting the evidentiary demands that the demonstration of cause entails. They have been forced to tolerate explanations which show considerable error. Their conclusions, however, are not considered rules but imperfect laws, for it is assumed that better methods will reduce the failures.

Rule-oriented scientists, for their part, have had difficulty in convincing the community that their findings generalize at all. This difficulty has led some practitioners to abandon the arguments for external validity (that the finding applies to cases other than the one under study) and to claim as their goal the full description of the single instance. Their goal is right interpretation. This application has been attractive to the qualitative researcher, for it permits a "traditional look" to an argument while still presenting a bounded, contextually embedded claim. The qualitative researcher's use of rule is expanding the meaning of that term to a sort of handbook statement—the rules of the game if you will. The rules perspective then is being stretched across objective and subjective approaches. As a concept it varies, in maddening invention, from "soft-law" to "etiquette."

Stories   A story as a valid conclusion from a scientific argument is neither a fictional account nor journalism. It is, however, the insightful telling of the relationships among empirical facts in a manner that connects those facts to some larger discourse about the world in which we live. Stories are found in both objective and subjective perspectives. The cosmological disciplines of astronomy and geology make extensive use of stories. The story is the presentational form of understanding as an explanation.

The story has a particular affinity, however, for the arguments that use interpretive narratives. The "telling of a good story" is a hallmark of that research. Such stories (and I am underlining that there are different forms) are in clear contrast with laws. Laws are reductionistic, universal, and enduring. Stories are expansionistic, specific, and contingent. Laws are said to be understood naturally; stories must be understood in their context.

In this section, then, we have seen that there is a wide spread in the valid conclusions that can be drawn from explanation which is considered scientific. For some, the ultimate goal is the universal generalization. For others, it is the contribution to our ability to discourse about the world around us. These different goals, as we should now understand, usually imply a much different world-view which itself is part of the assumptions of the research.

COMMENTARY:

This chapter presents what is undoubtedly a bewildering array of assumptions and perspectives. An understanding of this array is necessary to locate oneself within the multiple epistemologies which now characterize the human sciences. One's position on this array makes sense out of science in very different ways. If my sense of my respondent's insights into the practice of science is correct, one's position on these issues is often uncertain and over the years open to change. In spite of a public image of confidence, we all do struggle with who we are, how should we do what we do, and, in the end, what is it that we really know. In the remaining text of this book, I will confidently describe a set of methods acceptable to the scientific community and useful to accomplish reasonable goals. You should remember the struggle.

EXERCISES

1 How does the nature of facts demonstrate that science must have a perspective?
2 A scientistic researcher would reject the notion of argumentation in science. Why?
3 The number of warrants with at least some legitimation in science has increased dramatically in the past decade. How does that increase affect what is considered factual and what is considered evidence of fact?
4 Consider the warrants presented under "Forms of Argument." Which ones appear valid to you?
5 What is the difference between a universal generalization and a stereotype?
6 "Phase Y will follow phase X 60 percent of the time" is a conditional generalization. I now observe phase X; exactly what will happen next?
7 How does your answer to question 6 demonstrate the limits of conditional prediction?
8 What is the difference between expansionistic and reductionistic science?

SUMMARY

In this chapter, we have considered the presuppositions which are the foundations of our methods. We looked at them in the manner of our engagement with the human object, in our formulations of meaning, and in argumentation in science. A short review of the arguments presented in each follows.

Engagement

To engage the human object of our study requires a model of the individual. Two such models were discussed—the individual as the sum of a set of attributes and the situated individual. In the attribute model, an individual is generally seen as a collection of attributes (characteristics such as personality, intelligence, etc.) which have a common nature and an individual expression. That is, we all have a personality but each individual's personality is unique. The set of attributes that define human nature can be seen as finite and fixed, material and objective, or as ever-expanding, socially constituted, and subjectively understood.

The model of the situated individual sees the individual as a contingent expression—one dependent on the context of performance. Who depends on where not as a matter of latent traits appearing but as the re-creation of the person within time and place. The individual has to be understood holistically within the setting.

Individuals are engaged within aggregates or memberships. Aggregates are collections of individuals (people or things) which meet the definitional requirements of a common classification. Aggregates can be described by their characteristics which arise from the traits of the individuals that compose them. Aggregates are used to control for the confusion of individual differences and thus reveal the common qualities of the elements. Aggregates do not act. They do not have methods and practices. The practice of reifying classifications or making entities out of aggregates leads to explanations of coordinated action which are debatable.

The concept of membership was described as the shared understandings held by individuals who identify themselves and are identified as members. The concept of membership is often used to explain the characteristics, methods and practices, and causes and consequences of member behavior. Others resist the notion of a membership as a special thing seeing member behaviors as the responses of individuals to the sum of the influences of others.

Dyads as a particular class were contrasted as an aggregate, an imperfect group, or as the site of the relationship of friendship.

Meaning

The major comparison was between the ideas of objective meaning which is delivered in commonly understood content characteristics and subjective meaning which is constructed from the mix of content and the individual as contained in a context. Shifting between the strong positions of these different conceptualizations of meaning radically changes the explanations possible from standard research designs.

Our interests in behavior was shown to be less in the physical act than in its interpretation as action. The meaning of behavior, then, is equally as problematic as content. An extended example of the interpretive processes of research was given.

Direct observation in natural settings through the participation of the researcher in the behavior under study has been suggested as a better means of understanding human behavior than measurement instruments for collecting data in artificial settings. The argument was seen as another expression of the differences between objective and subjective formulations of reality.

Argumentation in Science

Science is concerned with the advancement of claims about empirical facts. The notion of a fact, its definition in terms of direct experience, and the character of a factual statement was discussed.

An argument was described as composed of grounded claims supported by warranted evidence. The warrants of quantitative and qualitative research were considered.

Finally, the kinds of valid conclusions used in scientific explanation were considered. Researchers in the study of communication were seen to seek different explanatory goals. Some consider the ultimate goal to be the specification of universal generalizations or laws. Others see laws as an unlikely outcome because of the inherent lack of order in human behavior and seek contingent generalizations or rules. Still others opt for holistic understanding provided in stories.

RELATED READINGS

Recent Research Using Aggregates

Kapp, J. E. and Barnett, G. A. Predicting organizational effectiveness from communication activities: A multiple indicator model. *Human Communication Research*, 1983, *9*, 239–254. [Uses the organization as the unit of explanation.]

Pingree, S. Children's cognitive processes in constructing social reality. *Journalism Quarterly*, 1983, *60*, 415–422. [Directed toward the explanation of cognitive attributes of children.]

Webster, J. G. and Wakshlag, J. J. The impact of group viewing on patterns of television program choice. *Journal of Broadcasting*, 1982, *26*, 445–455. [Uses group as an independent variable to explain the effect of viewing in a group on individuals.]

Recent Research Using Memberships (Groups)

Hirokawa, R. Y. Group communication and problem-solving effectiveness: An investigation of group phases. *Human Communication Research*, 1983, *9*, 291–305. [Considers phase as a group attribute.]

Poole, M. S., McPhee, R. D., and Seibold, D. R. A comparison of normative and interactional explanations of group decision-making: Social decision schemes versus valence distributions. *Communication Monographs*, 1982, *49*, 1–19. [Provides comparison between group-as-process and sum-of-members perspectives.]

Taylor, K. P., Buchanan, R. W., Pryor, B., and Strawn, D. U. How do jurors reach a verdict? *Journal of Communication*, 1981, *31*, 37–42. [Conducted from the sum-of-members perspective.]

Recent Research Using Dyads

Applegate, J. L. The impact of construct system development on communication and impression formation in persuasive contexts. *Communication Monographs*, 1982, *49*, 277–289. [Uses the dyad as an efficient method of assessing the effect of face-to-face communication.]

Hopper, R., Knapp, M. L., and Scott, L. Couples' personal idioms: Exploring intimate talk. *Journal of Communication*, 1981, *31*, 23–33. [Views dyad as unique setting for special forms of communication.]

Rawlins, W. K. Negotiating close friendship: The dialective of conjunctive freedoms. *Human Communication Research*, 1983, *9*, 255–266. [Views friendship as a dyadic relationship.]

Recent Research Using Different Perspectives on Meaning

Hocking, J. E. Sports and spectators: Intra-audience effects. *Journal of Communication*, 1982, *32*, 100–108. [Considers the effect of context in the meaning of a sporting event.]

Stovall, J. G. Foreign policy issue coverage in the 1980 presidential campaign. *Journalism Quarterly*, 1982, *59*, 531–540. [A traditional content analysis based on the assumption of equivalence of meaning.]

Wolf, M. A., Meyer, T. P., and White, C. A rules-based study of television's role in the construction of social reality. *Journal of Broadcasting*, 1982, *26*, 813–829. [An examination of how media content comes to have meaning within a social framework.]

Analytical Comment on Different Perspectives on Explanatory Objectives and Methods of Reasoning

Copi, I. M. *Introduction to logic.* New York: Macmillan Publishing Co. Inc., 1982. [A standard introductory text in the methods of logic.]

Cushman, D. The rules perspective as a theoretical basis for the study of human communication. *Communication Quarterly*, 1977, *25*, 30–45. [Commentary on rules.]

Fisher, B. A. *Perspectives on human communication.* New York: Macmillan Publishing Co. Inc., 1978. [A where-are-we-now analysis.]

Keat, R. and Urry, J. *Social theory as science.* London: Routledge and Kegan Paul, 1982. [A Marxist, critical theory view of science.]

Lakatos, I. Falsification and the methodology of scientific research programmes. In I. Lakatos and A. Musgrave (Eds.), *Criticism and the growth of knowledge.* Cambridge: Cambridge University Press, 1970, 91–195. [An examination of how change is introduced in science.]

Lull, J. A rules approach to the study of television and society. *Human Communication Research,* 1982, *9,* 3–16. [Adopts the middle ground between laws and interpretation.]

Mandelbaum, M. Social facts. In Ryan A. (Ed.), *The philosophy of social explanation.* London: Oxford University Press, 1973, 105–118. [Examines the reality of the constructs of social institutions.]

Nicholson, M. *The scientific analysis of social behavior: A defence of empiricism in social science.* New York: St. Martin's Press, 1983. [A defense of traditional science updated.]

Popper, K. *The logic of scientific discovery.* London: Hutchinson, 1959. [Examines the structure of argument in science.]

Putnam, L. L. The interpretive perspective: An alternative to functionalism. In Putnam, L. L. and Pacanowsky, M. (Eds.), *Communication and organizations: An interpretive approach.* Beverly Hills, CA: Sage Publications, 1983, 31–54. [Presents the assumptions of the interpretive approach in particular contrast with those of objectivist schools of thought.]

Suppe, F. (Ed.). *The structure of scientific theories.* Urbana: University of Illinois Press, 1977. [An extensive reader in the philosophy of science covering most of the issues.]

Wann, T. W. (Ed.) *Behaviorism and phenomenology.* Chicago: The University of Chicago Press, 1964. [A collection of commentary and debate concerning objective and subjective approaches.]

QUANTITATIVE RESEARCH

Quantitative research leans heavily on the presuppositions of a material, objective reality which can be decomposed into independent attributes which become the object of study. We call it quantitative research because it describes behavior in the terms of quantification theory. Using this theory, behavior is seen as discrete, functionally equivalent units which are amenable to analysis under the rubrics of mathematical logic.

Most quantitative research is both positivistic and reductionistic. It is positivistic because most quantitative researchers would hold that we can have positive knowledge of the empirical world about us based upon our experience of that world. It is reductionistic because its practitioners generally seek explanations which cover broad classes of entities and events, thereby reducing the number of explanations necessary to understand the world.

In this section of five chapters, we first examine the deductive model of quantitative research in Chapter 4. Chapter 5 explores measurement both as a process of observation and as a process of quantification—the redefinition of behavior as numbers. Chapter 6 looks at the logic and methods of sampling. Chapter 7 considers the statistical analysis of numerical sets which stand for human behaviors. Finally, Chapter 8 examines the use of statistical decision rules as evidence in hypothesis testing.

AN INTRODUCTION TO QUANTITATIVE RESEARCH

SYNOPSIS

This chapter presents an overview of the quantitative approach. Quantitative research has a deductive character in which new knowledge is gained through the analysis of existing theory. Quantitative research starts with a theoretical position and moves to support or falsify that position by testing hypotheses which are derived from it.

In testing a hypothesis, the researcher devises a protocol which provides a fair test of the relationship between the variables of interest claimed by the hypothesis. This protocol typically involves the quantification of behavior or the artifacts of behavior through some process of measurement. Measurement generates data which, in turn, are analyzed to reveal empirical facts. These empirical facts are used as evidence to verify or falsify the hypothesis.

The final move within this paradigm is the reconstruction of theory. As an empirical science, the court of last resort is the empirical evidence. Theoretical constructs will, over what might be a very long run, finally comply with that evidence.

THE TERMS AND TECHNIQUES OF QUANTITATIVE METHODS

The heritage of quantitative research in the human sciences is a quest for universal generalizations which will describe the characteristics, practices, causes, and consequences of human behavior. Rationalistic science in communication seeks a set of universal statements which will define and describe the characteristics, practices, causes, and consequences of human communication.

Quantitative research follows a **deductive** model in which our understanding of any particular action is derived from universal, covering premises. In an immature science such as communication, there is a bootstrap character about this reasoning. We, of course, do not have a well-developed set of covering premises from which to derive our research. What we do have is a partially integrated set of insights, intuitions, and accepted truths—some of which appear brilliant and others tiresome. This is our stock of knowledge from which we practice our craft. This stock of knowledge contains the **constructs** and **concepts** of the field and the relationships among them.

For example, persuasion is a construct—it is a relatively coherent organization of ideas about communication behavior. It contains lesser constructs such as: "Content can be distinguished by the intent of the sender." This construct itself is composed of the concepts of content, sender, intent, and the implied receiver. In organizational studies an example of a construct might be job satisfaction. This construct incorporates the notions of a job as a defineable activity in time and place and, of course, of satisfaction which might include the concepts of pleasure, evaluative criteria, and so on.

Violent content is certainly a construct in media studies. Perhaps you could add other examples of your own.

Constructs and concepts are abstractions of varying scope which organize our understanding of sense data. Two things you might note about them: (a) They seem so ordinary. Certainly there are senders and receivers and types of content in communication. There certainly are if we say so. That is, if we determine that organizing the empirical data into those constructs is useful, then we will create those constructs to accommodate that use. How odd that sentence sounds; it is almost too glib, too trivializing. We take the constructs of our field so much for granted that to hold them up for inspection of what they are is a bit shocking.

The second notable aspect is (b) that our understanding of what a construct covers is heuristically loose. Concepts and constructs are generalizations which have to cover a manifest of particulars. It is not very useful to require that the concept of content be applied only to a specific string of words. To be useful it has to point out the communality among what is printed on this page, the turns of a conversation we might have, and what we might watch on television. As is appropriate with a very useful concept, where the notion of content begins and ends remains equivocal. We can enlarge and contract its meaning for good ends as when we include the medium of presentation as part of the content or when we exclude all but the spoken words in a conversation. Both of these applications help us to discover something about the data we are analyzing.

The constructs and concepts of communication get passed on in our courses, textbooks, journal articles, and conversations. Each lecture, each review of the literature is a partial reconstruction of what we know and serves to maintain that knowledge. This knowledge gives us our world-view, our global understanding of what communication is, how it functions and why. Knowing the constructs and concepts of the field, we can make sense of particular forms of human behavior as acts of communication.

Developing New Constructs

The process of adding to that stock of knowledge begins when we question that knowledge, when some discontinuity appears between what we see and what we understand, when we are dissatisfied with the confusion in the internal structure of this knowledge, when we find it lacking some answer. That is, when something occurs which renders which we know problematic. This questioning is on the order of a revision like editing a text. Although any part of what we know is open to change, the change that occurs will be *within* the whole of that knowledge. We don't throw everything out, but we polish and add to what we have.

Perhaps our contribution starts with some nagging doubt: "I don't understand how there can be senders and receivers in face-to-face dyads when both members are obviously continually communicating. There must be a better way of making sense of what is going on."

Or: "I don't think 'seeking information' is a useful way to describe the primary purpose readers have for subscribing to the newspaper. It seems to limit our understanding of goals and may even be counter-productive."

Or perhaps, the contribution begins as an extension of what we know through a new application: "How can the principle of interaction in interpersonal communication be applied to mass communication settings?"

Or, the problem may arise in a move to reduce the diversity of explanation: "There must be a way of reconciling these five hypotheses concerning organizational effectiveness. They all seem to concern the same concepts."

Whatever the source, we begin by asking something that cannot be answered out of our stock of knowledge or that brings into question what we know. The next step is to propose an answer. This proposed answer is derived from that portion of our stock of knowledge which is not brought into question. For example, our earlier questioner was dissatisfied with the concepts of senders and receivers as constructs for describing face-to-face communication. A likely method of attack would be to show that these concepts are not compatible with other constructs in interpersonal communication such as "process," "the emergent nature of conversation," and "mutual participation in the formation of conversational content." A reformulation of the description of the communicants in face-to-face communication could be proposed as a more integrative approach than that provided by the notions of senders and receivers. This proposed answer is called a **hypothesis**. The process of research now proceeds to consider the standing of this hypothesis, to determine its worth as explanation. We will proceed to consider the nature of the hypothesis and its role in this research process.

HYPOTHESES

A hypothesis is a *statement* which poses a *relationship* between two or more *variables*. A **variable** is a concept which can take more than one value; it is any distinguishable and distinguishing property which is of interest to the researcher. Examples are height, weight, gender, intelligence, personality traits, attitudes, cognitive styles. The relationship is one of the four kinds of relationships found in scientific explanation: X is a characteristic of Y; X is a practice of Y; X is associated with Y in a predictive relationship; or X is dependent on Y in a conditional relationship. The statement is a tentative answer to the problem discovered within the fabric of our knowledge. Here are three examples of hypotheses:

Hypotheses: Examples

Tardy et al. (1981) became interested in the construct of agenda setting and its function across individuals exhibiting different levels of political participation. Agenda setting is a well-accepted construct in media studies. It claims that one of the function of the media of a society is to establish what it is that the members of the society hold to be important. Tardy and his coauthors felt that this statement could be refined by adding the modifying notion of political expertise. They reasoned that individuals with greater experience in political activity should show less effect of the agenda setting function. They hypothesized, "As political participation increases, the influence of television agendas decreases" (p. 625).

The variables in this hypothesis are political participation and the influence of television agendas. An inverse relationship is stated so that as one increases the other decreases. Note that at this point we are not sure of what either political participation or the influence of television agendas is. Here, they are large concepts which could vary in innumerable ways. Their definitions await refinement in the methods that will be used to study them. Note also that the relationship is one of implied dependency (although it will be tested for association only). In the hypothesis, the presence of high levels of political participation serves as an index for the presence of low levels of influence. No mechanism of connection is explicitly stated; the intent of the theory is, however, clear.

Lustig and King (1980) had an interest in the relationship between communication apprehension (one's level of fear in anticipation of oral communication) and the situational adaptiveness of one's communication strategies. Their review of the literature suggested to them that while individuals generally show a wide range of communication adaptations to situations at hand, individuals with high levels of communication apprehension may be less adaptive.

They hypothesized that situational adaptation of communication strategies "is a function of the level of communication apprehension" (p. 77). This hypothesis has three variables: communication situations, communication strategies, and communication apprehension. There are two relationships contained in it. The first is the relationship between situations and communication strategies. The relationship is contained in the word "adaptation," which implies that communication strategy will change as the situation changes. The second relationship is between the first relationship and the level of apprehension. Lustig and King hypothesize that the relationship between situations and strategies will take different forms at different levels of apprehension.

In this hypothesis, the first relationship becomes a variable which might be called situational adaptiveness. It is the degree of variation within strategies across situations and is composed of the changing relationship between the variables of strategies and situations. In describing the variable of situational adaptiveness, Lustig and King have provided an additional property by which communication can be understood.

Putnam and Sorenson (1982) bring a process perspective to the study of communication accuracy in organizations. Their concern was with the methods subordinates used to interpret ordinary but ambiguous messages received across organizational lines. They believed that a message could be ambiguous both in content and in the context in which it was received. (An example of a message with ambiguous content is: "We need to build a strong sense of togetherness.") A key to their argument about context was the conceptualization of hierarchical levels of a work community as a specific context for interpretation. They argued that a message sent across hierarchies (a memo from the boss) would gain ambiguity because it would be read out of context.

Putnam and Sorenson assumed that the level of organization (number of contexts) and the content ambiguity of the message would affect the number of rules or methods subordinates would use to interpret those messages. They were, however, uncertain as what that effect might be. Their hypothesis, therefore, was nondirectional. It stated: "Organizational level will influence the number of rules employed to process Hi and Lo E [Equivocal] messages" (p. 118).

This hypothesis contains three variables: organizational level, equivocality (message ambiguity), and rules of interpretation. There is an implied relationship between the level of equivocality and the number of rules, but the hypothesis does not inform us of what that relationship might be. The expectation is clear that the number of rules will vary across equivocality (as a later hypothesis clarifies) and that this pattern will be affected in some way by organizational level.

Two things to note about this hypothesis: (1) The variables involved come out of a particular perspective and body of literature in organizational communication. They have to be understood within that intellectual lineage. Within this perspective equivocality, for instance, is present in all messages as meaning is always in doubt. The reader has to be aware that these concepts organize reality in significantly different ways from concepts with similar names in other perspectives. (2) This hypothesis lacks specificity which grants the researchers considerable freedom in determining if the hypothesis has been supported. In fact, any change in the number of rules that can be associated with levels of organization can be interpreted as support. (In the Tardy et al. hypothesis, only an inverse change would be accepted.)

Putnam and Sorenson are aware that their hypothesis is incomplete. It is incomplete because they can find no justification for specifying a direction of change given the present state of explanation. Of course, they could just specify a direction, but a precipitate choice could bring the entire hypothesis into question in two ways. (1) They could guess wrong, which would put them in a weakened position for having created an argument for a failed hypothesis. (2) Their choice might appear idiosyncratic without sufficient standing within their community of practitioners, in which case, even supporting evidence might be discounted. In either case, they put their hypothesis at risk for little gain. Acceptable hypotheses must make sense within the community of practitioners.

Implied Hypotheses

In the usual case, the more precisely I can state my hypothesis, the stronger the case I can make for its acceptance should it prove to be successful. The Putnam and Sorenson example demonstrates, however, that the state of our knowledge may be such that a hypothesis of any but the most general is difficult to justify. There are, additionally, many circumstances where it is not possible to explicitly state a hypothesis of any kind.

For example, when there has been sufficient work in an area to suggest the presence of certain variables, but not sufficient to define a relationship, the researcher may pose an initial question of the sort, "What is the relationship between this variable and that variable?" The possible relationships to test for the answer to this question are three: Is X present in Y; is X predictable by Y; and is X dependent on Y? The choice of which of these to test implies the researcher's best bet as to which can be supported.

In even a less apparent manner, hypotheses can be contained in the literature cited as justification for the researcher's present interest. The earlier studies become the implied hypotheses for the current effort. For example, Barwise, Ehrenberg, and Goodhardt (1982) questioned the rate of viewing of successive episodes of daily and weekly programming. Their question was not plucked from the air, however. Their interest developed from their doubt of the generally accepted industry belief of high repeat viewing ("90 percent or more") and their earlier studies which showed a much lower level of repeat viewing. The results of these earlier studies formed their expectations and were the implied hypotheses of this study.

Finally, in examining implied hypotheses, we get into those areas of descriptive and exploratory research, where hypotheses begin to slide into presuppositions. Presume that we wish to conduct a descriptive study outlining the characteristic opinions individuals have concerning some political issue which has just arisen. On the face of it, this study may show the least derivation from what we presently know. We certainly can't make any predictions about the values or valences of the opinions we wish to measure. The issue around which these opinions are formed has, after all, just arisen.

Nevertheless, the measurement instruments and methods used contain the presumptions of an answer. They are, first of all, predicated on the construct of "opinions," which is a way of conceptualizing unobservable cognitive processes.

These opinions, further, are assumed to be of a certain nature accessible through the asking of particular questions. The instruments and methods, then, form an implied hypothesis about the properties of the human behavior in question.

The design of a questionnaire, the development of an experimental protocol, and the application of methods all involve a claim that reality is how the researcher would have it within that design. Questionnaires, indeed all methods, should be considered as hypotheses in need of evidence that reality is what they claim.

The Purposes of Hypotheses

Hypotheses serve several purposes: (a) As we have noted, they are a proposed answer to some problem within our understanding of phenomena; (b) they also specify the empirical observations required for the test of the proposed answer; (c) and they provide protection against **self-evident reasoning**. A word or two on each follows.

Hypotheses as Proposed Answers   Hypotheses develop from the careful study of what it is we know about the phenomena of interest. As we test that knowledge for its coherence, completeness, utility, and goodness of fit with our observations, we learn of its weaknesses. In solving those weaknesses, we make use of those successful constructs and concepts already in place and add new notions and new relationships. Even revolutionary hypotheses flow out of our present knowledge. To some extent, then, every hypothesis must be acceptable within our present framework. The process of acceptance begins when the scientist conducts a **fair test** of the statement.

Specification of Required Observations   The hypothesis, itself, identifies the observations needed for its test. If we return to the hypothesis proposed by Tardy et al. (1981), we can see how the statement identifies these observations. The hypothesis was: "As political participation increases, the influence of television agendas decreases." The two variables, political participation and influence of television agendas, are abstract concepts with no empirical content or, better, with a wide potential for empirical content. One of the first tasks, then, is to provide empirical meaning for the variables.

That task will be in the purview of measurement. The measurement device which is used to collect data on political participation becomes the empirical definition of participation in the same manner that the ruler one uses provides the definition of length. This definition is called an **operational definition**.[1] In it, a concept is defined by the methods used to measure that concept. In their study, Tardy et al. used self-reports to define participation classifying those who reported acts of campaigning as "Actives" and those whose participation was limited to occasionally voting as "Inactives." Political participation was opera-

---

[1] A good operational definition of a concept is a major contribution in and of itself. We can make no progress without adequate measurement. Specific operational definitions are always problematic. You can anticipate a discussion of these issues in the chapter on measurement.

tionally defined by the answers to the self-report items on the researcher's questionnaire.

The relationship investigated by Tardy et al. is one of association. The association is an inverse one which indicates that low values on one variable will appear in conjunction with high values on the other. In the terms of the hypothesis, low values of political participation will be associated with high values for influence of television agendas. This relationship requires, then, some measure of association which itself will be an operational definition of association. This requirement establishes the design of the **statistical analysis**. (It is, of course, the question you ask which defines the method you use. It should not be the methods you know which define the questions you ask.)

What we have seen in this analysis of the Tardy et al. hypothesis is that part of the conditions for a test of the hypothesis were found in the requirements for acceptable operational definitions for the variables and for the relationship proposed between them. There are many solutions to these requirements. The research team of Tardy et al. argues for one set of them. The success or failure of a hypothesis using one set of solutions to its empirical requirements does not predict a similar outcome with a different solution set. The performance of a hypothesis is directly linked to the operations which define the terms and the relationships. The move, therefore, from the outcome of a test of a hypothesis to a statement of **theory** can be considered pure **induction**—a particular instance is used in support of a universal statement. The limitations implied by such a move are often ignored by those who use research findings.

Hypotheses as Protection against Self-Evident Reasoning   Finally, hypotheses protect us from self-evident reasoning (sometimes called post hoc reasoning). The analysis of a collection of **data** will always reveal patterns. Our problem is to distinguish between those which are trivial and those which are informative. Trivial patterns are those which are solely the result of the collection or analytical process; informative ones report the effect of one variable on another.

For example, collecting economic data from college students will reveal an average income. The question remains as to whether that average is predicated on the particular methods used and individuals asked or reveals a relationship between the state of being a college student and earning power. The methods used and the individuals asked will always provide an average income. They will not always reveal a relationship. It is the ability to predict the outcome from a rationally developed position which gives some leverage against this confusion. That is precisely what a hypothesis proposes to do. It predicts what the data will show and gives an acceptable reason for that performance. If the data match the prediction, I have a case for my argument because the hypothesis has been successful. If they do not, I must, at least, temper my claims.

The Nature of Hypothesis: Summary

The deductive character of quantitative research is shown in the way that it moves from the known to the unknown. The unknown can be reduced by applying and extending what is known deriving new knowledge from known premises. The basic assumption involved is that knowledge is of a single fabric, is continuous and unified. The discontinuities that we perceive are not discontinuities in reality but only of our present knowledge. The starting point of quantitative research, then, is theory because the theory contains the premises from which the hypotheses will be derived. Theory is an explanation of how things are. It may follow a particularly logical organization (thereby becoming a formal theory), but more likely it is a collection of assumptions embedded in methods and perspective combined with explicit statements about the subject matter at hand. In the ordinary research report or journal article, the theory becomes apparent in the references cited, the methods used, and the arguments which justify the hypotheses and conclusions. In order to fully understand a hypothesis and the evidence for its support, the reader has to piece together the underlying theory from these sources.

The hypothesis itself is a statement composed of variables in some relationship. Hypotheses serve three purposes: (a) They are a proposed addition or refinement of the theory from which they are derived. (b) They define the observational requirements for the research to follow. And (c) they enable us to distinguish between trivial and useful relationships. Hypotheses enter into theory when sufficient evidence is presented for their acceptance by the science community. The process of gathering that evidence occurs in the test of the hypotheses. The procedures for testing hypotheses are nested within the accepted protocols of analysis, an explanation of which follows.

EXERCISES

1 Identify three constructs held within your specialty in communication.
2 What are the concepts within these three constructs?
3 Why does a variable have to vary to be of interest?
4 How is a relationship defined by change in the variables?
5 What would be the likely result if a communication scientist proposed a hypothesis which used an entirely new set of constructs and concepts?
6 How does an operational definition give empirical content to a concept?

PROTOCOLS IN QUANTITATIVE RESEARCH

As with any established activity there are a number of practices of investigation which define the ordinary conduct of research. There are, to begin with, two major classes of protocols—survey and experimental.

Survey Protocols

Survey research collects observations on the characteristics of categorical entities—kinds of people, performances, content, and the like. Its intent is to explain those characteristics, their nature, and, often, the relationships among them. Examples of survey research are public-opinion polls, broadcast ratings, readership audits, content analysis, and any questionnaire.

Survey research examines things as they stand without an intent to effect some outcome. It can be seen as a passive (nondisruptive) examination made by an outsider looking in. It considers the whole population of a class or a representative sample of that population (see Chapter 6), and applies some system of measurement to determine selected characteristics of that class.

Survey research is based on the presuppositions of aggregate analysis (see Chapter 3)—that there are defineable categories; that the categories are defined by the characteristics the member elements hold in common (converge reality) and that these defining characteristics will not be shown by nonmember elements (distinguish reality). Studying the characteristics of these categories, obviously, informs us about the class of elements being studied.

Sex in America Today was a recent headline in a mass-distributed Sunday newspaper supplement (Ubell, 1984). The accompanying article described eight different sexual styles which were identified by differences in the answers to such questions as "my sex life is happy" given by 1100 American men and women ranging in age from 18 to 60. The research team offered an explanation of the sexual style characteristics of American men and women. One can see the journalistic nature of this study in that little attempt is made to connect results with theory. It is presented primarily as a method of comparison for readers.

Greenberg and Atkin (1983) in a study funded by the National Highway Traffic Safety Administration examined the portrayal of driving on prime-time television shows. From a sample of 223 programs collected over a four-year period, they classified driving portrayals according to frequency, who performs it, and what happens as a result. The motivation for this survey was not a desire to describe television driving (which is what it does, but that alone might be considered trivial), but was their belief that "frequent exposure to depictions of driving in entertainment programming may encourage behavioral modeling on the part of viewers" (p. 44). Here, knowing something about television content might be useful in understanding the effects of that content.

The Anderson and Avery presidential campaign studies introduced in Chapter 3 are an example of surveys used in a panel administration. A panel is a sample of respondents which is surveyed more than once during the study period. (A **panel study** is one form of **longitudinal research** which investigates change over time—see Janson, 1981.) In our studies, we have timed the administration of the questionnaire to take advantage of notable events during the campaign such as the debates. We, of course, don't manipulate those events, and our measurement though repeated is assumed to have no significant effects on the outcome.

Richmond, Davis, Saylor, and McCroskey (1984) surveyed the use of power strategies in supervisor/subordinate relations. They examined two separate groups (teachers and bankers) because the researchers felt that the groups represented substantially different positions on an organizational hierarchy. Throughout the study, the analysts compared the two groups' responses to measures of power and satisfaction. It is implied that the characteristics found for each group identify that group as a valid category and that the differences between the two groups distinguish the categories used. They also examine the relationship between use of power, perceived use of power by others, and satisfaction.

In this latter element of the study, they found that the increased use of behavioral alteration techniques (positing a reward, appealing to norms or higher authority) led to decreased satisfaction among subordinates. Let me draw your attention to the wording of that last sentence.[2] First of all, the words "led to" imply a conditional relationship between use of power by supervisors and satisfaction held by subordinates. Second, the modifiers "increased" and "decreased" indicate the mechanics of the relationship. Turn up the power; turn down the satisfaction.

I'm emphasizing the wording here to discuss the limits of survey research. A survey can demonstrate the presence of characteristics. It cannot demonstrate the operation of a dependent relationship. What we actually know, as the authors of this piece point out, is that high scores on one measure appear in conjunction with low scores on another, and that low scores on that first measure are associated with high scores on the second. All of these scores, however, come from different people reporting on different situations. It is possible that the processes that relate high scores to low scores are different from the processes which relate low scores to high, even though they appear as a single mechanism. We have no evidence that changing the conditions of the use of power within a single setting will result in reduced satisfaction for the subordinates within that setting. That evidence requires some form of the experimental protocol.

Experimental Protocols

The distinguishing characteristics of experimental protocols are control and **manipulation**. The idea of control is to limit the influence of everything else while investigating the effects of a particular variable set. For example, in the Richmond et al. survey, respondents are presumably in a variety of work settings with different styles of management, subordinate relations, primary tasks, and the like. Perhaps, one or some combination of those variations is the source of the apparent relationship between power and satisfaction. Introducing **controls** for those variations would eliminate them as possible explanations. Hypothetically, in the Richmond et al. example, the researchers could have used respondents only from the same or similar settings.

Even greater control could be exercised in **invented settings** because the researcher can, with some latitude, select the influences to be present. The researchers, in our example, could have devised a particular setting to test a simulated or actual supervisor-subordinate relationship. There is, of course, a

---

[2]"Led to" is my wording for instructional purposes; the authors use the more appropriate "was related to."

trade-off. One risks the trade of a better study in a situation so contrived as to have little correspondence to the actual settings to be explained.

Manipulation involves some act of change in a variable which is seen as controlling a relationship (X is dependent on Y). Again this change can be invented or naturally occurring. Invented manipulations are, typically, a highly specified set of procedures or presentations. Naturally occurring manipulations are, simply, changes introduced in the controlling variable by some agent other than the researcher. A management team may be implementing a new system of employee appraisal which is thought to have an effect on productivity, for instance.

Manipulation in the Richmond et al. study would probably involve different levels of power use. The hypothesis might be that as one increases the use of power, subordinate satisfaction decreases. The manipulation would involve increasing the use of power and comparing the effect of these increases on subordinate satisfaction. Of course, the relationship might be the other way around. That is, as a supervisor recognizes decreasing employee satisfaction, he or she increases the use of power. The manipulation to be performed would depend on which theory is in place.

The purpose of the manipulation is to determine the effect of change in one variable on the performance of another. If increased use of power decreases job satisfaction, then changing the conditions of power use, while controlling for all other variations, ought to result in changing satisfaction scores.

The study of **experimental design** investigates the methods which can be used to isolate the effects of the manipulation and to control for the effects of other variables. An extensive treatment of the design of experiments is provided by Campbell and Stanley (1963) among others. In this text, we will consider some exemplar experiments to briefly consider their design components for isolation and control.

Isolation of the Treatment Effect

The identification of the effect of a manipulation requires an experimental design which separates that effect from all the other elements in the event. Such design components are said to isolate the **treatment effect**. This isolation of treatment effects is accomplished in one of three ways—through the comparison of independent groups, pre- and post-manipulation measures on the same group, or a combination of the two. In my reading of the communication literature, the **independent groups design** is the most common of the three.

Tan and Scruggs (1980), for example, were interested in pursuing the effect of violent content on tendencies for subsequent aggression in children. Their medium of presentation was the comic book. Children in the fourth, fifth, and sixth grades were given comic books on either violent or nonviolent subjects (the manipulation) to read in a classroom setting within a 25-minute period (controlled setting). At the conclusion of the reading period, each child completed a set of measures of aggression. Comparison of the two groups isolated the effect of the violent content. No difference was found between the two groups.

This is a simple design, the effectiveness of which is dependent upon the two groups being similar in respect to the **criterion measure**. If there were some pre-existing condition of difference, the effect of the manipulation might be masked. The use of independent groups is a common method of isolating the effect of the manipulation. It can be extended to any number of groups depending on the complexity of the manipulation. For instance, in studying the effects of five levels of suspense, three levels of liking-of-the-protagonist, and the gender of viewers on the evaluation of televised drama, Comisky and Bryant (1982) used 30 (2 × 3 × 5) separate groups. (E.g., females watching low suspense drama with a positive protagonist.) The greater number of groups used would seem to increase the likelihood that some group might differ from the others on the basis of an uncontrolled variable.

When it is likely that an argument of equivalence of groups on the criterion measure cannot be sustained, the independent groups design must be abandoned for a **pre/post design**. In this design, respondents serve as their own comparison group in that their performance prior to treatment is compared with their performance after the manipulation.

Anderson and Ploghoft (1980) investigated whether skills in the critical reception of television programs could be increased through a year-long instructional program specifically designed for the third, fourth, fifth, and sixth grade levels. They used a pre/post design in which the criterion measures were given at the start of the school year and then again at the conclusion of the curriculum. They found increases at all grade levels. The pre and post design of this study eliminates the need for the groups to be alike—an impossibility in this case—because it specifically measures the change in each individual.

The design has its own problems, however, such as practice effects or other changes in the individual being read as the effect of the manipulation. Anderson and Ploghoft were particularly susceptible to the latter charge as they were using children in rapidly changing stages of maturation. To test for this effect, they compared the postscores from a lower level with the prescores from the next higher (third-grade postscores with fourth-grade prescores). If the differences they found over the year were simply due to maturation, then no differences should be found between the groups. Differences were found for third and fourth graders but not for fifth and sixth. The two older groups would have increased their skills even without the instruction, apparently through the sophisticating processes of maturation.

In combining the pre/post design with a comparison of the independent grade groups, Anderson and Ploghoft were able to control for both differences between the groups and for intrasubject variations which were not the result of the instructional treatment.

Combination designs are the most powerful of the three. For example, **combination designs** can isolate differences between groups, changes within subjects, the effects of practice generated by repeated administrations of the criterion measure, and the treatment effect. They are also the most costly in the demand for respondents, time, and effort.

Control Variables

Characteristics of the respondents which are nonmanipulated properties or natural attributes are often used as control variables when it is suspected that the manipulation will have different effects across these attributes. Age, gender, education, income, media consumption, self-esteem, and similar traits are examples of these variables. They result from natural processes not from an intervention by the researcher. They are called control variables because when they are effective, they control the variability of the criterion measure. These controls work through statistical partitioning techniques given the information gathered on the respondents. That is, when the criterion measure is investigated under the separate classifications of the control variable, the variability of the criterion is reduced. It is then held that some of the variability of the criterion is due to the effect of the control variable and is, therefore, explained by that effect.

Control variables have less explanatory power than experimental or manipulated variables. Because they are not the result of some direct action by the researcher, but rather are merely imperfectly measured by the researcher, the mechanism of association between the control variable and the experimental variable always remains in doubt. The evidence of the effect is from correlation which can be spurious or the result of some other variable (consequences more thoroughly discussed in Chapter 7). Control variables, then, can be very useful, but they don't have the causal character of explanation given to experimental variables.

Control Given by the Protocol

Experimental designs provide a control function by partitioning out the effects of other variables to isolate the treatment effects. Additional control functions can be provided within the larger setting of the protocol by (a) restricting or defining the environment, (b) specifying the properties of the stimulus materials, and (c) limiting the mode and context of response.

Environmental restrictions eliminate distractions and alternatives. If the analyst wants the respondent to attend to the stimulus materials, a simple insurance is to provide no alternative. This was the policy taken by Tan and Scruggs who essentially required their respondents to sit and read the comic books. Equally important, the social environment was defined in such a way that the respondents were not permitted to interact with one another which eliminated the possibility of social support for deviant aggressive behaviors.

By developing stimulus materials with detailed specifications, the researcher is attempting to identify the particular source of the effects measured. In the Comisky and Bryant study, an attempt was made to vary the drama only in its level of suspense. Other components of drama, such as humor, were presumably held constant. Changes in the evaluation of the materials, therefore, could be attributed to the variable of suspense. If, of course, all other elements of the drama were not constant, then the effect given to suspense could be a misattribution.

The measurement used in the study is itself a form of control. Ordinarily, measurement is designed to be responsive to the other conditions of the test. Anderson and Ploghoft devised a critical skills test which met the academic context of the instructional program. A much different outcome might have been found had they gone into homes to examine program choices made by the participants. To pursue this a bit to show the effect of controls, Anderson and Ploghoft would then be faced with the bewildering task of determining which acts of choice were directed by what was learned and which were directed by all the other influences in the household (parental rules, status among siblings, better picture on given channels, and so on).

The controls we have examined in these paragraphs are restrictive controls. That is, they eliminate the presence or effects of other variables. The restrictive nature of control is obviously beneficial, but also leads to the prime criticism of experimental protocols—that they lack **mundane realism**. For example, if Anderson and Ploghoft's program of instruction in the critical use of television can't be shown to work in the home where most television viewing gets done, then its benefit is in question.

Additionally, restrictive controls provide no information about the effects that have been eliminated. For instance, if the effect of violent content in comic books works through a context of social support, then eliminating that system suppresses the effect of the content on subsequent aggression. A finding of no difference results. Continuing hypothetically, if the analysts suspected the necessity of a social support system, a better approach would have been a design in which the support was isolated and its effects measured. On the other hand, if that support was not part of the theory which directed the study in the first place, the researcher would have no justification for its inclusion.

The benefit of controls is that they limit the possible explanations for a given effect. Abandoning controls returns the scientist to the situation of so many possible explanations that no choice can be made. Good design has to affect some balance between the benefit of controls and the problems they introduce.

Protocol Design and the Testing of Hypotheses

The purpose of a protocol is to provide a fair test of the hypothesis—a subject treated extensively in the next section. Once a hypothesis has been proposed, one sets out to demonstrate either that it is false or to add evidence for its support. (Note that I explicitly excluded the words "prove" and "true.") Protocols are designed specifically for one of those two ends—the **falsification** or **verification** of the hypothesis. This section considers those two methods of evidence and their influence on protocol design.

In falsification, one designs the protocol to show that the hypothesized relationship does not hold under, at least, one set of conditions in which the hypothesis claimed that it would hold. For example, a simple decision-making hypothesis—the fewer the number of alternatives, the faster are decisions made—claims a linear increase in speed of decision making as the number of alternatives decreases. The hypothesis would be falsified if one could show that this relationship was not true in all cases, as perhaps, when one alternative was much preferred.

In verification, one designs the protocol to provide conditions in which the hypothesis will most likely hold. That is, we add to the support of the hypothesis by finding one or more conditions in which the relationship will hold. Again considering our decision-making hypothesis, we might use a protocol in which we reduced the number of equally attractive alternatives presuming that decision speed will increase correspondingly.

Note that in falsification the researcher is trying to make the hypothesis fail and in verification trying to make it succeed, but in both cases the effort has to be fair.

If a hypothesis is falsified, it must presumably be abandoned or modified. If a hypothesis is verified, it should not be considered true, but only supported (not falsified) in the conditions tested. Falsification, therefore, is clearly the more powerful of the two reasoning methods. Falsification leads directly to an increase of knowledge because we know immediately what is not true. Verification adds nothing to our knowledge, for the hypothesis is still only proposed, albeit now with additional support.

Given this difference, one might suspect that the usual practice would be the use of the method of falsification. Such is not the case. Nicholson (1982) notes: "While scholars labour to produce refutable hypotheses . . ., they do not try to refute them but on the contrary try very hard to prove [verify] them. It is their professional rivals who try to falsify them" (p. 90).

In the ordinary practices of verification, it is not just any condition which is tested to see if the relationship holds, but it is, typically, an optimal condition that is tested. The literature is filled with studies which present hypotheses in their best possible light. The method of verification seems to match well with the psychological commitment to the hypothesis generated by the effort involved in its creative discovery. The act of formulating a hypothesis is an act which makes sense out of some part of the world in which one is interested. We are not likely to abandon this hard-won understanding. The method of verification permits us to continue to support a hypothesis even if we should find no support for it in a particular set of testing conditions. We are simply directed to find a better set of testing conditions.

Lest I overstate, the method of falsification is not nearly so cut and dried as suggested. Presume I decide to attempt and, unfortunately, succeed in falsifying the asserted relationship between perceived distances on issues and voter decisions that we claimed was evidenced in our campaign study. I need not abandon our hypothesized cognitive mechanism. All the conditions of the test are as open to attack as the hypothesis. I could argue that the test was contaminated, the measures inadequate, the findings equivocal. It is only the limits of my creativity which might force me to concede the hypothesis.

In spite of its lack of guarantees, the method of falsification suggests the popular image of the scientist—skeptical, questioning, always examining one's supposed truths. The method of verification shows what the practice is more nearly like—an effort to promote one's ideas, to gain ascendance for one's theories. I think this brings us around to a re-emphasis of the importance of the process of acceptance of an idea within the scientific community. As a scientist, I expect to do my best to present my ideas, and I expect others to do the same. I certainly intend to win any disputes, but it is the community that will judge. As a reader and, therefore, a member of that community, you should be aware that I intend to win you over—honestly, of course.

Protocols: An Analytic Summary

The two major protocols in quantitative research are the survey and the experiment. Surveys and experiments are not two discrete classes with nothing in between. On a continuum, they both involve measurement of some set of attributes of respondent groups. They are distinguished by the presence or absence of controls and manipulation. As control and manipulation come into play, the design begins to shift toward the experimental side. When subjects respond to well-defined stimulus materials, in a restricted environment on a limited task within a system of observation that permits comparisons between groups and/or across subjects, the design is clearly experimental.

Surveys tell us of the presence of characteristics and of the presence of relationships among those characteristics. Experiments investigate the nature of those relationships.

The design of both surveys and experiments is a creative solution to the demands of the purposes of the research, the implications of the directing theories, the methods of reasoning chosen, the resources available to the scientist, and the trade-offs that appear in decisions on control and manipulations. Application of survey and experimental protocols in the testing of hypotheses is not cut and dried. A discussion of the decisions which must be made follows in the next section.

EXERCISES

1 The panel design in our campaign study allowed us to take measurements immediately before and immediately after a presidential debate. Does this design make the study more experimental? On what criteria do you judge?
2 What is the manipulation in the Anderson/Ploghoft study? What controls are in place?
3 Describe the notion of mundane realism.
4 What is the difference between isolating an effect and controlling for an effect?

TESTING THE HYPOTHESIS

Having identified a problem in the state of our knowledge, proposed a solution, and become knowledgeable about the analytical protocols available, the next step in quantitative research involves the gathering of evidence concerning the acceptability of the proposed solution—that is, testing the hypothesis. A test of a hypothesis involves the analysis of **systematic observations** made under known conditions. The testing procedure can be examined in four steps: (a) devising the conditions of the test appropriate to the question asked and the method of evidence; (b) making observations within those conditions; (c) analyzing those observations into meaningful evidence; and (d) constructing the arguments in support of the hypothesis. As you might suspect, we will struggle through each of these.

Devising the Conditions of the Test

In ordinary practice, a test of a hypothesis proceeds through a process of verification or a marshalling of supporting evidence. In this process, conditions are sought in which the hypothesis can be shown to hold. The first step then is to identify or devise a set of conditions in which the variables can be shown to function in the hypothesized relationship.

A hypothesis establishes our interest in the relationship(s) of certain variables. These relationships will be observed under given conditions. "Conditions" include all those elements which are part of the context in which the data are generated. Conditions are never neutral but are instrumental in creating the data to be analyzed. They are, therefore, important choices to be made or evaluated in determining whether or not a fair test of the hypothesis has been conducted.

A fair test simply means that if the hypothesis is false, it will fail, and that if the hypothesis is true, it is true for the reasons advanced. The question of a fair test is never resolved. The signs of fairness that one looks for in the testing conditions are that (a) there is a reasonable chance that the hypothesis can fail—the outcome is not artificially fixed or methodologically determined—and (b) that no other equally credible reason for its success can be advanced.

Given that our interest is in human communication behavior, we can proceed in one of four ways: (a) The researcher can get people to act when they voluntarily agree to participate in **constructed settings**. This is the approach used in experimental and quasi-experimental studies. (b) People can be observed acting within a **mundane context** in a **natural setting** as is done in field observations or **field experiments**. (c) The researcher can get people to report on themselves (or others). These studies are surveys, questionnaires, and polls. Lastly (d), the products or **artifacts** of people's actions can be observed. Those studies which make use of the lists of society—birth records, voter registrations, deed transfers, tax records, and so on—fall into this category as well as most content analyses.

Choosing an Approach

The researcher must make a choice among these four condition sets. Unfortunately, there are no automatic decisions. The structure of the hypothesis and the ultimate explanatory purpose will only suggest one approach over another. Studies which are directed toward the description of characteristics usually start with surveys (c) or the study of artifacts (d). The examination of methods and practices almost always focus on naturally occurring action in mundane settings (b). The search for conditional relationships for prediction or explanation of control will often begin with surveys of people or artifacts (c and d), but ultimately must find its evidence in laboratory or field experiments (a and b).

Available Resources   There are a number of other criteria which come to bear on these choices. A substantial set is the pragmatic considerations of time, money, availability, and personal affinities. There is no question that the relatively low cost and little effort that are possible with a survey are two good reasons for its popularity. It sometimes seems that these are the only criteria, but there are others.

Sociological Level of Attack   The sociological level of one's explanatory purpose influences the choices that can be made. Experimental approaches are simply not viable when the unit of analysis is the institution or society. The examination of effects at these sociological levels must depend upon **survey protocols**.

Fortunately, society's functions produce prodigious amounts of data in the ordinary records of government which are of great explanatory value. Tunstall's (1982) examination of the British press in this age of television is a good example of the application of such data. Tunstall was interested in the changes that occurred within the institution of the British newspapers following the rise of television. Clearly, no experimental manipulation was possible. Even the initiation of a data collection was decades too late. Tunstall, however, had the benefit of the British government's penchant for statistics. From the reports of Royal Commission after Royal Commission, he was able to analyze the financial impact, consumer usage, and content changes through four decades.

The large sociological view is often required to even observe the effect of certain variables. These variables can be observed only at a large enough **scale**. My friends in advertising, for example, claim that a commercial message on television will result in purchases in about 1 to 3 percent of the exposures. Not a very powerful effect in a study of 100 people, but very significant with an audience of 60 million. Again, survey methods or the study of records is the only choice.

Laboratory Controls versus Mundane Realism

The choice between using subjects who realize they are under study in a constructed setting versus observing individuals acting in an ordinary context (shopping, conversing, whatever) in a naturally occurring setting is bound up in several values. Let me explain a few distinctions. Constructed settings are under considerable control by the researcher. Respondents enter these settings on a voluntary basis to provide a performance which is particular to that context.

Naturally occurring settings are those which are part of the ordinary concourse of behavior and not under control of the researcher. They are our everyday settings which are evoked in ordinary individual and social practice. Respondents are in these settings without the intervention of the scientist.

For some, the choice between (a) subjects in constructed settings and (b) individuals in natural settings brings them face to face with the question of the relationship between research and the naturally occurring world. If one selects conditions that are so unusual, the evidence gathered may be rejected because its connection with the natural world cannot be seen. A good example is the controversy which has swirled around the early media violence studies (Meyer, 1970). Those studies used the number of electric shocks given as a grade (A, B, C, etc.) for a written theme as the measure of aggression. The studies consistently showed that the number of shocks increased when the graders had previously viewed violent media fare. The critics replied: "So what? Who grades themes with electric shocks? How can that be considered a measure of aggression in the real world?"

That seems like a good question. Let's examine what the strong position of the rationalistic research argument might be: Rationalistic research is concerned with the explanation of the performance of attributes not individuals. Attributes are not sensate beings but are properties whose functions are determined by their nature. In order to gather evidence concerning the relationship between one attribute (variable) and another, it is only necessary to permit the full operation of each attribute. The particular setting in which this occurs is trivial. Therefore, it doesn't matter if one tests the hypothesis under laboratory conditions, with college freshmen or in the natural world. In fact, the laboratory setting gives greater control in permitting the full operation of each attribute; it is, therefore, probably better to conduct the research there.

A position closer to the middle might argue that unless one was going to construct a natural world by controlling the mix of attributes manifested by individuals, then the utility of understanding the purified operation of attributes is limited. There are always contaminants in the natural world. A more useful test is one in which the functioning of attributes can be observed under conditions which approximate the essential characteristics of naturally occurring situations.

We can return to Putnam and Sorenson for an example of this position. In their test of their ambiguous message hypothesis, they simulated the message interpretation methods of a hierarchical organization using a classroom setting with upper-division organizational communication students who held supervisory and subordinate positions within the simulated company. Clearly not General Motors, but a situation which, for Putnam and Sorenson, contained the necessary components for a valid test of their hypothesis. But is it? Could the findings from Putnam and Sorenson be used to explain what a mid-line manager does in Detroit when faced with an equivocal directive to raise morale in the shop? Yes, but only if the interpretation of the necessary components by Putnam and Sorenson match those in which the manager actually operates.

For Burgoon and Aho (1982), real world relevance was a guiding principle in the testing of their hypotheses on social distance (the space maintained between conversationalists). They wished to demonstrate that their hypotheses were applicable to the human communication we see around us. Given that goal, they selected a field experiment within the natural setting of a retail store. The researchers, posing as casual shoppers, recorded the responses of the sales staff, presumably unaware of the manipulation, to preplanned violations of social distance. In this study, the natural setting was a necessary part of the explanatory purpose. Its success in meeting that purpose was dependent on the maintenance of the naturalness of the situation.

The relevance of the conditions used to test a hypothesis are always open to debate. The terms of the debate change depending on the position from which the research is conducted. The hard-line rationalist is the least concerned with the question of artificial or natural settings. If one accepts the presuppositions of this research perspective, then arguments about the artificiality of the laboratory settings are actually inappropriate as the intent of this research is to study the attribute independent of its setting. Legitimate criticism within this perspective concerns the presence of **contamination** from uncontrolled variables. These uncontrolled variables primarily result from the fact that the individual must naturally participate in and, therefore, respond as a consequence of the procedures used to display and manipulate the attributes under study.

For those who seek a more direct connection with the natural world and use approximations of natural settings, contamination is less the issue than the quality of the approximation. If the approximation does not provide the essential characteristics of the natural settings, then its value is lost. The quality of the approximation is rarely tested in such studies, but always asserted.

Finally, for those who use natural settings as a necessary context of their explanatory purposes, contamination is again an issue, but instead of a concern of the natural world contaminating the laboratory procedure, the concern is of the procedure contaminating the natural setting. Had the respondents of Burgoon and Aho known of the study, then their explanation which was based on the natural operation of conversational distance would have been cast in doubt.

Selecting Conditions: A Summary

Hypotheses in our field concern human communication behavior. We are directed toward the study of action and its artifacts. In testing a hypothesis, we can proceed in one of four ways: (a) The researcher can get people to act in constructed settings (experimental and quasi-experimental studies). (b) People can be observed in a natural setting (field observations or field experiments). (c) The researcher can get people to report on themselves or others (surveys and polls). Lastly (d), the artifacts of people's actions can be observed (studies of content and natural records).

The selection of the conditions of a test of a hypothesis is dependent on a number of criteria. (a) The structure of the hypothesis and the explanatory purpose suggest certain choices over others. The examination of characteristics usually involves the analysis of natural records or surveys. Methods and practices are studied in field observations in natural settings. Studies considering the association between variables where the appearance of one variable is associated with the appearance of another either looking forward in time (prediction) or back in time (postdiction) generally use surveys or the analysis of natural records. Studies investigating causes and consequences or attempting control-type explanations may begin with survey protocols but should use experimental methods as their ultimate evidence. (b) The pragmatics of time, money, and personal interests are always a part of the choice. (c) The nature of the variable influences the choice. Some variables exist only in the function of institutions, societies, or cultures. Large aggregate analysis is required. (d) The values which define the relationship between research and the world in which it resides can direct the choices. Traditional laboratory research has been criticized for its supposed irrelevance to the natural world of communication leading some researchers to prefer natural world approximations or natural settings. A justification for any choice can usually be found, but one's selection is always open to attack.

Conducting Systematic Observations

Systematic observations in rationalistic research almost always involves quantification. Quantification is based on the concept of **equivalent units**. A unit is a discrete element separate from any other element. An equivalent unit can be substituted for another equivalent unit with no change. In short, a one is a one is a one and not a two—although there are three of them in this sentence (with apologies to Gertrude Stein). Individual human behavior, on the other hand, is usually considered continuous and unique. I am continuously acting in some way and although you may see differences in what I do from time to time, where those differences begin and end is arbitrary. Further, no one else can do what I do if for no other reason than I would not be doing it. The so-what of this is that human behavior doesn't occur in readily accessible, functionally equivalent units but must be re-created in these units. Seeing conversations as composed of functionally equivalent units of turn taking, group processes as functionally equivalent phases, the effects of advertising as functionally equivalent units of decision making are all acts of this re-creation. The pay-off of this re-creation is the ability to apply the powerful methods of mathematical analysis.

The quantification of a whole requires a set of rules which will distinguish units *of* something. Those rules are contained in the process of measurement. Measurement, then, is a process which defines a unit and assigns that unit a categorical value. We define the unit when we claim that there is an X, and it is a conversational act or an episode of watching television or a hierarchical level in an organization. We assign the categorical value when we describe the properties of X which distinguish it from other X's.

Observation in quantitative research is observation through some system of measurement. Measurement takes uniquely appearing individual behavior and transforms it into regular-appearing quantities of some attribute. The focus of the study, then, becomes that which is measured in this process.

Systematic observation involves the consistent application of the measurement instrument to the circumstances under study. That is, the performance of the measurement will be the same for each individual or incident. It does not mean that each individual or each incident will be the same. Actually, each is considered unique. Measurement is a filter which removes the attribute(s) of interest from this welter of individual differences.

Measurement removes the researcher from the naive, direct observation of behavior (see "Direct vs. Indirect Observation," Chapter 3). Behavior is seen through the screen of the rules of measurement. A group observation study, such as that conducted by Fisher and Drecksel (1983), is a good example of this reduction. These researchers had volunteers in a constructed situation attempt some group task. They audio recorded their interactions. A transcript was made following a well-defined set of rules. (Transcripts of free talk are relatively difficult to make as oral speech does not follow the same forms as written discourse.) Each **interact** (paired turns of talk) was then coded according to a set of definitions into one of five categories. In this manner, a unit was defined (the interact) and given one of five categorical values. The observations that are reported in the Fisher and Drecksel study were conducted over the data that were generated by this measurement process. The researchers never needed to be present during any group meeting.

While it was not necessary for these researchers to actually observe the behavior they wished to explain, for the measurement process to be valid, it is necessary that the data—in this case the frequency of appearance of each interact type—be the direct consequence of what the members of the group do. The properties of the data which are the focus of our explanation have to correspond with the properties of the behavior we wish to explain. When the behavior changes in some significant way, the data must change in some significant way.

Systematic observation in quantitative research, then, begins with the consistent application of a set of rules of measurement which results in data with properties that correspond to the behavior of interest. Systematic observation continues in analytical procedures which determine the facts contained within these data.

Systematic Analysis of Observations

Unfortunately, data do not provide us their facts without effort. A fact is the invariable consequence of some procedure of analysis. I know there are 25 elements in a particular set when I follow given rules of counting. There will always be 25 elements in that set according to those rules of counting, but change those rules and a different fact appears. Quantitative data are in the form of numbers which makes it possible to use the powerful procedures of statistical analysis to discover their facts. Statistical analysis will provide descriptive statements about the characteristics of a set of numbers, permit us to compare the characteristics of separate sets of numbers, and to determine the degree of association between numerical sets. When these numerical sets are the product of the measurement of human behavior, then the facts discovered by statistical analysis are convertible into facts about human behavior.

Each statistical procedure generates its own set of facts concerning the set of measurements. While there are some technical considerations in the applications of procedures to kinds of measurements, the real task of analysis is the determination of what facts are appropriate as evidence for the hypothesis under study (the issue we take up in Chapter 7). Presuming that I buy into your warrants and that you follow the rules (though technical errors are not uncommon), I can't dispute your facts, but I can always dispute what those facts mean. As with data, facts do not speak for themselves. They have to be understood within the explanatory purpose of the research. That understanding is gained in the evidentiary arguments that comment on the hypothesis.

Constructing Arguments

The last step in the testing of the hypothesis is the public presentation of the whole process as an argument in support of some claim. When verification is used as the method of reasoning, the positive outcome of a test is the claim that the hypothesis has been supported. (The negative outcome is inconclusive.) When falsification is the method used, then the claim is that the hypothesis has been denied. (The positive outcome is inconclusive.) In either case, acceptance of the claim is dependent upon the quality of the argument used to advance it. As a scientist I have to argue for that acceptance. The whole structure of a journal article, research report, and convention presentation is an argument for that acceptance.[3]

To begin with, the reader has to be convinced that there is indeed a problem in the fabric of our knowledge. The question raised has to be lacking an answer in the scientific community, not simply in the understanding of the individual writing. The import of the question has to be shown. The value of its answer in relation to the goals of science and society has to be demonstrated.

The author, then, has to show that the proposed answer—the hypothesis—is credible, that it is consonant with that which we already know. The hypothesis ought to be the best that can be drafted given our present knowledge.

The methods used to test the hypothesis must be justified as a fair test of the hypothesis. The reader must be convinced that the conditions of the test were relevant to the variables and the relationships involved in the hypothesis, that the measurements were the consequences of the human behavior to be explained and that the facts observed were appropriate to the test and meaningful for the explanation.

---

[3]Peter and Olson demonstrate this argument form so skillfully in their article "Is Science Marketing?" (1983).

Finally, the author has to demonstrate that the whole of the work functions as a unit to support the conclusions drawn—that claim that the hypothesis was supported or denied. In all of this, the author should expect the reader to be skeptical throughout the reading of the report. For science to work, there has to be a fair effort on both sides of the ledger.

Testing the Hypothesis: A Summary

Testing the hypothesis proceeds through four steps: (a) devising the conditions of a fair test; (b) conducting observations through the processes of measurement within those conditions; (c) analyzing those observations for the facts relevant to one's claims; and (d) constructing the public arguments for the acceptance of those claims.

There is no single set of conditions which are solely appropriate for the fair test of a hypothesis. Devising a testing protocol is a creative act involving judgments concerning the nature of the variables involved, the structure of the hypothesis, the availability of time, money and other resources, the explanatory purposes involved, and the relation of the research to the natural world.

Quantitative research makes its observations through the screen of measurement which transforms unique, continuous behavior into functionally equivalent units of some attribute. For measurement to be valid, it must be the direct consequence of the behavior to be explained.

Measurement generates data which contain the empirical facts that are the evidence for the claims to be advanced. Those facts are revealed in the processes of analysis. In quantitative research, those analytical processes are typically statistical.

The test of the hypothesis is concluded in the public presentation of the arguments for the verification or falsification of the hypothesis. Each step of the test must be justified to stand the scrutiny of the informed, skeptical reader.

THE RECONSTRUCTION OF THEORY

The final resort of empirical science is the empirical facts of the matter. While we are now aware of the layers of interpretation involved in the discovery of empirical facts, they do represent a particular foundation for theory which is different from that of other forms of analysis, creation, intuition, or inspiration. When the weight of argument from these empirical facts calls for an addition, deletion, or modification of theory statements, those existing statements will eventually give way. Their proponents may not do so readily, and they will not do so automatically. The task of theory reconstruction is a deliberate one undertaken, unfortunately, by all too few.

Research work which is not fed back into the living theory of the field through citations or the continued efforts of the researcher has little effect. Like some disconnected thought, it gathers dust on periodical shelves. There are several reasons for this fate. The research may be out of synchrony with the interests of the research community. Research ideas tend to cycle in 10-year periods. Introduce an idea at the perigee of interest, and it goes little distance. The research may be so radical that its utility is not apparent. Its presentation may be so obtuse that its contribution cannot be recognized. The idea may be too large or too small in scope or too near or distant from our present knowledge. Of course, the research might also be a mediocre thought or badly conducted or poorly written.

Whatever the case, the research never achieves a position within the community. It enters into a latency period of, perhaps, 20 years during which it still could be discovered and have its effect. After 20 years, the contribution may be recognized if the idea is promoted by another, but usually as a historical footnote.

A great deal of research never makes a contribution to theory. Some, as we have noted, because it is never assimilated. But more of it fails because it has little contribution to make *to theory*. This is not nearly as negative a comment as it might seem. Much research is directed toward current states which are not expected to remain constant over time. The individual opinion poll, content analysis, or audience study usually is of this sort. Its value to theory is not so much in its particular findings but as a datum point in longitudinal analysis. While its value to understanding the contemporary scene is clear, if it is not used in some analysis of, say, trends, it quickly disappears.

At present there is no single, commonly accepted body of theory in the field of communication. As we saw in Chapter 2, the field is composed of separate, but perhaps overlapping, communities of scholars, the members of which hold a common understanding of what communication is, how it works, and why. Theory in communication is this loosely knit conventional wisdom held by these different communities.

This makes the final step of research—the reconciliation of theory with empirical evidence—both more difficult and easier. It is more difficult because the terms of communication theory are rarely explicit which limits our ability to examine specific claims in formal analysis. This limitation impairs our understanding of just what is evidenced in the empirical facts revealed. Reconciliation is easier, on the other hand, because there is less organized resistance to contrary claims. Somewhere in the mix, one can generally find a community of acceptance for nearly any argument.

SUMMARY

Generally following a deductive model, quantitative research begins with the covering premises of our stock of knowledge. Motivation for inquiry is raised at those points where this knowledge is shown to be inadequate. In order to reduce that inadequacy, a proposed addition or refinement to that knowledge is posed in the form of a hypothesis. The hypothesis is typically a statement composed of variables in a relationship. The hypothesis is to be subjected to a fair test of its validity within accepted protocols of evidence. Conducting the test requires the researcher to devise a set of testing conditions, develop rules of measurement, apply methods of analysis, and construct arguments in support of the claims made for the hypothesis. If the hypothesis is supported by the test and accepted by the scientific community, the cycle of research is completed when its contribution to theory is made.

EXERCISES

1 Why is the question of a fair test always in doubt?
2 What might be an important difference in the actions of research volunteers compared with the naive actions of people in ordinary settings?
3 In the same context of question 2, how might surveys differ from natural lists?
4 Why does the study of institutions ordinarily preclude the use of experimental methods?
5 What is the notion of scale?
6 How far back in time could you place the starting point of your act of reading this sentence?
7 How does that starting point (in question 6) change as you change your definition of what is included in the act of reading?
8 What does the statement, "The distance of a yard is short in miles but long in millimeters," tell us about the relationship between measurement and observation?
9 What is the difference between data and facts?
10 How do facts become meaningful?

RELATED READINGS

Babbie, E. R. *The practice of social research,* (2d ed.) Belmont, CA: Wadsworth Publishing Co. Inc., 1979.

Bowers, J. W. and Courtright, J. A. *Communication research methods.* Glenview, IL: Scott, Foresman and Co., 1984.

Chadwick, B. A., Bahr, H. M. and Albrecht, S. L. *Social science research methods.* Englewood Cliffs, NJ: Prentice-Hall, 1984.

Dooley, D. *Social research methods.* Englewood Cliffs, NJ: Prentice-Hall, 1984.

Leedy, P. D. *How to read research and understand it.* New York: Macmillan Publishing Co., 1981.

MEASUREMENT

SYNOPSIS

This chapter is organized around three partial definitions of measurement. The first concerns measurement as a link in the relationship between the empirical world and our theoretical concepts. This definition leads us to consider the problems of validity. The second is concerned with the process of measurement —the activity itself. Here we are led to the concepts of an operational definition, accuracy, precision, and reliability. The third approach considers the quantification of measurement—the process of transforming observations into numbers. In this approach, we learn of the properties of numerical scales and of the notion of isomorphism. The chapter concludes with some household hints about developing and using the instruments of measurement.

CONCEPTS AND MEASUREMENT

The previous chapter introduced a number of concepts as we examined examples of research in communication. Some of those were agenda setting, political participation, message ambiguity, interpretive rules, repeat viewing, and communication accuracy, adaptiveness, strategies, and apprehension. We know that these concepts are interpretive devices which help us make sense of human behavior. They are not themselves acts of human behavior but are the interpretation of that behavior. As an interpretation, they are conceptual, not empirical. For these concepts to have utility in an empirical science however, some empirical content must be attributable to them. They must map onto something in the empirical world.

A theoretical concept, therefore, can be considered a categorical scheme which accommodates some set of empirical elements. The elements which are subsumed by the concept form the empirical definition or content of the concept.

The first problem in measurement, then, is identifying the empirical content of the concepts of theory. This identification begins with the determination of what behavior or behavioral artifacts the concept interprets.

For example, agenda setting is a concept which interprets the role the media play in the relative importance individuals place on topics for action. What it contains empirically might be acts of conversation in which topic choices are made, acts of decision making in voting behavior, and acts of information seeking in media use. Any of those acts might be an element of this concept, but none of them defines it alone. In fact, the substantive strength of this concept is its capacity to interpret diverse acts as being part of the same course of behavior.

You may have noted that I described what *might be* the empirical content of agenda setting. The reason for this equivocation is simply that the empirical content of any concept is problematic. Whether or not some action is an element of a concept is always a legitimate research question. How does one know if an act is an empirical element of a concept? That evidence appears if the action's properties are those specified by the concept and if the measurement of it performs as predicted. If the action fails this test, then it is not part of the concept. If no act can be found which meets this test, then the concept is empirically empty like the concept of a living unicorn.

Empirically empty constructs are not automatically expunged from theory. Because other measurement techniques may discover empirical elements for which the concept has explanatory power, the concept usually survives. The concept of subliminal persuasion is a good example.[1]

Synthetic and Naturally Occurring Components

There are essentially two ways in which I can find the empirical content of a concept: (a) I can invent some synthetic action and claim it as an element, or (b) I can claim some naturally occurring action as an element of the concept. Note that I am using the word "action" to indicate an interpreted act (see, "The Interpretation of Behavior," Chapter 3).

Synthetic Action   There is nothing unnatural about filling out a questionnaire or participating in some experimental protocol, but as actions of something, both are inventions by the researcher. An excellent example of this invention is provided in a study by Zillmann and Bryant (1982). As is typical of these researchers, this study is a well-crafted experiment which at the same time raises some of the most provocative questions in methodology. For our purposes here,

---

[1]The concept of subliminal persuasion involves persuasive messages presented below the threshold of recognition. The concept has great ideological power (evil media and all), but most would agree that it lacks reliable data.

it is enough to report that these researchers were investigating the relationship between exposure to sexually explicit films, identified by them as pornography, and the trivialization of the crime of rape.

Our present focus is on the concept of trivialization, although their concept of pornography raises a parallel question. The concept of trivialization as used in common language and as used by these researchers involves an act of evaluation which results in a judgment which is lower than what would be expected by some standard. Trivialization is obviously a complex cognitive act for which there may be no externally, observable components. The likelihood of finding naturally occurring instances of behavioral indices of this cognitive act ranges from slim to none.

Zillmann and Bryant, therefore, invent an index by having their subjects assign a prison sentence to a convicted rapist described in an ostensible newspaper story. The researchers claim the index as an element of trivialization because it works. That is, because it performs as they hypothesized an element of trivialization would perform.

The interest of Zillmann and Bryant is, of course, in explaining the consequences of massive exposure to pornography. But they have little interest at all in predicting their subjects' performance on their measurement instrument. That performance is a synthetic action, the value of which is as a surrogate for what naturally occurs. That is, the authors realize that few care if massive exposure to pornography results in different numbers being recorded on their paper-and-pencil test. While these different numbers are the facts of this study, their importance is in their standing as elements of the concept of judgments concerning rape as those judgments occur in matters of societal import.

Zillmann and Bryant's paper-and-pencil test is part of an invented, **synthetic action** which itself is claimed to be part of the concept of trivialization. At this point in their research program, their claim is supported only by the evidence that it performed as predicted. The researchers are unable to provide the supporting evidence of its membership within the concept of trivialization as it finds its expression in the judgments that people make in everyday life.[2]

What we have seen is that two separate claims have to be made in the use of synthetic action: (a) that the action is an element of some construct; and (b) when the intent is to explain behavior in society, that the synthetic action is an adequate proxy for what people actually do.

Natural Action **Naturally occurring action** is what people actually do, which relieves the need for evidence for this latter claim, but the researcher must still demonstrate that the behavior chosen for study is an element of the construct which forms the explanation.

Burgoon and Aho, as you will recall, made use of naturally occurring behaviors in their study of social distance. They measured the naive reactions to cohort violations of conversational distances between customers and sales

---

[2]Given the caliber of the research it is likely that that evidence will be sought.

personnel. While the behaviors of the sales staff were freely occurring,[3] the meaningfulness of the action is still dependent on its interpretation as an empirical element of the concept of conversational distances. Burgoon and Aho must make the same kind of initial claim as Zillmann and Bryant. Their only advantage is that the action under measurement is also part of each reader's experience.

VALIDITY

When one sets out to measure something, one accepts the task of showing the validity of the instruments used. These instruments are valid when they measure what is claimed that they measure. There are three slightly different facets to this claim: (a) The measurement will perform as predicted by the research (internal validity); (b) the measurement is an empirical element of theoretical concept under study (conceptual validity); (c) the measurement generalizes to the conditions to be explained (external validity).

Internal Validity

The concept of **internal validity** relates to the purposes the researcher has for measurement. The general purpose of research is the description of the world around us. We use that description to predict, control, and understand that world. Description involves two processes, distinction and convergence. In distinction, we separate properties one from another. In convergence, we develop our understanding of a property through our knowledge of the integration of the elements that comprise it. A measure demonstrates its internal validity when it accomplishes one of these two purposes with the contextual frame of the research protocol.

Zillmann and Bryant wished to distinguish individuals with differential exposure to sexually explicit films. Burgoon and Aho wished to distinguish different violations of conversational distances. The measures used by each were successful in making these distinctions. The validity of the measures within the boundaries of the research was demonstrated.

The question of internal validity is the first question of validity. If the measure fails to perform in the manner expected, we are usually left with an indeterminate condition. That is, we can rarely distinguish within a failure whether our measurement or our theory was invalid. The failure to perform as expected renders moot all other considerations of measurement validity as it forces the researcher to reconsider either the instrument or the construct from which it is derived.

---

[3] One *must* complete the questionnaire to fulfill the implied social contract involved in volunteering for the Zillmann and Bryant experiment; there is no such contract to move in response to the manipulation of Burgoon and Aho.

Conceptual Validity

Measurement, as we have seen, identifies some empirical component of the theoretical concept under study. The claim to be demonstrated is that whatever empirical element is selected, whether synthetic or naturally occurring, it is part of those empirical elements which comprise the set covered by the theoretical concept. This claim is the claim of **conceptual validity**. These validity claims are supported in three ways:

1 In the weakest, the claim is accepted simply because it does not appear to violate the generally accepted understanding of the concept. The element looks right, if you will. This argument of conceptual validity is called **face validity**. This is the level of validity that Zillmann and Bryant can claim.

2 Moving up, the validity claim can be advanced by showing that the present measure performs in a manner related to other measures previously accepted as being components of the theoretical concept. This argument has been given a number of names—concurrent, predictive, criterion related. As all of those are based on tests of association, the term **associational validity** covers them.

3 The highest level of support for the conceptual validity claim is developed when it can be shown that the performance of the test across all individuals is consonant with the theoretical performance of the construct involved. To use the Zillmann and Bryant protocol as an example, a minimum "prison sentence" of one year was given by a number of respondents in the massive exposure condition. The average sentence for that group, however, was a little over four years, and several respondents gave much higher sentences. If that variation between individuals can be accounted for by what the construct itself would predict, the researcher has additional evidence that the measure is performing as a component of that construct. This conceptual validity argument is called **construct validity**.

External Validity

External validity refers to the capacity of evidence to generalize to other actions, settings, and individuals. It has to do with the transfer of evidence from the conditions of the test to the conditions that we wish to explain. Neither Burgoon and Aho nor Zillmann and Bryant wish to explain only what happened within the particulars of their study. One pair wishes to comment on the characteristics of conversational distances, the other on pornography and rape in society. This transferability of research findings is the question of external validity.

Synthetic actions in constructed settings carry an additional burden of argument as to their external validity. If we compare the measurement of Burgoon and Aho with that of Zillmann and Bryant, we can see this additional burden. Whatever our validity concerns about the study of Burgoon and Aho, whether or not the behavior will occur in normal settings is not one of them. With the Zillmann and Bryant study, one must question whether the findings have relevance to rape in society. The researchers themselves recognize this obvious question and respond to it with an extensive assertion in favor of the external validity of the experimental protocol.

The question of external validity differs slightly from the question of measuring what one claims to measure. The sentencing measure can indeed be a component of trivialization without informing us of such events in society just as the conversational distances found in the appliance store may not generalize to any other social setting.

The reader needs to evaluate the claims for validity advanced by the researchers. All too often those claims are supported only by arguments of face validity augmented by references to those who have used the measure before. (Actually, that others have used a measure only repeats the face validity evidence that the measure is generally acceptable.) On the other hand, not everything can be demonstrated in a single study. The evidence for validity tends to develop over the total program of research. It is just as inappropriate to reject a study at the beginning of a program of research as it is to embrace it without doubt.

Evaluating Validity: An Example

In our campaign study, one of our concerns was the images of the candidates held by the voters. In order to construct the measurement instrument, it was first necessary for us to determine the image dimensions on which those candidates might vary. There are any number of ways that this determination might be accomplished. The one we used was to survey printed news reports for descriptive adjectives. These adjectives were then used as potential descriptors and rated by the respondents for the degree of application to each candidate. As with all such instruments, the images that could be described by our respondents were limited to the particular set of adjectives we used. This limitation is the obvious consequence of any set of adjectives no matter how large.

The point here is that in order to collect information on what the images of the candidates were, we first had to decide what the structure of those images would contain. Those decisions had to be made in reference to the purposes we had for those image data. In our case we were looking for mediated campaign influences which justified our method of selecting the adjectives from the print sources. Why not broadcast sources? We had no archive available to us. Did we lose something because of this lack? I would presume so, although I can't tell you what.

How should you as the reader evaluate our image measure? First of all by asking if it worked. Did it do what we wanted it to do? Did it clearly distinguish the candidates one from another? For each candidate, did it provide a coherent description of his or her image as generated by the adjectival set? Such were our purposes, and if those purposes were met, then we have demonstrated the internal validity of the measures.

The reader can begin to consider conceptual validity by asking whether the procedures used make sense in reference to the concept to be explained (face validity). Is it reasonable to look for the components of a candidate's image by considering the descriptions provided by print media? One can further evaluate the worth of the measure by considering its utility in explaining the performance of other measures (associational validity). Was it useful in understanding how individual respondents differed in the ways they dealt with other campaign influences? Did its performance integrate with the theory that was directing the questions of the study (construct validity)?

Finally, one needs to consider whether the measurement is limited to the particular circumstances of this study. Do the findings generalize to the condition under which actual individuals find themselves making decisions about candidate image and campaign issues (external validity)?

The reader is capable of making these judgments only if the authors assemble the evidence to provide sufficient information. If the evidence is not available or not reported, these judgments cannot be made. This limitation does not mean that the measurement of the study is invalid. It means that the study remains in considerable doubt. None of the three studies used as exemplars has provided sufficient evidence necessary to make informed judgments about the three issues of validity. Such is the usual case. Their contribution to theory, then, must be considered tentative awaiting further support.

EXERCISES

1 What is the role of concepts in measurement?
2 What evidence can be given that a particular act is an empirical element of a concept?
3 Why do we distinguish between naturally occurring action and synthetic action?
4 How could the measurement of Zillmann and Bryant have conceptual validity and not have external validity?
5 Why doesn't internal validity (a measure performing as predicted) tell us anything about conceptual validity?

OBSERVATION AND MEASUREMENT

Our second definition considers measurement as purposeful observation conducted according to a set of rules. This definition directs our attention to the activity of measurement, why we do it and how it gets done. The *why* is contained in our explanatory purpose and the *how* in the rules which literally define what is being observed.

Explanatory Purpose and Measurement

Measurement as purposeful observation simply means that the observation is directed by the theory which motivates it. Measurement is the selective collection of data according to some a priori scheme. Measurement, therefore, requires a prior understanding of that which is to be observed. If one wished to evaluate the quality of performance on some task, for example, the measurement process would begin by determining the dimensions on which the quality of performance might vary. If this task were within an organization, the researcher might begin by asking the shop managers for their evaluative criteria.[4] The researcher would then develop an instrument which would be responsive to variations along those criteria. The methods of measurement would obviously change, given a different set of criteria to conceptualize the quality of performance. The criteria that should be used depend upon the purposes of the study. If the researcher's intent in this example was to determine the satisfactions workers gained from quality performance, then the managers' criteria may well be inappropriate. At least the researcher should be prepared for an argument along those lines.

Defining What Is Measured

To pursue this example of evaluating the quality of performance on some task a bit further, the concept of "quality of performance" would become a variable of interest in a hypothesis or research question. (The move from concept to variable is simply a name change depending on its appearance in a statement of theory or in a hypothetic or problem statement.) With quality of performance as the variable of interest, the researcher must determine the action which will become the empirical content of that variable. This determination is made when the researcher selects the methods by which quality of performance will be measured.

The abstraction "quality of performance" can be applied to a wide variety of human behaviors. It will, certainly, be claimed that one such expression is the measurement that the researcher conducts. This claim is called an operational definition. An operational definition alleges that an empirical component of the concept under study (quality of performance, in this case) is the measurement used. That is, the concept is claimed to be empirically defined by the operations used to measure it. The operational definition establishes the connection between the conceptual domain and the empirical domain. The connection is not automatic, although **operationalism** (see following) would have it that way. The connection has to be demonstrated. As a claim, it will need evidence to establish its standing.

Operationalism The doctrine of operationalism is an extension of the notion of the operational definition. In this doctrine, the concept of quality of performance has *no* meaning other than the system of measurement used. Here, no claim is made for a concept beyond the empirical reality of the measure. In operationalism, the theoretical import of a concept is limited to its expression in measurement. The notion of "quality of performance," then, in our example, means only the items used in the instrument. The items comprise the totality of

[4]The selection of the manager's criteria can be seen as an example of managerial bias in an organizational study.

quality of performance and are not a surrogate for or an index of some larger concept.

Operationalism certainly simplifies the validity claims of measurement, but, at the same time, it spreads confusion by proliferating independent expressions of what a concept is each time a new measurement of it is devised.

The doctrine of operationalism does not appear to govern much of the research done in communication. Most researchers are not content with the explanatory restrictions of operationalism. Most analysts would appear to prefer to hold that concepts such as quality of performance maintain a consistent meaning in theory even though particular empirical expressions may differ. Nevertheless, operationalism still provides a useful refuge when one's measurement is under attack concerning its conceptual validity.

Consistency of Method

Measurement is conducted according to a set of rules to ensure that each observation is performed in the same manner. Those rules describe the set of operations used to collect the data. Those rules are not necessarily complex and often make use of "standard ingredients." Palmgreen and Rayburn (1982), in a typical uses and gratifications study, investigated the gratifications sought from attendance to television news. Their measurement procedure was a checklist of 14 statements which presented different reasons for watching the news (e.g., "I watch TV news to keep up with current issues and events" [p. 569]). Respondents were to rate each statement on a seven-point scale for their applicability to them. Their measurement rules then, are that each respondent will get the same 14 items; each will be asked to make the same judgment on those items and to record that judgment on a standard seven-point scale. On the other hand, the measurement procedures of a typical interact analysis, such as the one we saw in Fisher and Drecksel's (1983) study, will have a book of instructions and entail several hours of training for their application.

Accuracy, Precision, and Reliability

However complex, the rules of measurement determine the **accuracy**, **precision**, and reliability of the measurement. Accuracy is the degree to which the measurement procedure represents the concept under study. Precision is the fineness of distinction that can be made. And reliability is the consistency of measurement when observing the same conditions. (An extended discussion of reliability follows in the next section.)

Accuracy and precision are often confused. Accuracy is concerned with the validity of the measure—the degree to which it represents what it claims to represent and nothing else. Precision on the other hand is the capacity of the measurement system to respond to differences in the characteristics under observation. The smaller those differences, the more precise the measurement. Precision, however, does not inform us of what is being measured.

RELIABILITY

A major topic in any research study is the reliability of the measures involved. The question of reliability asks: Does the system of measurement provide the same response when the same thing is measured more than once? For example, if, at first, I measure the length of a board to be $27\frac{7}{8}$ inches and then to be $27\frac{15}{16}$ and finally 28 inches, I have to conclude that the measurement procedures of my carpentry skills are not very reliable. The rules that I have for measuring this board are not adequate to give me a consistent result.

There is an interrelationship between reliability and precision. A system of measurement can be very reliable at one level of precision and not at all reliable at another. In my carpentry example, I am perfectly reliable at quarter-inch intervals, all three measurements would be equivalent to 28 inches. But, unfortunately, I am not at all reliable at the level of precision that I presumably need to properly fit this bloody board!

As with precision, reliability does not tell us of the accuracy of our measurement. If I solve my measurement problem by learning to hold the tape straight and to keep my eye perpendicular to the surface of the board, I may become reliable in 64ths. But if my measuring tape is defective, having lost an inch, the board will be very reliably short.

On the other hand, reliability is a prerequisite for accurately representing some consistent property. Consider that my task is to measure the initial position of voters on some issue. Grant me a group of voters who are, in fact, all slightly positive toward this issue. If the instrument I am using to classify this group is unreliable, it will sometimes err in the negative and sometimes in the positive. Consequently, with my given group of voters, some of them will be classified as slightly negative, some neutral, and some quite positive even though they are all slightly positive. The unreliability of my measure inaccurately represents the characteristic property of the group.

Sources of Unreliability

Reliability is a hallmark of good measurement if it results from controlling variations in the value ascribed to observation, when the observed attribute remains unchanged. How can there be variations in values when the attribute remains unchanged? There are two sources: (a) Those which are the result of the measurement process; and (b) those which are contained within the conditions and individuals being observed.

Examples of the internal sources of measurement unreliability are incomplete instructions which permit differences in administration or interpretation of a measure; vague, ambiguous, or double-barreled items which can be validly answered in more than one way; or clerical errors introduced during the preparation of data.

Examples of the second source are temporary conditions within the respondent which mask the true character of the attribute, such as fatigue, hunger, illness; changing conditions within the environment which affect individuals differentially; or the effect of capricious performance by the respondents such as mismarking a test form and the like.

In considering the reliability of a measure, it is useful to think of each observation as composed of the true effect of the attribute and the effect of these internal and external factors which our imperfect measurement fails to control. When the sources of error account for too much of the observed value, two individuals with the same attributes (or the same individual observed again) end up with different values for no explainable reason. A measure which is unreliable, therefore, is not very useful because its evidence is confusing. That is, the researcher cannot distinguish between those differences which are the result of differences being studied and those which are the result of variations from other sources.

In order to determine if a measure is reliable, researchers test the measurement under conditions when the attribute under study is expected to remain constant so that the observed values should be the same. These methods are discussed in the following:

Measures of Reliability

There are several measures of reliability. They all involve the degree of comparability between a measure and its repeat. One can make this comparison (a) within a measure, (b) between repeated applications of the same measurement, or (c) between administrations of equivalent forms of the measure. From this list, note, first of all, that if the measurement is composed of a single, nonrepeated operation, there can be no measure of reliability. Discussion of the other circumstances follows:

• If the measure is composed of several operations which are designed to measure the same thing, the results gained from some subset of those operations can be compared with the results from the remaining subset. If a test form of 30 items all measuring the same trait is being used, a reliability estimate can be gained by comparing the even-numbered items with the odd-numbered ones. This estimate is called a split-halves reliability estimate. This single-test estimate of reliability has certain advantages and disadvantages. Its advantages are that the conditions of administration are the same across the two subsets to be compared. Variations within the environment and the individuals are controlled. Its primary disadvantages are that the reliability estimate is based on just half of the items rather than the whole test although the calculation methods make some adjustment for this problem. Also, the method can be used only when the items are considered to be equivalent. If the items are not homogeneous—one item measuring the same thing as another—then this procedure cannot be used.

• If two or more coders are categorizing the same behavior or its artifacts (e.g., transcriptions of conversations, memos, television programs), the degree of agreement between them can be used as a reliability estimate. This method is conceptually the same as the first, and its advantages and disadvantages are much the same. The principal advantage is the control gained in having the content exactly the same for all coders. The disadvantages are that the product of the whole procedure is not evaluated and that the measurement procedure itself is inefficient. Most coding procedures use the sum or average of the raters as the criterion measure. This reliability estimate is calculated over the individual ratings of the coders. The procedure makes an obvious demand on time and money in having more than one person repeat the entire measurement task or some sample taken from that task.

- If the same conditions are available, the same method of measurement can be repeated either immediately or with some time interval between repetitions. The reliability estimate is the correlation between the two measurements. This method permits the use of the entire test in calculating the estimate, but introduces other problems. Individual variations between the two observations will reduce the reliability estimate. These legitimate changes in score values, such as any learning that might have taken place, will be read as measurement error. In addition, the readministration may generate effects such as those of practice, familiarity with the test on the second administration and, possibly, boredom and fatigue, if the test is immediately retaken.

- If the same conditions and equivalent forms of the same measurement are available, the measurement can be repeated using the different forms either immediately or after some time interval. The reliability estimate is the correlation between the two results. This procedure controls for the effects of practice and perhaps boredom, but carries the burden of demonstrating the equivalence of the forms. To the extent that the forms are not equivalent, the reliability estimate is lowered. This procedure generally provides the most conservative reliability estimate.

- If equivalent forms of the same behavior or artifacts are available, then the reliability of a coding team can be determined from the degree of agreement over these equivalent forms. This method permits the reliability estimate to be calculated over the actual data used. It also permits a reliability estimate when only a single coder is used. It has all the problems involved in the use of equivalent forms over time, however.

Presumptions and Problems in Reliability

Any method of measuring reliability makes certain presumptions about what is being measured and has limitations as to the accuracy of its estimate. The fundamental presumption is that the attribute being measured remains the same over the repeated measurement. If the attribute changes between the repetitions, then the discrepancies between the two measurements will be incorrectly seen as error instead of as an accurate measure. The researcher must make a judgment as to the volatility of the behavior being measured. Volatility can have its effect even within the ongoing process of measurement. As a respondent works his or her way through a multi-item instrument, the cognitive domain of the respondent's judgments may be enlarged by the content of the items. By the end of the instrument, the respondent is making judgments from a much different cognitive context from that of the beginning. We have all had the experience of learning an earlier answer from a question later in the test. This effect is quite apparent in extended interviews where what the respondent said earlier forms the context for later excursions into the same territory.

The presumption of a consistent attribute becomes even more of an issue when the method of estimating reliability involves some interval of time. Time permits even greater opportunity for change in the attribute. An unthinking pursuit of reliability here would throw out those items, which change when conditions are presumed to be the same, without investigating the source of this change. In short, we would wreak havoc with our measurement instruments in pursuit of a consistency which isn't there.

In general, we improve the reliability of our measures in such cases by reducing their precision. That is, we make them less responsive to the differences which occur in the attribute. This is analogous to improving the performance of an unreliable firearm by increasing the size of the bullseye. Not ordinarily a fair or useful solution, but often an attractive one (see Figure 5-1).

A more subtle presumption is that the attribute being measured is in accordance with the rules governing the measurement. Let me return to my tape measure. The ordinary measurement of a board presumes that the board is cut square on each end. My unreliability in measuring the board is easily explained if the angle at one end is greater than 90 degrees. Over the width of the board, the board gets longer. I can certainly change my measurement rules to ensure a reliable measure. Turn the board on edge and measure across the top will do it. Now the measurement will always be 27⅞ inches, but the board still won't fit.

Each procedure of measurement and analysis in research carries with it some set of assumptions about the world it observes. When that world does not match

FIGURE 5-1
A bigger bullseye increases reliability (relationship between precision and accuracy).

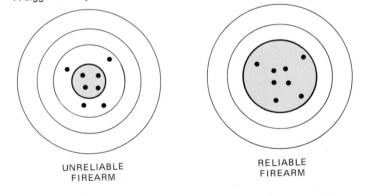

UNRELIABLE
FIREARM

RELIABLE
FIREARM

those assumptions, the descriptions provided by those procedures will be inadequate. My point is twofold: First, reliable measures are not necessarily valid ones; and second, variations, that have the appearance of random error, may be the result of accurate measurements taken on an attribute which is different from the assumptions we have of it. Reliability in research is a concern because if a measure is truly unreliable, it cannot be valid. However, a measure can be consistently wrong, that is, reliable yet invalid. It can also appear unreliable in our estimates when accurately responding to variations in the attribute. The problems of measurement are considerable. The chances of doing it right the first time around seem slim.

The Analysis of Reliability: Some Examples

Many studies aid the reader by reporting reliability coefficients for the measures used. In studying the effects of classroom instruction about the nature of television information, I developed a test of receivership skills which measured the ability of students to assimilate and interpret information presented via television (Anderson and Ploghoft, 1980). There were seven dimensions to that test. The first was visual skills which had a reliability coefficient of .70. How should you as the reader interpret this information? One rough-and-ready way is to square the reliability coefficient. This number approximates the percentage of correspondence between the two elements or two administrations of the test. In the case of my first dimension, the square of .70 is .49, indicating that approximately 50 percent of the variations in the scores is accounted for by some systematic skill effect, and 50 percent is unexplained. Well, again, is that good or bad? The answer to that question depends on two other questions: What else is available, and what are the purposes of this study? If no equivalent test of higher reliability is available, then this one is the obvious choice. In general, choose the test with the higher reliability.

The answer to the second question takes us back to the relationship between reliability and precision. One can increase reliability by lowering precision (it's easier to consistently hit a larger bullseye), but the result is less ability to distinguish an effect. To increase reliability *and* precision requires a genuine improvement in the measurement procedure. The way to tell which of these changes has occurred is in the results of the test. If the hypothesis fails, that is, if the researcher cannot distinguish between events which ought to be distinguishable, then it may be that the measurement lacks sufficient precision and not that the hypothesis is faulty. In such a case, a reliability coefficient of .70 would be good evidence that lack of precision ought to be the prime suspect. If the hypothesis is supported, as in our case, then the level of precision was adequate for the purposes of the research. Efforts to generate higher levels of reliability, in this case, given the possibility of merely lowering precision in the process, would have been inappropriate.

Research conditions are often such that the direct analysis of reliability is not feasible. In the Palmgreen and Rayburn study reported earlier, a 14-item scale was used in which *each* item measured a *different* component of the gratifications sought from attending TV news. The researchers report no previous history with the scale, the scale items were not equivalent and apparently no readministration was made. In a situation like this, the reader is limited to judgments of reliability which can be made from the performance of the measures. An unreliable measure will tend to dissipate the effects of a relationship between variables. Reliability is, after all, the ability of a measure to correlate with itself. If it won't correlate with itself, it won't relate to any other measure. Consequently, if the evidence for a relationship is coherent and robust, reliability is probably not an issue.

In our campaign study, we were working with conditions of judgment which were presumed to be highly topical and volatile. Our primary data collection came from four administrations of the same 16 items. We expected rapid change within our respondents. Variations over the administrations, even randomly appearing ones, were predicted by our theoretical stance. When our data met those expectations, we felt justified in offering a substantive explanation for findings that could have been dismissed as the consequence of measurement error. In short, the evidence we were able to provide for the validity of our claims obviated the need for evidence of reliability.

Coding studies present some particular problems in judging reliability. These studies generally use the degree of agreement among the raters as the indicant of reliability. Fisher and Drecksel (1983), for example, report an average reliability coefficient of .84, indicating a moderately high degree of agreement among their coding team. It also indicates that in some number of the judgments, the members of the rating team disagreed. What is the effect of this error? As long as the error is distributed over the different categories used and does not represent a consistent failure to deal with particular judgments, it has little effect. If it is associated with a single event, it can have a major effect. The reader should look for evidence, which must be supplied by the author, of the random distribution of error.

The reader has the least evidence of reliability in single instance studies which are descriptions of the qualities of individual variables. Many survey studies reported in the popular press are of this kind. Essentially, no estimate of measurement error can be made with these studies as each question involves a single administration of an independent item. Asking any question will, of course, generate some answer even if the respondents do not understand the question or are not competent to give an answer. These studies should be held in our lowest level of confidence.

Reliability: A Summary

Reliability is the consistent performance of a measure. Given the same conditions, a reliable measure will return the same observational values. Reliability is a prerequisite, but not a guarantee of a valid measure. Accuracy is the degree of correspondence between the description provided by measurement and the attributes of the variable observed. Precision is the fineness of distinctions that can be made between values of measurement.

Reliability is the degree of correspondence between repeated measures. Evidence of this correspondence can come from comparisons of subsets of a measure (split halves), of repeated administrations of the same test (test-retest), of separate administrations of the different forms of the same test, and the degree of agreement among raters with the same material or with equivalent forms. Lacking direct evidence of this correspondence, it can be inferred from the strength of the relationships between measures. Strong relationships between measures indicate high reliability for those measures.

Judgments of the adequacy of a measure in terms of reliability are based on the availability of similar but more reliable measures and upon the purposes of the study. Researchers should use measures of the highest reliability given the standard concerns of time, money, and the research situation. Nevertheless, even measures with low reliability may be sufficient for the purposes at hand. If, however, a hypothesis fails, the reliability of the measurement becomes problematic.

There is a relationship between precision and reliability. Precision establishes the limits of reliability. The higher the level of precision demanded, the more difficult the task of producing a reliable measure. In general, there is always an upper level of precision at which a measure will prove unreliable.

Reliability can be increased by lowering precision. Efforts to improve reliability may simply succeed at lowering the precision of what is measured. Reliability must be appropriate to the precision required for the test of the hypothesis.

There is a necessary relationship between unreliability and accuracy, but not between reliability and accuracy. An unreliable measure will be inaccurate at least some of the time. A reliable measure, however, can be inaccurate all of the time. Nevertheless, if a measure is consistently accurate, it will be reliable although it may not be recognized as such. Reliability can be a property of accuracy; it is not its cause.

EXERCISES

1 What is the relationship between measurement and the purpose of the research?

2 How does the research fail if the operational definition used is false?

3 How does operationalism remove the possibility of this failure?

4 I describe my carpentry skills as "within a 16th." How does that describe my reliability as a sawyer?

5 How does the volatility of an attribute affect a test/retest estimate of the reliability of a measure?

6 How can a measure be reliable and still not valid?

7 How can a measure be judged unreliable and still be valid?

OBSERVATIONS, MEASUREMENT, AND NUMBERS

Quantitative research proceeds from the premise that the analytical power of mathematics can be a useful tool for the understanding of human behavior. In order to use this tool, the properties of numbers must be associated with the properties exhibited within our observations. In short, measurement becomes the process by which we assign numerical values to our observations. We have seen that this transformation first requires us to interpret the properties of these observations as coming in distinguishable units of some categorical set, the elements of which are all equivalent. This interpretation is common and not difficult.

From this presumption, S. S. Stevens (1951) has suggested that there are four levels of **quantification** that can be used to describe observations, the nominal, ordinal, interval and ratio **levels of measurement**. As we rise through these levels, we assign more and more of the attributes of numbers to our measurement. We consider those attributes in the following sections:

Nominal Measurement

Nominal scales make use of the categorizing or naming functions of numbers. Measurement using this scale distinguishes qualities into mutually exclusive and exhaustive categories and uses a number for a name. A mutually exclusive category system means that the categories are independent of one another and that no observation would fit into more than one category. An exhaustive category system has a categorical home for each element under study.

Numbers come into play only in that we give the categories numerical names: category 1, 2, 3, and so on. The numbers do not imply nor give us any information about an ordering of categories or the distance between categories. In fact, there is no requirement that numbers be used as the verbal terms serve exactly the same purpose. Using numbers, however, simplifies data handling and computer analysis.

Examples of the use of the nominal scale in measurement are the identification of gender, marital status, religious preference, minority membership, and similar traits. The various categorical values of these traits are assigned a numerical name. In marital status, the researcher might establish the categories of *Never Married, POSSLQ,*[5] *Married, Separated* (including POSSLQ relationships), *Divorced, Widowed*. In selecting these categories, the researcher is attempting to account for all relationships within the domain of marriage that may have a substantive contribution to his or her study. Any useful set of categories can be used. Every possible relationship need not be represented; there may be no benefit in doing so. In fact, given the relationship between precision and reliability, the fewest categories necessary for the purposes of the research is a general rule of selection.

---

[5]*Persons of Opposite Sex Sharing Living Quarters* is the designation used by the Census Bureau.

The categories are exclusive in that no individual would be sorted into more than one category according to the rules used to define those categories. Those rules would have to take care of some obvious problems such as what defines a POSSLQ, what to do with the person whose history includes more than one category, and so on. The categories appear to be exhaustive. Every respondent would find one category to be most appropriate although neighboring lovers or a polygamist might object.

There will obviously be problems in precision as the categories are extensive in their coverage. *Never Married* covers both a two-year old whose marriage would be most unusual and a 50-year old whose marriage would not. There would obviously be substantial differences between individuals in this category. There may be problems in reliability as the actual categorization will probably be done by the respondent who may not understand the category system or may choose not to use the most appropriate one.

This system of categories could be improved by attacking the problems in precision and reliability. The greatest benefit from categorization comes when the separation between categories is maximized (precision) and the differences within categories is minimized (reliability).

From this example, we can see that a nominal scale is a set of categories within a domain of interest. The category set as a whole is an interpretation of that domain in that it accommodates and defines every element that can appear. The value of a category set is considered in two parts: The first is the clarity in which the domain of interest is defined. The domain is a conceptual unity of which the categories are particular and different examples. In our marital status example, the domain is a concept concerning committed heterosexual relationships. The more coherently that concept can be defined, the greater the understanding of the elements contained within it.

The comment "You are mixing apples and oranges" is heard when the conceptual unity of a proposed domain is considered weak. The comparison between "apples and oranges" is considered unfair because there is (according to the critic) no conceptual basis for that comparison. Apples and oranges are different because they are simply two different entities.

The second evaluation of the nominal category set is the extent to which the categories create useful distinctions among the elements within the domain. Each category that can be reliably defined adds a dimension of meaning to the domain. The fact that we can see a committed heterosexual relationship in marriage, in widowhood, and in POSSLQ's broadens our understanding of what that relationship means.

Some distinctions can be claimed, however, when there is no valid difference. A claim that "There is a difference between men and women in scientific competence" concerns the supposed distinction between two categories within the domain of competence in science. There are certainly useful categories of competence, but gender is not one of them.

Our marital category set divides the world of committed heterosexual relationships along a somewhat muddied dimension of formal and informal contracts in the hopes of accounting for some of the differences that are observed in individuals. I could have included other premarital and extramarital relationships in the exemplar scheme (e.g., *Dating before Marriage, Dating while Married*). The more dimensions I mix into the scheme, however, the more difficult it is for me to explain any substantive effect found along the values of the category set. The justification of a set of categories is in the explanation it generates. It is not simply being able to posit differences along a categorical value that counts; it is the understanding that is gained.

Ordinal Measurement

Ordinal measurement makes use of a mutually exclusive and exhaustive category scheme within some domain of interest in which the categorical values are arranged in some order. The additional property which is ascribed to this level of measurement is that of order. Order is defined by transivity. The transivity axiom states that if a < b and b < c, then a < c. Order is the organization of elements along some dimension according to some positional **rank**. The dimension might be satisfaction, importance, agreement, commitment, ambiguity, accuracy, or the like. The increase in magnitude may be in degree, intensity, size, strength, or the like.

Each rank along the scale is considered an exclusive position different in order from all other ranks. All the ranks together accommodate all possible instances. (I might note parenthetically that there is no measurement problem with more than one observation falling into a given rank. Some statistical procedures assume each observation will be a different rank, but that is not a measurement requirement.)

Ordinal measurement makes no statement about the distance between the ranks. Knowing that a is greater than b does not indicate how much the difference is. Technically, in assigning numbers to the ranks, it is only necessary that the number reflect an ordering. The ranks could be called 1, 3, 15, 35, and so on. Conventionally, we name them according to their order of appearance: 1, 2, 3, 4, and so on. Naming them in their order of appearance, however, does not mean that the distance between 3 and 4 is necessarily the same as the distance between 2 and 3. It is important not to confuse the convention with the attribute.

When an **ordinal scale** is used to classify observations, it is assumed that the dimension is relevant to the observations and that those observations can be ordered along this dimension according to the ranking scheme. It is also assumed that the ordering itself has some meaningful relationship to the behavior being studied.

In the 1980 campaign study, we asked our respondents to rank certain qualities that might be exhibited by candidates according to the degree of importance within their decision making. ("Rank the following qualities according to their importance in your selection of a candidate." See Table 5-1.) In doing so we assumed that the qualities listed would be relevant to the decision making of our respondents and that those qualities would vary along the dimension of importance.

TABLE 5-1
AN EXAMPLE OF AN ORDINAL
SCALE
Rank the following characteristics according to their importance for your selection of a candidate. The most important should be number 1; the least important number 11

Quality	Rank
Honest	_____
Intelligent	_____
Experienced	_____
Skilled	_____
Handsome	_____
Dynamic	_____
Devious	_____
Inconsistent	_____
Graceful	_____
Mature	_____
Clear	_____

The analysis generated by this ordinal scale was used in two ways: First, it allowed us to comment on the relative power that each quality had in the decision-making process assuming that a high ranking meant more influence in that decision. Second, it allowed us to identify subgroups of our respondents whose values, as reflected by their ordering of the qualities, differed one from another. Our interpretation of the ordering, then, was that it indexed a cognitive structure of values upon which decisions were based. The concept of structure is notable here because it makes use of the notion of positional ranking inherent in ordinal measurement. The concept contained in our theory matched our level of measurement.

Ordinal measurement rarely appears in research. The reason for that has more to do with lack of development of procedures for statistical analysis than the utility of the scale to describe behavior. Ordinal measurement would indeed appear to be more appropriate to our intuitive understanding of most judgmental behaviors than interval measurement. It loses out because of the benefits available from the more powerful methods of interval analysis.

Interval Measurement

Interval measurement orders a set of exclusive and exhaustive categories in equal intervals (distances) along some dimension. As with the nominal and the ordinal scale, the dimension is some attribute or domain of interest (quality of performance, success in class). As with the ordinal scale, the ordering is in magnitudes of degree, intensity, and so on. The added characteristic of this level of measurement is that the distances between points on the scale are considered

TABLE 5-2
AN EXAMPLE OF AN INTERVAL SCALE
In response to the following item: "Defense spending should be greatly increased"

I would:						
strongly agree	agree	slightly agree	neutral	slightly disagree	disagree	strongly disagree

John Anderson would:						
strongly agree	agree	slightly agree	neutral	slightly disagree	disagree	strongly disagree

Jimmy Carter would:						
strongly agree	agree	slightly agree	neutral	slightly disagree	disagree	strongly disagree

Ronald Reagan would:						
strongly agree	agree	slightly agree	neutral	slightly disagree	disagree	strongly disagree

equal. In a standard measurement form such as a bipolar adjectival scale (a scale with opposing adjectives on either end, e.g.:)

Good -1- -2- -3- -4- -5- -6- -7- Bad

the unit of distance between positions 2 and 3 is considered the same as the distance between positions 5 and 6. Or another way of putting it is that the amount of change (movement) between 7 and 6 is the same as the amount of change between 2 and 1.

Interval measurement allows us to use the arithmetic operations of addition and subtraction to describe the performance of the construct. (Operations on the numbers themselves are not being considered here.) This level of measurement is a requirement for any statistical analysis based on linearity. The zero point on an **interval scale** has no special meaning. It is just another position on the scale and does not imply the absence of the attribute. The metric of interval measurement extends infinitely in either direction using an **arbitrary zero** point. It does not require the discovery of a point of natural origin. Interval measurement is in distance, not quantities. The position 2 on our scale is not twice as good as 4 but is two units distant from 4.

I am emphasizing the notion of distance, just as I emphasized the notion of position in the ordinal scale, because what one learns from data collected under interval measurement is expressed in distances. The centerpiece studies of our presidential campaign research have all used interval scaling. (An exemplar item from the 1980 study is given in Table 5-2.)

Using this scaling technique, we could determine the relative positions of the three candidates as perceived[6] by the respondent and plot the distances from

---

[6]"Perceived" is a sort of code word which indicates that the measurement is all relative to the respondent's views and not to some absolute position.

those positions to that held by the respondent per se. In order to do that, we made a number of assumptions about the way our respondents use these response forms.

First of all, we assumed that the four scales were all centered on the same neutral point in cognitive space. It was as if we could stick a pin through the "t" in the neutral of the first scale and skewer the other scales in the same place. Neutral for the respondent has to be in the same place as the neutral for the perceived John Anderson, Jimmy Carter, and Ronald Reagan. We also assumed that the width of the scales was the same for all four—that the expanse of agreement possible for the respondent was the same as that perceived for each of the candidates. Finally, we assumed that the distance between each point on the scale was the same both within a scale and between the scales.

That's a pretty remarkable set of assumptions (for their graphic display, see Figure 5-2). Perhaps more remarkable is that we expected the behavior of each respondent to meet those assumptions, and they apparently did. I say "apparently" because we have no direct evidence of compliance. Our evidence is based on the orderliness of our findings, an orderliness predicted by our theory.

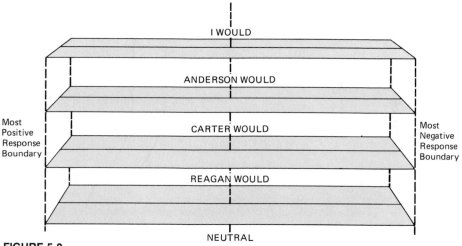

FIGURE 5-2
Semantic frame of measurement.

Ratio Measurement

The highest level of measurement makes use of **ratio scales**. Ratio scales have all the attributes of nominal, ordinal, and interval scales plus the added property of a true (**absolute**) **zero**. The ratio scale is composed of an exhaustive and mutually exclusive set of categories within some domain of interest arrayed in an order of equal intervals along a dimension which has a point of origin (zero point). Age is a ratio scale. The number of conversational turns, memos written, books read, television programs viewed, and magazines subscribed to are also ratio scales. Ratio scales are expressed in quantities of something. Ratio scales permit us to use multiplication and division as conceptual explanatory devices. Relative values within a construct can be three times as many or half as much.

Ratio scales measure the presence (or absence) of functionally equivalent units. In our exemplar ratio scales, one conversational turn, one memo written, and one book read are all assumed to be the same as any other. Obviously, each of these units has to be operationally defined. Further, the functional equivalence of these units is an interpretation which must be justified by the purposes of the research.

The ratio scale is the highest level of measurement because it makes use of all the properties of numbers—classification, order, distance, and quantity. The ratio scale is the only scale that deals with quantities of some property. To demonstrate the difference between a ratio scale and an interval scale, let's take another look at the interval agreement scale we used to position candidates and respondents:

Strongly Agree	Agree	Slightly Agree	Neutral	Slightly Disagree	Disagree	Strongly Disagree

The reason that this scale cannot be a ratio scale is because we have no theoretical conception of what a unit of agreement might be. Given that, we cannot recognize the true absence of agreement to "zero out" the *Strongly Disagree* position. It is this absence of a true zero which prevents us from talking about quantities of agreement although informally we often do.

Levels of Measurement: Review and Comment

The quantification of observations requires us to apply the properties of numbers to the phenomena observed. The properties of numbers are classification, order, distance, and quantity. Starting with classification and nominal measurement, each subsequent level of measurement assumes an additional property. A brief review of the levels of measurement follows:

• Nominal measurement involves the definition of categories which are mutually exclusive and exhaustive within some domain of interest. The particular categories used depend on the purposes of the research. The perfect set of categories maximizes the separation between the categorical values, minimizes the differences within those values, and provides an explanatory base for that result.

• Ordinal measurement involves the organization of observations along some dimension according to increasing ranks. It assumes that each rank is an exclusive category of the dimension that is different from every other rank according to some differential in amount, degree, intensity, etc. All the ranks exhaust all possible occurrences. The number of ranks is dependent on the precision needed and the reliability of the classification.

• Interval measurement specifies that the positions along the scale are an equal distance apart. This assumption permits the mathematical operations of addition and subtraction. Interval measurement is a requirement for many common statistical procedures.

• Ratio measurement has all four properties of numbers. Its attribute of a true zero permits the measurement of quantities of some property.

As a final comment, we should note that measurements taken at a higher level can always be treated as if they were at a lower level. One could ignore the property of quantity in the ratio scale and analyze it as an interval scale or ignore quantity, distance, and order to treat it as a nominal scale. On the other hand, it is a questionable practice to move up. The justifications for one level of measurement are ordinarily not adequate to support a higher level. The reasons why are in the idea of **isomorphism**, the concept we tackle next.

ISOMORPHISM

Isomorphism is a validity construct which holds that the properties of the level of measurement must match the properties of the phenomena being measured. When the concept of isomorphism is based upon an objectified, material definition of phenomena, it is presumed that phenomena exists outside the measurement process and that measurement should approximate that reality. An attitude measure constructed with equal intervals, for example, presumes that the cognitive structures of the attitudes can be interpreted through equal intervals.

As with all validity claims, there is no single way to directly evaluate the isomorphic relationship between measurement and phenomena. Phenomena, after all, are made visible through measurement and are not otherwise available to us to make a comparison. It is when we fail to support our hypotheses that we may call into question the isomorphic properties of measurement. At that point, the scientist will try something else in the hopes that a different form of measurement will isolate the relationship desired. The pragmatic test of the validity of measurement, therefore, is if it works to produce evidence in support of the hypothesis. While we don't question success, we also don't abandon our hypotheses at the first sign of failure, but rather begin to examine the validity of our methods.

The Demand Characteristics of Measurement

Another concern about the isomorphic relationship between measurement and phenomena develops from the ability of human behavior to accommodate different conditions of performance. This concern asks the question of whether the measurement properties conform to the behavior measured or the behavior conforms to the conditions of measurement. The case of behavior conforming to measurement is called **measurement demand**. In response to measurement demand, the respondent structures his or her behavior to meet the requirements of the measurement protocol. In our campaign study, for example, the structure of the questionnaire may have led respondents to decide that an agreement between self and candidate of choice was wanted by the research, and, therefore, they would comply (that didn't happen, however).

For those who want their findings to generalize to the natural world, measurement demand is a problem—a failure in measurement because it measures an "artificial" behavior. Much research is undertaken to comment on the character of our everyday life. Policy research, for example, investigates the circumstances which lead to some condition in the natural world and also, perhaps, the manipulations that can change those conditions. The studies of mediated violence are an example of this type of research.

In research of this kind, support of the hypothesis within the operational definitions of the research protocols is no longer sufficient to advance this argument. The research protocols must also represent—be isomorphic to—the conditions of interest. If the protocols used in research do not correspond to the conditions under study, *the findings cannot generalize to those conditions*.

The argument of generality is one of the most difficult to advance. Does giving electrical shocks to grade themes correspond to violence in society? Does a paper-and-pencil measure indicate the value of a crime? Does a questionnaire check mark represent a decision made? Our only answer to these questions is in the utility of the explanation to account for the natural world.

Evaluation of the Isomorphism of Measurement

The net of all this is that we need to make three judgments concerning isomorphism. First, we need to determine if the theory supports the level of measurement. To use the campaign study again, one needs to be satisfied that our conception of a cognitive space in which the positions of self and candidates can be plotted is sufficient to justify interval measurement. It is easy to construct scales: Take any declarative sentence and add a seven-point agree/disagree response, and there is the first item. The work is in the theory.

Second, one needs to determine the external validity claim being made by the researcher. Few would claim that human behavior actually comes in metric categories, but most make some claim that their findings are indicative of what is occurring out there. The reader needs to make the claim explicit and to examine the evidence (or lack thereof) offered in support.

Finally, the reader needs to consider the manner in which the observations, generated by the measurement used, give an accounting of the natural world. What better understanding of human behavior do we now have?

PRACTICAL METHODS OF MEASUREMENT

Measurement involves the methods and instruments by which individuals can sort, rank, estimate distance, or determine the quantity of some property. Measurement methods are the systematic procedures through which these activities get conducted. Measurement instruments are devices which aid these activities.

As we consider both instruments and methods, it is important to remember that quantitative measurement uses selected properties of numbers to describe the elements under study. The explanatory significance of the measurement—whether to explain characteristics, methods and practices or causes and consequences—is not contained in the measurement but in the design of the protocol in which the measurement appears. I can measure a piece of pipe to see if it is long enough for a plumbing repair or for a murder weapon. The measurement is the same; the purpose different.

Characteristics of Good Measurement

It is at this point that most books on research methods provide a list of the characteristics of good measurement: Items should be clear, unambiguous, short, purposeful, unbiased, positive, and relevant. The researcher should avoid items that are leading, double-barreled, embarrassing, worded at the wrong vocabulary level, have social desirable responses, or are unrealistic. Instructions should be complete, appropriate, logical. There is certainly nothing wrong with this advice. The problem is that good measurement is deeply embedded in the context of the study. The characteristics of good measurement are relative to this context. We can judge the goodness of an item or a procedure only in its application for some purpose. While examples to copy are not appropriate, there is a set of rough procedures which is useful to follow:

Developmental Steps Attaining good measurement instruments and procedures involves a process of successive approximations. One begins by looking at what others interested in the same research questions have done. Read the literature thoroughly. Write for exact copies of the instruments used in those studies which appear close to yours. Rarely does the published report contain the full instrumentation. (Unfortunately, many authors will not respond in spite of a public standard of access. Do not be discouraged; get what you can.) Check the encyclopedias and handbooks of measurement which provide examples and listings of published measurement instruments. (Access to some published instruments is limited to "qualified professionals." You may need a sponsor.)

But, unless one is replicating a previous study, duplicating the instrumentation and procedures of another is likely to be inadequate for your specific purposes. A published instrument may be exactly what is wanted, but its use has to be justified by the particular purposes of one's research. Specifically, that means that *each element* of the measurement plan should be justified, not simply accepted because it appeared somewhere in print. The researcher should ask: "What is the purpose of the item? Is there evidence that the item can accomplish that purpose? How is the item relevant to the theory directing my research? Does the theory suggest or require other items?" For good conceptual validity, one's theory should predict the outcome on every item.

Not every item in a good measurement plan will pass these tests. Researchers often include items for insurance or serendipitous findings. The practice is both legitimate and useful, but the character of the explanation is different. The researcher needs to be prepared to maintain that difference. It is dishonest to treat a serendipitious finding as if it confirmed a hypothesis.

The level of measurement used in an item must first be justified by the theory and then correspond to the level required by the analysis to follow. Researchers err both when they let the statistical analysis dictate the level of measurement and when they carelessly measure at the wrong level for the analysis proposed. The researcher should ask for each item: "How will I analyze that item? What will the possible outcomes of that analysis mean?"

Several different wordings of each item should be considered. The item is the connection between the theoretical construct and the empirical world. That connection is made in the construction of the item. Not only should the obvious characteristics of good writing be considered but also the subtle variations in what can be represented. Should a list of characteristics be ranked on the dimension of importance, usefulness, or value? The dimensions may appear the same, but they typically result in different ranking structures. Researchers decide among them by what they are trying to demonstrate in their theory.

Finally, the researcher needs to develop a history of experience with the measurement within the protocol of its use. The researcher should develop a trial measurement to use with a small group which can both represent the target respondent group and also provide a critique of the instruments and methods. The researcher will ask each respondent in this trial group to reinterpret the measurement back to the researcher. In this manner, the researcher can gain an understanding of how the respondents make sense out of the measurement and, therefore, what the measurement measures.

The careful construction of measurement is a time-consuming process. The best advice that can be given is, "pretest, pretest, pretest." A measurement instrument whose only merit is that it looks good to the researcher is rarely worth the effort of data collection. Avoid the write and run.

TABLE 5-3
AN EXAMPLE OF CONSEQUENCES OF MEASUREMENT CHOICES

Item	Percent selecting*		
	Print	**Radio**	**TV**
When you want to find out about local events, do you select:	66	23	11
If you wanted information about a fire in the telephone company, would you select:	33	56	11
When you want to find out about world affairs, do you select:	26	6	68

*Based on 575 respondents (Anderson, 1971)

What Difference Does It Make, Anyway?

A number of years ago, a bunch of us were arguing about research which claimed to report which medium was the most frequently used news source. Another promotional piece had been released indicating that TV was the most frequent source. The idea that people would rely on a single source for all the possible news of interest just didn't make sense. We decided to see if we could write legitimate source items which would result in different media being the most frequent. As Table 5-3 shows, we succeeded.

SUMMARY

This chapter presented a discussion of measurement based on three different facets. The first showed how measurement defines the empirical world in the terms of one's theoretical perspective. In this definition, measurement provides the empirical components of our understanding. The major issue discussed in this section was validity. Validity has three parts: The validity of the claims made by the study without reference to theory or the natural world; the validity of the connection provided by measurement between theoretical concepts and the empirical world; the validity of claims that findings generalize to conditions beyond the study itself. These parts are called internal, conceptual, and external validity. Conceptual validity has three characteristic forms of evidence: face validity—the measure appears acceptable; associational validity—the measure relates to other measures of the same concept; and construct validity—one's theory is adequate to account for the individual variations found in the measurement.

The second facet concerns the activity of measurement as purposeful, rule-governed observation. Measurement decisions must be justified by the explanatory purpose of the research. Measurement practices are systematized under the rubrics of operational definitions. Operational definitions are the rules which govern measurement and define the empirical content of measurement. They were distinguished from operationalism. Additional issues discussed were accuracy, precision, and reliability, and their interrelationships.

The final facet looked at the practice of quantitative measurement, which makes use of the powerful methods of mathematics to analyze observations. This application requires the assignment of numerical characteristics to the properties within the observations. Four levels of measurement were described: nominal, ordinal, interval, and ratio. The nominal scale makes use of the naming function of numbers and requires exhaustive and exclusive categories. The ordinal scale orders those categories in ranks along some dimension. The interval scales specifies an equal distance between those ranks. The ratio scale requires a true zero or absence of the property being measured in order to designate quantities. The problematic issue involved in measurement is isomorphism, or the relation between the properties of measurement and the properties of the thing measured.

The chapter concluded with a set of rough procedures for developing measurement instruments and procedures. These procedures start with a clear definition of purpose and a thorough reading of the appropriate literature. They end when the proposed measurement has been subjected to extensive pretesting.

EXERCISES

1 What is the difference in the relationship between categories in the nominal scale and that relationship in the ordinal scale?
2 What is the difference between an arbitrary and true zero?
3 How does one determine what properties of numbers can be legitimately assigned to a set of observations?
4 Why is moving the level of measurement up for purposes of analysis unjustified?
5 Outline the isomorphism claim implicit in the use of the ordinal scale of adjectives in the campaign study.
6 How is the criticism of experimental studies that they demonstrate only what can happen not what does happen, an example of a critique of isomorphism?

RELATED READINGS

Bailey, K. D. *Methods of social research*. New York: The Free Press, 1982.
Duncan, O. D. *Notes on social measurement*. New York: Russell Sage Foundation, 1984.
Kerlinger, F. N. *Foundations of behavioral research*. New York: Holt, Rinehart and Winston, Inc., 1973.
Miller, D. C. *Handbook of research design and social measurement*. (3d Ed.). New York: Longman, 1977.

SAMPLING

- *"Mary, will you taste this stew to see if it's seasoned enough?"*

- *Joe pushed the channel selector one more time. An action flick came up on the screen. He watched a few minutes and then said, "Nah. . . ." to himself and pushed the selector again.*

- *Professor Ramos outlined the technique to be used by her assistants. "We start with this transparent overlay which we put on the street map. Each quarter-inch square on the grid has a number. Here is a list of the numbers I had the computer select at random. Each chosen square on the map indicates a place where we will locate an observer."*

Each of these three illustrations demonstrates the process of sampling. The process of sampling involves the selection of some part of the whole in such a way that we can use the part to inform us about the whole. When Mary tastes the stew, she'll first give it a good stir to make sure all the ingredients are mixed. She will assume, probably without thinking about it, that the spoonful she takes will be the same as any other spoonful in the stew, at least as far as the taste of the seasoning is concerned. Her spoonful then can represent the taste of the whole pot.

Joe was taking samples of the television programs that were being presented at the time. He assumed that the few minutes that he viewed would be representative of the whole program.

Professor Ramos was taking a sample of places. She assumed that the places she selected would provide her with places representative of the whole geographical area.

We sample, then, when it is less useful, impractical, or impossible to deal with the whole of something. You can imagine the cook's consternation if Mary ate the whole stew just to be sure that the last spoonful was as well-seasoned as the first, or the technical problem Joe would have to watch all the programs at once or the number of observers Professor Ramos would need to cover the whole city.

SYNOPSIS

The whole is called a "population," which is any definable set of elements. An element is a single member of a population. An element may be a person, an interact (two turns of talk), a TV household, an organization, or a spoonful of stew. Sampling involves the selection of elements to represent the population. A fully representative sample has the same characteristics as the population in the same proportion as the population. We are rarely concerned about a fully representative sample, but, rather, we need a sample representative on the characteristics we are interested in studying. These characteristics are called "criterion measures." Criterion measures may be attitudes, income, age, gender of the respondent, or voting behavior—basically anything of interest.

The selection of elements in a sample is done with a sampling frame which is a list or a procedure which identifies all the individual sampling units in the population. A sampling unit may be a single element or a collection of elements (e.g., a household). Typical sampling frames are telephone directories, voter registration lists, plat maps (maps of residence locations), zip code lists, and so on. The sampling frame rarely includes all of the members of the target population. The difference is called the "gap." This gap typically widens during the collection process through the procedural loss of sampling units (a sampling unit may not be available or may refuse to participate). The elements that finally get analyzed are called the "in-tab sample." The representativeness of the in-tab sample is always problematic and should never be taken for granted.

Three kinds of sampling appear in the research literature: convenience sampling, judgment sampling, and probability sampling.

The convenience sample is aptly named. It corresponds to a readily available group of people who meet the definitional requirements of the population. For example, a class of college freshmen enrolled in a basic journalism class can be used as members of a population of adults.

Judgment sampling, which includes dimensional sampling and theory sampling, is the procedure used by the researcher when individual sampling units with specific characteristics considered necessary for the purposes of the research are deliberately, rather than randomly, selected.

Convenience and judgment samples do not permit the researcher to make statements about the precision of the method of selection, i.e., the rate of sampling error. Probability samples do.

Probability samples can be organized into four types: (1) simple random, (2) stratified random, (3) cluster, and (4) multistage.

Simple random sampling gives every member of the population an equal chance of being selected. Stratified random sampling is used when the population is organized in groups or strata which are homogeneous on the criterion measure(s). Simple random sampling is then conducted within each strata. Cluster sampling is used when the population is organized in heterogeneous units, each of which mimics the entire population on the criterion measure(s). These could be neighborhoods, schools, towns, clubs, classrooms, and so forth. The entire membership of each cluster is used. Multistage sampling involves the successive random selection of units starting with the largest unit and moving to the smallest. For example, a national sample of voters might start by selecting zip codes, then blocks within zip codes, then residences on those blocks, then voters in those residences.

As noted, probability sampling is the only method which contains evidence about the precision or error rate of the procedures. Sampling errors occur when the sample selected does not represent the population or the characteristics under study. In any set of samples drawn from a population, some proportion will contain erroneous information. That proportion is called the "rate of sampling error." Probability samples permit us to make estimates of this sampling error because in the long run, errors in random samples tend to array themselves in a particular shape. With many characteristics of interest to researchers (but not all), the errors fall into a normal distribution. The normal distribution in graphic form is the normal curve, the familiar bell shaped curve. It displays the relative frequency of occurrence of each error. The normal curve is actually a family of curves all with the same useful attributes. It is those attributes which permit us to make estimates of sampling error rates. Note that we know that sampling errors will occur and we can estimate the rate of error, but we cannot know *when* it occurs.

The use of a known distribution such as the normal curve to describe the distribution of sampling errors is called into question if there is sampling bias. Sampling bias is the systematic exclusion of a member or members of the population from the sample because of the procedures used (e.g., the exclusion of individuals with no permanent residence from a survey of individuals which uses households as its sampling frame). When the characteristics of the elements excluded are systematically related to the criterion measure(s), i.e., they are of a particular type, then additional error is introduced. Most samples are biased, and in most cases the effect of the bias is unknown but considered trivial.

POPULATIONS

The process of **sampling** involves the selection of a group of individuals or elements from a **population**. That group or **sample** can then stand for the whole. A population is any definable set. It certainly might be people as in the residents of Ohio or voters in a San Francisco election, but it also could be objects or events such as tape recorders on a production line, turns of talk in a conversation, programs shown on television, or memos distributed in an organization. All that is necessary to form a population is to develop an exclusive category to which members belong and nonmembers don't. This category of people, objects, or events may be "naturally occurring" as in the category of "employees in the SATCO Corporation" or constructed by the researcher as in "network television newscasts from April 1978 to March 1979." Members of naturally occurring populations generally show intrinsic characteristics which differ from nonmembers, while members of constructed population often are distinguishable only for research convenience. Employees would be recognized by the organization as members because of their working agreement not because the researcher defined them as such, but the newscast of March 31, 1978, is not intrinsically different from the newscast of the following day, although the former would not belong and the latter would.

Populations are defined and refined according to the purposes of the research. If the purpose of the research is to predict the outcome of the San Francisco mayoralty election, then the population is composed of the actual voters in that election. Here, a problem arises because that population does not exist until after the election is in progress. If we wish to predict the outcome prior to the official count but after the election process has started, then we can do exit interviews of voters as they leave the voting booth. But, if our intent is to predict the outcome prior to the election day, then we must redefine our target population. We may, instead, select registered voters who are further qualified by a declaration of a firm intent to vote. This substitution, however, must be recognized as an intrinsic, conceptual source of possible error in the prediction made.

The first step in sampling, then, as in all research activities, is to clearly articulate the intent of the research. What does the researcher want to say about what or whom. Oftentimes, one stakes out an imposing or impossible task as in wanting to "say something about the television program choices of children 6 to 12 years old." This intent posits the population of all children 6 to 12, a suddenly ambitious task. Further, the idea of program choice is dependent on the local availability of programming which varies from place to place. It is, therefore, a responsibility not only to represent all kids from 6 to 12, but also to represent all kids in all television environments.

When the critical reader discovers that what the researcher actually sampled was children enrolled in grades K through 6 of the Bureaugard Elementary School of Petowsky, Michigan, different judgments of the credibility of the research begin to form.

The net of this discussion is that populations are easily defined. But the match between research purposes and available populations is not always easily made. It's the match that counts.

Sample or Census

Once a population has been identified, the researcher has the choice of either taking a sample or conducting a **census**. To sample involves the study of members selected from the population; to conduct a census is to study the entire population. With large populations, it is almost always preferable to take a sample rather than a census. While a census eliminates sampling error, it does not follow that a census is error-free. A census offers no more control than a sample (i.e., none) over poor design, errors of measurement, or within procedures of analysis. Further, there is the problem of scale. Every individual in a study costs time and money to contact, collect data from, record, and analyze. Every individual added increases the possibility of processing errors and reduces the ability of the researcher to verify each step. Reducing scale by working with a sample no larger than needed for the purposes of the research often permits the reseacher to minimize these errors.

Representativeness

The purpose of taking a sample is to use the information in the sample to generalize about the population as a whole. It is, therefore, necessary that the sample represent the population on the characteristics under study. The notion of **representativeness** has some pitfalls and is in fact rejected by at least one author on sampling (Raj, 1972). He rejects the notion of representativeness because there is no way of knowing whether a sample is representative of a population on the criterion measure—the characteristic of interest—without knowing the population value. Of course, if one knew that value, one wouldn't sample in the first place. Statistical procedures give us no insight as to the representativeness of an estimate; they tell us only its precision in approaching an **expected value**. It is usually presumed that this expected value (which is derived from the sample) is also the population value. The expected value is, in fact, our best guess as to what the population value actually is. Nevertheless, this expected value will vary from the population value when systematic errors due to sampling bias, faulty measurement, inadequate collection procedures, poorly defined constructs, and similar difficulties are present in the data. Our expectations don't always match reality.

Researchers sometimes present arguments for the representativeness of the sample by showing that it matches census information on some subset of descriptive characteristics. The ratio of males to females in the sample or the breakdown of socioeconomic, income, or age groupings are often used. Certainly, the reader should be wary of samples that are badly unbalanced on known characteristics. Unfortunately, however, representativeness on one property such as gender is no assurance of representativeness on another characteristic such as job satisfaction or whatever the criterion measure might be. The inherent inability of the researcher to demonstrate representativeness should leave the reader with a healthy skepticism of claims of wide generality.

TYPES OF SAMPLES

Research in communication generally makes use of three kinds of samples: the convenience sample, the judgment sample, and the probability sample. A discussion of each follows:

Convenience Samples

As its name suggests, a **convenience sample** is one which is readily available to the researcher. Convenience samples are usually "prepackaged" groups such as classes or work teams, but they can also be overheard conversations, volunteers for experiments, available collections of objects, and the like. The convenience sample is probably the most common of the three groups of samples. Its relative ease of selection and low cost make it very attractive. The convenience sample makes the fundamental assumption that the characteristic under study is common to all members of the target population. Therefore, any member or group of members will serve as a base of study. Our campaign studies provide us with a good example of the convenience sample. In essence, we asked four colleagues at other universities to select 10 families each for inclusion in the study. The initial sampling, then, was of cities—the cities where our colleagues lived. The cities were selected because they represented different types and because we happened to have colleagues who would agree to the task of data collection. In our publications, we have specifically disavowed any intent to represent all families, but, rather, presumed that the information gathered on the families available would be useful because all members of the voting public have to deal with persuasive messages during the course of a campaign.

Convenience samples do give us useful information, and, at times, they are the only ones possible. Nevertheless, the convenience sample contains no evidence that it informs us about any group other than itself. The reader must carefully evaluate any claims of generalization to a larger population.

Judgment Samples

When the researcher has expert knowledge about a population, it is possible that a **judgment sample** whose elements have been deliberately chosen will better serve the research purposes. James and McCain (1982), in their study of nursery-school children's use of TV in play, selected a particular nursery school because the students enrolled there were racially and socioeconomically diverse and because the school used television as part of its daily curriculum. Both of these characteristics were considered important to the purpose of their research. A nursery school selected at random might not have given those characteristics.

Dimension sampling and **theory sampling** are other forms of judgment sampling. Dimension sampling involves the formation of exclusive and exhaustive categories which encompass all members of a population. The researcher then selects available elements from each of the categories. The purpose of such a study is to show that the dimensions formed in the categories are indeed an adequate description of the different kinds of elements in the population. Arnold (1970), for example, describes a dimension sampling technique to demonstrate the unique categories of deviance in a culture.

Theory sampling is the successive enlargement of a population description through the selection of elements, each of which is different from the preceding case. When no "different" element can be found, the description of the population is considered complete. Theory sampling is espoused by Glaser and Strauss (1967) as a way to "ground" one's theory in empirical data rather than in a priori conceptualizing. Note that dimension sampling and theory sampling are approaching the same task—the description of a population on some characteristic of interest, but one argues for the benefits of the deductive method and the other for those of induction.

Probability Samples

Convenience and judgment samples can provide no internal evidence for the likelihood of sampling error—the deviation of the sample from the population on the criterion measure(s). In the convenience sample, we must accept that all elements are alike on the criterion measure and in judgment samples, that the judgment is expert. There is, then, a rather dissatisfyingly large measure of faith needed to accept such samples. **Probability samples**, on the other hand, provide the research with direct evidence of the degree of precision with which the sample approaches the expected value of some population characteristic, although it must be noted that more than a little faith will be needed here too. We will deal with four types of probability samples: (1) simple random samples, (2) **stratified random samples**, (3) cluster samples, and (4) multistage samples.

Simple Random Samples   The **simple random sample** is a probability sample where each member of the population has an equal chance of being selected. Simple random sampling requires that each member of the population be dealt with in exactly the same way. There can be no biasing, no stacking of the deck in favor of certain members or against others.

To say that selection is random means that an individual, examining the method used, could make no prediction as to which element would be selected and which would not. If one could predict, for example, that no one with an unlisted telephone number would be included in the sample, then it would not be a random sample from a target population of phone subscribers. Randomness means, then, that chance alone should operate to select the elements from the population.

The requirements for a random sample are stringent: First, every member of the population must be available for selection; second, the method of selection must not discriminate among the members; and third, once selected, the element must be entered into the sample without regard to the elements already in the sample or those left out of the sample. So strict are these requirements that we rarely meet them, particularly when dealing with human populations. With such populations, we are typically dealing with varying approximations of randomness.

Gantz (1983) gives us an example of the common difficulties in sampling human populations. Interested in studying the diffusion in a large population of news about the Reagan assassination attempt, Gantz selected a random sample of resident telephone numbers listed in the Indianapolis phone directory.

Six-hundred entries were drawn. He reported that "309 interviews were conducted. This represented a completion rate of 56 percent (62 percent when disconnected numbers are discounted). One-fourth of the potential sample either was not home or already on the phone when called; one-tenth of the potential sample refused to be interviewed" (p. 59). Critical readers are left to their own devices to determine whether the 44 percent of the sample not reached represented a substantively different portion of the population. In order to present his argument, Gantz must presume that it does not. In doing so, he is following standard, accepted practices of research, but he does not meet the requirements of a random sample.

Stratified Random Samples   When prior knowledge permits, the entire population can be divided into subgroups or strata. Simple random sampling can then be conducted within each of the strata. Like populations, strata may be naturally occurring, as say gender, or researcher-defined as in dividing a population into income categories. Strata are most useful and become meaningfully different when they contain elements that are relatively homogeneous on the criterion measure. There are three major benefits to be gained from stratification: (1) Sampling from strata ensures that at least some members of the total sample will come from each strata. It is possible in simple random sampling that some strata would not be represented. (2) Because the procedure can be considered as taking independent samples from each strata, different collection methods can be used for one or more of the strata. Broadcast rating companies have found that certain respondent groups are better reached through the mail, others via telephone, and still others by personal interview. With stratification, the most efficient collection procedure can be used while maintaining control of collection costs. (3) Stratified sampling reduces sampling error because each strata is assured representation in the sample (compare with (1)) and because the strata restrict the spread of values contained within them. Consequently, the elements within each stratum are more like one another. The fewer different properties that have to be represented, the less likely the occurrence of error. (If all elements in the population were exactly alike, no sampling error would occur.)

Reardon (1982) was interested in investigating the ability of children from different age groups to provide scenarios for how they would deal with different communication situations. Because the purpose of her study was to say something about children of different ages, she randomly selected her subjects from each of four age groups ranging from 3 to 11 years. Her age groups were defined to provide separation in ability within strata. By comparing the strata over her criterion measures, she was able to isolate the effects of the maturation variable, cognitive complexity, on the accounts of children.

Cluster Sampling   It is often easier to identify organizational or geographic units than individuals in a population. For example, I know that most of the incoming freshmen seeking to major in communication will be enrolled in one of the sections of the "Introduction to Communication" course. Should I have an interest in this population, it is much easier for me to sample whole sections of the course rather than to try to identify, throughout the university, individuals interested in becoming a communication major.

Classes within schools, schools within districts, clubs of various kinds, political groups, towns, plots of land—all can be considered clusters for particular research purposes. Insect and plant surveys often are conducted by first laying a string gridwork over a field and then selecting individual squares for study. I followed much the same procedure in studying the communication processes involved in pickup dating in the beer bars of Wisconsin. Gaining the tavern owner's permission, scaled drawings were made of the public areas and a grid work drawn on them. This grid was transferred to the tavern floor by marking the intersections of the grid with masking tape. Cells were randomly selected for sampling at different times during the evening. Individuals in the cells selected were interviewed. That study demonstrated, among other things, that a variety of purposes can be accounted for in research.

Cluster sampling is a technique which makes use of the fact that in some populations, elements assemble in easily identifiable units. The sampling is conducted over these sampling units. A key difference between cluster sampling and stratified sampling is that the clusters should maintain the spread of differences rather than make them more homogeneous as is desired with strata. The clusters should be able to be considered on the criterion measures as populations in miniature. The entire membership of the chosen clusters is used in the sample.

Multistage Sampling   **Multistage sampling** is a procedure which makes use of nested **sampling units**. Sampling is first done from the most encompassing units called the "primary units." Secondary units are then selected from within each of the primary units. Sampling continues from within each larger unit until the smallest units are selected. Multistage sampling is most common when the population of elements is very large or when the elements are not individually identified. In attempting to sample a large organization, it may be simpler and less prone to error to begin by sampling divisions or departments rather than attempting to develop a list of all employees.

O'Keefe, Nash, and Liu (1981) used multistage sampling in doing a three-city study on the perceived utility of advertising. Within each city, residential territories were first selected, then street blocks within these territories, then residences within the blocks, and, finally, individuals within those homes to complete their sample.

In multistage sampling, each stage is a separate sampling task. The separate stages, therefore, can be approached with different methods. For example, in a large population, stratification may be useful within the initial steps and simple random procedures in final ones.

EXERCISES

1 A researcher wishes to study the rules which govern turn-taking in conversations. Define the population of interest.

2 A cable television company wants to raise its rates for new subscribers. It takes a sample of current subscribers to test their reaction to the rate change. Is this population appropriate to the research purpose? If not, where could it find a better sample?

3 Professor Wilkomann had volunteers sign up for his experiment on the persuasive effects of certain message constructions. What type of sample was used?

4 Many national polling institutes contact individuals residing in selected households on selected streets within selected census tracts. They are using what form of sampling?

5 What would be an efficient way to draw a random sample of third graders in your school district?

6 What is the sampling unit and population element in the sample of third graders you designed for question 5?

7 I have determined that there are "air heads," "jocks," "intellectuals," and "preppies" in a population. I select four individuals from each of these categories. I have conducted what form of sampling?

8 Still working with the population in question 7, I take a random sample from each group. Have I changed the form of sampling?

SAMPLING ERROR

Sampling error occurs when what we measure in the sample does not match what exists in the target population. Consider that we wished to measure job satisfaction for workers on an automotive subassembly line. Presume in this hypothetical case that on this particular job satisfaction measure, all the workers together on any given day averaged a 3.0 on a five-point scale, indicating that they were "usually satisfied" with their job. As this is a typical, albeit made up, workforce, not everybody is equally happy about his or her work. Some don't like it at all; some like it almost all the time. Most enjoy their work but have good days and bad days. It is this variability of job satisfaction across the workforce which sets the conditions for possible sampling error. For, if every worker, every time he or she was asked, scored the scale a "3," then any sample of workers, in fact any one worker, would give us an error-free estimate of the population. (Of course, such information would be trivial as it would not be helpful in explaining other variations across workers.)

As our population does vary across job satisfaction, it is now possible to misrepresent it by drawing a sample which includes too many of one kind of worker. That is, proportionately too many of, say, satisfied workers than what actually reside in the population. The type of sample does not matter. Whether convenience, judgment, or probability sampling is done, the possibility of error always exists when population members vary and something less than the entire population is drawn. With convenience and judgment samples, we can do nothing more than live with that possibility. With probability samples, we can estimate the **rate of sampling error**, thereby giving us an idea of the risk assumed in accepting the sample as true.

TABLE 6-1
RESPONDENTS FROM A WORKFORCE OF NINE AND
THEIR JOB SATISFACTION SCORES

Respondent:	1	2	3	4	5	6	7	8	9
Score:*	1	2	2	3	3	3	4	4	5

*Job satisfaction measured on a scale from 1 to 5. 1 = never satisfied; 2 = usually not satisfied; 3 = mixed; 4 = usually satisfied; 5 = always satisfied.

This estimate of the rate of error is possible because the process of random sampling imposes constraints on the samples drawn. The effect of those constraints is described in the **central limit theorem (CLT)**. The CLT states that as many successive samples are drawn from a population, the sampling distribution of an estimate of some population characteristic will tend to form around the true population value. The sampling distribution itself will approach a known distribution called the normal density distribution.

To break this concept down, let's first of all see what a sampling distribution is. A **sampling distribution** is the set of all possible samples of a given size. The sampling distribution of an estimate of some population characteristic is the set of values for that estimate calculated from each of those samples.

Here's a small example. Because the number of possible samples gets very large very rapidly with even very small populations, we'll set our workforce *population* at nine individuals. Table 6-1 lists those individuals and gives their job satisfaction score.

We'll take a sample of size 3. Sampling without replacement—for each sample we will use a given element only once—there are 84 different ways a sample of 3 can be drawn from a population of 9.[1]

The reader can inspect Table 6-2 to verify that no possible sample is missing—remember no duplicate samples are permitted, and samples with the same elements drawn in a different order are considered duplicates. The sampling distribution of all samples of size 3 taken from a population of 9 begins in the second column of the table. The third column shows the job satisfaction values which were collected from the individuals in each sample. The **mean** of these values is calculated in the next column.[2]

[1]That value, should you need mathematical assurance, is given by the formula:

$$\begin{matrix} N \\ n \end{matrix} \frac{N!}{n!(N-n)!}$$

Where N is the size of the population (9) and n is the size of the sample (3).

[2]The mean is given by:

$$\overline{X} = \frac{\Sigma X}{N}$$

Where X is each individual score and N is the number of scores added.

TABLE 6-2
ALL POSSIBLE SAMPLES OF SIZE THREE TAKEN FROM A POPULATION OF NINE,
RESPONDENT ID NUMBER, JOB SATISFACTION SCORES FOR THOSE
RESPONDENTS, AND MEANS OF THOSE SCORES

Sample	Subjects	Scores	Mean	Sample	Subjects	Scores	Mean
1	123	122	1.67	43	259	235	3.33
2	124	123	2.00	44	267	234	3.00
3	125	123	2.00	45	268	234	3.00
4	126	123	2.00	46	269	235	3.33
5	127	124	2.33	47	278	244	3.33
6	128	124	2.33	48	279	245	3.67
7	129	125	2.67	49	289	245	3.67
8	134	123	2.00	50	345	233	2.67
9	135	123	2.00	51	346	233	2.67
10	136	123	2.00	52	347	234	3.00
11	137	124	2.33	53	348	234	3.00
12	138	124	2.33	54	349	235	3.33
13	139	125	2.67	55	356	233	2.67
14	145	133	2.33	56	357	234	3.00
15	146	133	2.33	57	358	234	3.00
16	147	134	2.67	58	359	235	3.33
17	148	134	2.67	59	367	234	3.00
18	149	135	3.00	60	368	234	3.00
19	156	133	2.33	61	369	235	3.33
20	157	134	2.67	62	378	244	3.33
21	158	134	2.67	63	379	245	3.67
22	159	135	3.00	64	389	245	3.67
23	167	134	2.67	65	456	333	3.00
24	168	134	2.67	66	457	334	3.33
25	169	135	3.00	67	458	334	3.33
26	178	144	3.00	68	459	335	3.67
27	179	145	3.33	69	467	334	3.33
28	189	145	3.33	70	468	334	3.33
29	234	223	2.33	71	469	335	3.67
30	235	223	2.33	72	478	344	3.67
31	236	223	2.33	73	479	345	4.00
32	237	224	2.67	74	489	345	4.00
33	238	224	2.67	75	567	334	3.33
34	239	225	3.00	76	568	334	3.33
35	245	233	2.67	77	569	335	3.67
36	246	233	2.67	78	578	344	3.67
37	247	234	3.00	79	579	345	4.00
38	248	234	3.00	80	589	345	4.00
39	249	235	3.33	81	678	344	3.67
40	256	233	2.67	82	679	345	4.00
41	257	234	3.00	83	689	345	4.00
42	258	234	3.00	84	789	445	4.33

The mean of our *population* of workers is, of course, 3.00. Looking at the
sample means in Table 6-2, we see that quite a number of the *samples* do not

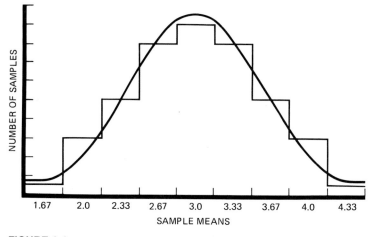

FIGURE 6-1
Histogram of sample means from Table 6-2. Normal curve (the expected distribution) is superimposed.

generate means of 3.00. This variation is caused by sampling error. That is, these samples are not a precise representation of the population.

If the central limit theorem is useful, however, we should expect that the distribution of all these sample means will tend to form a normal distribution around the population value. Figure 6-1 presents a histogram of the **frequency distribution** of the sample values. A **normal curve** is superimposed.

The match is not perfect (the CLT describes a tendency), but it is quite good. (It is even better under more typical research conditions using samples of, say, 30 or more from much larger populations.) There's nothing mystical about the CLT. The CLT simply describes a property of numbers that is useful. It is useful because when sample values distribute in a normal curve, we can use what we know about the normal curve to describe the characteristics of the sampling distribution. All normal curves are symmetrical about the mean; that is, there will be an equal proportion of scores on each side of the midpoint. For each normal curve, a standard unit of distance based on the midpoint can be calculated. This unit of distance, called the **standard deviation**, always accounts for the same proportion of scores as one moves away from the midpoint of any normal curve. In the interval of $+/- 1$ standard deviation, one will find 68 percent of all the scores. In $+/- 2$ standard deviations, slightly more than 95 percent of all the scores will appear. Figure 6-2 gives some examples within the family of normal curves.

Let's now apply what we know to our exemplar sampling distribution. Our population parameter (numerical characteristic) is the mean; our distribution is the set of sample means calculated from all possible samples of size 3 drawn without replacement from our population of nine. The CLT specifies that the

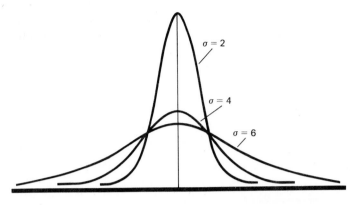

FIGURE 6-2
Three normal curves with the same mean but different dispersions (σ's).

grand mean of these sample means should be 3.0 and that 68 percent of all the sample means should fall between $+/-$ 1 standard deviation around the mean. We calculate the grand mean of the samples by adding up all the means listed in Table 6-2 and dividing by 84 (the number of means). It is 3.0.

The standard deviation of this set of means is given by:

$$SD_{\bar{x}} = \sqrt{\frac{\Sigma(\bar{X} - \bar{\bar{X}})^2}{N}}$$

Where $\bar{X}$ is the sample mean and $\bar{\bar{X}}$ is the grand mean of all the sample means.

Plugging our values into this formula we get:

$$\sqrt{\frac{(1.66 - 3.00)^2 + (2.00 - 3.00)^2 + (\ldots)^2 + (4.33 - 3.00)^2}{84}}$$

$$= \sqrt{\frac{28.0006}{84}}$$

$$= \sqrt{.33}$$

Solving that we get:

$$SD_{\bar{x}} = .58$$

Therefore, 68 percent of all the sample means should fall between the values of 2.42 (3.00 − .58) and 3.58 (3.00 + .58). Checking Table 6-2 and counting the number of mean values which fall between 2.42 and 3.58, I get 50 out of 84, or 60 percent. This is lower than we would expect, which shows the quality of our approximation. (I might note that statisticians have worked on this small sample problem to give us even better fitting curves, but our example is not too bad.)

We should also expect that approximately 95 percent of all the scores will fall between $+/-$ 2 standard deviations. This time I count all the scores which fall between 1.84 and 4.16. (Why?) I find that 82/84, or 97 percent, of the means fall into that interval.

Introduction to Sampling Error

In this discussion, I have been using the complete sampling distribution from a known population to demonstrate the way an actual distribution of sample means approximates the formally defined model of the normal curve. We have seen that even with a very small population and even smaller samples, the approximation is good enough that we can use the model to investigate the performance of samples as estimates of population values. In this section, I will introduce the concept of sampling error still using this known population and complete sampling distribution. In actual research practice, of course, the population is not known, and the sampling distribution is not available. The concept of sampling error remains the same.

As we have seen, sampling error occurs when the characteristics of the sample do not correspond to the population. The error occurs because by chance or by faulty procedures the proportionate mix of elements in the sample is different from that in the population. When probability sampling is used, *the rate of chance errors can be specified because of the relationship to the normal curve.* The term "sampling error" generally refers only to the rate of chance errors. The rate of procedural errors—called "sampling bias"—cannot be modeled and is, therefore, always unknown.

Sampling error rates are calculated by using a formal model—in this case, the normal curve—and some interval of acceptable values. This interval is called a **confidence interval**. It is an important concept because it establishes the definition of an error. We could, with our data set, argue that any mean other than 3.00 is an error. In our distribution, there are 66 samples that have means other than 3.00. With this definition of error, our error rate is about 79 percent (66/84).

That definition of error, however, is wastefully precise. Many useful conclusions can be drawn from samples which vary considerably from this value. Researchers, therefore, specify an interval of values acceptable for the purposes of the research. That interval—the confidence interval—is assumed to contain all the useful samples. We might note that the word "confidence" indicates the probabilities involved and not any sense of "true value" or believability.

Confidence intervals are expressed in standard deviation units. In using the normal curve approximation, the researcher knows that with an interval of $+/-$ 1 standard deviation, the probabilities are that 68 percent of the samples will produce estimates that are within that distance ($+/-$ 1 standard deviation) of the population value. By defining an error as any estimate that falls beyond $+/-$ 1 standard deviation, the researcher knows that the rate of error will be 32 percent. That is, 32 percent of the samples will produce estimates that will deviate from the population value by more than +/− 1 standard deviation. We would say that this researcher is using the 68 percent confidence interval. In our distribution of job satisfaction means and using this confidence interval, the researcher is accepting all values between and including 2.42 and 3.58 as useful estimates of the population value.

We can reduce the rate of error by simply casting a wider net and using an interval of +/− 2 standard deviations. Within this confidence interval, slightly more than 95 percent of the samples will produce acceptable estimates. The error rate would drop below 5 percent. Thinking about this a bit, it seems obvious that an error rate of less than 5 percent is a whole lot better than an error rate of 32 percent. Why wouldn't the researcher always use the interval of 2 standard deviations? The answer lies in the utility of that definition of an error.

To return to our example, the 95 percent interval defines any value in the interval of 1.84 and 4.16 as acceptable estimates of the population value. Interpreting these values by using the meanings supplied by the measurement instrument, 1.84 means that the workers are "rarely satisfied" with their jobs and 4.16 means that they are "nearly always satisfied" with their jobs. Is it useful for the purposes of the research to say that a sample which indicates that the respondents are "rarely satisfied" with their jobs gives the same information about the population as one which indicates that the respondents are "nearly always satisfied"? I think not. There is a trade-off trap here. If one decreases the rate of sampling error, one stretches the interval of acceptable values, and if one shortens the interval width of the estimate, one increases the rate of sampling error.

Methods for Controlling Error

The way out of this trap is to increase the precision of our sampling procedures. The precision by which a sample approaches the expected value of the mean is shown by the size of its standard deviation. In our example, the standard deviation is .58, which is quite large relative to the scale we are working with. If we could reduce the magnitude of the standard deviation, then the confidence interval would more closely locate the expected value of the mean.

To use our example again, if we could reduce the standard deviation to, say, .10, then the 95 percent confidence interval around the value of 3.00 would include only those responses ranging from just slightly dissatisfied to just slightly satisfied—a pretty good definition of "mixed."

TABLE 6-3
STANDARD DEVIATIONS FOR SAMPLES OF DIFFERENT SIZE
TAKEN FROM A POPULATION OF NINE

Sample size:	1	2	3	4	5	6	7	8
Standard deviation	1.15	.72	.58	.46	.37	.29	.22	.14

TABLE 6-4
SUBJECTS AND SCORES FOR EACH OF THREE
STRATA

Stratum one ss. scores		Stratum two ss. scores		Stratum three ss. scores	
1	1	3	2	7	4
2	2	5	3	8	4
4	3	6	3	9	5

Increasing Sample Size   How could we reduce that standard deviation? One of the simplest ways is to increase the size of the sample. Table 6-3 presents the standard deviations for samples of size 1 to 8. Note how rapidly the standard deviation decreases as the sample size increases. This increase in precision by increasing sample size will generally work for large populations also as it is only slightly dependent on the proportion of the population sampled.

Partitioning Variability   Unfortunately, in the world of actual research, every increase in sample size means an increase in the time and money needed to collect the sample. It often is not possible to increase sample size. There are other ways to increase precision. Partitioning the variability of the population characteristic under study is one of the most successful. In sampling, we accomplish this **partitioning** through stratification. Stratification, remember, involves the selection of elements from groupings which congregate members with similar values. Looking at our example once again, presume that from discussions with the managers of the assembly line, the researcher was able to distinguish three sections of the line with increasing levels of built-in frustrations. The researcher may well expect that those workers within each subsection would tend to be more similar to one another than to workers in a different subsection. For purposes of instruction, place workers 1, 2, and 4 in subsection A—the most frustrating; put workers 3, 5, and 6 in B; and 7, 8, and 9 in C—the least frustrating. Table 6-4 gives the respondents and scores from each of the strata.

To construct a sample of 3, randomly select one worker from each stratum. There are, of course, only three samples-of-one possible from each stratum. It takes one element from each of the three strata to form the total sample. These restrictions give us 27 possible samples of three respondents, drawing one from each of three strata. (Why?) The smallest mean value would be given by a sample with respondents 1, 3, and 7 shown in the first row of Table 6-4. The values 1, 2, and 4 would give a mean of 2.33. The largest mean value would be obtained with a sample containing respondents 4, 6, and 9 as in the bottom row of Table 6-4. Given the values of 3, 3, and 5, the mean would be 3.67. Comparing this range of values (2.33 to 3.67) with the range of values in Table 6-2 (1.67 to 4.33), we see that we have gained a definite advantage. In fact, the standard deviation for this set of 27 sample means is .37. Using stratified sampling, the researcher in this example can adopt the $+/-$ 2 standard deviation interval and be assured that 95 percent of all the samples will generate estimates of the population mean within the interval of 2.3 and 3.7—which would appear to be a useful interval.

SINGLE SAMPLE ESTIMATES OF SAMPLING ERROR

One might have guessed that in the actual practice of research, things are not as neat as all this formal theory would have it. As we know, the researcher would not have available all possible samples from a population which would, of course, require total knowledge of the population. The researcher is typically in the position of making estimates about sampling error rates from a single sample rather than from an entire sampling distribution. The manner in which these estimates are made, however, follows the reasoning used when the distribution is known.

In the research situation, both the population mean and its standard deviation remain unknown but are estimated from sample values. A few statistical notions are needed here. First, given a random sample, the expected value of the population mean is the sample mean. The sample mean is an **unbiased estimate** of the population mean and is, therefore, our best guess of what the population mean actually is. An unbiased estimate is one whose technical calculation from a sample does not introduce systematic error into the outcome, although other sources of error are possible.

The standard deviation of the sampling distribution of all means drawn under the same conditions as the sample in hand can also be estimated from the sample itself. This estimate of the standard deviation of a distribution of sample means is called the **standard error of the mean** ($SE_{\bar{x}}$). The estimate is given by:

$$SE_{\bar{x}} = \sqrt{(1 - n/N)s^2/n}$$

Where n is the sample size; N is the population size; [3] and s^2 (var) is the **sample variance** $\Sigma(x - \bar{x})^2/n - 1$.

We now have all the pieces necessary for estimating the rates of sampling error generated by the probability sampling procedure being used. We will use one sample to estimate the entire sampling distribution presented in Table 6-2. We can make this jump because (1) the expected value of the population mean is the sample mean and (2) the expected value of the standard deviation of the sampling distribution is the standard error of the mean and (3) the expected distribution is normal.

It is important to note that these are expected values, not true values.

---

[3]As our mythical, discerning reader would quickly grasp, in most situations the population size is never known but presumed to be very large. The first term, then, approaches the value of 1 leaving the estimate as simply $\sqrt{s^2/n}$.

Expected values are generated by probability theory. We have no better guess of what the true value is, but these theoretical values do not account for errors introduced in the actual practice of research. We do know that sampling can introduce error. Sampling error is the single source for which we can specify the rate of occurrence. (The rates of other sources are always unknown.)

To determine the rate of sampling error from a single sample, we first assume that the obtained mean—the one calculated from the sample—is at the center point of a theoretical sampling distribution which approximates a normal curve and has a standard deviation of the same value as the standard error from the sample. With these assumptions, for which there is good empirical support, we can, then, determine what is the likelihood that the true value resides in some interval around the sample estimate.

Presume that the sample estimate deviates by 1 standard deviation from the population value; then a confidence interval of +/− 1 standard deviation around the sample estimate will contain the population value. Of course, we do not know where the population value is, but we do know that the probabilities of drawing a sample further than 1 standard deviation from the population value is 32 percent and the probability of drawing a sample further than 2 standard deviations is less than 5 percent. It follows, therefore, that when sampling, 68 percent of the time the true value will be no more than 1 standard deviation away from the sample estimate, and 95+ percent of the time it will be no more than 2 standard deviations away from the estimate. This relationship gives the confidence interval its name. That is, we are confident, at a given probability, that the true value is in the interval specified. These statements, however, specify only the rate of error of estimating a true value. Whether an estimate is true or false *on any given occasion,* of course, we can never know.

We can demonstrate the procedures by using the 95 percent confidence interval and sample 14 from Table 6-2. This sample contains persons 1, 4, and 5 with values 1, 3, and 3. The sample mean would be ⅓ or 2.33. To find the $SE_{\bar{x}}$, we first calculate the sample variance (s^2):

$$s^2 = \frac{(1 - 2.33)^2 + (3 - 2.33)^2 + (3 - 2.33)^2}{3 - 1}$$
$$= \frac{1.768 + .448 + .448}{2}$$
$$= 1.332$$

Plugging this value into the formula for the standard error of the mean we get:

$$SE_{\bar{x}} = \sqrt{\left(1 - \frac{3}{9}\right)\left(\frac{1.332}{3}\right)}$$
$$= \sqrt{.667 \times .444}$$
$$= \sqrt{.296}$$
$$= .54$$

Our probabilistic claim then is that in 95 percent of the samples taken in the manner of the one we have obtained, the sample mean will be within the interval of 1.25 (2.33 − 1.08) and 3.41 (2.33 + 1.08). We would not know what the true mean is, but would bet that it also resides in the interval between 1.25 and 3.41. And, of course, we're right.

But before we get too confident, let's take sample 78 from the same database. That sample contains persons 5, 7, and 8 with scores 3, 4, and 4. Using this sample information, we will specify a normal curve this time with a mean of 3.67 and $SE_{\bar{x}}$ of .27. Again, we would not know what the true mean is, but would bet that it falls in the interval between 3.13 (3.67 − 54) and 4.21 (3.67 + 54). Ouch!

How can we distinguish between these two situations? Actually, we can't. We are somewhat protected from this problem, however. While it is true that the probability of selecting sample 14 is exactly the same as that of selecting sample 78, the probability of selecting a sample which contains the population mean in the 95 percent confidence interval is much greater than selecting a sample like old number 78. In our sampling distribution, there are 70 samples that contain the population mean in the 95 percent confidence interval and 14 that do not. We are, therefore, five times more likely to get a sample with correct information than an erroneous one. In the final analysis, however, I can tell you that sampling error will occur. I can tell you the rate of its occurrence, but I cannot tell you when it occurs. The potential of error in the sample selected is simply a fact of sampling no matter what the procedure. It is necessary to reserve judgment about any single sample and seek confirmation in repeated sampling.

SAMPLING BIAS

If we can be wrong when we do everything right, what can happen when we do things wrong? The answer—**sampling bias**. Sampling bias refers to a sampling procedure which systematically excludes some member or members of the population. Whereas convenience and judgment samples are by definition biased samples, true random samples are freed from sampling bias (but not error) by their nature. Most probability samples are not truly random, however, because of the difficulty of effecting random selection. One, of course, may not intend the bias, but it occurs because the procedures are inadequate (e.g., using a telephone listing as a sampling device for a population that has members without listings). Sampling bias is also the consequence of respondents refusing to participate in a study even when drawn in a sample or any other circumstance where selected elements do not enter the **in-tab sample**.

Fortunately, it is not automatically true that biased samples are nonrepresentative samples. What is true is that ordinarily a biased sample increases the rate of sampling error. We can get an idea of the effects of bias by systematically excluding person number 3 from our sampling procedure. Perhaps this worker was absent on the day the instrument was administered. As a result, we throw out all samples from Table 6-2 in which person 3 occurs. Table 6-5 gives the new

TABLE 6-5
ALL POSSIBLE SAMPLES OF SIZE 3 TAKEN FROM A POPULATION OF NINE WITH ONE
ELEMENT EXCLUDED, RESPONDENT ID NUMBER, JOB SATISFACTION SCORES FOR
THOSE RESPONDENTS, AND MEANS OF THOSE SCORES

Sample	Subjects	Scores	Means	Sample	Subjects	Scores	Means
2	124	123	2.00	42	258	234	3.00
3	125	123	2.00	43	259	235	3.33
4	126	123	2.00	44	267	234	3.00
5	127	124	2.33	45	268	234	3.00
6	128	124	2.33	46	269	235	3.33
7	129	125	2.67	47	278	244	3.33
14	145	133	2.33	48	279	245	3.67
15	146	133	2.33	49	289	245	3.67
16	147	134	2.67	65	456	333	3.00
17	148	134	2.67	66	457	334	3.33
18	149	135	3.00	67	458	334	3.33
19	156	133	2.33	68	459	335	3.67
20	157	134	2.67	69	467	334	3.33
21	158	134	2.67	70	468	334	3.33
22	159	135	3.00	71	469	335	3.67
23	167	134	2.67	72	478	344	3.67
24	168	134	2.67	73	479	345	4.00
25	169	135	3.00	74	489	345	4.00
26	178	144	3.00	75	567	334	3.33
27	179	145	3.33	76	568	334	3.33
28	189	145	3.33	77	569	335	3.67
35	245	233	2.67	78	578	344	3.67
36	246	233	2.67	79	579	345	4.00
37	247	234	3.00	80	589	345	4.00
38	248	234	3.00	81	678	344	3.67
39	249	235	3.33	82	679	345	4.00
40	256	233	2.67	83	689	345	4.00
41	257	234	3.00	84	789	445	4.33

sampling distribution. That distribution shows 56 possible samples as we have discarded a total of 28 samples.

Looking at those discarded samples, we find that 24 of them fell within the 95 percent confidence interval, thereby giving acceptable information, and four did not. Our new error rate, then, is $^{10}/_{56}$, or 18 percent. Consequently, the rate of sampling error has increased because of biased sampling procedures. Nevertheless, we see that even with biased procedures we are still more likely to get a sample with a good approximation ($^{46}/_{56}$) than not, even though the rate of error has increased.

The single exception to the rule of increase in error rate occurs when the biasing characteristic (say, not having a telephone listing) is not related to the criterion measure. That is, when the excluded portion of the population is the same as the included portion *on the criterion measure,* the bias does not raise the rate of error on that measure. This exception is the basis for researchers arguing for acceptance of samples which are clearly nonrandom and biased (such as Gantz's). They presume that there is no difference between those elements included and excluded.

We often have to accept procedures inherently biased. It is not unusual for samples of the general public to systematically exclude more than half of the population starting with those dropped by the sampling procedure, moving to those not available for contact, then to those unwilling to participate, to those whose data are lost or unusable. For all of one's good intentions, it is only the in-tab sample—the elements the researcher can actually analyze—which gives any information about the population. As researchers, we have a responsibility to investigate the effects of the inevitable sampling bias. Readers presented with studies without such analysis should carefully consider the possibility of substantial error.

EXERCISES

1 Why is a trait that has a constant value usually of little interest?
2 What is the source of sampling error?
3 Calculate the grand mean and standard deviation of the means taken from samples 1 to 25 in Table 6-2.
4 What is the 95 percent confidence interval of the mean of samples taken in exercise 3?
5 How does a confidence interval define sampling error?
6 Calculate the $SE_{\bar{x}}$ using sample 38 from Table 6-2.
7 What is the 95 percent confidence interval of the mean for this sample?
8 Why are convenience and judgment samples always biased?
9 When are probability samples biased?

METHODS OF CONVENIENCE SAMPLING

Convenience samples are often treated as if they were approximations of probability samples. While no estimate of the "goodness" of the approximation can be given, certain procedures can be used to eliminate more obvious sources of sampling bias such as researcher/interviewer preferences and respondent self-selection.

Researcher preference comes to bear in a number of ways. The "quickest" and "easiest" are always preferred. Academic researchers will use classes in their own departments. Nearby organizations are preferred to those which would require some—even minimal—travel. Interviewers prefer to interview people who are like themselves. They will avoid the differently dressed individual or the run-down house. To control the potential bias in these automatic preferences, the researcher should work to define all available samples possible within the constraints of time and money. The attraction of the wider draw is that it may limit the homogenizing effects of the researcher's immediate knowledge of what's at hand.

Interviewers need to be given specific instructions for identifying respondents in order to eliminate as much choice as possible. For example, if the interviewer is to contact individuals at library study tables, instructions such as "Take the first person going clockwise from the lower left corner" are preferable to, "Interview two people at each of the tables."

Quota sampling is another method by which convenience samples can attack inherent biases. Quota sampling is a nonprobability form of stratification which divides the population into categories or types and samples according to quotas set for each type. If one were sampling a population of undergraduate students, one might set quotas for each of the class levels—freshman through senior. The quotas would be based on information about the relative proportion of each class in the entire university. Available respondents would be drawn until the quota for each class was met. Note that this is still a convenience sample as the researcher is simply using what is readily available and not accessing all undergraduates.

Respondent self-selection is a potential problem in any study where the respondent is given the choice of participation. Every interview situation or experiment using a volunteer protocol involves this choice. In order to lessen the effects of self-selection on the criterion measure, the researcher should make the choice of participation as attractive as ethically possible. Attractiveness can be raised by giving incentives such as gifts, token payments, extra credit in academic settings, and the like. Even simple language as "I have some interesting questions for you to answer" helps. Attractiveness can also be raised by contacting individuals in groups and gaining the approval of the group leader. Participation by the members of classes, clubs, and even families is usually complete once leadership approval is given.

The ethical consideration in this attractiveness manipulation is simply the question of **informed consent**. The participant must be aware of the task to be completed, the potential risks if any, the costs involved (including time), as well as the inducements.

METHODS IN JUDGMENT SAMPLING

When time and cost considerations severely limit the size of the sample, the judgment sample is often preferable to a random sample. Beginning researchers may have little opportunity to work with sample sizes adequate to ensure representation across a number of categories. Valuable information can be gained from studies in which **population elements** are specifically selected in line with the purposes of the research.

Three research purposes which justify judgment sampling are apparent in the research literature: the identification of "pure types," the representation of diversity, and the elimination of sources of variation. In the identification of "pure types," the researcher wishes to demonstrate the existence or performance of a particular class of respondent. Individuals are selected specifically because they meet the type criterion. Working to develop a measure of alcoholism which could be applied to a general population, I used a judgment sample of 15 admitted alcoholics to develop the initial set of items.

Congalton (in press), in his dissertation study of the relational uses of television among siblings, deliberately selected *diverse* family situations in order to show how different family groups might use media for purposes of power, status, and the like. His method was to review the available volunteer families and to select those which appeared to him (and his committee) to be most different from one another.

On the other hand, Stoll (1983), in her dissertation on interactive talk in classroom settings, selected only high school classes in order to *eliminate major variations* across age groupings. In all three of these examples, the researcher constructed the argument for the particular elements selected based on the purposes of the research and made no attempt to argue beyond the scope of those purposes.

METHODS OF PROBABILITY SAMPLING

The first requirement of any probability sampling method is to identify all the elements within the population to be sampled. This identification is done through a **sampling frame**. The sampling frame is either a list of all the elements or a procedure which makes all the elements available for selection.

Examples of lists are telephone directories, city directories, voter registration rolls, tax rolls, employee payrolls, class attendance lists, plat maps of real estate lots, road maps, subscription lists, and the like. Examples of procedures are sampling behavior through time windows, systematic sampling of residences on a city block, sampling units of distance, and the like.

The sampling frame defines the actual population sampled. There is often a considerable difference between the target population and the actual population within the sampling frame. This difference is called the **gap**. The purposes of the research defines the targeted population; the sampling frame defines the actual population; the difference between the two is the gap.

This gap may result from simple circumstances such as workers not yet entered onto the payroll or from the more complex circumstances of sampling a population which is only an approximation of the targeted population as in using registered voters to stand in for actual voters. It is normally a matter of judgment rather than evidence that the gap is not a serious impediment in the attainment of the research purposes.

The next several paragraphs consider common sampling frames and the methods that can be used to develop samples from them. The methods considered are those appropriate to the smaller scale research project and are useful for any of the four random approaches. An additional section specifically discussing stratified sampling is included.

Selecting Samples from Lists

Random sampling can be quite easy when every member of the population or every sampling unit can be identified on a list. The entries on the list can be numbered, and a sample of these identification numbers can be drawn from a table of random numbers or from computer-generated random numbers. When the list is large, such as a telephone directory of a city, the task of numbering and counting becomes tedious unless machine aided. Faced with hand selection from an extensive list, one may do a form of multistage sampling by using random numbers to select page numbers and then using them again to select an entry on a page.

Systematic sampling is often used with lists. Systematic sampling involves the selection of every k^{th} entry where k is some fixed interval, usually the ratio of the sample size to the population size. If one wishes to draw a sample of 250 from a population of 100,000, then the selection interval would be every 400th entry (100,000/250). The use of a random starting point for the first entry—a random number in the interval of 1-400—ensures the equal likelihood of all elements.

There is a danger in sequential sampling if the lists are arranged with periodicities or cycles of values. If the cycle length approximates the length of the sampling interval, then the sample will be biased.

Random selection from a list requires a procedure which is fully describable and repeatable—not one which is unknown. Throwing the list down a flight of stairs and using the pages that fall on the uneven treads, or dropping a pencil with eyes closed from a height of 2 feet are not random selection procedures.

Sampling from Pictorial Material

Samples can be drawn from pictures or pictorial representations such as maps by using a grid drawn on a transparent overlay of the same size as the pictorial material. The grids are numbered and a random selection is made. The cells within the grid define the elements within the population.

Procedural Sampling from Unknown Populations

We often have to sample finite but unknown populations. In order to do so, a procedure must be developed which will make accessible all the elements based on what information is available. We will consider three such procedures: random sampling from numerical populations, sampling over time, and area sampling. Although these procedures will be presented through specific applications, they can be applied to research problems with similar circumstances.

Random Sampling from Numerical Populations   There are many numerical populations which can be useful to the researcher. There are populations of Social Security numbers, employee numbers, student ID numbers, addresses, telephone numbers, and so forth. The total population within any of these sets is often unknown by the researcher. The problem of sampling telephone numbers from a directory is a good example. In most urban areas, about 35 percent of households with telephones have unlisted numbers. This population is finite, but unknowable to the researcher. One does know (1) the possible exchange numbers—the three-number prefix—and (2) that some set of four digits will follow the exchange. Exchange numbers can be matched with randomly drawn sets of four-digit numbers. In this manner, all possible telephone numbers are made available. The obvious drawbacks are that some of the numbers will be nonworking numbers, others for businesses and the like. If one were interested only in residence phone numbers, oversampling would be necessary.

Sampling over Time   Certain populations arise sequentially over time— decisions by a manager, interacts in a play group, moments of attendance to media. Sampling of these behavioral events is another example where the total population is usually unknown. A population of behavioral events, however, can be conveniently defined by time boundaries. The population, then, is every event that occurs within time 1 and time 2. Time interval sampling can be used to select the behavioral events into the sample. In this procedure, an observation is made every k^{th} interval of time where k is some unit of time—usually the ratio of the number of sampling events desired to the total time. (That is, a sample of 240 events over a 2-hour time period requires an observation every 30 seconds.) As with systematic sampling from a list, time interval sampling must be concerned about possible cycling of events over time. Merely claiming that such **periodicity** is unlikely should not be sufficient.

Area Sampling   Physical space can also be used to define populations. Wanting to learn about the media usage habits of rural residents, I defined a rural resident as an individual living at least ½ mile from a town of under 5000 inhabitants, the town itself being no closer than 10 miles to a town of over 5000. Residences were then sampled by using odometer readings on specified roads with randomly selected distances between ½ and 7 miles from the town boundaries.

Methods for Stratified Samples

Stratification of a population can be accomplished by any variable that groups elements more alike than unlike. (Remember that the sum of the members of all the strata must equal the entire population of interest.) Each stratum can be treated as a separate random sample, and the most effective selection methods for that stratum applied. Each stratum will have its own sampling frame (and gap), its own sampling error, and its own sampling biases.

The strata may be sampled proportionately to the population or equally to one another. If the independent samples are taken proportionately, the elements can be merged into a single sample while still retaining the benefits of the increased precision offered by stratification. If they are sampled equally, then the sample elements must be weighted to account for the oversampling in some categories and the undersampling in others.

For example, presume one were sampling three strata of management—floor, middle, and upper—with floor management accounting for 60 percent of all managers, middle for 30 percent, and upper for 10 percent. With a population of 5000 managers, a proportionate sample of 600 participants would have 360 floor managers, 180 middle managers, and 60 upper managers. The researcher may consider a sample of 60 upper managers as too small for his or her purposes and yet be unable to afford more than 600 respondents. One solution is to take 200 respondents from each stratum and then to weight each element for the over and under sampling. There is an information loss incurred in weighted samples. In essence, one must use a smaller sample to stand for a larger one. In our example, a sample of 200 floor managers must stand for the proportionate sample of 1200. Formulas for merging proportionate samples and for weighting nonproportionate samples are beyond the scope of this text but are readily available in several of the references (e.g., Raj, 1972).

Sample Size: Some Choices

Sooner or later, every sampling procedure must deal with the question of how big a sample to draw. Unfortunately, this simple question does not have a simple answer. The size of the sample needed is dependent on three properties of the study: (a) the complexity of the characteristics under study, (b) the precision required to approach these characteristics, and (c) the resources available.

The complexity of a characteristic depends on the number of categories used to measure it. For example, we could approach the question of the likelihood of a respondent voting in the next election by asking a "Yes/No" question, or we could ask: "On a scale from 1 to 100, indicate the probability of your voting in the next election." We can represent the relative proportion of "Yes" and "No" answers in a population with a much smaller sample than that needed to represent the proportion of all 100 probability categories. But even simple measurements can become quite complex. If we became interested in those "Yes/No" responses and decided to investigate them over, say, political party (Democrat, Republican, Independent, and other), sex of the respondent, and 6 levels of socioeconomic class, we would have a $2 \times 4 \times 2 \times 6$ categorical scheme, or 96 different cells.

Precision is determined by the efficiency of the statistical procedure to be used and the variability of the characteristic under study. It does not involve the size of the population.

And, resources are the researcher's time and money.

Characteristics which are very complex and must be approached with high precision require large samples and considerable resources. Characteristics which are measured by two or three well-defined values or studies which can tolerate substantial sampling error may be very well served with small samples.

A very rough rule of thumb for the novice researcher is that samples of less than 30 are generally considered inadequate except for pretesting; samples in the 100 to 200 range are rarely brought into question on the basis of size; and few (although certainly some) research questions require samples of greater than 500.

There are, of course, a set of procedures for estimating sample size based on complexity, precision, and the technical requirements of the analysis. Their discussion is beyond our scope here. Those procedures, however, are much less useful in determining the balance between a study's demands and the researcher's resources than an examination of what has been generally accepted. Again, the community establishes what is considered adequate workmanship.

SUMMARY

Sampling is a process by which members of a population are selected to represent the population on some set of criterion measures. Information from the sample is said to generalize to the entire population. We have examined three methods of selection: convenience sampling, judgment sampling, and probability sampling. Of the three, only probability sampling can give an estimate of the rate of sampling error and, therefore, provide an estimate of the precision of the **population estimates**.

Convenience sampling is used when a relatively small proportion of the population is available to the researcher. For the reader to accept any claim of the sample generalizing to the larger population requires the assumption that all members of the population are reasonably alike on the criterion measure and, therefore, any sample of elements is as good as any other.

Judgment sampling applies to samples of elements selected specifically because of characteristics held by those elements. Three purposes have been used to justify judgment sampling—the identification of pure types, the representation of diversity, and the elimination of sources of variation within a sample.

Probability sampling requires the identification or availability of every member of the population for selection into the sample. Most probability samples, in fact, are approximations because they cannot meet this test. A sampling frame is a list or procedure which makes the population elements available for selection. The difference between the members in the sampling frame and the total population, called the gap, establishes the character of this approximation. Probability sampling can be simple, stratified, cluster, or multistage.

The advantage of probability samples is that they provide estimates of sampling error. Sampling error occurs when the sample value of some criterion measure is not equivalent to the population value because the population elements selected into the sample do not represent the population characteristics. The estimate of sampling error is *an estimate of the rate of error* generated by a sampling procedure; it is *not* an estimate of the "rightness" or "wrongness" of any particular sample.

As a sample stands for the population, the sample value of the criterion measure is the expected value of the population characteristic. One can increase the precision by which a sample approaches an expected value generally by increasing sample size and/or controlling variations among elements in the sample.

Sampling bias occurs when the sampling procedure systematically excludes members of the target population from the sample. Convenience and judgment samples are inherently biased. Probability samples can be biased when the sampling frame used is defective or when population elements selected cannot be entered into the in-tab sample—e.g., a selected individual refuses to participate. Biased samples do not necessarily give false information, but generally raise the rate of sampling error.

Taking a sample is often the only way that one can get adequate information about a population. It is important to remember, however, that samples are estimates of population characteristics and are always subject to procedural error. In order to account for this error, the researcher does not make absolute claims from sample information but rather makes probabilistic ones. A single value may be reported, but that value is always to be interpreted as being the center point of a range of values which is likely, but not certainly, to contain the population value. When examining research, the reader should place the least confidence in studies which report the findings from a single sample. As every gambler knows, anything can happen once.

EXERCISES

1 Mail surveys often include a quarter as payment for completion of the questionnaire. Why?
2 How does enlarging the pool of available population members help control the potential bias?
3 Does the notion of a pure type differ from the notion of a stereotype?
4 Why is the researcher at risk using a small random sample to represent a diverse population?
5 Describe a procedure that could be used to draw a random sample of 10 means from Table 6-2.
6 Describe a procedure to draw a systematic random sample of 10 means from Table 6-2.
7 Is there periodicity in Table 6-2?
8 John takes a stratified sample of 10 names from each letter of the alphabet in a telephone directory (270 respondents). Mary claims the sample is biased. Is she right?
9 Presume that you had a 30-page transcript of an extended conversation. How could you take a random sample of 30 pairs of turns?
10 What sample size would you recommend for the Wisconsin beer bar study?

RELATED READINGS

Cochran, W. G. *Sampling techniques,* (3d. Ed.) New York: John Wiley and Sons, Inc., 1977.

Glaser, B. G. and Strauss, A. L. *The discovery of grounded theory.* Chicago: Aldine Publishing Co., 1967.

Raj, D. *The design of sample surveys.* New York: McGraw-Hill, 1972.

Williams, B. *A sampler on sampling.* New York: John Wiley and Sons, Inc., 1978.

STATISTICS

Susan: *"So, what's your problem?"*

Jim: *"Well, Susan, I've got more than 45 books on stats in my library alone. The longest one has over 1200 pages. I'm having a hard time figuring what to say about stats in less than 40 pages."*

Susan: *"What's the content of most of those books?"*

Jim: *"Formulas, recipes—that kind of thing."*

Susan: *"And you're not doing formulas."*

Jim: *"I'm trying to avoid them."*

Susan: *"So, drop out all the formulas and write about what's left."*

Jim: *"OK. Here goes."*

SYNOPSIS

Statistics is the science of probability. In research, statistics is the principal method by which the sets of numbers generated in measurement are analyzed. In this analysis, statistics performs any of three tasks:

1 Statistics provides methods for determining the properties of a set of numbers. The properties most often examined are measures of representative values or central tendency, the distribution of occurrences of the possible values, the spread or dispersion of the number set, and, when two or more variables are contained in the set, the structure of association between the variables in the set. These methods of analysis are usually called "descriptive statistics."

2 Statistics offers a method by which the characteristics found in a sample of measurements can be applied to the population from which the sample was drawn. These methods generate estimates of population characteristics (called "parameters") based on the information made available in the sample.

3 Finally, statistics can be used as a decision rule in determining whether a characteristic found in sampling can be reasonably attributed to sampling error. If it is determined that sampling error is not a reasonable explanation, then an alternate explanation—usually the hypothesis—is considered a significant candidate. This use of statistical analysis is considered in Chapter 8.

In the actual practice of research, analysts are most often concerned about the latter two applications. In our discussion, I will combine (1) descriptive and (2) inferential statistics in that the characteristics I will present are those which are also population estimates. In short, I will be assuming that the number sets analyzed are observations over samples randomly drawn from a population. You should be aware that there are many more descriptive statements that can be made given a set of numbers and, for that matter, even more population estimates, than those we will discuss.

DESCRIBING NUMERICAL OBSERVATIONS

Descriptive and inferential statistics are methods by which we can discover the properties of sets of numbers. When those numbers themselves are the product of the measurement of human behavior or of its artifacts, statistical analysis is another set of tools to aid our understanding of that behavior. Let's create an example:

Presume a general interest in the dissemination of information about street drugs. Our interest is in the level and quality of knowledge that college students have and the manner in which that knowledge is connected to various information networks. We begin by developing a hundred-item "Drug Knowledge Test" with items like:

Barbiturates (downers) are available in:

1 White tablets only
2 Any color tablet
3 Yellow powder only
4 None of these

The opiates (narcotics) are used by:

1 Smoking
2 Injecting in the arm
3 Swallowing
4 Snorting
5 All of the above

This instrument is scored by the number correct. For this example, we will presume that it was administered to 100 upper-division undergraduates, all

TABLE 7-1
DRUG KNOWLEDGE TEST (DKT) SCORES FOR 100 COLLEGE
STUDENTS

Ss*	00	10	20	30	40	50	60	70	80	90
00	30	42	48	62	33	51	35	78	58	93
01	81	25	75	47	92	57	88	65	38	59
02	51	56	45	85	44	36	31	26	70	83
03	42	41	66	58	44	53	57	50	93	63
04	82	82	73	29	49	67	33	44	64	35
05	90	68	48	58	70	53	33	84	46	86
06	65	50	89	91	58	53	43	28	81	67
07	77	62	69	73	94	54	56	87	72	48
08	49	79	52	68	79	45	23	81	69	61
09	38	85	46	32	34	21	46	37	66	71

*Scores are arranged by respondent ID number (00–99).

enrolled in a senior-level organizational communication course at a small western college. We now have 100 scores which can vary from zero (none correct) to 100 (all correct). Table 7-1 shows what that set of scores looks like.

In this array the first score (30) is for respondent 00 and the last score (71) is for respondent 99. This array is called a "univariate data set" because there is one observation (score) on one variable (the DKT) for each unit of analysis (individual). For most people, an array of numbers such as this one is not very meaningful. We need some techniques to make some sense out of that array. How can that set of numbers be characterized? Three qualities are most often used to describe a univariate set of numbers: (a) typical or representative values, (b) the distribution of values, and (c) the dispersion or spread of the scores. A discussion of each of these follows over the next several pages.

REPRESENTATIVE VALUES

The most widely used representative values are given by the averages: the mode, the median, and the mean. The **mode** is the most frequently occurring value; the **median** is the score value which divides the set of scores in half with 50 percent of the scores falling below the median and 50 percent being above it; and the mean is the arithmetic average with which we are familiar—i.e., the sum of the scores divided by the number of scores [$\Sigma X/N$].

There is a relationship between the level of measurement and the averages. Because the mode requires us to simply count the number of occasions of each categorical value, it can be meaningfully used with any level of measurement, including the nominal. The median, however, requires that the numbers represent order and can therefore, be used only on measures that are ordinal or higher. The mean, in order to be a meaningful representation of a measured characteristic, requires the properties of interval or ratio scores. In our example,

TABLE 7-2
DKT SCORES IN ASCENDING ORDER

21	33	42	46	51	58	65	70	79	86
23	33	42	47	52	58	65	70	81	87
25	34	43	48	53	58	66	71	81	88
26	35	44	48	53	58	66	72	81	89
28	35	44	48	53	59	67	73	82	90
29	36	44	49	54	61	67	73	82	91
30	37	45	49	56	62	68	75	83	92
31	38	45	50	56	62	68	77	84	93
32	38	46	50	57	63	69	78	85	93
33	41	46	51	57	64	69	79	85	94

we are using an interval instrument. Consequently, all three averages can be calculated.

To find the mode and to figure the median, we will have to put the DKT scores into order by magnitude. Table 7-2 presents those scores in ascending order.

In examining Table 7-2, we find that the most frequently occurring score is 58 with four instances. That is the mode. Had there been other score values with four occurrences, then there would have been more than one mode. The median is 57.5. Although that is not an actual score, splitting the difference is the conventional solution for calculating a median with an even number of scores. The mean is 58.44 [(21 + 23 + . . . + 93 + 94)/100].

The Meaningfulness of Observations and Averages

In order for the measured observations to make sense as explanations of human behavior, we have to make the assumption that there is an attribute (in this case, drug knowledge) which can be meaningfully used as a descriptor for each member of the aggregate (in this case, college students). In order for the averages to make sense as representative values, there has to be a core of common values associated with the aggregating category. That is, scores at and near the averages have to be more likely than scores at greater distances. If that assumption is true, then what the average explains is the most likely value that the attribute will take for that class of individuals, and it is fair to make a statement like, "For college students, the mean drug knowledge is 58.44."

That statement is not a statement of fact, but, rather, a claim that the category called "college students" can be characterized by the value of 58.44 on the DKT and further that the value of 58.44 will distinguish the category of college students from other categories that can be devised. If the assumption on which it is based is not true, then all that has been done is to perform some technical manipulations on a set of numbers.

How could that assumption be false? The assumption is false if (a) there is no convergence or tendency for convergence of the elements in the category on some common value of the attribute. If there is no convergence, then 58.44 does not characterize college students but is simply the result of the chance collection of measurements determined only by the happenstance of the individuals tested. Or (b), if the value of the attribute does not distinguish college students from other classes, then its attribution as a characteristic of college students is wrong. It may be that some other larger classification such as the 18-to-25-year-old age bracket, of which college student is a partial subset, is the better explanation.

It is important for us to remember that regardless of the quality of our measurement or explanation, the statistical characteristic can always be calculated. Performing $\Sigma X/N$ will always generate a mean, but it will not always be meaningful. Once again we are forced to make judgments. The burden of proof is always on the research. It is up to the researcher to provide a convincing argument that there is a characterizing attribute the value of which is distinguished by the aggregating classification.

DISTRIBUTIONS

Powerful evidence for the claim for this attribute can come from the distribution of the scores themselves. The distribution of a set of values is simply a list of the values in the set and the number of times each occurs. The distribution curve can be given by plotting the frequency of occurrence of each score value on a set of coordinates. (Table 7-3 and Figure 7-1 present the frequency distribution and **distribution curve** for the DKT example.) Our interest in the shape of the distribution stems from certain expectations concerning that shape which arise when measurements are taken on a characteristic of a class of elements.

To show the relationship between distribution and characteristics, let's first examine the claim of the existence of an attribute which is a characteristic of a given set with some care. The claim is that there is a core property which is common to all elements of the aggregate (see Figure 7-2). It is assumed, however, that the actual values shown by the individual elements will vary from the core due to particular circumstances. That is, circumstances can occur which will cause the value for certain individuals to differ from the core value. Given

TABLE 7-3
FREQUENCY DISTRIBUTION FOR THE 100
DKT SCORES SHOWN IN INTERVALS OF 5

Score	Freq.	Score	Freq.	Score	Freq.
21–25	3	26–30	4	31–35	8
36–40	4	41–45	9	46–50	11
51–55	7	56–60	9	61–65	7
66–70	10	71–75	5	76–80	4
81–85	9	86–90	5	91–95	5

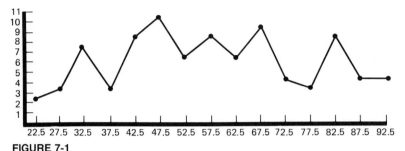

FIGURE 7-1
Distribution curve for the DKT scores shown at the midpoint of the frequency interval.

that those circumstances are chance effects and not related to the protocol of the research, these deviant values should show no pattern but should distribute equally around the core, some higher and some lower. That is, the variations should distribute randomly throughout the aggregate of individuals. This random distribution means that we should expect these additions to balance out (see Figure 7-3).

Further, we might expect that major variations will be unusual; most variations will be minor. These expectations mean that most of the scores will be clustered around the core value and that there will be a decreasing number of scores as one moves away from this core value. The distribution ought to look something like that shown in Figure 7-4. In that figure, the relative frequency is shown on the ordinate (the vertical, or *y* axis), and the scores are shown on the abscissa (the horizontal, or *x* axis).

The curve shown in Figure 7-4 is called the "normal curve." It is a formal, mathematical model of probability. It shows the theoretical probabilities of variations from an expected core value. We see that in the normal curve, the mean, median, and mode are all the same, that most of the values cluster around

FIGURE 7-2
Notion that measurements congregate around the core property being measured.

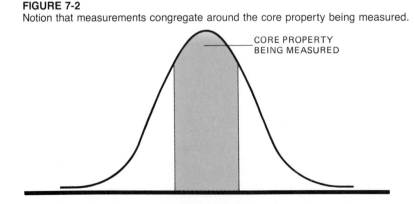

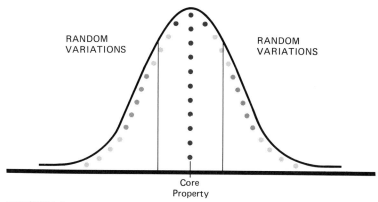

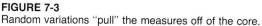

Core
Property

FIGURE 7-3
Random variations "pull" the measures off of the core.

these typical values, and that as the deviations from them get larger, their relative frequency rapidly gets smaller, but that all possible values do appear.

The normal curve has been shown to have great utility in describing empirical events which are random in nature, such as the value that individual differences contribute to the core value of some attribute.[1]

Let's see if we can pull this all together to evaluate the data from the DKT. We are claiming that these data represent an attribute of the classification of college students. For the moment, we are concerned with the problem of convergence: Do these data show the qualities that indicate a property which is a valid description of the classification college student? If they do, given our reasoning of the past few paragraphs, we would expect the distribution of the scores to look something like the normal density distribution (normal curve). If the distribution of the DKT scores is rectangular, skewed to the right or left, or shows some other major departure from normal (Figure 7-5 shows these and other nonnormal curves), then typicalness becomes difficult if not impossible to define.

Figure 7-6 presents the comparison between the DKT distribution and the normal distribution. As we can see, the data curve and normal curve do not match, but the data curve looks more like the normal curve than several other ways it could look. Here we are faced with another decision. Is this deviation

---

[1]A **random event** is one without pattern. Or, to put it another way, it is one which requires its own, individual explanation as in the case of the individual differences which appear in an aggregate. Random, then, does not mean the event is unexplainable but that a separate explanation is needed for each event. When a set of random events shows a pattern it is an error of interpretation. For example, the outcome of the toss of a fair coin is a random event. If one were to toss this coin 10 times and come up with 10 heads and no tails, it would be an error to claim that this coin always results in heads or to make any prediction at all about the next outcome. We simply need a larger event space (set of events) for the randomness to appear.

FIGURE 7-4
Normal curve.

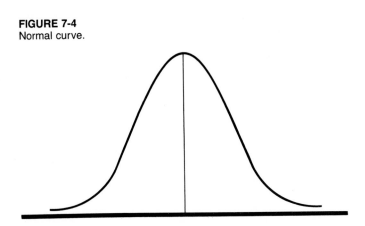

from the model an indication that we have problems in convergence, or is it just the happenstance of a restricted event space—after all, it is impossible to get a normal curve out of all 100 possible values and only 100 respondents (why?)? In the end, this is a judgment call, one in which the researcher would use inferential statistics as a public way to justify that decision.

DISPERSION

Our concern for convergence around a core value sparks our interest in dispersion. The concept of dispersion can quickly be shown by returning to Table 7-2, which presents the DKT scores in ascending order. Looking at the first and last entry, we find the lowest value to be 21 and the highest 94. By subtracting these two we get the **range** (73), an indicator of dispersion. Note that the obtained range is less than its possible value (which is?), suggesting that there may be some convergence.

FIGURE 7-5
Some non-normal distribution curves.

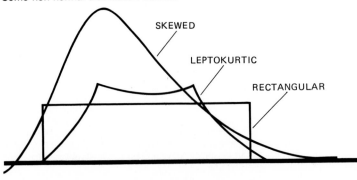

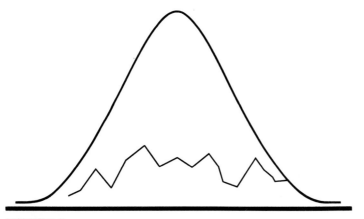

FIGURE 7-6
DKT scores with a normal curve superimposed.

Variance and Standard Deviation

Probably the most important measures of dispersion are the **variance** and the **standard deviation**. The variance is the average squared differences of the raw scores from their mean; or:[2]

$$\text{var} = \frac{\Sigma(X - \overline{X})^2}{n - 1}$$

And the standard deviation is the square root of the variance; or:

$$\text{SD} = \sqrt{\frac{\Sigma(X - \overline{X})^2}{n - 1}}$$

Applications of the Variance

The utility of the variance lies in the fact that it is a measure of dispersion based on averaged deviations from the central value of the mean. Variances which are small relative to their maximum possible value give good indication of convergence.

We calculate the variance by taking each raw score and subtracting the mean of the scores from it, squaring that difference, adding all those squared differences together, and then dividing by the number of the score. We calculated the mean in the previous section as 58.44. Therefore:

---

[2]A word on notation: There is no standard notation system in statistics. The one I am using works with English abbreviations and acronyms. Other systems will use English, Greek, and sometimes German letters to stand for the same concepts as presented here. When there is a choice, I will use the formulas for population estimates.

$$\text{var} = \frac{(21 - 58.44)^2 + (23 - 58.44)^2 + \ldots + (94 - 58.44)^2}{100 - 1}$$

Which gives us:

$$\text{var} = \frac{37148.64}{99}$$

Or:

$$\text{var} = 375.24$$

Nothing terribly exciting so far except, perhaps, for those who don't care for numbers of any sort. But now, let's consider whether 375.24 is a big number or a little number. In comparison with the maximum value possible (2500; why?), it is small. But it is still big enough to suggest that there is more that explains a respondent's DKT score than just being an upper-division college student.

Remember that our purpose in this example was to explain the drug knowledge of upper-division college students. If the characteristic of being an upper-division college student was perfectly related to drug knowledge, we would expect all the scores to be the same value with just minor variations for **measurement error**. The value of 375.24 is too large to be reasonably assigned to measurement error. (For those of you who are thinking of Chapter 6, sampling error is not an issue in this discussion; why?) We would conclude that being an upper-division college student is only partially or imperfectly related to drug knowledge and that there may be other traits systematically related to drug knowledge. There is more to be learned about the attribute of drug knowledge and about the class of people called "college students." We will pursue that task in the section on the analysis of association. For now, we turn our attention back to the standard deviation.

Applications of the Standard Deviation

The value of the standard deviation, other than as another measure of dispersion, is in its application in the inferential process of describing populations. Most data collections in the realm of science are not concerned with describing the data in hand, but in using those data to draw inferences about the larger population from which they were selected. Our interest in the 100 individuals in our sample of college students is not restricted to those 100, but is in those 100 as representative of all such college students. The chapter on sampling shows that when a sample has been properly selected, the statistical characteristics of the sample can serve as effective estimators of the **population parameters** (characteristics).

The relationship between samples of data and the population from which they were drawn is shown through the use of formal, mathematical models such as the normal curve. I want to emphasize that the models used in statistics (normal density distribution, t distribution, Chi Square distribution, etc.) are first derived from mathematical principles. It is then shown that empirical data collections, developed under certain provisions, will approximate those models. This approximation permits us to use them in making the move from samples to populations. The reasoning is straightforward: There is evidence that statistical characteristics X distributes according to model Y. Model Y can then be used to describe an otherwise unknown population of which the sample in hand is a subgroup. The standard deviation has a special role in all of this because it is often the link between the formal model and the data collection.

For example, any normal curve can be determined if one knows the center point of the curve (mu) and a measure of dispersion (sigma) around that center point. By using the mean of a sample as the center point and the sample SD as the measure of dispersion, then a normal curve can be drawn which will represent the entire population from which the sample was selected. We make two assumptions in this application: We assume that the population is, in fact, normally distributed and that the sample values of $\overline{X}$ and SD are representative of the population parameters of mu and sigma. If these two assumptions are true, we now have a complete model of the entire population of values.[3]

In its application within the normal curve, the standard deviation is a measure of distance from the center point (mean) of the curve. As we remember from our previous discussion of the normal curve in Chapter 6, the distance between the center of the curve and one SD to the right (or left) always accounts for 34 percent of the area under the curve no matter which member of the normal curve family is used. The distance between 1 SD and 2 is always 14 percent of the area and the distance between 2 and 32 is always 2 percent of the area. Figure 7-7 diagrams these relationships.

When the normal curve is used to model a population based on information from a sample, the standard deviation of the sample characteristic is used as sigma, the center is held by the mean, median, and mode, and the area under the curve represents the relative frequency of population values. Given that all possible values of the population are defined in the measurement process and that the relative frequency of any value can be determined from the normal curve model, I can reproduce the entire population of values.

The reasoning is exquisite, but it is based on a fairly complex string of assumptions which makes it very fragile. For example, if we apply these rules to our DKT scores, we find that the description indicated by the model doesn't make much sense. Going two standard deviations away from the mean (2 × 19.37 + 58.44) leads us to a score value (97.17) which does not occur within our data, and three standard deviations yields a score value (116.55) that is not even

---

[3]This definition of "sigma" first appeared in one of Pearson's works published in 1894 more than 160 years after the publication of the formula for the normal curve. In fact, the calculation design of the standard deviation was chosen for this application (Walker, 1929, p. 188).

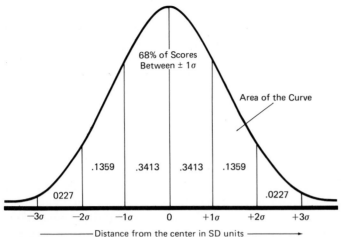

FIGURE 7-7
The relationship between the normal curve and the standard deviation.

possible. These errors occur because our sample does not provide a very good approximation of the normal curve model—something we discovered earlier when we compared distribution curves.

At this point, we can decide that the population is not normally distributed, and we should therefore abandon the use of the normal curve as a model. Or, we can decide that the sample is a poor approximation because of sampling error—the chance selection of the particular 100 subjects that we got. If we take the first option, we're pretty much out of the business of making inferences about the population as we have no commonly accepted basis for describing the population. If we take the second option, we can still draw inferences even though we are aware that they are, at best, very rough estimates. Most often we take the second option, and frequently, unfortunately, without much thought.

The connection between the standard deviation and distribution models allows us to draw inferences about the population from which our sample data were drawn. Not all of these inferences will be accurate. No alarm bells will ring when our inferences about the population are inaccurate. The use of a formal model has to be deliberately evaluated in each application. There is not much we can do about inaccurate estimates except limit the conclusions we draw from our study and try again.

Relationship between Averages and Measures of Dispersion

Measures of central tendency (averages) and measures of dispersion are independent of one another. Knowing the mean of a set of numbers tells you nothing about its variance and vice versa. This independence means that each of those measures tells us something new about the set of numbers in question. In fact, with a measure of typicality and one of dispersion, we have completed what is ordinarily said (with the occasional addition of a comment on distribution) about a set of numbers where each value represents a single observation on an individual unit of analysis. Number sets of this kind can have no internal structure. Sets of multiple measures, however, can show structures of interdependence or association. A discussion of the concepts and methods of the analysis of association and structure follows.

RELATIONSHIPS AND STATISTICAL ASSOCIATION

In our earlier discussion, we noted that the true nature of the scientific revolution was the worldview of relations among phenomena—the notion that the presence and performance of phenomenon A can affect the presence and performance of B. Present day science seeks to explain the variations within an attribute by discovering the relationships that invoke those variations. In the section that follows, I present an extended sample of the search for relationships using analysis of variance as the statistical procedure of evidence.

Connectedness and the DKT

At the end of our introduction to the variance, we had determined that the category of college students was inadequate as an explanation for differences found in drug knowledge across individuals. We decided that there must be other traits which affected the extent of drug knowledge.

What other traits? What about being connected with the community of drug users? I would expect those who have contact with those who use drugs on some regular basis (operational definition?) would be more knowledgeable than those who did not (note implicit theory). Anticipating this possibility, we, of course, asked our respondents this question in spite of its formidable measurement problems. (Research on paper is a lot easier.) The following item would be typical:

I have contact with those who use drugs other than alcohol:

1 Never
2 Sometimes (two or three times a year)
3 Regularly (about once a month)
4 Often (once a week or more)

Ignoring the fact that knowing someone who takes aspirin for arthritis might legitimately place a respondent into category 4, we can now separate our 100 students into the four subgroups of "Never," "Sometimes," "Regularly," and "Often." One of the important properties of the variance is the fact that it can be **decomposed** to identify different sources of variation within a set of scores. What do we expect to happen here? If connectedness is related to drug knowledge, we would expect the subjects within a given category to be more like

TABLE 7-4
DKT SCORES FOR THE FOUR CONNECTEDNESS SUBGROUPS

		Group										
		Never			Sometimes			Regularly			Often	
Scores	21	35	48	26	48	61	30	58	81	33	72	87
	23	35	50	36	49	63	41	62	83	46	73	88
	25	42	53	37	51	66	49	65	84	58	77	89
	28	43	56	38	52	67	50	67	85	62	79	92
	29	44	57	38	53	68	51	69	90	64	82	93
	31	44	65	42	53	70	54	71	91	66	85	94
	32	45	70	44	58	75	56	73	93	68	86	
	33	46	79	45	58	81	57	78		69		
	33	47	81	46	59	82						
	34			48								

one another (less dispersed) on the DKT score. As a result, the variance for each of the subgroups should be less than 375. If connectedness is not related, then each of the subgroups should show about the same dispersion as the total group given the error possible in measurement. The variance of the subgroups should remain around 375. Table 7-4 gives the scores within each subgroup:

Was our hypothesis successful? Just looking at the range of each group, it would appear so. The range of each subgroup is about 10 points lower than the total group. I think it's worth our time to calculate the four variances. Why bother, you say? Because it may tell us something about the attribute of drug knowledge.

Specifically, it may give us evidence that connectedness is a trait that contributes to the differences among individuals on the DKT attribute. Table 7-5 gives the variances and the means for the four subgroups:

Table 7-5 shows us that indeed the variances of the subgroups are smaller than the variance of the total group (375.24).[4] This reduction indicates that connectedness is related to drug knowledge. Individuals who show the same level of contact with the drug community tend to have similar scores on the DKT.

In all of this analysis, I have not changed the **total variance**. It will always remain 375.24. What has changed is the explanation for that variability. At the first step, the only explanation available to me for the variability among scores was that of **individual differences**. But in science, individual differences are the orderly consequences of the convergence of a set of attributes not the random emission of behavior. Individual differences are therefore explainable. At the second step, with the introduction of the connectedness attribute, I identified one element of that explanatory set. I was able to reduce the unexplained variations in the DKT scores by showing the association between

---

[4]These reductions are not due to the smaller size of the subgroups. The formula accounts for that.

TABLE 7-5
VARIANCES AND MEANS FOR THE FOUR
CONNECTEDNESS SUBGROUPS

	Group			
	Never	**Sometimes**	**Regularly**	**Often**
Variance	252.02	196.88	292.57	256.46
Mean	43.89	54.07	66.87	74.43

knowledge and connectedness.[5] Some of the variability is now explainable by demonstrating that individuals with different histories of social contact show different levels of drug knowledge.

If my theory were sufficiently sophisticated, I could continue to add variables which would partition the variance of the total group until I got a set of subgroups, each of which would contain only individuals with the same DKT score. The variances of the subgroups would go to zero. I would have accounted for all the sources of the differences between individuals on the DKT. Ignoring measurement error, my goal in this analysis, then, is to identify a set of partitioning variables which will account for *all* of the variability of the DKT scores. The perfect combination of variables (e.g., intelligence, the character of interpersonal networks, media content attended to, arrest record, and so on) would identify separate subgroups, within which each subject would have the same score. Most likely, however, measurement error will prevent this perfect solution. There will be some variability within the groups because the true scores on the DKT or the partitioning variables will not be given due to imperfect measurement procedures.

Statistical Evidence and the Relationship between Attributes

Let's look carefully at the evidence for the claim of an association between drug knowledge and connectedness. Our sole piece of empirical evidence is the reduced subgroup variances. What we know is that if one sorts DKT scores into subgroups formed by the connectedness measure, the DKT scores show greater convergence. Any relationship between the attributes of connectedness and

---

[5]The variability explained is contained in the differences between the connectedness subgroups. I can demonstrate this by examining the numerical components of the **sums of squares**—the name given to the numerator $[\Sigma(X-\bar{X})^2]$ of the variance. (I cannot easily add and subtract variances because of the operation of division, common denominators and all that, you know.) The sums of squares for the total group is 37148.64 (99 × 375.2388). The sums of squares for each subgroup is 6804.67, 5315.85, 6436.60 and 5129.14 respectively. The total of these four, 23686.29, must still be dumped into the unexplained category of individual differences. The remaining portion, 13462.35, is what we would now (if these data were not made up) claim is explainable by differences in connectedness. Our one partitioning variable has accounted for about one-third of the total variability (13462.35/37148.64).

drug knowledge within college students that we might posit, however, has no direct support from this evidence. The evidence is permissive—that is, it allows explanations of this sort to be developed, but it is not supportive. What we have been able to demonstrate is evidence for a statistical association—a relationship between sets of numbers. We have not been able to demonstrate the mechanism which relates these human attributes to one another.

The evidence for that relating mechanism must come from outside the statistical analysis itself. It usually is provided in the form of an experiment in which the relationship between connectedness and the DKT could be manipulated. In our example here, we would probably be arguing that increased contact with drug users increases drug knowledge. (The opposite relationship is also possible but not as attractive.) In some way acceptable to a "Committee on Human Subjects," we would need to devise an experimental protocol which would subject individuals to different levels of contact and then look for change on the criterion DKT. Note that the statistical analysis would be exactly the same, although the force of its evidence would be quite different.

EXERCISES

1 What is the mean, median, and mode(s) of the data set from respondent 00 to respondent 49?
2 What is your judgment as to whether the DKT data set represents a characterizing attribute?
3 How would a judgment of nonconvergence (that DKT is not a characterizing property) affect the research process?
4 Given that effect, what is the likelihood of a judgment of nonconvergence?
5 Given three sets of 50 scores from zero to 100, one is a rectangular distribution, one is leptokurtic (sags in the middle), and the other is a normal distribution. Which of these three distributions has the smallest variance; which has the largest? Why?
6 In a perfectly representative draw of a hundred scores from a normal population, how many will fall between 1 and 2 standard deviations from the mean?
7 Why is the explanation of individual differences less than satisfactory?
8 How do you think the DKT scores would be partitioned over a measure of intelligence (say, high, moderate, and low)?
9 Now apply this theory to the subgroups presented in Table 7-4 by sorting the scores of each of the subgroups in the way that you think intelligence would affect the DKT.

MORE ON RELATIONSHIPS AND STATISTICAL ASSOCIATION

Having seen a specific example, let us now approach the general properties of relationships and statistical association. When a data set is composed of two or more measures collected from each respondent, there is the possibility that the data set will show patterns of relationships based on the associations among the measures. There are many statistical procedures which investigate patterns of internal structure. All of them do so by determining the degree to which the values of one variable tend to congregate the values of the other variables into distinguishable groupings.

We discovered such an association when we partitioned the variance of the DKT scores over the variable of connectedness. The values of the connectedness variable tended to congregate the DKT scores into distinguishable groupings. These groupings were distinguishable because (a) scores within each of them tended to be more similar to one another, and (b) the means of the collections were different from one another. We can say that the connectedness scores were associated with the DKT scores. Therefore, particular values on the connectedness variable were identified with particular values of the DKT test, and as the values on the connectedness variable changed, the values of the DKT scores also tended to change.

The analysis of internal structure can be conducted over data of any level of measurement. The statistical procedure and some of the information gained change, but the basic notion of association remains the same. That is, statistical association can be variously described as (a) the degree to which one variable distinguishes another, (b) the degree to which the values of one variable congregate around the values of another, and/or (c) the degree to which change in one variable is related to change in another. In the next section, we will take a look at these three forms of association.

THE CHARACTER OF STATISTICAL ASSOCIATION

In our campaign studies, we found that about two-thirds of our respondents fell into one of two categories of cognitive mechanisms. (The notion of "cognitive mechanisms" describes the methods people use to maintain a choice in the presence of the conflicting persuasive messages of a campaign.)

In the first category, respondents reduced the differences between the candidates, perhaps to lessen the importance of the choice. In the second category, respondents increased the difference between the candidates and moved the candidate of choice closer to their own position perhaps to strengthen their selection.

We wondered if characteristics of media use would distinguish between these two categories. Our data set included measures which identified the usual media source of campaign information that the individual used. The question we asked was, "Is the use of print media rather than television as the usual media source associated with one of the cognitive categories?"

The Condition of No Association

Let's explore what patterns we would expect to appear within the data if this hypothesis is true. Thirty-six respondents (48 percent) fall into cognitive category 1, and 39 (52 percent) into 2. If there is no association between membership in a category and preferred media source (PMS), then one of two conditions will occur. First, PMS might be an independent variable with no explanatory power in this application. In this case, the same relative proportion (48/52) should appear when we look at the relationship between the two groups of media users. That is, in both media groups, 52 percent of the respondents will be from cognitive group 2 because the PMS variable will simply divide the cognitive groups randomly in half.

In the second condition, PMS will have an effect, but its effect will be consistent across both cognitive groups. That is, PMS will distinguish the entire sample in that the aggregate will favor one medium over another. It will, however, make no difference in what cognitive group the individual respondent belongs. To show you these conditions, Table 7-6 presents two **cross break** or **contingency tables** which give the number of respondents that are classified in each combination of cognitive group and preferred media source for these two effects.

What we see in these 2 × 2 contingency tables is that when PMS is an independent variable, the cognitive groups divide as equally as possible, and that when PMS is a consistent variable, an equal percentage of respondents from both cognitive groups appear in the PMS categories. In both of these cases, there is no association between PMS and cognitive group membership, although in the second case PMS has explanatory utility.

The Condition of Perfect Relationship

The condition of a perfect relationship between two variables occurs when each value of one variable is uniquely related to a separate, single value of the other variable. That is, each value of one variable is congregated around a different value of the other variable. In our example, a perfect relationship would occur if all members of one cognitive category chose the print medium and all members of the other category chose television as the preferred medium.

The Condition of Intermediate Relationship

When there is a relationship which is not perfect, the unique relationship between categories of the associated variables will be lost. Categories of both variables will have elements from more than one of the categories of the variable associated with it. Applying this definition to our example, categories of the PMS variable will be filled differentially by the individuals classified in the two

TABLE 7-6
AN EXAMPLE OF TWO CONDITIONS OF NO
ASSOCIATION (INDEPENDENCE AND GENERAL
EFFECT) BETWEEN THE VARIABLES OF PMS
AND COGNITIVE GROUP

	Independence		General effect	
	TV	Print	TV	Print
Group 1	18	18	10	26
Group 2	19	20	12	27

TABLE 7-7
THREE EXAMPLES OF INTERMEDIATE ASSOCIATION

	Greater/Lesser		Greater/None		Opposite	
	Group 1	Group 2	Group 1	Group 2	Group 1	Group 2
Print	90	60	80	50	63	37
Television	10	40	20	50	37	63

cognitive groups. There are three ways that this differential shift can appear: In all three, one group will show a greater preference for one of the media; the other group, however, will show a lesser preference for the same medium, a greater preference for the other medium, or no preference. (Each group showing no preference or each group showing the same preference are the conditions of no relationship; each group showing a unique preference is a perfect relationship.)

The three examples in Table 7-7 all show the same level of association (significant but quite weak), but the theoretical import of the three are quite different. In the first case, the researcher might begin looking for some inhibiting function which lowers the preference for print in the second cognitive group. The second case of our example suggests that information seeking may not be a function of the structure of Group 2. And the third is the one most directly explained by the concept of association, as it suggests that the different qualities of print and television may be informative of the differences between the two groups.

Sources of Intermediate Levels of Association

We might wonder how intermediate levels of association can occur in the first place. If X is actually associated with Y, how is it that in a data collection, individual bivariate pairs will sometimes show that association and sometimes not? Why, in the first case of our example in Table 7-7, do those 10 individuals show a preference for television when the other 90 in their group choose print? There are four useful explanations and a "garbage can" for what's left over. These five explanations with the four useful ones first are:

1 The variables as defined are actually composite properties which vary internally. A given observation, therefore, can be arrived at in different ways.

2 The relationship between X and Y is spurious. Its appearance is an artifact of the relationship between X and Z and Y and Z.

3 The relationship between X and Y is affected by other variables (inhibiting and facilitating).

4 The deviant cases are the result of measurement error.

5 The garbage can is the explanation of the particular instance which holds that any data collection will have unique occurrences which affect the relationship between variables but which have no explanatory utility for future instances.

A discussion of each of these explanations follows:

Composite Variables Many variables with which we deal are not unidimensional but are the composite of several properties. A particular observation, therefore, such as a given score on a testing measure can be the result of different combinations of those properties. Most classroom essay tests, for example, not only measure the knowledge of content but also the ability to use that content in producing a solution to the question and the ability to coherently write the answer. A particular score on the test, say 67, may reflect lack of knowledge, poor application of knowledge, poor writing skills, or any combination. What predicts that score, however, depends on its source. A given predictor may be associated with one property within the composite but not the others. It will be useful, then, only for those observations within the data set which are the result of the associated property.

The Third Variable Problem The third variable problem is usually cited as the reason that the finding of a significant correlation between variables cannot be used as evidence of causation. That is, what is seen as a relationship between X and Y is actually a relationship between X and Z and Y and Z with Z being the controlling variable in both cases. If Z is the cause of both X and Y, then X and Y will tend to be associated, but controlling X will have no effect on Y and vice versa. Consequently, evidence of association is not evidence for cause, but causes will be associated with their effects.

When the relationship between X and Y is the result of a third variable, the association between X and Y will be perfect only if their separate relationships with Z are exactly the same. If the conditions necessary for the relationship between Z and X are different from the conditions necessary for the relationship between Z and Y, then the relationship between X and Y will start to decay as cases showing these differences appear in the sample. You can quickly create your own example by simply presuming that Z works in association with Q to affect X, and independently to affect Y. Next, vary the appearance of Q to see what happens to the relationship between X and Y.

Associations Modified by Other Variables A relationship may be modified by another variable or variable set. Other variables may inhibit or facilitate the relationship between bivariate values. For example, category 1 respondents may always choose the print media as their preferred source except when they lack the financial resources for the subscription costs. When the modifying effect is uncontrolled, the relationship between X and Y will show some indeterminance.

Measurement Error Measurement error can be a potent source of intermediate associations. Individual cases can be misclassified through poor instrumentation or inadequate protocols.

We, perhaps, think of poor instrumentation as poorly written items which are confusing to interpret or permit multiple answers to occur. But good instrumentation is more than avoiding rubber rulers. It involves the relationship between the measurement device and actual structure of the variable. For example, it is quite common to use the physical sex characteristics of the respondent as a measurement device for classifying individuals along social dimensions of masculinity and femininity. Gender classifications are very reliable, but poorly represent the social variable of sexual acculturation. (Researchers are aware of this problem, yet routinely collect information in this manner; why?)

The relationship between two variables is dependent on the number of categories in each. When there are fewer categories in one variable than in the other, the strict definition of perfect association cannot be met as categories cannot be uniquely associated. Unequal categories cause technical problems in the indices of association as most will not report the actual level of association. Assuming that the technical problems are recognized, however, unequal categories cause no problems in theory construction as long as the number of categories validly represent the structure of the variable. But what if they don't? Start with two variables (*P* and *Q,* for variety) with four categories each which are perfectly associated. Unfortunately, the researcher's insight into these variables conceives of but two categories each. What happens to those respondents in those unseen categories? Figure 7-8 shows the result. The first error distributes the respondents randomly between the two remaining categories of *Q.* The second error again randomly distributes them over the remaining categories of *P.* The result is an intermediate level of association which is the consequence of poorly conceived measurement.

Lowered indices of association can also occur if the researcher proposes too many categories within a variable. Start this time with two variables with two categories each. Our intrepid researcher, however, devises four categories. The additional categories would be no problem if they were simply independent additions as they would show up with empty cells. It is unlikely that such categories would be acceptable, however, because they would be fanciful— without connection in common knowledge. It is much more likely that the researcher will devise four categories out of the actual two, thus destroying their independence. As no category could then clearly distinguish a set of elements, the elements will tend to distribute into all categories, and the level of association would decline.

Protocol design can be an agent in the weakening of an association. Remember that the protocol is devised to provide a known environment in which explanation can be developed for what is observed. If the protocol provides inadequate control or gives an incomplete description of that environment, then unknown sources of variation can come into plan.

Let me give just one example. Protocols which make use of simulations presume that each respondent plays the game equally well. If the scenario is not equally engaging, then, the behavior observed will be expressed from differing levels of motivation.

FIGURE 7-8
Intermediate association due to poor measurement design.

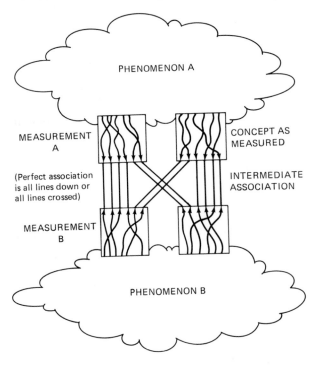

The Particular Instance Scientific explanation is designed for general application. It is not concerned with the variations that occur in the individual case. In
fact, a rationalistic distinction between scientific knowledge and common
knowledge is that common knowledge focuses on the individual variations and
scientific knowledge on the underlying patterns. Scientists generally concede
that in any theory there will be some variations which will simply go unexplained. Those "leftovers" tend to fall into the explanation of the particular
which is why I call it the "garbage can." I have not called it useful because it
doesn't motivate any additional discovery. The four previous explanations ought
to lead to new models, better measurement, and improved protocol design, but
the catchall of individual differences, the unexplained, the disturbance, and
error, as these leftovers have been called, gives us no future direction, although
it may save a good deal of frustration.

The End of the Example: Findings from the Campaign Study

This section began by outlining an interest in the relationship between two major
categories of cognitive style and the preferred media sources of campaign
information. This analysis is a post hoc analysis. That is, we don't have any
theory on which to base a hypothesis. We do have an interest in media, and past

experience has shown us that media preference is a fruitful variable which may be useful to explain the differences between these cognitive categories. Our data show that respondents who typically converge opposing candidates by reducing the perceived differences between them (category 1) tend to select television as their preferred medium. Those who increase the distinction between opposing candidates (category 2) tend to select the print media.

Our job now is to determine what is it about the differences between television and print that will explain the differences between the two cognitive categories. We might speculate that television's presentation homogenizes the issues and therefore category 1 respondents prefer that medium to accomplish their convergence task. Whereas print underscores the differences on issues, which supports the efforts of those in category 2. (Note the "uses and gratifications" perspective here. How would a traditional "direct effects" theorist argue this relationship?)

Let me emphasize what that previous paragraph did. The finding of a statistical association is a technical result which is, in itself, meaningless. The result is made meaningful by the theoretical constructs which define the variables and specify the mechanism of the relationship. In this post hoc analysis, I created a statement of theory which explained an empirical finding. The empirical finding gave me reason to pursue this theory construction, but did not provide the content which made sense of the relationship.

There are, of course, any number of differences between the media that could be used to explain the differences between the respondent groups. I focused on the treatment of issues. I could have selected differences in image treatment, quantity of material, print's dependent on the verbal symbol, and so on. Had the finding been reversed, I would have developed a sense-making statement by looking at the media in some other way. The point is that that theoretical statement is quite vulnerable. The work ahead is to find the empirical support for its claims.

Summary: Analysis of Association

Statistical association occurs when the units of analysis that show the same value on one variable also tend to show a common value on some other variable. Perfect association occurs when each value of one variable is uniquely identified with a particular value of the second variable. Independence or the absence of association occurs when the units of analysis with the same value on one variable show no pattern on the second, but rather, distribute randomly over all the values of the other variable.

Our interest in association stems from the two explanatory purposes of prediction and control. If two variables are associated, then knowing the value of one informs us about the value of the other. If two variables are causally related, they will also be associated (although the reverse is not true). Therefore, the finding of an association can be a material element in the development of a causal explanation.

The presumptions of scientific theory require that if X is related to Y, that relationship must be orderly and not capricious. It should hold for each unit of analysis. Of course, it often does not. When it doesn't, it signals that our understanding of the relationship is incomplete. A better understanding may lead us anywhere from abandoning the claim of a relationship to rethinking the definition of the variables to developing new methods or new models.

STATISTICAL MEASURES OF ASSOCIATION: CORRELATION COEFFICIENTS

Correlation, as a generic term, refers to those procedures which generate a value which can be interpreted as an index of the strength of the relationship between two variable sets. (Each set may contain one or more variables.) These values are designed to run from zero (to report the condition of no relationship) to 1.0 (to report a perfect association; a −1.0 will report a perfect inverse relationship in linear models) and to increase as intermediate levels of association increase. Not all indices accomplish these tasks equally well. Particular care must be taken in interpreting intermediate values for nominal or ordinal data. Table 7-8 lists the common bivariate (two-variable) indices for each level of measurement and offers a comment on potential problems. The section following the table presents an examination of the product-moment **correlation coefficient** in order to show how this most popular index responds to patterns of association.

TABLE 7-8
BIVARIATE CORRELATION COEFFICIENTS

Nominal measures	
Index name	Description and problems
Yule's Q	Useful in 2 × 2 tables only. Uses the most liberal definition of perfect association. Varies from 0 to +/−1.0 to indicate the direction of association within the table.
C	The contingency coefficient can be used for any size cross break. Upper limit is less than 1.0 (in a 2 × 2 table a perfect association is reported as .70). Not comparable to other correlation indices and not comparable across different sized contingency tables.
Ordinal measures	
Spearman Rank or Kendall's Tau	Both correlations compare pairs of rankings. Vary from 0 to +/−1.0 although not all intermediate values are possible with small samples. Both require correction for tied ranks. Tau will tend to give lower intermediate values on same data (Siegel, 1956).
Interval and ratio measures	
Pearson's Product Moment	Assumes normal distribution and a straight line relationship between variables. Varies between 0 and +/−1.0.

TABLE 7-9
X/Y PAIRS FOR LOW, MODERATE, AND HIGH
CORRELATIONS

Low correlation		Mod. correlation		High correlation	
X	Y	X	Y	X	Y
1	1, 2, 3	1	1, 2, 3	1	1, 1, 2
2	2, 2, 4	2	2, 2, 3	2	2, 2, 3
3	3, 4, 5	3	3, 4, 5	3	3, 3, 4
4	4, 5, 4	4	3, 4, 4	4	3, 4, 4
5	3, 4, 5	5	4, 4, 5	5	5, 5, 4

An Analysis of the Product-Moment Correlation Coefficient

The Pearson product-moment correlation is historically the first and, presently, the most popular of the correlation coefficients. Because it appears so often in our literature, we will spend some time with it.

To begin with, the product-moment correlation examines the structure within a bivariate data matrix. A bivariate matrix is one in which each respondent or object of study has a pair of measures. Matching income and social class or education and media choices or job satisfaction and level of productivity are all examples.

The Pearson product-moment correlation is a **parametric measure**. It assumes a normally distributed population and a **linear relationship** between the two variables in the correlation. The requirement of a linear relationship places constraints on the way that the values of the variables associate. Extreme values must be associated with extreme values, and moderate ones with moderate ones. As the values of one variable increase, the values of the other variable must either increase in a direct relationship or decrease in an inverse relationship. **Nonlinear relationships** may result in spurious values for the correlation coefficient.

The product-moment correlation is a ratio of the degree of **covariation** between two measures and the total variation within those two measures. Covariation occurs when change in one variable is matched with change in the other or when the deviation from its mean in one variable is matched by the deviation from its mean by the other. That is, extreme values are matched with extreme values and moderate ones with moderate ones.

When the match is perfect, the ratio of the covariation to the total variation is 1.0. The correlation coefficient, then, can vary from zero, no covariation, to +1.0, a perfect direct relationship, or −1.0, a perfect inverse relationship—both conditions of total covariation. Table 7-9 gives three sets of numbers which will generate low, moderate, and high correlations, respectively.

Note that I have "messed around" with the usual way of displaying columns of numbers by pooling all the Y values on each X value—all the pairs with an X value of 1 are shown together and so on. I pooled them in this manner to show

how the relationship between X and Y affects the correlation coefficient. As the values of Y paired with a given X value become more like one another and less like Y values paired with other X values, the correlation increases.

I can offer two descriptions of what a correlation shows. First, it shows that as the value of one variable changes there is a concomitant change in the other. To demonstrate this relationship, we can match the X value with the mean of the corresponding Y values (e.g., $1 + 2 + 3 / 3 = 2.0$) for each score in the low and high correlation data sets. Table 7-10 provides this match.

We see that in the low correlation set, when X changes from 1 to 2, Y changes from 2.0 to 2.4. Therefore, change in X is associated with change in Y, but it is not the same amount of change. The amount of change in X does not have to correspond to the amount of change in Y for perfect association. As long as the amount of change in Y is the same for each unit of change in X, the association will be perfect. Of course neither of these two sets shows that. As we look down the low correlation pairs, we see that the amount of change is not consistent and, in fact, even the direction of change reverses itself at the top. In the high correlation set, we see a much more consistent relationship. One unit of change in X is matched with one unit of change in Y for three of the four possible changes along the increase. We also see why this is not a perfect correlation in the change at X values 4 and 5.

One cautionary note must be sounded when we talk of correlation and change. Change in correlation is the examination of the X/Y relationship at the different values of X. The different values of X also involved different individuals in the ordinary design of these tests. In short, we look at the X/Y relationship over those individuals who have the first value of X then at that relationship over those individuals who have the second value of X and so on. The design does not effect some change in the individuals to have them achieve a different X value. What we know, then, in correlation, is the degree of agreement between change in X and change in Y. What we do not know is what happens when an individual changes his or her characteristic X value.

Although not an uncommon error in our literature, it is not legitimate, therefore, to conclude from a strong, positive correlation that increasing one's X value will increase one's Y value. To use just one contrary argument as an example, if the relationship between X and Y were mediated through a third variable, then effecting a change in an individual's X score may have no effect whatsoever on that individual's Y score. Correlation is a measure of concomitant change in paired numerical values, not change in individuals.

The second description of the correlation coefficient deals with the nature of a linear relationship in deviation scores. A deviation score is the difference between the raw score (the actual score value) and the mean of that set of scores. A linear relationship means that an extreme case on one variable will be an extreme case on the other variable. Therefore, a strong correlation will show a match between equivalent deviation scores on the X and Y variables.

We can demonstrate that description by calculating a deviation score for each X value in our example by subtracting the mean of X from each of the X values (e.g., $1 - 3.0 = |2.0|$) and calculating a deviation score for each Y value by

TABLE 7-10
LOW AND HIGH CORRELATIONS
FROM TABLE 7-9 USING THE
MEAN OF THE Y VALUES

Low correlation		High correlation	
X	Y	X	Y
1	2.0	1	1.30
2	2.4	2	2.30
3	4.0	3	3.30
4	4.3	4	3.67
5	4.0	5	4.67

TABLE 7-11
DEVIATION SCORES IN
ABSOLUTE VALUES

X deviation scores	Y deviation scores
2.00	2.07, 2.07, 1.07
1.00	1.07, 1.07, 0.07
0.00	0.07, 0.07, 0.93
1.00	0.07, 0.93, 0.93
2.00	1.93, 1.93, 0.93

subtracting the mean of Y from each of the Y values (e.g., $1 - 3.07 = |2.07|$). These values are given in Table 7-11.

Table 7-11 repeats much of the information of Table 7-10. We see where the scores don't match and where the relationship starts to decay at the upper end. What is new is the view of the relationship in terms of equivalent amounts of deviation. For a relationship to meet the requirements of **linearity**, it must show both characteristics of matched change and matched deviation scores. The requirement for matched change is the basic requirement of association. The requirement for matched deviations establishes the relationship as linear. If the deviation scores don't match (in relative size, not actual value), then the association cannot be described in a straight line model.

Correlation and Partitioning Variability

Given this analysis of the correlation coefficient, we can see that the coefficient is responsive to exactly the same kind of partitioning of the variance that we explored with the variables of drug knowledge and connectedness. Remember that the intent of partitioning was to arrive at a set of categories within which the variability of the criterion measure would be reduced to zero. When variables are correlated, the action of one variable is to provide classifications for the other. Within these separate classifications, the values of the second variable are more compact, more like one another, less dispersed. When linearity is present, these classifications will move in a single direction, either uniformly upward or downward. To see this effect, take another look at Table 7-4. There, as one moves from one classification of connectedness to the next, the value of the DKT mean increases in good order. We know, therefore, that the DKT and connectedness are linearly correlated.

MEASURES OF STATISTICAL ASSOCIATION: LINEAR FUNCTIONS

Correlations provide an index of the strength of the relationship between sets of variables. **Linear functions** provide a description of the relationship between variables. Functions which are valid permit the prediction of the value of the Y variable when the value of the X variable is known. In devising valid functions, it is up to the researcher to use the appropriate model (straight line, parabola, ogive, etc.). The statistical procedures which produce the values of the function coefficients are based on the characteristics of the model assumed. Unfortunately, these procedures will always provide a solution even if the model on which it is based is inappropriate. The researcher will find the evidence for the selection of a particular model by plotting the X/Y values from the bivariate sample.

Most of the work in statistics has made use of the linear function which describes a straight line and is of the form:

$$Y = bX + a$$

In this model, each unit of change in X is always associated with b units of change in Y. The function coefficient, b, describes the relationship between change in X and change in Y. The constant a in this model is the value of Y when X is zero and is called the "Y intercept"—the point at which the line crosses the Y axis on a set of coordinates.

The application of this model in statistical analysis is called **linear regression**. It assumes that the relationship between X and Y can be plotted on a straight line called the regression line and develops a solution for $(Y = bX + a)$ based on the information contained in the collected bivariate data set. That solution is, of course, presumed to generalize beyond the sample at hand.

The **regression coefficient** (b) called the **beta weight**, is the ratio between the covariance of X and Y and the variance of X. When X and Y covary perfectly, the beta weight is unity times some constant which accounts for any difference in the scales on which X and Y are measured. It will be positive or negative depending on whether the relationship between X and Y is direct or inverse. When there is no covariation in X and Y, then the solution to the function will always be the mean of Y, which is the best single predictor of the Y variable set.

The worth of a function devised to describe the relationship between variables is dependent on the degree to which it improves one's rate of success in prediction. For some purposes, even very small improvements can be very valuable. The amount of improvement possible is indicated by the strength of the relationship between the variables. A good rule of thumb is to square the correlation coefficient. This value, called the **coefficient of determination**, is the proportion of the Y variance explained by X. A correlation of .30 indicates that less than 10 percent of the Y variance is explained by X. It takes very high levels of association to get powerful predictions.

EXERCISES

1 Describe the condition of a perfect association between the variable of connectedness and the DKT. (Hint: It will maintain the independence of the four categories of connectedness.)

2 Which of the three conditions of intermediate relationships can show the strongest association?

3 Devise a diagram which would show the effect of an inhibiting variable on an X/Y relationship.

4 Why is a finding of intermediate relationship (any value between 0 and 1.0) an indication of an incomplete explanation?

5 Plot the relationships shown in Table 7-9.

6 Tardy and his colleagues found a significant inverse correlation between participation in political campaigns and the influence of media agendas. Why can they not conclude that one affects the other?

7 With the values of one to five show a perfect linear relationship and a perfect nonlinear relationship. Figure the deviation scores; how does the relationship differ?

8 What descriptive advantage does the assumption of linearity give the researcher?

9 How does plotting the X/Y values provide evidence for the selection of the model curve?

10 When the coefficient of determination is low, around what value will the predicted values of Y tend to cluster?

ANALYSIS OF STRUCTURE IN MULTIVARIATE DATA SETS

Measures of association indicate a structural relationship between and among phenomena. We have an interest in these associational indices because the presence of a relational structure helps the analyst understand the performance of phenomena. In the search for these structures, there is a growing presumption that the human behavior we see in the natural world is the product of a complex of influences. **Multivariate analyses** provide us ways of understanding these influences by studying a relatively large number of variables simultaneously. The greater the number of observations on each unit of analysis, the greater the number of relationships that can be discovered and, potentially, the more complex the structure that will appear. Statistical procedures in multivariate analysis have developed primarily because the simpler analyses have not been successful in providing adequate explanation. The analysis of multivariate data sets holds the promise of explanation which can approach the intricate interrelationships which seem to characterize human behavior.

As we have seen, **univariate data sets** are those with one observation per unit of analysis. **Bivariate data sets** have two observations per unit. **Multivariate data sets** are simply those which have at least three observations on each unit of analysis (see Figure 7-9).

Multivariate analysis (a) may examine the internal structure characteristics within a single multivariate data set in order to describe the structural characteristics of that set, or (b) may use one multivariate data set to explain another set (which itself may be univariate, bivariate, or multivariate) in order to support explanations of prediction or control. The next two sections look at these two purposes respectively, introduce the more common statistical procedures which provide for them, and consider some examples from the literature.

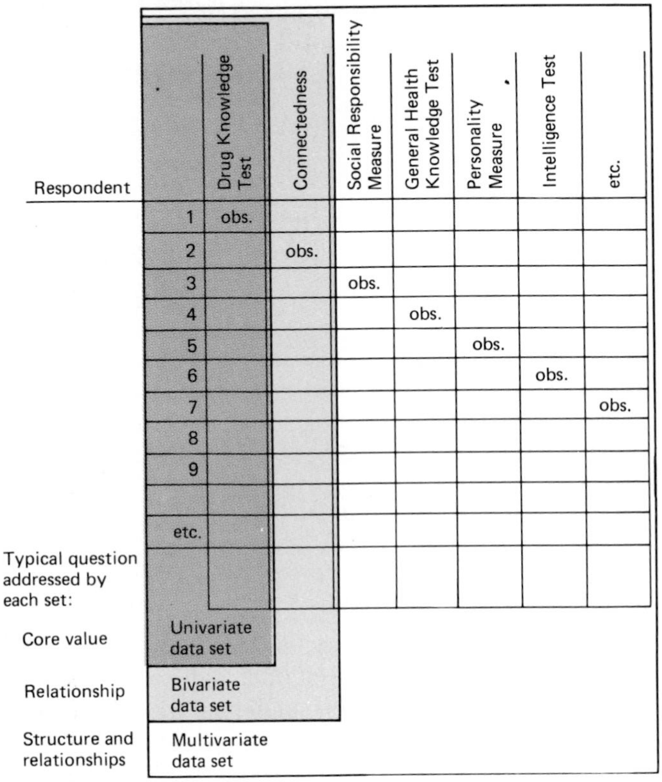

Respondent	Drug Knowledge Test	Connectedness	Social Responsibility Measure	General Health Knowledge Test	Personality Measure	Intelligence Test	etc.
1	obs.						
2		obs.					
3			obs.				
4				obs.			
5					obs.		
6						obs.	
7							obs.
8							
9							
etc.							

Typical question addressed by each set:

Core value	Univariate data set
Relationship	Bivariate data set
Structure and relationships	Multivariate data set

FIGURE 7-9
Nature of different types of data sets and the typical questions addressed by each.

Multivariate Analyses over Single Multivariate Data Sets

The approaches which investigate structure within a single multivariate data set are procedures such as **factor analysis**, **multidimensional scaling**, **cluster analysis**, and **Markov analysis**. These methods seek the underlying relationships between elemental variables in the set. All of these procedures start with a relatively large number of observations on a unit of analysis which may be an object of judgment or a common event. The analyses seek to discover the structural fabric in which these elemental observations are woven.

A factor analysis, for example, begins with a large number of individual items (such as **Likert-type statements** or **bipolar adjectival scales**), all evaluating a common object of judgment. The analysis presumes that the information contained in these several items can be reduced to a few **core dimensions** which are the generalizeable constructs. Each individual variable is, in effect, seen as a composite of (a) at least one core dimension, (b) its own specialized information, and (c) an error component. In using factor analysis, one is concerned with discovering the core dimensions. Arntson (1982), for instance, interested in the question of how speech style was associated with social class, developed a set of 15 speech style indicators. The subsequent factor analysis showed that four factors of speech style composed the underlying structure of these 15 indicators.

Whereas factor analysis uses covariation among the elemental items as the basis for determining the dimensions of structure, multidimensional scaling (MDS) uses **proximities**, or measures of the degree of similarity (or difference), among the elemental items as its structural basis. In factor analysis, the respondent considers each item independently. In MDS, the respondent considers each item in a paired comparison with every other item. The result is a map of the cognitive geography of the judgments.

In one of the studies which popularized this technique in the discipline, Woelfel, Cody, Gillham, and Holmes (1980) showed how the cognitive space between concepts such as "Marijuana High," "Good," "Intense Concentration," "Me," and two ostensive message sources—Timothy Leary and Linus Pauling—changed after reading a statement relevant to these concepts. The MDS analysis first presented a "map" of these concepts in cognitive space and then "redrew" that map to show the structural changes resulting from exposure to the message.

Both factor analysis and MDS are parametric analyses assuming normally distributed, linearly related internal data. Cluster analysis, on the other hand, is a nonparametric analysis which can be applied to any level of measurement. Cluster analysis considers the similarity among objects which have been evaluated on a common set of attributes. These elemental attributes each form one dimension of an attribute space. The cluster analysis starts from the principle that two objects cannot occupy exactly the same space and then considers how large the attribute space would have to be to include first the most similar and finally the most dissimilar objects.

Cluster analysis, while a common statistical procedure in agronomic research, is making its first appearances in communication research. Baxter (1983) used cluster analysis to determine the similarity groupings of 40 items measuring communication behavior. In this application, cluster analysis performed the same task as factor analysis. In a different application, we could in our next campaign study consider the amount of similarity among presidential candidates on a set of attributes which might include physical characteristics, cognitive traits, personality measures, value judgments, and so on.

Finally, Markov analysis is a nonparametric procedure which makes use of nominal data which are the measure of events in a series. Markov analysis displays the presence of a relational structure in which the preceding event affects the likelihood of the events that follow. An example is the Fisher and Drecksel (1983) article we examined in Chapter 3. These researchers coded turns of talk on a five-category measure of relational communication. The question they investigated was how the preceding appearance of a given type of conversational turn affected the probability of the type of turn which followed. For instance, they found that a domineering turn was more likely to be followed by a symmetrical domineering turn rather than a complementary submitting type of conversational turn.

Markov analysis is becoming the common method of analyzing communication interacts—the combination of initiating act and responding act of paired communicants.

Multivariate Analysis over Multiple Data Sets

Multivariate analyses over a single multivariate data set are directed toward the description of the characteristics of that set. Analyses which make use of two data sets are concerned with prediction and control. When one data set is used to explain another, the explaining set is usually called the independent and the explained the dependent. The independent set always contains two or more variables; the dependent, one or more. The analysis of structure in these data sets proceeds in one of two ways: (a) Each elemental variable is considered to have a unique contribution to the explanation of the dependent; or, (b) the elemental **independent variables** are assembled into **composite variables** which contribute uniquely to the explanation of the dependent set which itself may be subject to dimensional analysis.

Independent, Elemental Variables   The first approach is an extension of the notion of simple regression analysis with the model now looking like:

$$Y = b_1X_1 + b_2X_2 + \ldots + b_nX_n + C$$

Where b_1 is the amount of change in Y given a unit change in X_1 holding all other X variables constant; b_2 is the amount of change in Y given a unit of change in X_2, all other variables held constant and so on. In these analyses, the X variables are presumed to be independent of one another. Any dependence between them is controlled by the method of partialing that we discuss in a later section. Multiple regression and the general regression model of analysis of variance are examples of the approach that we will touch on briefly.

Multiple regression is a model building procedure that seeks the straight line function, which minimizes the differences between what a set of independent variables would predict the dependent's value to be and what the value actually is. It assumes that the outcome—the **dependent variable**—is associated with and explained by the values of the independent variable set.

Zuckerman, Singer, and Singer (1980) give us an example in their study of children's television usage and classroom behavior. Their independent variable set (which included selected demographic variables, the child's television viewing, the parents' television viewing, and the IQ of the child among others) was used to predict five independent variables, each in a separate analysis. In the analysis of average daily reading time, for instance, the researchers found that the child's IQ and education level of the child's father were positively related and the number of fantasy violent programs viewed was negatively related to time spent in reading each day. As a set, the three independent variables were a better predictor than any one of them alone. Given this finding, of course, the researchers were then faced with the problem of generating an explanation for the coherence of the set.

Analysis of variance (ANOVA) is a statistical procedure which uses explanatory variables to decompose the variability of a criterion measure. Our decomposition of the variability of the Drug Knowledge Test through the use of the connectedness variable was an example of a simple analysis of variance. Modern analysis of variance follows the general regression model with the control and treatment variables becoming the independent variable set. The criterion measure used in the protocol becomes the dependent variable. When more than one explanatory variable is being tested, analysis of variance based on the regression model is generally to be preferred to the classical analysis of variance. The modern version establishes the required independence among the predictors through **partialing** techniques (though, we will see that partialing introduces its own problems). Classical ANOVA simply assumes that independence.

Composite Variables   The second approach we will consider in multivariate analysis presumes an underlying structure to the independent data set (and to the dependent set when it is composed of more than one variable). These analyses, which include **discriminant analysis**, **multiple analysis of variance**, and **canonical correlation**, begin by extracting the structural functions composed of the information which is shared among those elemental variables. The reasoning parallels that which we saw in the discussion of factor analysis. These constructed factors or functions are then used to test for association or to develop an explanatory model.

I can show how this procedure works with an example drawn from our 1980 campaign study (Anderson and Avery, 1983). In this study, we used discriminant analysis to determine whether categories of individuals we thought utilized different cognitive techniques for managing campaign information could be distinguished one from the other by other variables. That is, we wanted to see if identification with a cognitive category could be predicted by the other information we had on our respondents. We selected 25 independent variables from five categories of information: (1) political salience—probability of voting, perceived importance of the outcome, knowledge of the candidates, average interest in politics over the campaign period; (2) attitudes toward the government—judgments on equality, honesty, wastefulness, trustworthiness, and the like; (3) ratings of the candidates averaged over the four data collections (Anderson, Carter, and Reagan); (4) demographics—age, education, income, etc.; and (5) attendance to the televised debate—part 1 and part 2. The dependent variable was the cognitive category. Note that we had 26 observations on each individual, 25 of which were used to predict the value of the 26th.

In the analysis, the 25 independent variables were reduced to five composite variables called "discriminant functions." (The first function was composed of the variables: marital status, age, viewed part 1 of the debate, changed candidate of choice during the campaign, education level, viewed part 2 of the debate, and governmental honesty rating.) These functions were then used to classify each individual into one of the six cognitive categories. The success of our hypothesis that the cognitive categories were coherent attributes depended on the success of the classification procedure. The classification was significant, but not as conclusive as we wished.

Issues in Multivariate Analysis

Multivariate analyses are powerful tools for displaying the structure of data sets. In some respects, the technical genius of them has exceeded our ability to use them to develop the constructs of theory. Though a thorough analysis of these problems is beyond the scope of this text, I can introduce the major difficulty of assigning meaning to **partialed variables** and to statistically **constructed composite variables**.

Partialed Variables   When two or more independent variables are used to explain a dependent variable, the variability of the dependent measure is first partitioned by the independent variable which shows the highest level of association with the dependent. The next variable is added, and new information is gained if that variable can further partition the variability of the dependent within the partitions established by the first.

This explanation is most clear when the independent variables are not correlated one with another. Figure 7-10 shows a relationship between two independent variables and a dependent variable when the independents are not correlated. The degree of overlap of each independent with the dependent

FIGURE 7-10
Diagram of two independent variables that each share information with the dependent variable but not with each other.

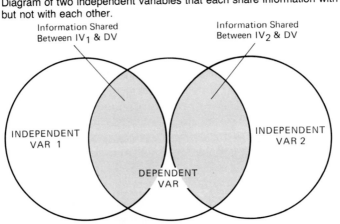

shows the correlation between the two variables. Note that there is no overlap between the two independent variables.

The figure shows that some of the sources of variation within each of the independents is related to some of the sources of variation within the dependent variable. This relationship suggests that the variables themselves are composites of empirical phenomena. In this situation, our explanation is limited to the sort that says that there are some empirical elements in variable X_1 and X_2 which are related to some empirical components of variable Y. Unfortunately, the analysis cannot tell us what those sources are. In this case, however, the conceptual meaning of the independents remains distinct one from another. At least we know that there are two different things mapping onto a third even if we are not exactly sure what those two things are.

When the independents are themselves correlated, some of the information that each has about the dependent is common to both. Figure 7-11 shows that relationship. The shaded area in the center shows the correlation between the independents which is shared in relation to the dependent. In order to get rid of the duplication, the method of partialing is used. In the process of partialing, all of the shaded area is assigned to the first of the pair to be entered in the analysis. What the second explains is that lesser amount left.

The vexing problem is that in this situation the independent variables, as originally defined, are no longer conceptually distinct. Instead, the statistical analysis has restructured the second variable into something else. We are now dealing with empirical evidence for which we have little, clear conceptual meaning. As more and more variables are entered into an analysis of this kind,

FIGURE 7-11
Diagram of correlated "independent variables."

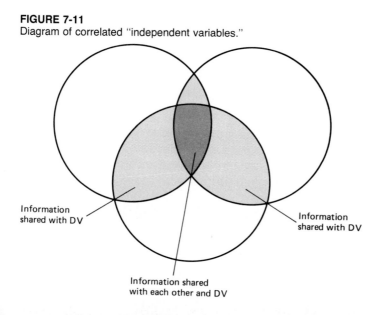

Information
shared with DV

Information
shared with DV

Information shared
with each other and DV

less and less of the composite of each gets used which leaves the resulting empirical variable with little correspondence to its defining concept. That is, we no longer know what it is that we are calling by the original variable name.

Partialing is a technique which is designed to protect the researcher from a failure to meet the assumption of independence among the predicting variables. When a variable is "partialed out," it is strong evidence that the conceptual validity of that variable was weak and that the researcher's theory is underdeveloped.

Statistically Constructed Composite Variables In partialed variables, our problem is that our initial concept of the variable is inadequate and fails. With statistically constructed variables, the researcher rarely has any a priori understanding of the function which is extracted. For example, as I have reported to you, we used discriminant analysis in our campaign study to demonstrate that the cognitive categories we discovered had structural integrity. That evidence appeared when we were able to predict membership in those cognitive categories through functions derived from a variety of items included in our instrument.

To set the problem, let me repeat the variables in the first function: marital status, age, viewed part 1 of the debate, changed candidate of choice during the campaign, educational level, viewed part 2 of the debate, and governmental honesty rating. What the discriminant analysis tells me is that those six items are particular representations of a core dimension which is itself useful in identifying membership in our cognitive categories. For purposes of theory construction, the items themselves are trivial. What is important is that core dimension. But what is it? The statistical procedures do not inform me.

In order for me to advance my understanding here, I have to create a description of that dimension which will account for the structure revealed in the analysis. Then, I will have to seek evidence to prove that description is valid. More often than not, the steps that make the actual contribution to knowledge are not taken.

SUMMARY

This chapter began with an examination of the descriptive statistics of typicality (measures of central tendency), dispersion, and structure. We found that the measures of typicality or averages were dependent on the notion that there was a common attribute being measured within the data set. The average makes sense because it describes this core property. The variations observed in the data set were assumed to be random variations due to individual differences that will distribute in equal proportion around this core.

Two measures of dispersion were described. The variance, or the mean squared deviations around the mean, was shown to be responsive to the analysis of individual differences. Useful partioning variables would show reduction of the variance within the partioned subgroups.

The standard deviation, or the square root of the variance, had its utility in making the connection between the sample in hand and formal models of distribution. As that connection, it provided for the use of those models to describe the population of values from which the sample was drawn.

When two or more observations are made on each unit of analysis, internal structure can arise with data sets. These structures are based on the notion of association, meaning that the values of one variable tend to congregate the values of another into coherent categories and that as the values of the first variable change, the values of the second change also. Strict perfect association occurs when the values of one variable are uniquely identified with the values of another. No association or independence occurs when the value of one is equally likely to be associated with any value of the other. Three conditions of intermediate association were shown and five reasons for that condition given.

When several observations are made on each unit of analysis, multivariate methods are used. These methods can be used over a data set considered as a single unit to discover the underlying dimensions or core properties. They are also used when the data set is considered to be composed of a set of explaining variables (the independent set) and a set of variables to be explained (the dependent set). Such approaches are applied to explanations of prediction and control.

EXERCISES

1 Test your ability to name core dimensions. Draw four overlapping circles. Title one "Good-Bad," another "Competent-Incompetent," the third "Witty-Dull," and the last "Honest-Dishonest." The area circumscribed by all four circles is the core dimension. What would you call it?

2 Redraw your figure of one above with the circle labeled "Competent-Incompetent" directly in the middle and the other three overlapping it. Now what do you call the core dimension?

3 Explain why you did or did not change.

4 What construct do you think is being measured by the first discriminant function we found in the campaign study (pp. 207–208, 210)?

RELATED READINGS

Kerlinger, F. N. *Behavioral research: A conceptual approach.* New York: Holt, Rinehart and Winston, 1979.

Nunnally, J. C. *Psychometric theory* (2d Ed.). New York: McGraw-Hill Book Co., 1978.

Willemsen, E. W. *Understanding statistical reasoning.* San Francisco: W. H. Freeman and Co., 1974.

Wright, R. L. D. *Understanding statistics.* New York: Harcourt Brace Jovanovich, Inc., 1976.

CHAPTER

STATISTICS: DECISION MAKING AND METHODS

SYNOPSIS

In the last exciting episode, we learned about using statistical analysis to discover the characteristics and in polyvariate data the internal structure of sets of numbers. The importance of that analysis is held in the fact that in research the set of numbers are generated from observations of human action. Given an isomorphic relationship between the numerical observations and human behavior, the characteristics and structures found in the data sets represent the characteristics and structures present in the behavior itself.

In this chapter, we will look at the use of inferential statistics as decision rules in hypothesis testing and consider some practical methods of analysis for the more common statistical routines. We begin with a look at inferential statistics in general and specifically in their role as decision rules. We resurrect the job satisfaction example of Chapter 6 to help in this discussion. The end of the first section presents an evaluation of statistical decision making. The second section presents a set of recommendations for the analysis of chi square, *t*-tests of the mean, ANOVA, correlation, and multivariate analysis.

INFERENTIAL STATISTICS

Descriptive statistics are analytical procedures developed to make meaningful statements about a set of numbers in hand. **Inferential statistics** permit us to extend those descriptive statements to a theoretical set or population of numbers. They are called "inferential" because they are based on a set of assumptions concerning the nature of the numbers, the statistics, and often the population itself. From those assumptions, we draw conclusions about the unknown.

In the paragraphs that follow, we briefly visit the notion of inferential statistics as estimates of population characteristics and structures and then move to the larger discussion of inferential statistics as decision rules.

Inferential Statistics as Population Estimates

Inferential statistics can provide population estimates of typicality, dispersion, and of internal structure in appropriate sets of measures when the samples from which these estimates have been figured are drawn in an unbiased method (see Chapter 6). It is rare that the purpose of a data collection would be to describe only the sample in hand. In most cases, the statistical characteristics of a sample are of interest because they are held to represent the characteristics of the populations.

There is nothing tricky about the argument: Random samples are more likely to be representative of the population from which they are drawn than not. Therefore, the properties of the sample ought to approximate those of the population. What gets tricky is that most samples are not random samples; many samples are not drawn from the population intended to be represented (such as using college students to represent personnel managers) and some populations to be represented do not exist at the time of the sampling (such as voters in an upcoming election). The technical procedures of inferential statistics assume a perfect sampling process. They do not address the question of representativeness but rather presume it. Most researchers behave in the same manner.

The population estimates are of one of two types: (a) parametric and (b) nonparametric. Parametric estimates assume that the population has certain characteristics (such as being normally distributed) and that the sample approximates those characteristics. Estimates of the population mean and standard deviation are parametric statistics because theory assumes a normally distributed population. Nonparametric statistics, such as chi square and lambda, make no assumption about the characteristics of the population. Parametric statistics carry an additional burden of proof—that the population characteristics meet the assumptions. In practice, as it has been shown that the violation of those assumptions has little effect, it is rare to see much concern for this burden.

Inferential Statistics as Decision Rules

The word "significant" has a special meaning in statistical analysis. It refers to the outcome of procedures that test for the likelihood of sampling error affecting the value of the population estimate derived from the sample in question. When a study has been properly designed, a **test of significance** can provide the public verification of a research hypothesis.

In the chapter on sampling, we learned that any estimate of a population parameter has to be considered probabilistically. The estimate given by the sample was not considered absolutely true but likely to be true within some range of confidence. We learned that the reason for tempering our claims was that any sample is subject to sampling error, which by the chance selection of particular respondents could produce an estimate considerably different from the true value.

In the analysis of hypotheses, we are once again concerned about sampling error (for a thorough discussion of sampling error, see pages 154–160 in Chapter 6). In this situation, however, instead of considering how far off an estimate might be, we are involved in demonstrating that the value received is sufficiently removed from an expected value that sampling error cannot credibly account for the difference and that an alternate explanation—usually the hypothesis—should be accepted. Let's look at the sampling chapter's job satisfaction example in another way:

The original example involved a set of job satisfaction scores which ranged from 1 to 5 and had a mean of 3. Presume that we wished to test procedures which were designed to increase a worker's job satisfaction. One test might involve changing the working conditions for a sample of workers in order to increase their job satisfaction. In order to set up that test, the researcher would have to design a protocol in which the only way job satisfaction would increase would be the result of the changed working conditions. In this best of all research worlds, we will grant the researcher control of all influences on job satisfaction. Even with this control (which, of course, is never granted), the researcher cannot prevent sampling error from producing a result which looks like the one hypothesized.

Let me explain: If the changes were successful, we would no longer expect the mean to be 3, but rather, some value larger than 3. Our problem is that values larger than 3 can also occur just by the chance selection of particular respondents (For example, see the mean for sample 74 on page 156.). That is, just by chance the sample selected for the hypothesis test might contain more satisfied workers. As a result, the particular sample would be the reason for the increase, and not the changes in working conditions.

If the obtained value from our sample is larger than 3.0, we have to choose between two competing explanations for that occurrence: (a) That we just happened to select a sample of respondents with more high satisfaction values than low; or (b) our hypothesized effect—that the changed working conditions have increased worker's job satisfaction. These two choices have special names in our research lexicon: The first is called the **null hypothesis** because it states "there is no relationship only sampling error." The second is called the alternate or **research hypothesis**; it is the one we wish to verify.

We choose between these two hypotheses by considering the relative frequency of samples with means of 3.6 or greater that could be drawn from the original population. If the rate of such samples is low, we accept explanation (b). If it is more frequent, we accept explanation (a). How low? The convention is usually 5 percent or less.

The method used to make this decision contains three components: the *obtained sample characteristic* as an estimate of a population parameter, an *expected value* for that estimate, and the known, formal *probability distribution* which is applied to the population parameter. In our example, the obtained value is the mean job satisfaction score collected after the work changes were put into effect. The expected value would be the mean of the job satisfaction score before the changes were put into effect. The probability distribution is assumed to be the *t* distribution with sigma defined by the standard error of the mean as estimated from the sample. We are now prepared to test a particular sample estimate to see if it deviates from the expected value by a large enough margin to be considered significant.

An Example in Job Satisfaction

To continue our example, in the test of the hypothesis, we would initiate the new working conditions and after some time to let our respondents acclimate to those conditions, we would readminister the job satisfaction test, this time to, say, 15 subjects in an experimental section. Presume we got the following scores:

Respondent	1	2	3	4	5	6	7	8	9	10	11	12	13	14	15
Score	5	3	3	5	4	4	2	4	3	4	2	4	3	5	4

The mean of this set is 3.6, and the SD is .99. The value of the mean is larger than 3 as we hypothesized, but is it sufficiently larger than 3 that we can safely assume that it is not due to sampling error? The question that we are asking is: How often would a sample of workers with a mean of 3.6 occur in repeated samples drawn from a population of workers whose mean job satisfaction score is 3.0? If it happens rarely, we will claim that our 3.6 occurred not because of sampling error but because of the changed working conditions. If it is not rare, we cannot dismiss the explanation of sampling error for our result.

To answer the question, we need to first determine which testing procedure fits the requirements of that question. Table 8-1 lists the common statistical tests and the questions they approach. If you don't wish to turn to that table, you can take my word that we are to use either a *z*-test or *t*-test of the means.

Statisticians tell us that our sample size is too small to use the normal curve as our model (which eliminates the *z*-test). They substitute the *t* distribution (also known as "Student's" distribution) as the appropriate model. (Please note that the technical procedures are not what is important in this example; it is the logic that underlies them.) The *t* distribution is a family of curves. Each curve is defined by its degrees of freedom[1] (n - 1) which means that the characteristics of the distribution changes slightly as the sample size n increases. At a sample size of a hundred or more, it approximates the normal distribution. Many statistics make use of families of curves like this one.

Our distribution will have 14 degrees of freedom, a mean of 3.0 (Why?) and

---

[1]"Degrees of freedom" is a mathematical concept indicating the number of elements which must be known before a value is determined.

TABLE 8-1
COMMON STATISTICAL TESTS OF SIGNIFICANCE

Statistic	Distribution	Research question
Chi square 1 sample	Chi square	Do the obtained frequencies in a category set differ from the expected?
Chi square 2 or more samples	Chi square	Do the relative frequencies within a set of categories differ across samples?
z or t 1 sample	Normal or t	Does the obtained mean differ from the expected?
z or t 2 samples	Normal or t	Do the means of the two samples differ from one another?
F-test or analysis of variance	F	When applied to means: Do the means of the groups differ one from another? When applied to multiple regression and other structural analyses: Is there an association between the dependent and independent measures?
t (applied to r)	t	Does the obtained correlation differ from zero?
Z (comparing 2 or more correlations)	t	Does the index of association between X and Y differ between samples?

"sigma" defined by the standard error of the mean. Assuming a large population, the standard error or standard deviation of the mean is given by:

$$SE_{\bar{x}} = SD\sqrt{N}$$

In our case, the standard error is:

$$SE_{\bar{x}} = .99\sqrt{15}$$
$$= .25$$

If the distribution of means drawn from samples of our population is defined by a curve from the t distribution and if .25 is a good estimate of the standard error of this distribution, then we can establish exactly the rate of occurrence of means of 3.6 within this distribution. We first determine the distance in standard error units that the obtained mean of 3.6 is from the expected mean of 3.0. We call that distance t and it is defined by:

$$t = \frac{(\bar{X} - \mu)}{SE_{\bar{x}}}$$

Where $\bar{x}$ is the sample mean, μ is the expected value of the mean, $SE_{\bar{x}}$ is the estimate of the standard error of the mean.

Here:

$$t = \frac{(3.6 - 3.0)}{.25}$$
$$t = 2.4$$

Figure 8-1 displays the t curve for 14 degrees of freedom and shows the location of our obtained and expected means. Because the curve is a frequency distribution, the proportion of the curve to the right of 3.6 will tell us the rate of means 3.6 and higher. Because the curve is symmetrical, 50 percent of the area lies to the left of 3.0. All we have to do is to solve for the area under the curve between 3.0 and 3.6 and compare that with the total area. If your trig is a little rusty, there are a number of handbooks with tables that do all the work for you. (They give the area for each t value to three places after the decimal, but such information is only marginal to this discussion.) In our example, the t of 2.4 accounts for the 50 percent below the mean and 48 percent above the mean or a total of 98 percent. That is, 98 percent of all the mean scores for samples of 15 drawn from our population will be less than 3.6. Well, now, what do we want to conclude? Is the 3.6 the result of a chance effect or is it the result of the changes we instituted in the working conditions.

Let's examine exactly what the evidence is for this decision. What we have learned by this test is that a mean of 3.6 rarely occurs by chance within random samples drawn from our original population. Could this be one of those rare instances? Of course. We know only the rate, not the occasion. But we could also claim the alternate explanation, that we can conceive of a set of samples

FIGURE 8-1
t distribution for 14 degrees of freedom (normal curve superimposed).

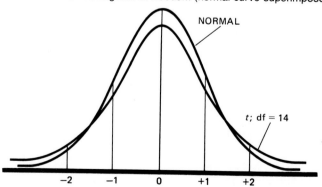

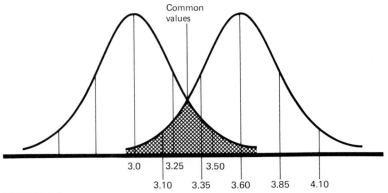

FIGURE 8-2
Two populations of numbers, each with a $SE_{\bar{x}}$ of .25 and one with a mean of 3.0, the other with a mean of 3.6. Question: the researcher has a sample with a mean of 3.6—from which population is it most likely to have been drawn from?

drawn from the original population and subject to the experimental working conditions which, indeed, increase job satisfaction by an average of .6 point. This set of samples would have a mean of 3.6 and a standard error of .25 as demonstrated by our sample in hand.

I now have two "homes" for my obtained mean of 3.6: One is the original population, which is centered around 3.0; the other is the hypothesized population centered around 3.6. The relationship between the two populations is shown in Figure 8-2. The shaded area under the two curves shows the area of overlap. In this area, the same numerical value can belong to either population, but it cannot belong to both. The explanation for what that value means depends on its parent population. If it belongs in the original population, then the 3.6 is a happenstance of selection; if it belongs in the hypothesized population, then the 3.6 is an indication of increased job satisfaction among the workers. Unfortunately, there are no distinguishing characteristics which permit one to identify a 3.6 belonging to the hypothesized population from a 3.6 belonging to the original population. The researcher has to make the assignment on the basis of the probabilities of membership.

Certain conventions have developed around this assignment. The point of maximum confusion between the two populations is always at the point where the two curves cross. If probability was the only issue, all values to the right of that point should be assigned to the hypothesized explanation and all values to the left to the chance explanation. The value defined at the point should be indeterminate. The scientific community is more conservative. It requires that area of acceptance of the chance explanation extend up to at least 95 percent of the values from the original population. Only values at or beyond that point are ordinarily to be assigned to the hypothesized population.

This conventional decision rule is called "setting the **alpha level**" or "setting

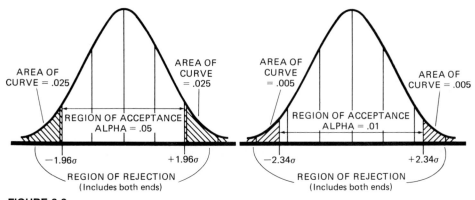

FIGURE 8-3
Regions of acceptance and rejection for alpha = .05 and .01.

the **level of significance**." Setting the alpha level establishes the conditions under which the null hypothesis will be accepted or rejected. It defines two areas on the distribution curve, the **region of acceptance** and the **region of rejection**. Figure 8-3 shows these areas for our testing situation using the alpha levels of .05 and .01. Test values falling at or beyond the alpha level indicate rejection of the null. Those falling within these levels indicate acceptance.

Alpha, or the level of significance, controls the risk of rejecting the chance explanation when it is true. If alpha is set at .05, then a true null hypothesis will be mistakenly considered false 5 percent of the time. If it is set at .01, this **Type I error** will occur 1 percent of the time. The selection of alpha also involves another kind of error. This error, in the poetic language of statistics, is called **Type II error**. Type II error is the rejection of the alternate explanation (research hypothesis) when it is true. The relation between Type I and Type II error is pernicious. Selecting a small value for alpha decreases the probability of Type I error but increases the probability of Type II error.

Figure 8-4 shows this relationship using our exemplar curves. I have set the decision point at alpha = .05 (the solid line in the figure). The crosshatched area in the original curve indicates the likelihood of rejecting a true null hypothesis. The shaded area in the alternate curve is the probability of Type II error or **beta**. In this relationship, and beta is definable only within a particular relationship between the null and alternate, beta is .25. If the researcher reduces alpha by 4 points and uses the .01 level of significance (the second figure), given the circumstances of this relationship, beta would increase to .38. That is, in more than a third of the decisions, the researcher would be rejecting a true alternate.

When these technical methods are applied to problem solving, the relative costs of Type I and Type II errors need to be carefully considered. The selection between them should control for the more costly error. A consultant evaluating a current but expensive business practice might wish to lessen the risk of a Type

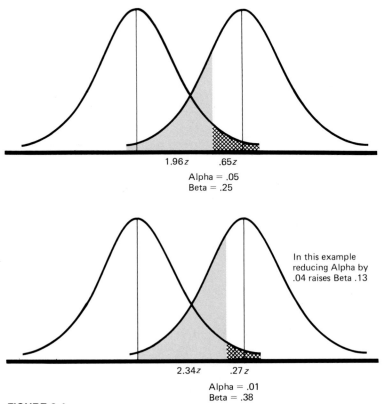

FIGURE 8-4
Relationship between Type I (alpha) and Type II (beta) errors.

II error (as it would be the more costly error by preventing change) by using an alpha of .10 or .20. In the practice of science, however, Type II errors are generally considered much less costly than Type I errors. Although Type II errors result in the continuance of ignorance, Type I errors permit false claims.

Tests of Significance with Other Statistics

Tests of significance have been developed for all of the major questions of association and difference. These tests all involve the same logic as our example with the t-test. That is, they all determine the probability of the obtained value of a sample statistic drawn from a population appropriate to the null hypothesis. If the obtained value is a rare event in such a population, it is then assigned to an alternate population appropriate to the research hypothesis. Setting the level of significance (alpha level) establishes the decision point of this choice. These tests establish the expected rate of error in selecting between the null and research hypothesis that is due to sampling. They do not control this error or identify the occasion of it or have any relevance to any other source of error. Table 8-1 presents a listing of the main statistical tests, the corresponding distributions, and the research question approached.

Issues in Tests of Significance

From the preceding discussion, it would appear as if inferential statistics provide a regularized procedure for decision making. Unfortunately, in many respects the procedures have the appearance of a house of cards and have come under continuing criticism (see Babbie, 1983 or Dooley, 1984). In the first place, the probabilities of error are simply the description of the pattern that should occur over a large number of repetitions of the exact conditions involved in the test. Just as we cannot predict the outcome of a particular coin toss even though we know the likelihood of each alternative, these probabilities tell us nothing about the rightness or wrongness of a particular decision. Again, they inform us about the rate of error but not the occasion of error. A given decision to accept the null or alternate cannot be 95 percent right. It is either all right or all wrong. This exclusionary consequence would be less of a problem if the normal practice of science in communication was characterized by repeated studies or research programs. Actual practice, however, is more likely to be individual studies conducted but once.

A second problem attacks the validity of the whole process. The decision procedures are dependent upon the assumptions of a random sample, valid measurement, and in the case of parametric statistics, of the properties of the population being met. We rarely get past the first assumption. It is, indeed, nearly impossible to get a random sample of the populations we wish to describe. Most samples are samples of convenience for which the rate of error is unknown.

Finally, even if conducted correctly (which it ordinarily is not), the test permits us to make a reasonable choice between an explanation based on sampling error and one based on *something else*. That "something else" will necessarily be the research hypothesis only if the protocol is perfect. If the protocol design is only human, then the something else could be measurement error or a potentially endless set of variables functioning within the protocol. The most that can be said after a successful test of significance is that sampling error is not a likely explanation.

These problems must reduce the confidence one places in any finding of significance. Such statements as "I'm 95 percent certain that I am correct" are simply foolhardy. In fact, tests of significance primarily represent a public way of making decisions based on criteria which have come to be accepted by the scientific community. They do not represent any real control of error.

Alternate Decision Rules

In my work as a consultant, I rarely use statistical decision rules *to make decisions*. The reason is that in that work it is not sufficient to simply provide a public decision-making process. The alternatives chosen must also make a difference in terms of what people actually do. Therefore, I help my clients work up a set of a priori rules about the conditions necessary for them to choose one course of action over another. The job satisfaction example can work for us again here. Statistically, in that example, a change in job satisfaction becomes significant at a difference of $+/- .5$.[2] Whether that amount of change is also a call for action on the part of management has almost nothing to do with the fact that it is significant. Action could be taken on much less change or even more change could be required. Presume that initial scores were much lower than 3.0, say, 2.0 or 1.5. Action taken on the finding of even very small, nonsignificant positive change may be well justified. On the other hand, if satisfaction scores were high—4.0 or above—no action may be justified even with significant change. A question that I would ask of management, then, is given present conditions, at what level of change in a satisfaction test would they be willing to adopt the proposed working conditions. In essence, you have to build a constituency of confidence for an alternative rather than measuring its statistical confidence.

Of course, I would also run the standard statistical tests simply because doing so is good workmanship. The unthinking use of statistical significance, however, cheapens the whole process.

Summary Analysis of Inferential Statistics

It has been shown that the sample statistics which commonly appear in research—the mean, variance, standard deviation, correlation, and other measures of structure—can also be used to provide estimates of population characteristics. Samples, therefore, can be used to draw inferences about populations.

Inferential statistics also provide methods by which an obtained population estimate can be tested to see if it is the likely result of sampling error or of some other source of difference from an expected value. These tests of significance all make use of some known, formal model of distribution to determine the rate of occurrence of the value in question. When that rate is low, usually 5 percent or less, then sampling error is rejected as a likely explanation and an alternate, usually the hypothesis, is advanced.

These testing procedures are strictly appropriate only when applied to a random sample which meets all the assumptions of the test. As this requirement is rarely met, tests of significance are primarily public methods of decision making accepted by the scientific community.

EXERCISES

1 Can a significant finding be without theoretical import?
2 Four distribution models accommodate all the tests of significance listed here. Can you name them?

[2]Remember that the standard error of the mean was .25 in our example and significance is reached at a difference of roughly 2 standard deviations.

3 Studies termed "exploratory" often use alpha levels of .10 or .20. Why?
4 Medical researchers are testing a new drug which may have serious side effects but which promises a cure for a disease you now have. What balance between Type I and Type II errors would you like them to take; how would their insurance agent view the choice?
5 What "alternate decision rule" might you suggest for those medical researchers in question 4?

SOME PRACTICAL THOUGHTS ON STATISTICAL APPLICATIONS

For most of us who use statistics, their application involves selecting the right routine appropriate to our research question and level of measurement from one of the many computer packages available. From there, it is simply a matter of keying the data with a few control commands. In a few seconds, the data are analyzed according to our wishes. The ease with which anyone who can follow step-by-step instructions can run even the most complex multivariate analysis can lead us to be careless of the information provided—a sort of take the significance and run. This carelessness can result in an overemphasis on tests of significance and an underemphasis on analysis. The sections that follow contain recommendations for the analysis of common statistical routines and for applying statistical analysis to survey and experimental protocols. They are presented in the best Betty Crocker tradition full of dos and don'ts but little debate.

ANALYZING THE BASIC TESTS OF SIGNIFICANCE

Tests of significance, as we have seen, evaluate the probability of particular values in populations under study. They are used as decision rules to choose between explanations of "chance effect" versus "significant effect." There are three general guidelines which direct the interpretation of all such tests.

First, a significant effect is not necessarily an important one. "Significance" means only that whatever effect occurred cannot be reasonably explained by chance. It does not mean that the effect will result in a substantive or even noticeable change in behavior or outcome. The interpretation of a substantive effect is not addressed by statistics, but by the scientist (and, of course, the critical reader) in design and measurement. (Note the substantive effect comments in the survey analysis under the next heading.)

Second, the finding of nonsignificance means only that sampling error cannot be dismissed as a possible explanation for whatever effect is being investigated. It does not have a substantive interpretation. If, for example, a researcher investigating the difference between two treatment groups finds no significant difference between them, the conclusion cannot be drawn that the two groups are the same. It is possible, of course, that they are the same. The test, however, provides no evidence of that similarity. The reason is that tests of difference depend on the precision of measurement and the sensitivity of the test. Both of these are, in turn, dependent on methodological decisions. True differences can be masked by failing to institute appropriate controls. The NSD finding, then, is a confounded outcome for which a single interpretation is not possible.

Third, significance is a decision rule not a property of the measurement protocol. The decision rule should be based on the relative costs (economic, social, epistemological) of the two types of errors. There is no particular merit in achieving significance at a smaller alpha level. The finding is not "more significant," "more important," or "more credible" at the .001 level than it is at the .05 level. Because the probability of any single event is 0 or 1, a single finding can be just as wrong at .001 alpha as it can be at .10. Significance, substance, and importance are three separate judgments, but they are each judgments, not objective characteristics.

Chi Square

Chi square tests nominal data for the difference between a set of obtained frequencies and their expected values. The obtained values can be drawn from a single sample or several samples. The expected values can come from one of three sources. They can be generated by (a) assigning an equal proportion to each of the categories in the set—called the "chance expectations." The expected values can be based on (b) some external knowledge on how the categories should fill. Or, they can be based on (c) information in the samples selected. The first two are used with tests over single samples; the last are used with tests over multiple samples. For example, if I were to test the relative proportion of Democrats, Republicans, and Independents in the campaign study, I could use the expected value of ⅓ for each (chance) or I could use national or regional rates of membership (external information). The expected values I select will, of course, affect the outcome and must be consistent with my theory.

The expected values in multiple samples are based on the assumption that the contribution of the cells along a row or down a column to their row or column total should be proportionately the same. I won't dissect that statement too far, except to say that although the size of the samples might differ across columns or down rows, the proportion from each sample that falls into each cell along a row or down a column will be the same when there is no relationship between the variables being studied. The expected value, then, is one of equal proportions.

Although we talk of testing differences in chi-square analysis, what is actually being studied is the relationship between two variables. For instance, I could take three categories of income—say, high, medium, and low—and test to see if the relative proportion of Democrats, Republicans, and Independents changed as the income category changed. If it does, then there is a relationship between party membership and income. Because chi square is a nonparametric test, it makes no assumption about the curve that describes that relationship.

Chi square is a conservative test in that it is not very sensitive to weak relationships (small differences). From one point of view, that means it wastes information because small effects that are genuine are treated as if they were by chance. From another point of view, that means it protects the analyst from mistaking a weak but significant finding from a significant and important one. From an applications point of view, the conservativeness of chi square means that when it will be the primary form of analysis much larger samples are required than when, say, ANOVA can be used. In fact, samples of 300 to 400 are preferred.

A few technical notes: χ^2 is always a positive number. Its expected value increases as the number of cells in the crossbreak increases. Consequently, the significant value for a large crossbreak is much greater than for a small one.[3] (Bigger is not always better.) When a crossbreak is found to generate a significant χ^2, the whole table has contributed to that finding. The analyst cannot, legitimately, single out particular cells as the source of the significant effect. Additional analysis is required.

Tests of the Mean

We can use t-tests of the mean to determine the significance of the difference between an obtained mean and its expected value or between two sample means. Analysis of variance (F-test) is used to test the differences between two or more sample means. These two routines come from the same logic family (when testing two sample means, t is the square root of F). We have spent some time with both of these; therefore, just a few comments are necessary.

Both of these routines assume that the difference effect (the treatment or categorizing variable) is a constant effect. That is, it affects everyone in approximately the same way. If it is a differential effect—some people change more than others—then a significant treatment difference is likely to be masked by these individual differences.

I can best demonstrate this by examining the makeup of analysis of variance. ANOVA is a ratio of two independent estimates of the population variance. The estimate in the numerator of the ratio is based on the differences between the subgroup means, the denominator on the subgroup variances. For our purposes, here, think of the numerator as an estimate of the variance which can be biased by the treatment or categorizing variable. (When there is no difference between the means, the ratio goes to zero.) That is, that variable adds something to that estimate. Whether or not the effect is significant depends on the value of the treatment effect relative to the total variance. To demonstrate, presume that we have a treatment effect of +4. If the total variance is 1, then the F-ratio is 5; or:

$$\frac{\text{Variance} + \text{Treatment}}{\text{Variance}} \quad \text{or} \quad \frac{(1 + 4)}{1}$$

[3]For instance, the chi-square value of 3.84 is significant with a 2 × 2 table, but 16.92 is the significant value for a 4 × 4 crossbreak.

But if the total variance is 10, then the F-ratio is 1.4; or:

$$\frac{(10 + 4)}{10}$$

The true effect of +4, then, can be masked by conditions which lead to variances larger than the effect. Those conditions might be a poorly designed protocol, measurement error, a small sample, and so on. When the treatment effect operates with different results over the subject groups to produce an averaged effect (of, say, +4) rather than a constant, then the treatment itself is also likely to increase the variability of the scores. (All of this demonstrates my earlier claim of no substance in NSD.) The moral is that the assumption of a constant effect should be investigated particularly when nonsignificance is indicated.

This investigation involves the examination of individual respondents in the subject pool. It is particularly important to become knowledgeable about the most deviant observations. Go back through the data set and identify those individuals for follow-up interviews if possible.

As with chi square, we talk of testing differences in t-tests and F-tests of the mean, but it is, perhaps, more useful to think of testing a relationship—the relationship between the treatment or categorizing variable and the criterion. Our analysis of the DKT over the connectedness variable showed that the DKT scores were related to the values of connectedness. It is that relationship which resulted in the subgroup means being different. Both the t-test and the F-test can be thought of as the correlation between the independent (treatment or categorizing) variable and the dependent criterion.

Correlation

As a critic of research, I am always fascinated by the differences between what we teach and what we do. Every statistics textbook I've read dutifully records the necessity of plotting the relationship between the X and Y variable to check the viability of the linear assumption. Here, as a rule, we do not practice what we teach. Although I have taken to that on occasion, no polemic follows here. What is interesting is an interpretation of why practitioners do not follow the "rules." Consider what happens if the scattergram—the plot of the X/Y pairs—does not appear to be linear. What happens is that the analyst's neatly ordered progression of analysis comes to a halt. The analyst must apply some linear transformations to the data or switch to polynomial analysis. The former is beyond the mathematical ken of many and the latter lacks the power of conventional meaning in the community. Well, who's to say that scattergram doesn't appear linear anyway.

In most of our analyses, the level of abstraction (or distance from a criterion of utility) is great enough that the actual shape of the relationship has little import for our understanding of behavior. It is enough that a significant relationship has been found. But not always. Working as a consultant for a chain of broadcast stations, I was asked to determine when the chain would become profitable. Television stations make their money from advertisers who pay for audiences delivered. It made sense, then, that income could be predicted from audience ratings.

At the time, I was working for an organization which had a concession from the Federal Communications Commission which granted access to privileged income data. It was a simple matter to regress income on audience ratings. The market-by-market correlations were very high—all above .90. I was prepared to make my predictions: "Generate X audience, collect Y dollars." I still do not know what prompted me to plot those data. Nevertheless, I did; the curve looked like that in Figure 8-5.

The curve shown is not a linear relationship but one of the third order. As you might suspect, the chain I was working for was at the lower end of the audience scale where an increase in audience had minimal effect on income (later determined to be the result of national advertiser buying practices). Had I predicted profit from the straight-line model, I would have been a false prophet, indeed. At least, when your job depends on your being right, plot the data.

Multivariate Analyses

Because our typical measures are verbally based proxies and, therefore, embedded in a common language structure, any large collection of such verbal items will produce linear composites. The finding of factor dimensions, path coefficients, discriminant functions, and the like, is the expected outcome from

FIGURE 8-5
Curve showing general relationship between income and audience size.

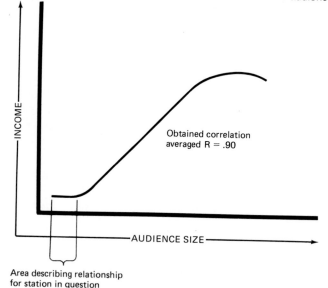

Obtained correlation averaged R = .90

INCOME

AUDIENCE SIZE

Area describing relationship
for station in question

these analyses. That is, it is not of a high order of discovery. The contribution comes when the analyst is able to specify the number and structure of such vector variables in a reliable, prior fashion. Our literature contains numerous exploratory multivariate analyses which hold promise, but, at this point, demonstrate only the obvious.

In order to confirm a vector variable, it is necessary to use the first analysis as the hypothesis for a second, independent test. As practice is not likely to change here either, it is up to the reader to see these findings as potentially disposable.

ANALYZING SURVEY DATA

Many will have their first experience with statistics in the analysis of survey data. The statistical analyses that can be performed depend, in large part, on the design of the survey instrument (which, of course, depends on the purposes of the study). However, all studies should begin with an outcomes analysis. Collecting data imposes a responsibility of analysis. Out of respect for the respondents' effort, the researcher should be prepared to evaluate each item on the questionnaire. After constructing the survey form, therefore, the analyst should establish the expected outcome for each item in terms of one's theory and level of measurement. An analysis of that sort would look like Box 8-1 for nominal data and Box 8-2 for interval data where I have first presented the questionnaire item (from our campaign instrument) and then our expectations and proposed analytical procedure.

When the analyst cannot specify an expected outcome, the possible outcomes and their interpretation should be listed as in Box 8-3.

Following this recommendation accomplishes several purposes. First, it forces the analyst to read the questionnaire once more, which increases the likelihood of catching errors and improving the wording. Second, it helps to ensure that the appropriate level of measurement is being used in the response form. Third, it establishes a basis for identifying notable outcomes—such as 70 percent of the respondents voting in the last primary election. Fourth, it raises the probability that the results from each answer will be considered. And last, it directs the analyst to actively consider the evidence for the validity of the measurement by developing explanations of the meaning of the items for the concepts under study. For example, the explanation for the candidate evaluation item shows that a midrange mean might be an ambiguous finding as it may be interpreted as an artifact of the response form or an actual rating of "fair."

As the second step, all analyses of association and structure should be specified along with their expected outcomes and interpretation. Boxes 8-4, 8-5, and 8-6 provide examples using chi square, correlation, and analysis of variance, respectively.

By laying out each analysis in this manner, the researcher can check to see that the procedure appropriate to the research question and level of measurement is being used. Further, specifying the expected outcome serves to state the hypothesis governing the test. In this manner, positive and negative evidence can be identified. It also serves to alert the researcher to alternate explanations which may need additional information items added to the form itself. The practice of automatically selecting the option of analyzing every question against every other question should be avoided. Too often, the researcher ends up selecting the significant ones as if they were theoretically important and ignoring the rest. Alas, the recommended procedure is a lot of work; the automatic option is none at all. Even experts fail this test.

BOX 8-1

NOMINAL DATA DESCRIPTIVE ANALYSIS

Item

Are you registered to vote?   Yes   No

Interpretation

In this county, 70 percent are registered. Should be that high or higher. Record percentages.

Item

Did you vote in the last primary election?   Yes   No

Interpretation

35 percent voted in the last election. More than 50 percent calls for investigation of the sample. Record percentage.

BOX 8-2

INTERVAL DATA DESCRIPTIVE ANALYSIS

Item

Do you think you'll vote in the election coming this November?

Very Likely   Likely   Not Sure   Unlikely   Very Unlikely

Interpretation

Expect the mean at "Likely"—these are politically interested; SD slightly more than 1.0 because of the skew. Record mean and SD.

BOX 8-3

Item

Looking at all the choices available to you, how do you rate the entire field of presidential candidates?

1 2 3 4 5 6 7 8 9 10

Poor   Fair   Excellent

Interpretation

Normal response behavior would suggest a midrange mean (endpoints rarely used). Might also result from dichotomous aggregate (winners and losers); check SD. If at the poor end, the lesser of evils might be the basis of judging candidates. If at the excellent end, then have unusual group of committed voters.

BOX 8-4

CHI SQUARE CROSSBREAK

Item

Would you describe yourself as a

Are you registered?	Democrat	Republican	Independent	Other member
Yes	High	Highest	Lowest	High
No	Low	Lowest	Highest	Low

Interpretation

Cell expectations match previous data. Expect significant chi square due to differences between Republicans and Independents. That difference would have to be about 10 points to have a substantive effect because of fewer Republicans.

BOX 8-5

CORRELATION

Item

Do you think you'll vote in the November election?

Very likely	Likely	Not Sure	Unlikely	Very Unlikely
5	4	3	2	1

Item

Looking at all the choices available to you, how do you rate the entire field of presidential candidates?

1 2 3 4 5 6 7 8 9 10

Poor   Fair   Excellent

Interpretation

Correlate intent to vote and rating of candidate field. Expect moderate positive (.30 to .50) correlation. Restricted range on either item will lower the correlation. Might be inverse if field ratings are generally low.

BOX 8-6

ANALYSIS OF VARIANCE

Item

How do you rate Anderson as a candidate?
1 2 3 4 5 6 7 8 9 10

How do you rate Carter as a candidate?
1 2 3 4 5 6 7 8 9 10

How do you rate Reagan as a candidate?
1 2 3 4 5 6 7 8 9 10

Even if you won't be voting or are ineligible to vote, if the election were held today, do you think you would vote for:

Anderson_____   Carter_____   Reagan_____

Interpretation

Divide the respondents into three groups by candidate choice (last question). Analyze rating for each candidate. Expect highest rating for chosen candidate (Anderson voters will rate Anderson highest and so on). All tests should be significant; should be a two-point difference for a substantive effect.

ANALYSIS OF EXPERIMENTAL PROTOCOLS

The application of statistical analysis in experimental protocols should be approached in the same a priori manner. Once the design has been determined and the statistical routine selected and the criterion measure(s) adopted, but before the collection of data, the experimenter should conduct a dry-run analysis. In this mock analysis, the researcher should go through all the steps from coding the criterion measure to preparing the data for computer analysis to evaluating the possible statistical results. To evaluate the possible statistical results, the analyst should list all possible decision outcomes of the test and develop a tentative explanation for what each outcome implies both substantively and methodologically.

For example, Bostrom and White (1979) were studying the effect of alcohol on logical reasoning. In their protocol, they tested subjects' logical reasoning abilities after an alcohol dossage which brought each subject's blood alcohol to the legally defined intoxication level. I piggybacked a study on the effect of alcohol on reported sexual behavior codes by giving respondents a sexual behavior code measure one week prior to the experimental trial and one hour after the dossage. The design I was using was a pre/post design with controls for gender and marital status. This design gave me four separate groups—female, single; female, married; male, single; male, married. In laying out the analysis, I had to consider sources of differences in all the possible combinations not just the ones that were suggested by previous work. This process forced me to make explicit my expectations for criterion differences between males and females between the married and single states, and the interaction between gender and marital state. When I discovered that I could not readily express my underlying theory, I realized that the evidence would be equivocal. That is, whatever I found my theory would adapt to it.[4] Consequently, I found myself without a hypothesis that could be fairly tested. The study had to be considered an exploration. The dry-run analysis, while its results were disappointing, prevented me from extending a poorly constructed study for review.

The most telling criticism of any statistical analysis is "so what?" If the researcher can't get the "so what" in place, the research is not likely to be worth doing. Prior analysis forces the researcher to explicitly state the meaning of the possible outcomes. Prior analysis does not prevent failure. It does help understand what that failure means for the analysis and for the theory which motivated it. Finally, prior analysis does not restrict the serendipitous finding— that "eureka" experience. Rather, it prepares the researcher to recognize it.

READING STATISTICS

Statistical tables and language can be an impenetrable barrier in the reading of social science research. This section is intended to be a guide through the thicket. The first step in understanding the role of the statistical analysis in a study is to identify the question that directs them. Often, that question is explicitly stated as a hypothesis, and at times, it must be inferred. Basically, there are three types of questions that can be approached in statistical analysis: questions of difference, questions concerning the level of association, and questions of structure.

• Questions of difference usually involve a greater frequency of one thing rather than another or a higher mean score for one group rather than another.

• Questions of association are directed toward the strength and direction of that association.

• Questions of structure are concerned with developing the underlying model that shows the relationship among several elemental variables.

Each of these questions has characteristic statistical analyses associated with them (see Table 8-1). Questions of difference over frequencies will be analyzed by chi square, over interval measures by *t*-tests of the means or ANOVA. Questions of association will use a correlation coefficient (see Table 7-8). Questions of structure will use one of the multivariate approaches.

The next step is to identify the protocol being used. First, within the general categories of survey and experimental, and then, specifically, what was done in what order. The protocol is the key to understanding the statistical analysis as evidence for some claim. As we have seen, the reader must evaluate its validity.

---

[4]Of course, even the most malleable theory can have limitations. The outcome that I was not prepared for was the finding of absolutely no change from the pretest to the posttest. Subjects, to a person, reproduced their performance on the pretest—item for item. Alcohol had no effect on their reported sexual behavior code measures. The testing scene, however, was bedlam. But, from that experience a theory of the social meaning rather than the physical effects of alcohol vis-à-vis sexual behavior began to develop.

Once you've matched question to statistical method within the protocol in place, identify the criterion measure(s). Unfortunately, little information is ordinarily given on the measures used. Nevertheless, even such statements as "a 16-item questionnaire was developed" are instructive. They tip you off on how to interpret significant and substantial effects.

Finally, put it all together by restating in your own language what the researcher is doing. Example: She expects students who take computer aided instruction to score higher on the final exam; he expects to find the core dimensions in a set of 100 items. Then examine the evidence to confirm or deny. You may well avoid much of the technical display with little loss. In the end, the author still has to convince you of the compelling case in favor of his or her claim.

SUMMARY

This chapter began with an explanation of the use of sample statistics as estimates of population parameters. It was found that when the sample can be considered to be free of systematic bias, many sample characteristics are unbiased estimates of the corresponding population characteristics. Such use ordinarily requires the acceptance of assumptions concerning the nature of the sample and of the population from which it was drawn.

The topic of inferential statistics as decision rules was then considered. When probability samples are used, inferential statistics can provide the basis for choosing between the null hypothesis and the alternate research hypothesis as explanations for an outcome. We found three components necessary for this use: the obtained sample characteristic as an estimate of a population parameter, an unexpected value for that estimate, and the known, formal probability distribution of that population parameter. This method generated information about the rate of Type I errors (accepting the alternate when the null is true). It does not inform us of the occasion.

Finally, we considered some practical methods of approaching and interpreting statistical analysis.

RELATED READINGS

Henkel, R. E. *Tests of significance.* Beverly Hills, CA: Sage Publications, Inc., 1976.
Lovejoy, E. P. *Statistics for math haters.* New York: Harper and Row, 1975.
Mueller, J. H., Schuessler, K. F. and Costner, H. L. *Statistical reasoning in sociology* (3d Ed.). Boston: Houghton Mifflin Co., 1977.
Runyon, R. P. and Haber, A. *Fundamentals of behavior statistics* (4th Ed.). Reading, MA: Addison-Wesley Publishing Co., 1980.

ISSUES AND METHODS IN QUALITATIVE RESEARCH

Having struggled through one research approach, it is now time to examine another. I would like to underline that qualitative research is not merely another set of methods. It is rather a different way of thinking about research in the human sciences. Quantitative and qualitative researchers find themselves in separate communities with different intellectual traditions, different normative practices, and different explanatory purposes, but both are directed to the creation of human scientific knowledge through theory based on empirical evidence.

Qualitative research in communication is much less conventionalized than quantitative research in our discipline. That is, there is general agreement on what the major methods of quantitative research should be and the meaning they should have in reference to theory building. In qualitative research, the major methods are those of participant observation, but there is considerable variation in what is permitted under that rubric and in the rules that connect evidence to theory. In this section, I have attempted one consistent view. Not all would agree with every point.

Chapter 9 presents an overview of qualitative research—its intellectual foundations, its major tenets and the broad outline of its methods. Chapter 10 examines design requirements which must be met before a research project reaches the field. Chapter 11 traces participant observation methods from one's entrance into the research site through the writing of field notes. Finally, Chapter 12 considers the route from field notes to theory.

AN INTRODUCTION TO QUALITATIVE RESEARCH

The qualitative community is small; in communication it is barely incorporated.[1] At this writing, communication's qualitative community is populated more by immigrants than native borns. That is, most of the people practicing qualitative research in communication received their training in traditional rationalistic research. They moved for various reasons. Nevertheless, in talking to many of them, I sensed an initial dissatisfaction with what could be accomplished in quantitative research followed by an excitement generated in their immersion in the lives of others. Researchers defend their hometown communities and argue over which is better. We will continue to bypass those arguments (until Chapter 13) and to simply consider what characterizes the research performance.

To begin, this chapter considers the intellectual heritage of qualitative research by briefly examining the founding texts and traditional concepts to which most members adhere. We then move to the normative characteristics which identify the purposes and justify the methods of current research. In the third section, the chapter outlines a set of practices which is true to the main lines being developed. Finally, the chapter introduces the common forms of argument used to move from evidence to theory.

INTELLECTUAL TRADITIONS OF QUALITATIVE RESEARCH

Prior to the 1700s, the study and comment on human behavior had been the province of metaphysics and theology. The 1700s saw science moving into this

[1]A survey of recent communication literature (Anderson, 1984) showed that out of an estimated 1100 articles published in the last five years, only 16 research pieces (as opposed to theory or commentary of which there were many more) appeared to be from this community.

reserve as proto-statisticians began to assemble their social facts. By the 1800s, with metaphysics and theology in full retreat, writers, particularly from the positivist school founded by Auguste Comte (1796–1857), were proclaiming that science (as exemplified by nineteenth-century physics) was the only legitimate intellectual activity. The aborning disciplines of psychology and sociology were beginning to apply natural science methods to the study of human behavior.

At the same time, there was a reaction to this extension of the perspective of the natural sciences into the study of human life. A loyal opposition was arguing that the natural sciences were all well and good at what they did, but the study of human behavior required a special insight and special methods. It is to these writings that we trace the modern **intellectual traditions** of qualitative research. These are the writings of Edmund Husserl (1859–1938), Max Weber (1864–1920), and Alfred Schutz (1899–1959). These writings all take a backward look to the seminal works of Immanuel Kant (1724–1804) who in his turn had been influenced by Descartes' meditations on the human mind. Beginning with Kant, I will touch very briefly on the central ideas of these four writers as they provide the foundation of qualitative research.

Immanuel Kant

In the context of these few paragraphs, the importance of Kant was his forceful argument that reality does not write its meaning on the human consciousness, but rather, that human consciousness approaches reality with certain embedded interpretations such as space and time. For Kant, our *knowledge* of the external world can exist only within those interpretations, but that world itself need not have those characteristics. Kant's conclusion was that our knowledge of the external world, which can be gained through strict empirical science, has definable limits. Certainly, *some* knowledge can be gained empirically, but not *all* knowledge.

Edmund Husserl and Phenomenology

Husserl, a mathematician turned philosopher, while "not rejecting science in any way," set out to demonstrate that science as an epistemological method was incomplete. His phenomenological epistemology is the intellectual touchstone of most qualitative methods. Phenomenological philosophy is the study of the manner in which experience is made meaningful within the human mind. As such, it seeks the axiomatic foundations of human knowledge. Of Husserl's many ideas, two are most apparent in the contemporary qualitative perspective: his emphasis on the lebenswelt and his method of the **epoche**.

Husserl believed that a person's fundamental connection with knowledge occurs within the trivial truths of everyday life—"that I am a person, that others exist, and that there is a world around me." The study of the human condition, including human knowledge, had to begin within the **lifeworld (lebenswelt)** of everyday existence. That emphasis on the mundane has been carried into qualitative research as a dictum that the lifeworld is *the* source of valid information about human action. The closer the analytic effort is to this lifeworld, the more direct its observation; the more it uses the concepts and language of this lifeworld, the greater its validity.

The epoche is Husserl's epistemological method by which we bracket or set aside what it is that we think we know about an object of inquiry in order that we may get to the essence of its nature. That essence or eidetic character is held in our consciousness—the meaning of things are contained within us—and is revealed as we perform the epoche on our experience. It is an exquisitely inductive method which begins empirically in the experience of things. It does not rest on this empirical evidence, but rather, ends in the intellectual grasp of the human mind. I would not pretend that these few lines interpret the method, but, then, the epoche, as Husserl developed it, is not the practice of contemporary qualitative scientists. Its modern-day translation is that each time the scientist approaches the study of human experience, she must set aside what she "already knows" and enter that study without supposition of what she will find. The epoche, then, is a purified form of scientific induction.

What is important to take from these few spare lines on Husserl for our understanding of present-day qualitative approaches is that their philosophical grounding is inductive, empirical idealism. That is, the phenomenological argument moves from particular experiences to an eidetic understanding which is the product of the human mind. The ultimate source of our knowledge is not "out there" pressing upon us, but is in our own consciousness.

Max Weber

Max Weber was a practicing sociologist concerned primarily with the explication of social policy. He was not a phenomenologist and would likely be uncomfortable with much of the literary effort in naturalistic inquiry. He is referenced by contemporary qualitative researchers for his declaration that **social action** was a proper subject matter; his insistence on an **empathic understanding** of social action (verstehen) in both its objective meaning (the meaning that can be viewed from the observer's perspective) and its subjective meaning (the meaning for the action held by the actor); and for the concept of **ideal types**.

Social actions are those behaviors which are produced by the individual in recognition of others. For example, as I type this page, I am involved in social action even though alone in my office. My act of pressing buttons is made meaningful by my intent to communicate. It is not the acts which are significant, but the meanings held for those acts.

Social action, therefore, is understandable not solely in the separate events of its acts, but more importantly, in the meanings that the individual and society hold for the action. The job of the analyst is not to describe the events (objective meaning) but the meaning of the action as held by the actor (subjective meaning). It is in these subjective meanings that one finds the causes and consequences of social action. In human behavior, phenomena are connected through the meanings held for them.

Weber's concept of verstehen or empathic understanding required the scientist to set aside his or her own normative rules of thinking and to "feel himself empathically into a mode of thought which deviates from his own" (Weber, 1949, p. 41). It is in this method of empathic understanding that one can achieve propositions about human behavior which can account for meaning.

For Weber, one form of these propositions is in ideal types. Ideal types are theoretical constructs which embody the essence of a social actor—a military commander, bureaucrat, teacher, student. These ideal social actors, within their own meaning context, "must act entirely without error and in a logically 'perfect' way" (Weber, 1949, p. 42). It is through the analysis of ideal types that we can come to understand the actions of individual commanders, bureaucrats, teachers, students.

Qualitative researchers have wholeheartedly accepted Weber's emphasis on meaning rather than behaviors as the proper object of study. Whatever the branch, and there are several, the understanding and explication of the meaning of social action is central to qualitative research. Verstehen is a virtual talisman within qualitative research with a meaning so expanded that it represents little of Weber's notion. It does signify, however, a dedication to the actor's rather than the observer's viewpoint. The concept of ideal types finds less direct representation in present-day qualitative research, although the composite characters that regularly appear in qualitative narratives are conceptually the same.

Alfred Schutz

Husserl and Weber provided the conceptual material from which Schutz constructed the foundation of a genuine phenomenological sociology. Schutz's primary contribution is his orderly argument from phenomenological philosophy to the nature of theoretical constructs in the human sciences. In this argument, he interprets Husserl's notions of the natural attitude by which individuals make sense of the lifeworld and of levels of conscious reality. Further, he clarifies and expands on Weber's ideas of social action, meaning, and ideal types. Having presented these ideas, he adds his own conception of the structure of the social world detailing the substantive differences between our direct experiences in face-to-face relationships and the indirect, objectified knowledge we have of our contemporaries and predecessors.

I can expand on this table of contents listing just slightly. Schutz provides three fundamental concepts which are held by current qualitative researchers: the **constitutive interpretation of experience**, the **intersubjectivity of meaning**, and his expansion on the theory of ideal types. A short presentation of each follows.

The Constitutive Interpretation of Experience   For Schutz, actual experience is a continuous flow, a flux with endless horizons extending into the future and into the past. That experience becomes consciously meaningful to us "after the fact" in constitutive acts of interpretation. In these acts, we isolate segments of the continuum of experience in space and time, ascribe to it motives which connect it with the past and the future, and give it the meaning which describes who we are and what we are about. The answer to the question of "What are we doing now?" is an interpretation based not on the behaviors we are exercising, but on the actions (activity which is meaningful to us) that we are performing. For experience to be meaningful, it must be interpreted, and what experience signifies is dependent upon that interpretation. Our common-sense knowledge is based upon the accumulated stock of these interpreted experiences. We further act upon this stock of knowledge interpreting its components to a higher level of generality. These interpreted constructs form the facts of our world.

As you can see, we have rapidly departed from primitive empiricism to a form of empirical idealism where knowledge is a synthesis of experience and the interpretive acts of consciousness. Further, what directs those acts of interpretation is not the experience but the character of the human mind.

Of course, the individual operating in the everyday world attends to none of this. In the natural attitude of everyday living, we take for granted the facts provided by our interpretations. That natural attitude assumes five primary interpretations to be unquestionably true:

1 *The preexistence of the social world.* The social world, *as the individual knows it,* existed prior to him or her and will continue after his or her death.

2 *The conformance of the external world.* The external world is ordered and meaningful in the way that the individual knows it. That is, objective reality conforms to one's understanding of it.

3 *The validity of experience.* One's understanding of one's own experience and the experience of others is essentially correct. What I experience is true and directly knowable.

4 *The correspondence of perspective.* Others come to know their experience in the same way that I do. If we were to trade places, life would have the same meaning for each of us.

5 *The world is defined within the individual's purposes.* All elements of the world are not significant; those which attend to our purposes are. The character of the world for the individual, then, can, in kaliedoscopic fashion, change as one's purposes change.

As Leiter (1980) points out, Schutz's interpretation of the natural attitude formulates it *as an object of scientific study.* Qualitative scientists have shown different concerns as they investigate the natural attitude.[2] Phenomenologists (or interpretivists as they are coming to be known in communication) are primarily concerned with explicating the content of the meaning structures that develop within a social system. Ethnomethodologists focus on the methods and practices which create and maintain these meaning structures. And symbolic interactionists have been more interested in the performances of individuals in their presentation of the roles contained within a society.

---

[2]Monica Morris (1977) provides an insightful review.

The Intersubjective Nature of Meaning   The second major concept drawn from Schutz's synthesis is his detailed analysis of how intersubjectivity develops. If one's understanding of reality is a constructed interpretation, how is it that members of a society can share common views? Why do we not each develop our own idiosyncratic understanding of reality? The answer for Schutz is that we spend our lives in face-to-face relationships in which we share a common, lived experience continually reflecting on each other's interpretation.

Schutz's concept of intersubjectivity,[3] along with the theorizing of George Hubert Mead, has led to the Berger and Luckmann (1967) thesis of the **social construction of reality**. This thesis is a central theme within most of qualitative research. It holds that what an individual's experience signifies is a function of the social system in which he or she resides. This concept does not imply that we all get together to determine what the characteristics of the physical world will be. It does mean that the manner in which we respond to those characteristics— our explanation for them, our uses of them, the value we place on them—is the result of the negotiated constructs we mutually hold. In short, our understanding of life is relative to the system in which we live.

The concept of the social construction of reality has some far-reaching implications for the character of scientific explanation. First, it places in jeopardy the reductionist goal. One must wonder whether there can be a finite set of principles which will explain human behavior if the causes and consequences of such behavior are dependent on the meaning system in which that behavior appears. The possibility of an infinite number of combinations stretches before us.

Second, the explanations that can be developed would appear to be limited in generality. That is, I may be able to develop an explanation for a system at a point in time, but that explanation would not transfer to another system or to the same system in a different era.

Finally, the social construction thesis places heavy emphasis on the relativism of all explanation, including scientific explanation. For example, if one happens to live in a society in which the structure of matter is considered to be best explained by atomic theory, then, as that explanation is used (it could, of course be ignored), certain consequences will occur within that society. If, on the other hand, one lives in a society where the structure of matter is explained through spiritual essences, radically different consequences will occur. It is not that one is a better explanation of physical reality; they are both, after all, inventions. It is that they enable the different societies to accomplish different things. Consequently, traditional notions of intrinsic validity are no longer appropriate for many qualitative researchers.

---

[3]Note the important difference between the meaning of intersubjectivity here and the way it was used in quantitative research. For the quantitative researcher, intersubjective agreement was the method by which one controlled idiosyncratic views of reality—what could be reported reliably by several observers met the standard of objectivity. Here intersubjectivity is the method by which we create the ability to see our common view of reality.

The Theory of Ideal Types   That intersubjectivity would lead to the rejection of three pillars of rationalistic science (reductionistic, generalizeable, and true) was not envisaged by Schutz. He argued,

> that the interpretive schemes of the social sciences must be compatible not merely with experience of the social world but with scientific experience as a whole. The original and fundamental scheme of science, the expressive scheme of its propositions, and the interpretive scheme of its explanations is, therefore, essentially that of formal logic (1967, p. 223).

To accomplish this task, Schutz expanded on Weber's notion of ideal types. For Schutz, the way I know my contemporaries—the people I know to be out there but with whom I have no face-to-face relationship—and my predecessors is through the construction of ideal types. Ideal types at this level are the subjective understandings that one has of people not known as individuals. I am knowledgeable about students at the University of Utah in a way that someone at Michigan or Frieberg cannot be. However, I know only relatively few students; my knowledge resides in a typification from my stock of knowledge which arises from the many experiences that I have had with Utah students.

Scientific ideal types are developed within known methods (more likely formal logic than empirical inquiry for Schutz) using public evidence. The scientific ideal type is a model of an individual performing perfectly to type. It is a "puppet," to use Schutz's analogy, whose every response is determined by the logical strings of motive attached to it by the scientist. Through these puppets we can model pure social action.

In this formulation, Schutz emphasizes a sharp distinction between scientific knowledge and common-sense knowledge (the living knowledge of the individual). Common-sense knowledge falls within a subjective meaning context; scientific knowledge in an objectified meaning context. Only in the subjective meaning context can we have direct knowledge of human experience. Of scientific knowledge, Schutz writes:

> All scientific knowledge is indirect. It is knowledge of the world of contemporaries and the world of predecessors never of the world of immediate social reality. Accordingly, the social sciences can understand man in his everyday social life not as a living individual person with a unique consciousness, but only as a personal ideal type without duration or spontaneity. They can understand him only as existing within an impersonal and anonymous objective time which no one ever has, or ever can, experience (1967, p. 241).

To many qualitative researchers who consider the writings of Schutz to be a touchstone, this quotation is a shock. One of the many directions pursued by qualitative researchers is to make explicit the lived experience of the individual. Denzin (1983), for example, argues that his purpose is to achieve an expression of "the first order, primary lived concepts of everyday life" (p. 132). He continues:

This world does not stand still, nor will it conform to the scientist's logical schemes of analysis. It contains its own dialectic and its own internal logic. This meaning can only be discovered by the observer's participation in the world (p. 133).

His is a much different standard than Schutz's.

Phenomenology and "Normal Science"

The movement of **phenomenology** presents one other legacy to qualitative research. It is a tradition of opposition to "normal science." As I noted, it was not Husserl's intent to reject science but to properly define its place within human knowledge. In phenomenology, science is a second-order, limited epistemology which has shown great success within its own territory. As phenomenology gathered strength, the rival position of Comte was being extended by a group of philosophers called "Logical Positivists." The positivists were and still are primarily concerned with the role of evidence and logical argument in science. Their vigorous commitment to empirical science has, on occasion, been associated with scientism.

Phenomenology's criticism of positivism has led it to be associated with an antiscience position. At the heart of both philosophies neither association is true, but in the political maneuvering for station within the institutions of both philosophy and science, these two communities have found themselves in opposition.

A Closing Thought

Certainly, part of the excitement in qualitative research is that conflicts over the objects of study and explanatory purposes abound. In this developing community, there is no idealized form of research to which we can point as a model. Most members, however, would recognize Husserl, Weber, and Schutz as part of their intellectual tradition while reserving the right to move on from them. What we reviewed here traced the sources of the underlying concepts of that tradition. In the next section, we discover the manner in which these concepts form the foundation of contemporary qualitative research.

BASIC CONCEPTS OF QUALITATIVE RESEARCH

First among the fundamental concepts of qualitative research is the axiom that the study of human life is an interpretive science. The causes and consequences of human behavior are not in objectified attributes but in the meanings that are held by individuals. It is the purpose of the social scientist to make explicit those meanings by interpreting the social action of others. Toward this end, the scientist is both aided by and responsible for that special empathic understanding which is possible because we are both the analyst and object of our own study.

All experience, including the experience of the scientist, is made meaningful in constitutive acts of interpretation. These acts segment the continuum of experience to create "sequences of action" which are infused with purpose and cause. These interpretations by which experience is brought into consciousness are ingenuous, practiced by the natural man and woman. They result in the taken-for-granted facts of everyday life.

The meanings that direct these interpretations arise within the intersubjective alliances we form in face-to-face relationships. An individual's view of the world is not idiosyncratic but developed in the multitude of social negotiations we call "relationships."

The natural person practicing the natural attitude in everyday life creates and maintains the world *as we know it*. It is the purpose of science to explicate these taken-for-granted facts.

The scientist must approach the lifeworld within the natural attitude first as a naive participant and then as a critical observer because socially constructed meanings become most apparent when we participate in their construction and reflect on those constitutive acts.

Scientific knowledge can explain common-sense knowledge, its characteristics, the methods by which it is produced and maintained, its causes and consequences. Scientific knowledge, however, cannot replace common-sense knowledge. We must live from that stock of interpreted experiences not from scientific explanation, although our experiences may include ones involving science.

Common-sense knowledge, therefore, is not a flawed form of scientific knowledge. Common-sense knowledge exists in the subjective meaning context of experience. Scientific knowledge exists in an objectified meaning context of abstract symbols. In experience, we can know the individual directly. Science can never reach knowledge of the individual, but only of ideal typifications.

NORMATIVE CHARACTERISTICS OF QUALITATIVE RESEARCH

Given its phenomenological undergirdings, qualitative research has developed a set of normative characteristics which distinguishes it as its own scientific approach. These characteristics do not appear in every qualitative research study. In fact, many a qualitative research study will show only one or two of these norms. The value of these norms is that they permit us to formalize what an ideal type of qualitative research ought to look like. They also permit us to show that the differences between this research and rationalistic research are more than the appearance of numbers or a particular method, but rather, are inherent in the intellectual structure of the two approaches. In my listing of these norms, I have provided the contrasting norm in parentheses.

Inductive (Deductive)

Qualitative research places primary emphasis on inductive methods. This emphasis is derived from the proposition that each social system is uniquely constructed. In order to be responsive to these unique qualities, the initial analytical attack must be free from distorting expectations of a priori constructs. The analyst's responsibility is to provide an interpretation from the member's viewpoint. To do so, the analyst must first discover and, then, adopt that viewpoint. If one investigates social action with a preconceived set of interpretive templates (such as a generalized theory of social action), the member's viewpoint will be lost.

The term "presuppositionless research" is often used to describe this characteristic. This term does not mean that the researcher is somehow a cultural blank without norms, values, and ideology. It means that the researcher makes his or her own norms, values, and ideology apparent and does not assume that they are those of the members. We can contrast this approach with that of, say, a survey where the researcher must assume that the meanings and ideology embedded within the questions are shared by the respondents. In a survey, the researcher's meanings are the only meanings permitted to appear.

The inductive emphasis does not mean that theory is absent. Beyond its metatheoretical axioms (the primacy of meaning, etc.), qualitative research uses theory to define its objects of interest. For example, Pettigrew (1982) was concerned with the manner in which leadership got expressed within the management style evident in an academic center. His theories of leadership and management, both explicit and implied, clearly directed his investigation. The empirical content of those constructs, however, was not presupposed. Pettigrew allowed the organization to show him what it meant by leadership within the management style expressed in that system.

Deduction, too, makes its appearance within properly designed qualitative research. The analyst's interpretations of the member's viewpoint can be profitably used as hypotheses seeking confirmation. For example, if I hear a "hierarchical manager"[4] say, "You might want to take action on the Jenkins problem," I am presented with a number of possible interpretations. The statement could be a simple command stated indirectly. The statement could be a directive with an invitation to participate in the decision process. The statement could be the presentation of an alternative with no imperative implied, and so on. How do I choose among these possible interpretations? First of all, I may not be able to as they may all be true at different times or even simultaneously.[5] But, by observing the response to the statement and the response to the response, I may begin to build a tentative description of a characteristic of this manager. That characteristic might imply certain outcomes, certain modes of behavior. These implications can be tested in spontaneously

---

[4]A manager can be described by office or action. Here, I am using the office as a definition. The example focuses only on the manager's meaning for the turn. The hierarchical subordinate's meaning for the turn is a separate analysis.

[5]An individual, for example, may discover what was wanted by what was received. It is a particular theoretical stance to presume that the initiator of a communication has a single or even an established meaning for the turn.

appearing or researcher-instigated episodes. These hypotheses are within the system. That is, they do not presume that all managers behave according to this characteristic (or even that this manager always behaves thus). On the other hand, it is presumed that there are useful regularities to the lives that are lived.

Eidetic (Atomistic)

The normative level of explanation in qualitative research is that of understanding. It directs its attention to the "heart of the matter." Understanding what is going on is not a matter of cataloguing the component elements. It involves that *voilà* insight which puts it all together. Beginning qualitative researchers sometimes substitute a rendition of their field notes for this insight. The field notes will document the sequence of acts, but it takes the insight to understand what action is being completed.

Wolf, Meyer, and White (1982) provide a good example of eidetic analysis. They document the integration of television use within the social interactions of a middle-aged, childless couple. The analysis is not limited to simply the times when the set is on, but attempts to show how the content of the medium and the activity of viewing are part of the context of this couple's lives. For these authors, television viewing is not something that happens independent of, or in a manner irrelevant to, everything else. Rather, it is an activity which is made meaningful by its relationship to every other activity. The authors give a good example of the rule of eidetic analysis, which states that the analyst must understand the totality before the meaning of the parts becomes apparent.

Subjective (Objective)

The normative explanatory purpose of qualitative research is to explicate the commonly held meaning of things. It is directed toward the subjectively held realities of social action. It considers social action from the meaning perspective of the actors. Meaning obviously resides at a number of levels. It would be difficult to think of any middle-class urbanite who would be unaware of the concept of the technological revolution occurring as the microcomputer enters more and more of our offices and homes. We can certainly consider what is the common meaning of this concept among a general population group such as this one. On the other hand, we would not expect those meanings to be indicative of the meanings held by the soldiers in this revolution—the individuals who use the micro in their work and leisure. Further into these layers of meaning, we would expect individual work groups to develop particular meanings for the revolution according to the manner in which it gets expressed in their day-to-day contact with the technology. As one of those latter individuals, I can abstractly talk about the social implications of computers with my neighbors and more directly compare notes with those who work with other computers in other applications, but my most intensive and extensive conversations will be with those who do the work I do on the same type of machine I use, for it is with them that I share the most.

The analyst may choose to explicate any or all of the layers of meaning. Hiemstra (1983) chose to study the common meanings of information technology held by operators in four different organizations. Working at this level, he is trying to explain the meanings that an individual would share with workers of the same type. These are clearly not all the meanings that the individual would hold. In my work environment, for example, there are continuing discussions about who can use the computer for what purposes. I would not expect these particular shared meanings about this technology to be common with others in other environments, although the fact of conflict may be.

In pursuing the actor's perspective, the notion of the actor requires a thorough specification. Who the actor is and what the actor represents changes the nature of the subjective. My perspective on the technological revolution as the actor in a dyadic relationship with my associate is not my perspective on this revolution in a party conversation on computers. The shared reality of technology is quite different in these two contexts.

Hiemstra's actors are typified operators, not individuals. The meanings he explains are those that transcend a particular work environment. One of the meanings, for example, that he describes is a quality of magic. In that description, there is no claim that all hold technology as a magical concept, nor is the claim that every organization will have someone who believes that technology is magical. The claim is, rather, that the idea of magic can be used meaningfully by those who work with information technology. The statement "Information technology is like magic" would be seen as an acceptable statement to make about info tech even if believed to be incorrect. The statement "Information technology is like a toad" would not, because the reality of the toad-like qualities of information technology has not been developed (but, remember, you read it here first).

The norm of subjectivity is the demand that the scientist be responsible through systematic analysis for the meanings held at the level of social action approached. The analyst is specifically enjoined from taking for granted the interchangeability of the perspectives of researcher and respondent.

Contextual (Generalizeable)

The meaning structures that integrate into social realities are formed within the holistic envelopment of a context. There are, therefore, multiple realities which govern the relationship among phenomena for the individual. Context is not merely the setting in which the action takes place. It is the interpretation of that setting by the actor. Whether in my room at the office building or in the office in my house, I am "at work" in these different settings. My responses are governed by the contextual meaning of being at work rather than the location of the action.

The concept of contextually embedded, multiple realities implies that explanation, too, is contextually bound—what is true for one context is not necessarily true for another. There are definitive limits on the extensibility of explanation. These limits are not like the quantitative researcher's idea of middle-range theory. Middle-range theory is an attempt to be realistic about what range of explanation can be achieved by the social sciences. If we can't achieve "grand theory," then settle for "middle-range theory." For the qualitative researcher there is no possibility of a grand theory of social action (except its own metatheory, of course)—theory is contextually bound. Instead of being directed to reduce theory by integrating narrow range theory into broader range theory, the qualitative researcher is directed to proliferate theory. The qualitative researcher's aim is to add to the library of discourse on human life—this library is ever expandable.

James and McCain (1982) give us a good example of contextually bound explanation. They studied the children of a preschool which made use of television viewing as a regular part of the program. James, who was responsible for creating the ethnographic record, was specifically interested in the manner in which the content of television would show up in the games these children played. In their analysis of the record and interviews, the authors found that the children used the content to create characters and story lines to fill primal themes of good guys/bad guys, house and family, and the like. The value of the study is that it shows the reader one method that children can use to solve the problems presented by play. Further, it describes the circumstances under which this method emerged. The authors point out that their analysis is exactly one example of the use of television in play.

The context in this study is more than the preschool program, more than the presence of television. It is also the teachers, the researchers, the specific children enrolled, and, most importantly, their shared understanding of what is proper in play.

Mundane (Purified)

If the purpose of qualitative research is to explain social action in everyday life and if explanation is contextually bound, then clearly the ordinary and everyday must be the context of qualitative inquiry. The researcher has to be where it happens. Experimental protocols, simulations, and other constructions are not considered unless the intent is to explain performances within them, e.g., the social action of responding to a survey.

Mundaneness also expresses an attitude that what happens in everyday life is important to know systematically, explicitly. That the way ordinary people conduct their affairs is not brutish but elegant, even in its pain and sorrow, with finely drawn variegations in meaning. The human consciousness is not the consequence of social action but its creator. It is an attitude which should replace academic elitism with wonder.

Of all the normative characteristics of qualitative research, the argument for the mundane (at least in settings, if not in attitude) seems to be most attractive to the human sciences in general. It is the *sine qua non* of qualitative research—other characteristics are likely to be missing, but not this one.

Textual (Measurable)

The analysis of the meaning of social action cannot be conducted directly. Meaning is a fact of consciousness, not of behavior or its artifacts. What is present to the analyst is a text—a text of behavior and its artifacts—from which the intentional meaning must be read. That text is itself removed from experience. It is not the moment-by-moment flow of energy, but is experience captured within some notational scheme. That notational scheme may be one's memories, field notes, audio or video recordings, and/or the products created in couture, cuisine, performance, or manufacture. Each text is a transformation of experience, not its representation.

The first job of the analyst, then, is to create the text, whether by observation and its record in memory and notes, or recordings or collections of artifacts. The next step is to explicate its meaning. The text is not the behavior; it is not the experience or the meaning of the experience, but it contains some form of all three. The scientist will sort all that out and then make that analysis accessible to the reader.

The metaphor of text, that I am using here, is intended to force the recognition that science does not contact experience directly, that there is not a one-to-one correspondence between what I experience as an individual and what I analyze as a scientist, and that the meaning of social action is as problematic as the meaning of any text. Textual meaning, is, after all, both **promiscuous** and **prolific**. The text has some meaning for everyone, and each time we contact the text, new meanings arise.

Anderson and Eastman (1983) in their study of the meanings of computers for a group of eighth-grade science students give a good example of the textual quality of naturalistic data. This study was part of a number of studies all of which used some aspect of the classroom performance of teachers and students as the text of analysis. In the Anderson and Eastman study, the aspect was the interactive conversations between either of two teachers and the participating student(s). Each teacher was wired to record these conversations. It was my job to create a transcription and to search the conversational episodes for those which evidenced the meanings held for those classroom computers. Here is an example:

> *T:* And you're having all this problem, huh?
> S: Yeah, cause it stuu . . . God, these stupid computers.
> *T:* They really frustrate you.
> *S:* I'm not ready for the computer age yet.
> *T:* You're not ready for the computer age.[6]

---

[6]These four lines demonstrate many of the technical problems of transcription. People do not ordinarily speak in grammatical sentences or even in whole words. These characteristics are accepted in speech but are startling in print.

Without attempting a full exegesis, consider the phrase "these stupid computers." Computers are indeed stupid—fast but stupid. Is that what is meant here? Or is the student expressing irritation because she cannot master the sequence of commands necessary to use the machine? The teacher seems to interpret her response in that way, but she neither confirms nor denies his interpretation. You can certainly grasp a meaning of those five lines (meaning is promiscuous), indeed, probably several (meaning is prolific). But can we determine the meaning of these lines for these actors? And can we determine what social action is being accomplished? The best and only thing that can be done is to give an interpretation. The analyst cannot find the meaning through the application of better and better methods. The analyst must create a meaning which is sensible to the reader and possible within the shared understanding of the actors in this conversational episode.

Preservationistic (Aggregated)

Qualitative explanation attempts to preserve the individual within the context of the social action. It does this by using the actual words, providing lengthy descriptions of performances, showing the artifacts or detailed representations of the artifacts that emanate from the individuals observed. The naturally occurring behavior of the individual is the fundamental evidence in the arguments of qualitative research.

Unlike quantitative research, which aggregates what are determined to be functionally equivalent responses by ignoring individual differences, qualitative research avoids aggregation to detail the individual. Quantitative research emphasizes the aggregate because its explanatory intent is reductionistic. Qualitative research emphasizes the individual because its explanatory intent is expansionistic. In quantitative research, a theoretical construct gains import when more of the individual behavior can be aggregated within its definitional confines or when the rate of behavior so defined is relatively high. In qualitative research, a single occurrence establishes the place of a theoretical construct.

Qualitative research's celebration of the individual does not imply that there can be no categorization, no identification of communalites among individuals. It does mean that the categories will be defined inductively rather than operationally. **Inductive categories** are defined by the exemplars contained within them. They arise after the observational text has been created. Stoll (1983) in her dissertation gives a good account of this process. She was interested in the one-on-one, interactive conversations between teacher and student in the high school classroom. She recorded and transcribed several hours of classroom talk and then identified each interactive episode. (Note the creation of the text.) Sorting through these episodes (all of which were on separate pieces of paper), she asked herself, "What happens when I bring these episodes together; can I make sense of them as a group?" When she could, a category was formed[7] made up of her initial set plus any additions from all the other episodes.

---

[7] This is a creative act of insight, not an inevitable consequence.

The meaning of that category was entirely contained in (her interpretation of) the episodes grouped under it. If the episodes were dispersed into other groupings, the category would disappear. There are no empty sets in inductive logic.

In Stoll's study, there was no miscellaneous category for all the single case events as there would be in a rationalistic study. Those episodes which needed to stand alone were left alone as an individual category of an event which happens rarely or perhaps uniquely in her classrooms. There were, of course, episodes which made no sense to her. Episodes which drew upon but did not reveal the history of interaction between the actors, or which were not true interactions (turns contiguous on a tape were not necessarily intended to be interactive), or which were marred by production errors (people misspeak), or were beyond Stoll's interpretive capacity. Leftovers such as these occur in both quantitative and qualitative studies.

Interactive (Independent)

Qualitative research focuses on the interactions among social actors. The scientist, regardless of his or her presence, is always one of those actors. It is an axiom of qualitative research that the investigator is the instrument. The investigator creates the data in the text to be analyzed. Given this axiom and the axiom that to deeply understand the meanings of social action one must participate in their creation and/or maintenance, the qualitative scientist is strongly encouraged to be part of the action to be analyzed. The analyst is directed to become a member or, at least, approach member status of the group in which the social action occurs. This directive translates into the primary method of qualitative research—participant observation. In qualitative research, both participation and observation must be demonstrated.

Pure observation cannot reveal the perspective of the actors. If, for example, I were to watch a videotape of a Nepalese dance, it is my estimation that I would have no idea of its meaning. The meaning is expressed; it's there for all to see, but my ignorance is so complete that anything I said would be a simpleton's guess. Perhaps I could go to the library, read all there is on Nepalese dancing, and then analyze the videotape. The analysis that I could then provide would be lexigraphical—I could define the terms of movement. I would still have no idea of what was being expressed by those dancers in the context of that performance.

Pure participation will not reveal the perspective of the actors either. A perspective can be grasped only when it is rendered problematic, when it is no longer taken for granted, when it is held in contrast to some other perspective. To do that, I have to step outside of my participation and to examine the carefully created text of that participation. In the analysis of those observations, I now have the tremendous advantage of having experienced the meanings revealed.

Participation can occur on many different levels. Physical presence as a member is typically considered best. It's not always possible; one does what one can. One cannot be a member of another family. I was not present during the science classroom conversations that took place 1500 miles away. The loss in interpretive ability was noticeable. There were episodes that I could not understand because I had not been there. For my coauthor, the meaning of these episodes was clear because she had participated in them.

Interpretive (Material)

The explanation derived from qualitative inquiry is considered an interpretation. This interpretation is a function of the interaction between the analyst and the observational text. Vary the text or the analyst and the interpretation will vary. Once again, we meet the postulates of meaning: Meaning is promiscuous and prolific; it is the product of human consciousness and is not contained in objects. If explanation is one interpretation among many, what can be the truth value of any given interpretation? Generally, truth with a capital "T" is considered unknowable if not impossible. An explanation can be true relative to its own system of evidence. As there are many interpretations, there can be many truths. That there can be many true interpretations does not mean that every interpretation is true. Some are frivolous, incomplete, flawed, or deceptive.

In science, the frivolous interpretation is one that proceeds from inadequate data, perhaps derived from shallow penetration into the social action, insufficient observation, or a lack of participation. The incomplete interpretation shows a deficient analysis—usually the failure to account for the observational text. A flawed or defective interpretation is one which fails the test of evidence. Claims are advanced for which there is no meaningful connection to the observational text. Deceptive interpretations are those which fail to be true to the perspective they claim to represent. They occur when the scientist has not performed the epoche but has insisted on a position of foreknowing. They occur when a priori constructs masquerade as **inductive categories** or when no effort has been made to reveal the standpoint of the social actors.

Qualitative research is unabashedly interpretive, but it is not idiosyncratic. It is not a chaotic, "anything goes" endeavor. It appeals to intersubjectivity within its rules of evidence. Its explanation must derive from the empirical evidence presented and must be sensible to all who are equally literate in that evidence. That other sensible explanations can arise from that evidence simply confirms, for the qualitative researcher, the nature of human knowledge.

A Summary Analysis of Qualitative Norms

The ideal form of qualitative research is inductive, eidetic, subjective, contextual, mundane, textual, preservationistic, interactive, and interpretive. Little of what is currently available in the communication journals approaches this ideal form. That is not the case in all journals. But there is little doubt that the form of qualitative research is currently distorted by the overwhelming presence of the rationalistic perspective. Most of what we see is not the interpretation of social action, but the content analysis of mundane data.

Nevertheless, there is wide subscription to these nine norms. Their importance to us is that they set the parameters for the methods to be used to conduct scientific inquiry from the perspective of qualitative research. The outline of those methods is the subject of the next major section.

EXERCISES

1 How can the writings of Kant and Husserl be seen as reactions to scientism?
2 Empiricism holds that experience delivers reality to the human consciousness; idealism holds that reality precedes experience in the human consciousness. What is the relationship between reality and experience for the empirical idealism of Schutz?
3 How is a dictionary an artifact of the intersubjectivity of meaning?
4 What is the significance of the notion of the social construction of reality for understanding human behavior?
5 Contrast the starting points of quantitative research and qualitative research.
6 Why can an eidetic understanding of social action never be reached by the careful study of the component behavioral acts?
7 What does the dictum, "The explanatory responsibility of the subjective is the actor in context" mean?
8 Does the concept of "nonobtrusive measures" have any meaning in qualitative research?
9 The statements "My data are valid observations of reality" and "My text is a valid interpretation of social reality" exemplify what characteristics of the two research perspectives?

DOING QUALITATIVE RESEARCH

Qualitative research[8] begins in our own experience. It is in our own lifeworld that we discover that the lifeworld of others is different from our own and, therefore, worthy of our study. It is because of this principle that studies typically have an "Us-Them" property about them. Western anthropologists study island cultures; middle-class academics study the urban poor. This research, then, is an encounter with "others" in an attempt to discover and publicly document their meaning of the world. I describe the process in four steps: (1) encountering the other, (2) creating the research text, (3) composing episodes, and (4) moving to theory (see Figure 9-1).

Encountering the Other

Our scientific encounters can vary in the same way that our everyday encounters can vary. A study might start with the chance realization that something is going on, or the encounter may be motivated by a general desire "to get to know those folks," or it may be directed by specific interests about given people in particular

---

[8]At this point, I will drop the qualitative modifier except where I am specifically contrasting the two perspectives. When research and its synonyms are used without modification, the qualitative perspective is implied.

SOCIAL ACTION

Becomes the intentional object of study in

> The experience of
> **PARTICIPANT OBSERVATION**

which is critically analyzed and structured to produce

> **THE RESEARCH TEXT**
> of field notes, interviews, artifacts, etc.,

from which abstract concepts are extracted in

> **EPISODES**

which are used as evidence for the knowledge claims of the

> **ETHNOGRAPHIC ARGUMENT**

FIGURE 9-1
The texts (boxes) and analytic moves of naturalistic inquiry.

settings. The Wolf, Meyer, and White study begins when a graduate student rents a room from a couple and lives in their home. Pacanowsky and Anderson (1982) begin their study on "Cop Talk and Media Use" with "a curiosity about the world of the police officer" (p. 741). Anderson and Eastman (1983) are specifically interested in the social meaning of computer technology within a given eighth-grade class. The first step, then, is to identify the encounter and to define the conditions under which it will take place.

In defining these conditions, the researcher can make use of the journalist's five "W's" and an "H"—who, what, where, when, why, and how.

The "who" (not a rock group) is first defined by the level of the encounter—with an individual (in a researcher/respondent dyad), members of a group, people in an organization, institution, or aggregated by action or purpose (e.g., standing in a ticket line). There follows, as the research progresses, the development of relationships with the particular individuals who, with the researcher, will "create" the **research text**. They are the individuals for whom the researcher has responsibility.

The "what" is the social action to be explained. The social action might be organizing, befriending, studying, going to school, conversing, working, reading the newspaper, and so on. The grammatical form here is noteworthy. It emphasizes that social action is an activity, not an object. Friendship is known in the joint acts of befriending enacted by the friendship pair, an organization in the constitutive acts of organizing generated by the members. The researcher is responsible for understanding the process of the action not merely cataloging the component acts.

"Where" identifies the locations or settings within which the social action will be studied. This concept is not quite as simple as identifying the place of study. The researcher has to consider the manner in which location is integrated into the action. The appropriate and inappropriate places of performance are an important part of the discovery.

"When" obviously concerns the schedule of contacts which will be maintained by the researcher. Not so obviously, it also concerns the timing of performances within the action. With an emphasis on naturally occurring performances in everyday settings, little gets done at the researcher's convenience. The researcher deals with the actors within a finite time frame. The significant contact times have to be identified—the important meetings, the special moments of disclosure.

"Why" identifies the purpose of the inquiry's explanation—(a) to specify the characteristics of the social action, (b) to reveal the methods and practices which create and sustain the social reality in which it gets performed, or (c) to determine the causes and consequences of the action within that reality. These, of course, are the three explanatory purposes of any scientific inquiry. Remember that in qualitative studies the characteristics, methods and practices, and causes and consequences are not objectified as being independent of the specific individuals involved in a particular time and place. The characteristics, methods and practices, and causes and consequences are understood from the perspective of the actor.

Finally, the "how" specifies the course the participant-observation will take. Specifying the conditions of participant-observation is governed by three requirements of research: The researcher must have access to the action, gain acceptance by the actors, and have the competence to participate. Each of these three can pose serious difficulties for the research plan.

Access is a problem with any social group whose performances are not public. Researchers cannot observe if they cannot be present. The researcher's access may be governed by choice, custom, policy, law, time, place, or finances. Interviews are often substituted when access is not possible. But, because interviews are themselves a performance, it is difficult to assay their value as a substitute.

The researcher *gains acceptance* when his or her presence has been legitimized. A researcher's presence has been legitimized when it is accommodated within the routine of the other. In aggregates and loosely organized groups, the researcher may gain all rights and privileges of membership. In more coherent groups, it is rather unlikely that this legitimate position will mean full-member status. Such is not necessary, but it is necessary for the researcher to know his or her place as the members define it. Our everyday experiences are clearly instructive about the difficulties of gaining acceptance in well-formed groups. It requires persistence, vulnerability, and resilience. The qualitative researcher is a peculiar animal who spends a professional life being the numbskull of the group.

The *level of competence* necessary to participate obviously varies according to the social action and membership. Competence may involve physical character-istics, certifications, language ability, specialized training, skill levels, and the like. I am not competent to participate as a team member within a women's softball league. I have to accept a different kind of insight available as a male associate. It is important for me not to mistake the two.

Competence is a persistent problem when dealing with a group widely different in age. Children remain a mystery because we can study them only as adults. Again, I have to accept a lesser insight.

Designing the qualitative study involves the solutions to the problems of access, acceptance, and competence. It is the rare study that successfully solves all three. Each moves from open access to restricted contacts to interviews to surveys or from acceptance to social invisibility to covert observation or from participation to audience to observer involves a loss in explanatory capacity. We often have to accept that loss.

In most research projects, our understanding of the manner of engagement emerges as the research progresses. Our encounter with another is a negotiated process. It is something that one ingratiates, not imposes. Nevertheless, that the researcher does not start with this understanding does not mean that he or she is not responsible for it. All six of these elements have to be explicated for the reader. They are an important part of the criteria of excellence.

Creating the Research Text

After spending sufficient time in a situation that the circumstances of the encounter can be reasonably well specified, the researcher can begin the process of creating the formal research text.[9] The research text is created by careful notation of the social action itself, the actors (including the researcher), settings, acts, and artifacts, the communication within and about the social action, and the experience of the researcher as a member. This careful notation will have **field notes** as its central feature and may also include audio and video recordings, transcriptions and other analyses of these recordings, photographs, sketches, objects, and the like.

Of this list, perhaps, field notes deserve the most comment here. Field notes

---

[9] I will warn the reader that different writers approach this process in different ways. The one I endorse rests the primacy of evidence on empirical events for which there is presumed intersubjecti-vity. In practice, this translates into a method which emphasizes detailed notes, careful transcription of words and acts, and attention to artifacts and settings. It is a plodding, bit-by-bit approach which is no less interpretive, or, I think, insightful, than the more impressionistic methods.

are the researcher's record of what was meaningful within some past experience. They are the researcher's recorded interpretation of what happened. They will include the significant observations made—what was seen, heard, touched, smelled, etc.—and what those observations meant to the researcher as a participant in that experience. Because they contain what was significant about an experience, field notes are deliberately constructed after the fact upon some reflection. The goal is not to record everything—that simply creates chaos—but to carefully note those critical moments when some meaning of the social action was revealed, however imperfectly, to the researcher. Field notes are indeed notes. They capture bits and pieces of the action. They do not produce a coherent picture of what is going on. They will, however, be a resource for that coherent explanation.

A common mistake of beginning researchers is the emphasis on the "hard" data of recordings. Apparently fearful of missing something significant, they want to "record it all." Aside from its impracticality,[10] this attitude misses the point of the research—whatever is seen or heard is useless unless it is understood as it is meant by the members. Recordings can be helpful, particularly when the social action is rich in conversation and restricted in locale. They are not, however, insightful and are, therefore, no substitute for participation and its analysis.

I have used the term "text" to distinguish it from "data." Unlike data which are presumed to be objectified, the qualitative research text is a personal product of the researcher's participation and observation of social action. It certainly contains physical notes and artifacts, but it is also composed of the first-hand experiences "written on" the researcher. Creation of the research text can continue indefinitely, but it has little public value in itself. For it to have public value, it must be critically analyzed in order to reveal the social action meanings of which it is an expression. Until that analysis is conducted, the research is essentially private in nature and not **public knowledge**. It is the next two steps which create that public knowledge.

Composing the Episode

Some authors move from the research text to the final argument form. I favor an intermediate step, when possible, of creating a public data bank in the form of descriptive episodes. An **episode** is the written, descriptive interpretation of an event of the social action under study. This example might clarify that definition. A group of us have been studying the way media get accommodated in family settings. One of us visits with a family, moves in, if permitted, sets the table, vacuums the rug, babysits the kids—in whatever way possible becomes part of that household. Our purpose is to find out the ways the media are accommodated within the lives of these families. As the research text nears completion, the

---

[10]The camera and the microphone each create a perspective and a frame of focus. The available performance is transformed by this unique view.

analyst begins to reflect on that text to discover the episodic narratives that can be composed from it. These narratives contain all the empirical facts of the event—detailed descriptions of the settings, actors, dialogue etc., but also, tell the "story"[11] of the social action. Composing the episode takes all the bits and pieces of the research text which relate to the event and integrates them into a connected narrative.

These written narratives are generally short, four to five pages long. An observational period of 8 to 10 weeks will reveal several episodes, though not the hundreds potentially there. The episode is not about just any event but about an event that makes sense, one that the analyst can grasp the story of.

The episodes that are composed can be evaluated to see if the narratives have a flow and if they provide the situation of the performance, identify all the actors, and give a richness of detail. The precision of the description has to be demonstrated in the closeness of the narrative relationship to field evidence. Who-did-what must be correctly identified. Quotes must be quotes. The exposition must use the language of the actors. The episode should be the actors' story. As an example, the opening paragraph of an episode follows:

> The father was slouched on the sectional couch in the corner of the family room. I had taken up my usual place at the table in the opposite corner. The television set formed the apex of a triangle between us. The set was tuned to HBO with a beach movie playing. The scene involved young women roller-skating by after which three young men would hold up evaluative rankings. As this scene was finishing, Angela, 15 years old, started down the stairs into the room. I watched the father straighten himself into a more formal position. "Watching some real dork TV aren't you?" she said. "Now, this is a socially redeeming sporting event," answered the father. She sat on the floor and watched with us. The movie introduced three middle-aged characters who had come to the beach to score and forget. "God," said Angela, got up and left.
>
> We watched a scene with some frontal nudity. As it concluded, the father said, "You know, I hate it when she comes down like that. I just can't enjoy this stuff then."

The ability to compose episodes from the research text gives the researcher evidence of the quality of the participant-observation. When the work is shallow at that level, few connections are apparent. Stories are hard to find.

What distinguishes the episode from the research text is that episodes can be criticized by others, the research text cannot. The episode can be approached from the criterion of intersubjectivity. Does the description hang together, make sense to someone else? Do others, knowledgeable about the situation, consider the narrative to have captured the essence of the event?

Composing episodes begins the move from private text to public knowledge. Episodes can be considered by others. The primary value of this process, however, is that it forces recognition of the weaknesses in the methods of the encounter and proves an evaluation of the quality of the research text while remedial steps may still be taken.

---

[11]The scientific story is empirical, not fictional, and involves a claim that it is a valid interpretation of experience.

Moving to Theory

The move to theory can be seen in two steps (a) the construction of the research argument—an **ethnographic text**—in which the claims about the social action analyzed are advanced and (b) the use of this ethnographic text as part of a dialectical (interactive) analysis of the terms and constructs of theory. Qualitative research has not achieved an operating consensus on either the proper form of the research argument or the role of theory in its science. Generally, however, the final research contribution is considered contingent, relative, and expansionistic. These are terms we have seen before. They ascribe to the theory the characteristics of being dependent on the time, place, and cultural milieu of development and of being a historical rather than transcendent contribution to an ever-increasing form of public discourse called "knowledge."

The arguments that are advanced and the subsequent analysis of theory depend on how hard the radical position of this stance is pushed. When it is strongly held, the story of what happened—the connected narrative of the researcher's participant observation—is the final contribution of the research process. The story tells it all; there is no move to analysis of higher abstraction. But few scientists are true to this radical position even though they may acknowledge it in some way. Many use the narrative as evidence for a set of inductive constructs or generalizations about the way things are in the action studied. Others will develop models or ideal types reminiscent of Weber or Schutz. These three—the narrative, inductive exemplar, and models and types—are the most common forms of the ethnographic argument. A few, but apparently growing number of researchers, take the next step in which the narrative is used as a device to inform us about the utility of an explanation given by theory. In the sections below, I comment first on the forms of argument and then on the dialectical analysis of theory.

The Narrative Form   The narrative form is an extension of the episode. It attempts to tell a coherent story of the social action. The story is not a description of the sequence of acts. It tells the story with characters in roles inspired by motives. In appearance, it is no different from the literary form of narrative. The scientific narrative, however, must be an empirical story founded on systematic evidence gathered in accordance with the rules of science.

The narrative presents what happened, how it happened, and, at some level, why it happened. Its value, as theory, is contained in its ability to capture human experience in symbolic form. Readers "who have been there" can find themselves reflected in the narrative. Naive readers can learn of the diversity of human life.

Benson (1980) gives us an example of the narrative form. His article is the story of his experience as a consultant to a political campaign. The people who appear in his narrative are shallow, venal men who treat voters as "marks" and candidates as commodities. His claim, by writing this narrative, is (1) that such is a fair interpretation of the empirical events in which he participated and observed (i.e., it is supported by his evidence), and (2) that to understand the notion of political campaigning one must include this description. He does not claim that this is the only description of political campaigning nor that the characters in his narrative (including himself) are always shallow and venal.

Because of its similarity to the literary form and its great dissimilarity with what we associate with science, the research narrative is often a confusing form for the reader. ("What the hell is this?" is not an uncommon response.) One obvious problem is that the reader has little or no access to the evidence that the author is using and consequently cannot "test" the argument in any way. One simply has to accept the fairness of the argument or reject the whole effort. Authors will sometimes attempt to lessen this problem by "wrapping" the narrative in an introductory and concluding exegesis in which the narrative's anchor points in the empirical are demonstrated.

The narrative presents an additional problem in the display of claims. Claims are not presented piecemeal or explicitly, but rather the narrative itself—the telling of the story—is the claim. In a straight narrative such as Benson's, the reader must grasp the claim by the critical appraisal of the narrative text. If the narrative is poorly formed—if it's not a good story—or if the reader fails to conduct a critical analysis, no claims appear.

The author can, of course, accommodate the lazy reader by providing that critical analysis. In doing so, the narrative text now becomes the evidence in a critical argument. It is no longer the author's private reserve (as the research text is). The reader can accept the narrative and reject the critical analysis just as we can accept quantitative data but reject the author's conclusions drawn from them.

The research narrative is a difficult form both to create and to read as science. The editors of our research journals do not appear to have discovered good solutions to the problems of presentation. Nevertheless, it is insightfully powerful, and, I suspect, will continue to force its appearance.

Inductive Exemplar   A more traditional form of scientific argument is shown in that which uses inductive constructs as explanatory devices. Inductive constructs are descriptive terms which create and display reference points within and between social actions. The very notion of "social action" itself is an inductive construct. Take any social action; for example, take marriage. The construct of marriage is composed of the performances and meanings which are referenced by (attributed to) the construct. It does not mean that my marriage necessarily has anything in common with my neighbor's (or even my wife's). It means that the construct of marriage accommodates what we do and what we mean when we reference our behavior by it.

Inductive constructs are explanatory terms which make sense of the research text and of the episodes composed from it. They are mundane categories used by the actors themselves as a reference for what it is that they do. They are defined by their contents and not by properties that are given to them.

They are formed in the process of the critical analyses of text and episodes. In an episodic analysis, the episodes are reviewed, compared, and examined for what the actors make important and appear to intend. The episodes may remain independent, but often the researcher will see a unity among them or some of them. This unity makes them episodes *of* something. That something is the inductive construct.

In the final research argument, the inductive construct is the claim and the episodes are the evidence which warrant the claim. In her dissertation, introduced earlier in this chapter, Stoll (1983) claims that classroom talk can be described by the set of constructs which include explanations, instructions, justifications, questions, threats, compliments, and accommodations. Her evidence for each of these constructs is in the exemplar episodes which she groups under them. She claims that those grouped in the same category are profitably like one another and at the same time different from those grouped in another category. For a given group, then, it makes sense to see them as, say, instructions and not as explanations. She would not, however, claim that all classroom talk will fit into these categories or even that an exemplar of one of these categories could not usefully appear elsewhere.

The inductive construct form of argument lacks the overall coherence and the deeply engaging quality of the narrative. It is, however, well suited to the episodic analysis of the research text. The steps of analysis are clear. The argument itself is explicit and its evidence is open to the reader. It adapts well to the journal article format and, apparently, for that reason is the most common form of qualitative argument.

Models and Types   Arguments of models and types make claims of relatively high generality. The claim for a model of the practice of marriage among Mormons, for example, would argue that the methods and meanings described in the model would be the expected methods and meanings among all who would consider themselves members. Similarly, the ideal type of an American college student would be a reasonable expectation for the performance of a person in that role. The word "expected" underlies the assumption that any particular example of what is modeled or typified can be located in the model or type but can also show substantial improvisation.

This type of argument has an inductive and deductive form. In the inductive form, it is pretty much an extension of inductive constructs to a higher level of abstraction. As you might suspect, some theorists have difficulty with the level of generality claimed, but the inductive form has standing in the traditions of qualitative research.

The deductive form is less consonant with the norms of qualitative research. The deductive form makes use of a priori constructs whose validity is evidenced by the appearance of exemplars in everyday life. The argument is hypothetic-deductive. The constructs used are essentially hypotheses about mundane performances. When mundane performances can be interpreted to match the properties of the constructs, the hypotheses are confirmed.

The primary difficulty with this form of argument is that there is no independence between the theoretical constructs to be tested and the "data" which are the evidence of success or failure. The researcher is the source of both. That is, the researcher both develops the constructs and provides the interpretation of experience that is the research text. A similar problem occurs when a survey writer presumes the world of experience to be encompassed by the choice of items presented. To press this comparison a bit, assume that I wish to demonstrate that parents think there are problems with their children and the presentation of sex and violence on television. I could (but only by violating the norms of research) write an item for a parent survey like:

I am concerned about:

1 My child's exposure to sex and violence on television
2 The values presented on action dramas
3 The glorification of sex on television
4 The trend toward adult programming during prime time

Unless my respondents rise up in revolt, whatever answer comes to the top, I win. That is, I can issue a report that parents are concerned about sex and violence on TV despite the fact that the questionnaire gave them no choice to indicate otherwise.

In quantitative research, the evidence of this deception, however unintended, is available in the questionnaire, if the reader can get a copy. The qualitative research text (the set of field notes and other evidence), however, is never available, only the researcher's interpretation of that text is available.

Qualitative deductivists will counterargue that the evidence they use—the conversational fragments, the episodes or anecdotes—are there to be inspected. They fail to point out that what theoretical construct (either inductive or deductive) a fragment represents is clearly a function of the way experience is punctuated. If the analyst had used one more or one less turn of talk, would the fragment be an interpretation of something else? Of course it would; that is precisely why those extra turns were not included because they did not make sense as part of the exemplar. Where the researcher makes the divisions within experience establishes the fragment as evidence for the claim.

Deductive approaches to qualitative research put the effort on the wrong end. The emphasis is on gathering evidence which will demonstrate the researcher's view of experience rather than the actor's view. Conversational fragments, episodes, and anecdotes which are developed according to qualitative research norms are punctuated by the divisions intended by the actors' meanings. Deductive fragments are punctuated to best represent the a priori construct. (This is obviously the argument for performing the epoche.)

In spite of this defect, a good deal of this style of research gets done, even with great care and technical expertise. The defect in argument does not necessarily render the claims false, but rather changes the nature of the argument from public science to one of authority based on privately held evidence.

The Dialectical Analysis   Qualitative research's contribution to theory comes in the form of a dialectic between the researcher's understanding of the social action as presented in the ethnographic text and the theoretical framework which is used to interpret the text for others. The concept of a dialectic sounds menacingly foreign. As I use it here, it means that the ethnographic text and theoretical framework are mutually informing. That is, in applying theoretical constructs to the ethnographic text, one gains an additional understanding of the scene. At the same time, it is in the power of the text to enlarge our empirical understanding of the theoretical framework.

The process of critical evaluation of the text through theory and of theory through the text examines the interaction between the ethnographic text and the interpreting constructs. The value of the theory as an analogue of social action is given in the way in which its constructs illuminate the action and in the way the social action illuminates the constructs. If the relationship is fruitful, the analyst should have a better understanding of both the social action and its interpreting theory. If there are few insightful returns in this situation, then, the theory, not the experience, is considered less valuable in this situation.

For example, there is a body of literature which defines the area of negotiation in organizations. That body of literature represents the terms of our current theory of negotiation. The ethnographic study of negotiation performances can help us evaluate those terms according to their success in providing meaningful interpretations of negotiating experiences.

The primary purpose of the dialectic is to improve one's theory through some new understanding of the constructs. Terms of the theory may be reoriented, dropped, or enlarged. If nothing else, the theory now has a new empirical component added to it in the form of the analyzed ethnographic text. At times, there may be a second major contribution in the addition of new terms to the theory or of a new perspective on the social action. In either case, a contribution can be made to the discourse of communication.

(To model this effort in your own mind, think of how the exemplar episode on p. 259, could be used to interpret the terms of a "direct effects" theory of mass communication.)

The process of critical evaluation is quite different from the process of hypothesis testing. In hypothesis testing, following the ordinary practice of verification, the intent is to strengthen the position of the hypothesis vis-à-vis other competing hypotheses. In a qualitative dialectic, the critical evaluation of the theoretical terms of a hypothesis begins by recasting the concept of what a hypothesis is. It must now be viewed as a potentially useful interpretive device rather than a potentially definitive epistemological statement. The evaluation then proceeds to discover the meaning of the terms of the hypothesis in the given social action and to determine the value of those terms as a means of understanding what is going on.

In this process, the constructs of the hypothesis are not validated; they are explained within the analyst's understanding of the situation. Instead of the terms of the hypothesis operationalizing experience, experience is used as the source of the empirical meaning of the hypothesis. There can be, therefore, many interpretations of the terms of the hypothesis.

For this to be a fair evaluation, the effort of creating the ethnographic text has to be independent of the effort of making the dialectical analysis through the deliberate suspension of the analytical frame until the social action is grasped.

Summary of the Qualitative Approach

The purpose of qualitative research is to explicate social action from the actor's point of view. It begins with an encounter of the other in the experience of the everyday world. At this point, we are acting as the natural individual. When we begin to systematically reflect upon that experience and to create a research text which can be critically analyzed, we start our scientific endeavors. The research text is a mixture of private and public knowledge, personal experience, and objective measures. We start the move to a fully public, objectified text in the composition of episodes or punctuated fragments of experience. The episode is the written documentation of these fragments.

Episodes are used as evidence of the claims that can appear in the ethnographic text as one of three forms of argument: the narrative, inductive constructs, and models and types. In the narrative, the episodes are embedded in the connected discourse of the story of what happened. Claims are implicitly contained within the narrative and are dependent on the whole of the narrative for their evidence. If the narrative fails to be credible, all the claims fail. The narrative form requires the reader to critically analyze its content to discover these claims and evidence. In the inductive construct form, the episodes retain their individual identity and are studied for the unifying principles (inductive constructs) they can display. Claims are explicit and are relatively independent of one another. Models and types in its inductive form is an extension of inductive constructs. In its deductive form, the researcher extracts episodes which will demonstrate the validity of a priori constructs.

A second move to theory can be made in the form of a dialectical analysis composed of the mutually informing interaction between the ethnographic text and theory. In this analysis, the explanatory value of the terms and constructs of theory are tested in their capacity to interpret the scene. The successful interpretation of a scene through theory, for its part, enlarges our understanding of that scene.

EXERCISES

1 The analytical subject of quantitative research is the data set; the analytical subject of qualitative research is the research text. How do the qualities of data and text differ?
2 Could data and text be developed over the same event? Would they lead to the same explanation?
3 A student wants to study a group of teenage computer hackers. What problems in the encounter can you foresee? What advice would you give?

4 Can one's personal experiences ever become public knowledge? If I told you the answer was "No," could you tell me why? (Hint: It has to do with the form public knowledge has to take.)
5 What is the relationship between experience and episodes?
6 Given what you know about this research, could Stoll use the same categories again with a different set of classrooms and be true to the perspective? Why?

RELATED READINGS

Clifford, J. and Marcus, G. E. (Eds.). *Writing culture: The poetics and politics of ethnography.* Berkeley: University of California Press, 1986.

Hammersley, M. and Atkinson, P. *Ethnography: Principles in practice.* London: Tavistock Publications, 1983.

Leiter, K. *A primer on ethnomethodology.* New York: Oxford University Press, 1980.

Morris, M. B. *An excursion into creative sociology.* New York: Columbia University Press, 1977.

Schwartz, H. and Jacobs, J. *Qualitative sociology: A method to the madness.* New York: The Free Press, 1979.

CHAPTER 10

DESIGN

An anthill is built by the cooperative efforts of each individual ant carrying a single grain of sand. The anthill is an artifact of that coordinated, individual activity. If you ever come across an anthill whether it is one of those one-holers in the crack of a driveway or an apartment complex in a pasture, you can sit down (not too close) to investigate its structure and function. At the end of it, you will know much about the anthill but almost nothing about cooperative methods of the individual ant.

Much of sociological research has focused on the anthills of human activity—the group, the organization, the institution. We know about phases, hierarchies, motives, and histories of these artifacts, but little about the socially constructed realities of the individual member.

Research from the qualitative perspective attempts to learn about the situated individual. Instead of investigating the anthill, it studies the ant as it goes about its daily effort.

This chapter examines the principles of design which govern the development of a qualitative research study. In the first two sections, I comment on characteristics common to all naturalistic studies: We start with the explanatory purpose with its focus on the social action of situated individuals and then move to consider the analytic metaphors which frame the explanation. The last section presents a method for determining the requirements of the study of a particular scene and a given contribution to theory.

EXPLANATORY PURPOSE OF QUALITATIVE RESEARCH

The design of any research project begins with its explanatory purpose. Qualitative research is directed toward the explanation of social action in order to unpack the jointly held meanings which constitute the reality of that action. Research accomplishes this task by examining the situated individual as a participant and architect.

The situated individual (SI) is a person who is conducting the everyday business of the maintenance and construction of the social realities in which we live. The SI is connected to others through a network of shared, mutually negotiated, and maintained meanings. These meanings provide location, identity, action, and purpose for the individual. They tell me where I am, who I am, what I am doing, how to do it, and why. These meanings also create objects out of things. They tell what things are and how to respond to them. The network of meanings is not independent of the SI. It is the product of the interaction among situated individuals.

The individual and the situation, which is composed of the influence of others within a cultural, social, and physical context, combine to constitute the meaning of social action. These meanings are expressed in the norms, values, mores, stories, myths, explanations, motives, names, labels, hierarchies, roles, characters, performances, rituals, procedures, methods, processes, activities, and the like that appear in everyday life.

A Focus on Social Action

The analyst's responsibility to explain social action from the member's viewpoint may still be some source of confusion. The confusion about what this responsibility entails arises because of four factors:

1 Social action does not constitute all of human behavior. The analyst, therefore, must determine what is social action and what is not.

2 The social action itself may be well or poorly governed by the meanings which underlay it, resulting in analytic confusion over personal acts and social actions.

3 The membership in which the meaning structure is constituted may be a broad, loosely defined public or an exclusive, private domain, raising questions about what membership is in the particular study.

4 The social action under study may be expressed in different ways by different memberships, making it difficult to identify what member knowledge is in place in any given performance.

Some discussion of the implications of these points follows:

Each of us is a physical entity and can be studied as such independent of any social component or notion of sensate consciousness. I will not understand the neuron's synaptic transmission of information through the observation of social action. I will understand how the explanation entitled "Synaptic Transmission of Information" is justified, how it is knowledge, how it is used in society, and so on, but the operation of neurons is not dependent on socially derived meanings. There are, therefore, behaviors to be studied which are not social action.

Each of us is an individual who separately interprets the world. We do not do it equally well or equally connected within a social meaning network. Some acts are unique to the person. Those acts may be indistinguishable from such that may appear in the performance of social action. The analyst, however, is responsible for the difference.

Each of us is a public person. We participate in the meanings which surround public actions. If we don't, we're likely to be removed to a prison or an asylum. If I step onto a public elevator in a public building, I feel confident in my understanding of what is getting done when my fellow passengers stand silently, facing forward. In this case, I am already participating with an insider's knowledge which can be made explicit through observation techniques. In these actions of an aggregated public (generic social action, if you will), we are all inside members, albeit with different degrees of competence within the publics to which we belong.

When the same individuals interact over time, however, even these public actions begin to move into a private domain. For example, as a faculty member, I am *the* insider for the first day of any class, supported by my credentials, here in the department of communication (note the implicit indexing of membership). By the second week of classes, I am an outsider for every class but my own.

Finally, there is an immense range of actions whose meaning context is available only to a restricted membership. They are those situations where each member has a history with every other member. My knowledge of public elevator riding, for example, may not be valid when riding the employees-only car in a private office building. People may be doing all sorts of things—arguing, dancing to the music, drinking—following some set of rules to which I am not privy. Those actions are not violations of proper behavior. I am the violation and am open to challenge ("Who are you?"). In this case, I have a very long period of study in front of me before I will be able to interpret those actions from the member's viewpoint.

The problem for the analyst, then, is to sort all this out. What is the physical behavior, personal act, social action? What is the meaning structure governing the social action under study? What are the characteristics, coherence, and relevant context of that structure? What membership is its source? Who are the members? What is the analyst's connection to that meaning system? When can one's own knowledge of an apparent situation be trusted? These are questions which must be addressed in the design of the study.

The focus on social action of situated individuals operating within a **semiotic system**, then, establishes what it is that we are about, sets the requirements for our methods and determines the criteria for evaluating our efforts. Essentially, we are directed toward the explication of meanings held in context. We are required to use methods which allow us to study people within the scenes of their performances. Our explanation is successful when we can make explicit some part of the semiotic system to which the situated individuals respond.

Four Types of Explanation

Explanation from this perspective has focused on four aspects of the situated individual. (a) It has looked at the individual biographically to present the other in a particular situation. It has looked to the individual as an informant who can reveal the workings of the network of meaning which forms his or her social reality. Within this focus, it has (b) concentrated on the content of that meaning network, (c) its structures and functions as expressed within the social order, or (d) on the processes which are used to negotiate and maintain those meanings.

Most of the examples of these types of explanation come from outside the discipline of communication, but communication has a significant contribution to make. Social action is, after all, inherently a communication process. The individual within it is a communicating animal. The study of the situated individual can focus on the communication content—its characteristics and qualities; the processes of communication—the rules that direct it, the functions it serves, the stages or phases that it transits; and on the methods and practices of communication through which the individuals create the scene. As we consider each characteristic explanation, I will indicate the communication focus that could be taken. Let's explore each of these just a bit:

Biographical Explanation   Biographical explanation, which is a hallmark but not the exclusive right of existential sociology (Fontana, 1980), centers on a particular person as an expression of the situated individual. Unlike traditional biography which typically attempts the ideological history of a culturally significant individual, biographical explanation tells the lived story of a person in significant situations. Here is a person *as part of the scene of* a nude beach (Douglas et al., 1977), television viewing (Anderson, 1983), a Hollywood story conference (Espinosa, 1982) or being a small-town cop (Pacanowsky, 1983).

This explanation approaches the answer to what does it mean to be a person in these situations. Biographical explanation is holistic; all three purposes of scientific explanation—characteristics, methods and practices and causes and consequences—are contained within it. One comes away from these explanations with an understanding of the thinking, feeling, and acting of the individual who is a legitimate part of the situation.

Content Explanations   Explanations which are directed toward the content of the meanings of social action are concerned with illuminating the attributes of the social self—the norms, values, symbols, and labels which identify me to myself and others as a person in society. Morris (1977) has identified this concern as the particular preserve of phenomenological sociologists. This type of explanation is concerned with the *characteristics* of meaning.

In communication, content explanations have made their appearance primarily in the study of the content of the meanings which define membership in organizations (e.g., Kreps, 1983). But there are other views that have been taken: Individuals are libraries of the signs, symbols, and images by which we constitute the social realities in which we live. What are the metaphors of everyday life (Lakoff and Johnson, 1980)? What themes appear in our points of conflict (Bormann et al., 1984)? What images constitute our understanding of ourselves, the other, and the objects of the world (Anderson et al., 1985)?

Structure and Functions   Explanations of the structure and functions of the meanings of social action are characteristic of those given from symbolic interactionism (Meltzer, Petras, and Reynolds, 1975) and the rules perspective as it appears in qualitative research (Toulmin, 1974). Structure concerns the manner in which meanings are held in the conscious mind, how they are incorporated, the relationships among meanings, and the like. Function concerns the manner in which meaning structures participate in the accomplishment of human purposes. Symbolic interactionism, for example, in part, views social meaning as incorporated in roles (structure). The role functions to provide identity, location, action, and purpose for the individual while within that role. That is, it contains the meaning of the situation. In a similar fashion, but now from a rules perspective, the structure of the interrelated rules contains the meaning of a situation and functions to direct the actions of the participants. Both adopt a dependent form of causal reasoning where purpose generates structure to provide for function.

Wilbrand and Rieke (1986) have begun what promises to be a series of studies of the structure and function of the logic of communication in everyday life. They are investigating the forms of argument, the nature of appeals, and the characteristics of evidence as they occur in mundane settings.

I have previously reported to you the efforts of our research team to find the points of accommodation at which mediated communication enters the social world of families. Instead of the traditional effects formula, we have considered the varying meaning structures which incorporate mass media content and its functional applications by family members.

Conversation analysis investigates the structures of conversation as shown in the relationships between turns of talk. The functions of these structures can be considered in view of the purposes of the communicants.

Other questions of structure and function can be addressed in the analysis of the communication processes of individuals in friendship pairs, marital contracts, small groups, organizations, and so on.

Processes   The manner through which individuals constitute and maintain the meanings by which they live is the subject of process explanations. The notion of the process of constitution and maintenance of meaning is sometimes difficult to grasp. Perhaps two examples will help.

As the first, two friends of mine just got engaged. They intend to be married at the beginning of next month. They have been living together, sharing bed and board, for the past two years. What is it about the practice of engagement that demonstrates a commitment to marriage that living together doesn't? How is it that these two states are distinguished both by the engaged pair and by society at large? The manner in which this couple now conducts itself as an engaged pair rather than as a POSSLQ (persons of opposite sex sharing living quarters) is the method by which engagement survives as a socially meaningful state.

For the second, Garfinkel's (1967) study of a male transvestite undergoing counseling for a sex-change operation, demonstrated that gender is confirmed in the practices of dress, social activities, employment, and so on. His study showed that the transvestite confirmed his femaleness in the everyday acts of passing as a woman. Being acknowledged as a female demonstrated the validity of his claim. (Note that my use of the male pronoun is itself a practice which confirms a social meaning of gender.) Process explanations document the methods and practices of meaning. Methods and practices have been identified as the particular preserve of ethnomethodologists (Leiter, 1980).

A Comment on the Individual in Individuated Analysis

In all four of the focuses of individuated explanation, the particular persons are both trivial and indispensable. They are indispensable because the **research text** could not be created without them, nor could anyone else be substituted to create that particular text. Each individual's lived experience is unique. On the other hand, each experience is trivial because a research text can always be created in the analysis of any SI. Certainly, there are some individuals who are more open, obliging, cooperative, and insightful into their own lives than others. Finding those people is striking gold.

Most analysis, however, is not identified by the individuals studied. It is, rather, identified by the situation. Even in biographical explanation, it is the scene that is explained through the actors. The scene is the unifying concept. The actors, the setting, and the time are all elements of the scene. We understand them as part of that composition. The identification of the significant scene or situation is generally the first step in the conduct of research.

ANALYTICAL METAPHORS

In this section, we discuss the analytical metaphors of qualitative research. **Analytical metaphors** give structure to the interpretation of the research text. There are a wide variety of metaphors in every type of research, and new ones are regularly suggested. In my treatment, the fundamental metaphor of narrative, the traditional metaphor of theater, and the relatively recent notion of culture in organizations are presented to demonstrate the idea of metaphor but not to limit the concept to them.

My colleague Leonard Hawes has written that science is "the exploitation of provocative metaphors" (1975, p. 7). Metaphors are interpretative devices in which we use our knowledge of one thing to understand another. Quantitative research is characterized by the metaphor of quantities and rates. The bulk of qualitative analysis is contained in three metaphors—the metaphors of the narrative, the theater, and of culture. These metaphors are tools for the analyst. They are notational schemes which permit the analyst to organize and display interpretations of experience. There is no necessary claim that experience is composed of the terms of the metaphor, although reification of these terms is not unusual in ideological debate.

We are concerned about these metaphors because the research you read and perhaps conduct will undoubtedly be structured by one of them. For example, if the metaphor of the theater is present, then the analysis will likely display individuals in culturally defined roles speaking from socially determined scripts or, from another view from the theater, as giving improvisational performances upon the stages of social action. On the other hand, if the metaphor is culture, then the analysis may focus on the myths, sagas, and folklore of organizations that show the proper order of the world in the telling.

The underlying metaphor establishes what is significant in the creation of the research text and the nature of the episode which is composed from it. The research text, you will remember, is the repository of interpreted experience available for analysis. What is understood, what is significant, what is collected, are all directed by the underlying metaphor. Episodes are documented occurrences of something. The something they are of changes as the metaphor changes.

In my discussion, I will present the generic form of each metaphor bringing in as many terms as are supported by it. Research will rarely use the whole of the metaphor. Terms will often be missing or irrelevant. Particular theorists will endow the terms with their own particular meanings. This analysis is meant as an introduction to the analytical metaphor, not a presentation of particular formulations within the metaphor such as the concept of role as developed by Mead (1934) or of culture as Geertz (1973) would have it, or the development of narrative by different documentarists. That is left to your own reading.

The Metaphor of the Narrative

Perhaps the fundamental metaphor of qualitative research is that of the narrative.[1] The narrative tells the story of the scene. A narrative has an internal structure which models our understanding of experience. The narrative structure implies that its paragraphs are to be understood as a whole, that sentences within paragraphs justify one another, and that the elements presented stand in some meaningful relationship.

The story contained in the narrative is bound together by the claims of relationships between people and events. The story occurs within time and over time. That is, it has a beginning, a middle, and an end.

A narrative is a frame which both includes and excludes experience to accomplish the display of something. That frame promotes a view from a given perspective—the **authorial stance** taken by the writer (see Strine and Pacanowsky, 1985).

Let me try to exemplify these principles by presenting and dissecting two examples. The first is an episode taken from our television viewing research. The second is a student's field notes from the observations of the eighth-grade science class.

---

[1]As Figure 10-1 shows, narrative can be implicit. A good place to start your consideration of narrative in research is in the collection edited by Mitchell (1981). See also Bakhtin (1981), Brown (1977), Clifford (1983), Sammons (1977), and Webster (1982).

FIGURE 10-1
A cultural narrative

An Episode of Television Viewing   During the summer of 1981 I had spent some time observing a mother, father, and 11-year-old daughter in their use of television. One practice of theirs was of particular interest to me. They would regularly gather in the family room to watch the late-evening news (which comes on at 10:00 in this mountain time zone) and to play competitive solitaire. Writing a paper for a convention presentation (Anderson, 1982), I was thinking of this practice as an example of the process by which news watching gets signified as an important adult activity. I was curious at the time if I had characterized Melissa's family's news-watching card-play correctly and contacted the family again, just six weeks short of a year of the time previous. I made four visits; I report the last one.

On this visit, Melissa (now aged 12) was upstairs in her bedroom reading another horse story. Her mother was in the living room reading a historical romance novel. Her father was in the basement workshop repairing the garbage disposal.

About 9:45, Melissa called out, "Mom, you want to play some solitaire?" Getting an affirmative reply, Melissa came down from her bedroom to the family room, got out three decks of cards, shuffled two of them and laid out two hands of solitaire. Her mother came into the room, and the two proceeded to play.

In the basement, the father bench-tested the disposer successfully. He immediately left the workroom, washed up, and came into the family room. "Well, it works," he announced.

"Good," answered his wife, still attending to the card display.

"You'll have to wait for the next hand, Dad," said Melissa.

The father, noticing that they had just begun to play the hand said, "No I won't," sat down and dealt his hand quickly.

The family was arranged around the table, as always, so that each member could face the TV. It was now about six minutes after 10 p.m. The late-evening news had started. Tonight, as for the past four nights, the set was not turned on. The set was in the repair shop. Yet, the family met at the same time in the same way as they had the year before and as they had for many nights of this summer.

A Critique We can see the episode as composed of three parts. The first prepares us for the significance of the action to follow; the second describes the action and its importance to the family members; the third comments on its meaning.

Paragraph 1 motivates paragraph 2 and the subsequent dialogue. If I don't start the episode with paragraph 1, the reader cannot grasp the significance of the coming together of the family members. The notion of a chosen activity which is well practiced by the family members would be lost.

In the final paragraph, several disparate elements are placed in relation to one another. The seating arrangement is related to the location of the television set. The time of the event is related to the time of another event—the presentation of the news. Both of these relationships are interpreted by the absence of the television set. All of these relationships are interpretations by the analyst based on his understanding of what it means for those three people to be gathered in that room. None of these relationships can be directly observed.

The authorial stance taken by the writer is of the unseen but all seeing narrator. The frame is a cut-away doll house where we can see all the rooms at once. To accomplish this simultaneity of view huge chunks of action are glossed—"Melissa was in her bedroom reading another horse story."

The beginning, middle, and end of this episode is defined by what the episode is about. The episode starts at 9:45 because it is about the practices of this family vis-à-vis the 10:00 news. It ends not with any act of the family members, but upon the revelation by the analyst that his original interpretation was inadequate.

In the telling of the story, the analyst makes sense of all that he has revealed to the reader. For example, the story starts with the actors separated in order that we may see them come together. The time of 9:45 is made meaningful by the reference to the 10:00 news, the seating by reference to another point in the room, and so on. I am not saying that any of this was made up. Melissa did speak up at 9:45, and all the rest. (She said something around 9:30 also, but that's not part of this episode. Why?) I am saying that what was observed is understood in the creation of the narrative which relates this scene to the reader. All of these elements make sense within the structure of the narrative. If they didn't, there would be no story to tell.

You might be wondering how this narrative is metaphorical. The purpose of this narrative is to make sensible a segment of social action. Nevertheless, none of the actors—including the researcher—experienced the narrative itself. The analyst uses the structure of the narrative as means by which we can come to know the structure of the social action. The narrative form was chosen by the analyst as the lens through which the social action could be observed. This, of course, is central to the construct of metaphor—that we use what we know about one thing to make another meaningful.

You might also wonder if this is a good narrative. The answer is yes and no. For its purpose in the short convention paper as a narrative argument, it adequately presented the picture of how the practices of a family can accommodate television viewing within other structures of behavior. As a documented episode, it is too refined. There is not enough detail in its presentation of the actors and situation. The evidence for the analyst's interpretation is missing. It is too much story and not enough observation.

In the next section, we can compare the televiewing narrative with a student's field notes. Here, we will see much more observation although it is still the appearance of the underlying, sense-making story that makes that observation meaningful.

The Implicit Narrative of Field Notes

This field note was written following an observation session of an eigth-grade science class which was learning how to search a computer-based encyclopedia for information helpful in writing their themes. There were nine computers each placed in individual carrels which are arranged in a semicircle in one corner of a media resource room (library). This note details about 10 minutes of elapsed time (the narrative above was close to an hour). The observer writes:

> I have been watching Rodney and Mark for several minutes, and when I look at Annette's screen, she is in the middle of rather detailed instructions on how to use all the commands available for running the encyclopedia. She is not reading them really, they're going by too quickly for that, and no one can memorize a bunch of instructions just by watching them go by. Her notebook is closed, and there is no paper out. There is also almost no room to write, The bays [carrels] are not much larger than the terminals. That means deep and narrow bins, almost on either side of the terminal.
>
> Annette then gets to an instructions page which says "GOTO AAE-110" in caps, unlike the rest of the page. "All right," she says, and types it in. This starts running her through the detailed list of instructions again. She didn't carefully read all her options, nor did she notice enough about the instructions to figure out how to prevent herself from seeing all the instructions again.
>
> Mark isn't doing so well, either. He says either the book or the terminal is bad and says he's "been here before," meaning some screen he's getting on the terminal.
>
> Annette, meantime, has gotten through the screens. I ask her where she is. She doesn't look too happy about how it is going. She says, "I'm back to where I started. I don't know what happened." She pushes number one (which she did before).

A Critique   In spite of the increased descriptive load, we can clearly see that this note is something more than the serial description of a sequence of events. The observer makes sense of the empirical events in a created, insightful narrative. The narrative is the story of Annette's failure to accomplish the task of getting to the source. The story is established in the first paragraph. The second sentence of that paragraph contains the claim ("She is not reading them really.") that will make sense of the events. This claim is followed by supporting claims and evidence: "They're going by too quickly." "No one can memorize. . . ." And, "Her notebook is closed and there is no paper out." We are now prepared to understand why she types in the repetitious command and why she looks unhappy at the end of the note. It is the story that makes sense of all that detail.

Again, you might ask whether or not this is a good field note. The answer is again mixed. The writer writes clearly with a descriptive eye, although I would encourage even more description. The main failure is that the observer extrapolates too much from his own knowledge. He knows that Annette cannot read the instructions (and should want to). He assumes that she wants to get to the next stage—that she indeed is attempting the task he has in his mind. He may be right. Her comment at the end suggests as much. On the other hand, he missed the opportunity to converse about what she was trying to do.

The Metaphor of the Narrative: A Summary

In this section, we have been examining the narrative as the fundamental metaphor of qualitative research. Given that our task is the meaning of social action, the narrative is fundamental because it provides a structure of discourse in which the meaning of things and acts can be made apparent. Neither Melissa nor Annette is acting in narratives, both are living life. But, our direct experience of life is unknowable, unspeakable. Narrative permits the disclosure of the hidden relationships among observable elements. It fixes what is observable in relationships of time and significance. It is in these relationships that the story of the scene is held.

The story to be told is, of course, the story as the actors hold it. Greater objectivity is not gained by increasing the precision by which the observables are described. They are not the object of study. Greater objectivity is gained by a better representation of the actor's perspective rather than the researcher's perspective. The field note of our second example can be criticized because the researcher's perspective is too apparent.

Not all narratives are equally coherent. Not all social action is equally well formed. The quality of the narrative ought to reflect the quality of the social action. On the other hand, not all stories are equally well told. Writing descriptively in narrative is a craft which requires training and practice. The researcher must create the experience in the written word. The quality of the contribution is limited by the quality of writing effort.

Finally, **research narratives** are documentaries and not fiction. They genuinely represent what happened. But what happened is a story told from multiple perspectives. The world of social action is a world of multiple realities. It is a fiction to believe that one has "told it like it is." It is, rather, that a **valid story** has been told.

The Metaphor of Theater

The theatrical metaphor is commonly used to describe the individual as involved in a series of performances the roles and scripts for which are determined by the social units in which they appear. The most-used terms of the metaphor are actor, character and characterization, role, performance, scripts, audiences, settings, and scene.

The term "actor," as we have been using it, is the individual in the performance of some social action. It identifies a person who is participating in meaningful behavior. This person can be contrasted with the individual acting reflexively or emitting behavior which is undefined.

The concept of "character" is a typification, a descriptive category, which exists within some social meaning network. It names the idealized properties of a type of performance in a role (e.g., the qualities of "nice guy" in the role of teacher).

"Characterization" is the **enactment** of a given character in a given role within a social action.

"Role" identifies the socially defined, idealized properties of a complex of activity. It is a typification, again defined within the social milieu. Its properties can include title, position, rank, status, rights, responsibilities, power, and so forth as described by the social unit.

"Performance" is the activity of a particular individual which is included in that individual's definition of a role. A performance is what is done when acting within a role.

"Scripts" are the action and dialogue which organize and define a performance. They contain what is typically said and done when performing as a character in a role within some social unit. Scripts arise from the joint expectations of the members about what a performance should be. Not all performances are considered scripted; some are seen as primarily improvisational.

"Audiences" are the referenced others of the performance. They are the individuals for whom the performance is provided. The metaphorical force of the term highlights the symbiotic relationship between the actor and the audience. Performances are made possible by audiences and must be viewed within the context of the audience.

"Settings" are the places of performance. They are composed of meaningful space—activity sites, territories, and the like; and of objects—things made meaningful within the social action.

Finally, the "scene" is the assemblage of all of these elements into an ongoing experience. It is an event of social action.

An Educational Example of the Theatrical Metaphor   The role of "teacher" gets defined within various social units of our society. It has different values and properties for teachers themselves, their students, parents of students, funding agents, administrators, and so on. One can see the conflict over what a teacher is at the intersections of these social units. As a teacher, I find my primary justification for my definition of that role within my fellow teachers, first with that small group of people with whom I would regularly discuss such matters, then perhaps with my departmental colleagues in review processes, then at higher levels of administration. I may modify or just defend that role as I am brought into contact with students, parents, and funding agents. The defined role is a set of attributes which may be integrated or contradictory (a teacher must be fair but compassionate). The role establishes the norms of a performance—the picture in our heads of the ideal teacher. When I step into the classroom to deliver a lecture, I am clearly identified as giving a performance of the role of teacher. What I do is understood from the vantage of that role.

As an example, we can compare the same ostensible behavior taken in two different scenes. It would be unusual if I were to hug all of my students as they entered the classroom. But not unusual if I were the host at a party within some social circles. That does not mean that hugging could not become part of the classroom performance. I could fairly easily negotiate that performance with my students. I could appeal to some norm within the role such as trust:

> This discussion class is founded on the principle that we trust one another enough to share our ideas and criticism. As a visual reminder of that trust, I would like to hug each of you as you enter the classroom. We can be as formal or as warm as you wish. As you gain trust for one another, I hope you will hug your fellow classmates as well.

Assuming that the students accept the principle, this behavior becomes an acceptable part of the performance. The action is open to challenge, however (That creep better not try hugging me!), in no small measure because it is not part of what students know to be the ordinary performance of the role of college teacher.

The nature of one's performance is dependent upon the audience for which it is played. As a teacher, I am aware that different class audiences will permit and encourage different performances and the appearance of different characterizations of the role. I am also aware that my performance changes when I am a guest speaker or when I have observers in my class because my audience is different.

We can consider character and characterization by contrasting that warm performance with the teacher who begins class with a formal calling of the attendance role, uses only last names or no names in addressing students, insists on being addressed as "doctor" or "professor," and the like. We have character names for the different approaches that are identified with a role. She's "hard-nosed" (or other portion of anatomy); he's "Mickey Mouse." The names and properties associated with the names vary with the social unit that uses them. The same performance can be identified with positive or negative names.

Our discussion leader may be simultaneously identified as a warm, open person, a touchy-feely, and a sexual pervert.

The manner of my performance of teacher which distinguishes it from that of some other teacher's performance is my characterization of the role. Characterization gets defined from multiple perspectives. I may see myself as quite different from teacher X; students may see us as pretty much alike.

When I walk into a classroom, I know what to do. I know what my rights and responsibilities are. The methods I use to provide for my performance of teacher can be seen as a script. Textbooks, assignments, lecture schedules, due dates, rules, typical dialogue, and my perception of role and character are all part of that script.

The setting of the classroom promotes the typical performance of teacher and student. There are teacher areas and student areas. There are individual territories and owned objects. As a student, try sitting in the teacher's chair or holding the blackboard pointer.

Finally, there is the scene which even if we come upon it on a grassy knoll, we can instantly recognize as a class. It has a beginning and an end. In between we give our performances as individuals in social action.

The Theatrical Metaphor as an Interpretive Frame If we step back from these concepts, we can see them as layers of interpretation. This interpretation begins with the moment-by-moment flow of experience as it becomes meaningful as social action. Social action is seen as a complex of activity by individuals who are identified with different normative roles. From this interpretive stance, individuals are actors giving performances of the roles contained within this social action. The various solutions given to the normative demands of a role generate the ideal of characters. Variations in performances between individuals in the same role (or the same individual in different performances) give rise to the concept of characterization. Role performances become linked with settings. For example, the scripts change when members move from the office to the pub in order that they can be freed from some normative standards and adopt others. Put together, the whole of social action becomes the scene.

Two Views from the Theatrical Metaphor When the theatrical metaphor is in place, attention is directed either to the roles that appear or to the performances that are given. Symbolic interaction theorists tend to emphasize role, dramaturgical theorists the performances.[2]

Particular theorists will use some of these terms and not others and will endow the terms they do use with their particular qualities. There is no particular merit in being bound by the limit of someone else's ideas. But, care must be taken not to confuse the reader. For example, Goffman (1959) is closely identified with performances. One can naively analyze performances without

---

[2]McCall and Simmons (1978) has provided a good review of the literature in which the theatrical metaphor is central (p. 56, footnote 26). The citations are also listed in this text's bibliography.

attending to Goffman. But if the researcher claims a Goffmanesque analysis, it must be true to the term as Goffman defined it.

Culture as Metaphor

Organizational communication scholars have adopted the terms of culture to interpret the joint acts of organizational members. The terms commonly used are culture, myths, sagas, folktales, explanations, rituals, and workways.[3]

The master notion of "culture" as applied to organizations directs us to see organizations not as means of production or used as systems of interlocking elements, but as the arena for the development and maintenance of networks of shared rules, beliefs, meanings, and symbols. This conceptualization suggests two foci of study: the structure of the normative systems as expressed in the content of meanings and the means by which the meanings are generated and sustained.

The myths, sagas, folktales, and rituals of a culture are an expression of the normative content of that culture. The manner of their presentation and performance serves to sustain them within the culture. Their entrance and extinction mark significant occurrences of the culture. Myths, sagas, folktales, and rituals can be part of the public face of an organization or used as signs of innermost membership.

Workways and the explanations for them are the expression of the individual within the organizational culture context.

A Critique   The metaphor of culture is of recent vintage in organizational studies. There is little research by which we can test its value. Some thoughts do come to mind, however. The notion of culture as well as the structure of a narrative or the notions of role, character, and so forth of the theater represent methods by which experience can be organized meaningfully. As such, they carry the danger of being solely the researcher's template. Evidence for culture (or narrative structure or theater) must be found within the actions of the members.

While the concept of an organization as a means for the development and maintenance of shared values in action is a useful one, it should not be held that every assemblage that calls itself an organization meets this characterizing definition. The concept of culture calls for a broad-scale influence on the individual and widespread involvement of the organizational members in the processes of socialization and acculturation. Coordinated activity, however, can be undertaken for many reasons. Individual membership does not need to be predicated on an organization's values. It is an easy gloss to assume that each person's activities are an expression of a common network of beliefs. The analyst needs a method of doubt—a healthy skepticism of the facility of the analytical metaphor.

[3]For a review of this application see Smircich (1983), Pacanowsky and O'Donnell-Trujillo (1983), and Pettigrew (1983).

ANALYTIC METAPHORS: A SUMMARY

In this section, we have considered three metaphors which are analytic lenses which can direct our view of experience. The most fundamental of these metaphors was that of the narrative. Other analytic metaphors will have narrative embedded within them. The documentary record of the scene is more than a collection of independent descriptions. Ordinarily, it is made meaningful through the structural devices of narrative which express the implicit relationships among the observables. The narrative places the observables in time and space and establishes their significance for the actors. In writing field notes, episodes, and the final argument, the analyst develops a story of what happened.

The metaphors of theater and culture have each been used to help construct that story. The metaphor of theater views social action as organized around roles or performances depending on how this metaphor is used. The metaphor of theater has been criticized for depicting social action as a pretense—a series of masks we don to hide our inner self. But it can be profitably viewed as a way to describe the different configurations of behavior and value that come into play in the different situations of our life. The metaphor of theater is a covering metaphor. That is, it has explanatory power for all conditions of social life.

The metaphor of culture has a more restricted scope. It has been promoted as a fruitful way of considering the integrating functions of organizations. As a tool of analysis, it directs us away from the structures of organizations and toward the network of beliefs, meanings, and symbols that are the product of the practices of the members.

The power of these metaphors is both their strength and our concern. Their strength comes from its capacity to interpret unruly experience. Our concern is that the metaphor has to be more than the researcher's view. It has to be meaningful to the social actors as well as the analyst.

In order to avoid the solipsistic explanation, the analyst must make the metaphor explicit, must use it in a knowing way—must know that he or she is telling the story; the actors are not living it—and must find the evidence for its terms in the discourse and action of the social actors. The analyst must practice a method of doubt by keeping the fact of interpretation always present and viewing the research text with a healthy skepticism.

EXERCISES

1 Different theorists have different ideas about the independence of the scene from the actors. Consider the answer to the question, "Can the scene be re-created with different actors?" What do you have to argue about the nature of the social meanings which form the basis of the scene to answer "yes"? How would you argue contrarily to answer "no"?

2 Contrast the beginning of a qualitative study with that of a quantitative study.

3 "Kilroy was here" is a famous narrative. What story does it tell? How do you know it is not about Kilroy?

4 Reread the story of Melissa's family, but change the time of Melissa's request to 9:00 instead of 9:45. How does that change of time change the meaning of the gathering of the family members?

5 What do you think is the significance of the news for Melissa's family?

6 How does the notion of analytical metaphor compare with the notion of traditional theory?

7 How does the analyst protect against solipsistic explanation?

8 Analysts who use the organizational culture metaphor do not consider efficiency, productivity, or profitability as useful criteria to evaluate an organization. Why?

DESIGNING THE STUDY: IDENTIFYING THE SCENE

Ethnographic studies most often begin with an interest in how things get done in the distinguishable situations of everyday life. An interest in classroom communication led Stoll (1983) to study the methods in interactive talk by which the members constituted the characteristics of the classroom scene. Rawlins (1981) studied the interactive practices that surround the notion of friendship—by what joint acts is friendship created and maintained. Pacanowsky and Anderson (1982) studied the way in which the content from television police dramas is integrated in the worklife of a cop. O'Donnell-Trujillo (1983) investigated the ways in which common symbols developed in the practices of a small work organization.

For Stoll, the scene was the relationships between student and teacher as they appeared in a classroom setting and were expressed in interactive talk. For Rawlins, the scene was the social contract of friendship which occurred in many settings. For Pacanowsky and Anderson and for O'Donnell-Trujillo, the scene was the world of work which was transcendent of place and time.

Scenes, then, are performances of social action. They describe what the actor is doing—teaching, working, being a student, a friend, or a cop. A scene is defined by the actors' understanding of the situation they are in, and not by settings, behaviors, or other objective characteristics. The analyst understands the scene of something as a social actor—a participant in that scene. We study scenes to make explicit our own understanding and to discover the understandings of others.

Scenes vary on a number of dimensions which are relevant to the research process. There are the observable characteristics: the number of actors in the interacting unit, the range of action in which they participate, the number and properties of the settings in which the scene appears, the level of involvement expressed by the actors, the requirements of membership, and the rate, duration, and frequency of interaction. Then there are the inner characteristics of the social meaning—its coherence, compactness or density, its intimacy, and emotional range. Finally, there are the researcher's own resources of interest, time, and money. These characteristics affect the analyst's ability to assess the scene in ways discussed in the following sections.

Number of Actors

The greater the number of actors in the interactive unit, the greater the observational load and the more demanding the requirements of participation. The analyst can lessen this load by selecting smaller interactive units. An "interactive unit" is defined in the social action by the actors' choices and the situational demands. In no practical way can I study the individuals in a large organization, but I can study self-connected work groups. A work group of four or five may be easier to study than one of 15 or 20.

A smaller number offers problems of a different sort. Groups of two or three can be more resistant to accepting the analyst as a member, and the effect of a new member can instigate radical changes in the relationship.

Range of Action

The greater the range of action either in the number of different actions or in its technical requirements, the greater competence demands on the analyst. The range of action for middle managers, for example, is quite extended by social, organizational, and technical demands (see Mintzberg, 1973). To understand the world of work in this arena, the analyst must be sufficiently competent to be responsive at all these levels.

A high level of technical knowledge can be part of the context for social action. Again, adequate understanding can be gained only with a competence within this context. Van Maanen, for example, in his study of the socialization of cadets (1973) into the world of police work, qualified for and completed the police academy course of training.

Settings

In each setting of social action, the researcher has to find a place which will accommodate the work of observation and permit the analyst to participate. Social action which takes place on the run or makes use of multiple settings or is performed in limited space is generally more difficult to study than that in a single setting with plenty of space. A conference table with just enough room for the conferees but not the researcher is an extremely difficult research site.

Level of Actor Involvement

A high level of involvement for the actors generally means greater time of participation, a greater range of action, and the appearance of more settings. Studying the leadership component of, say, a softball league will be more demanding than working with one team of players.

Conditions of Membership

Whether for the true member or the permitted outsider, each social scene will have conditions of joining. These conditions may include sex, age, race, relgion, social standing, dialect, length of hair, and so on. A serious mistake is made if egalitarianism is assumed. There are many social scenes that the researcher cannot join with full membership.

Interactions

Social meanings are constructed, maintained, and revealed in interaction. To understand social action requires that the analyst be privy to and participate in these interactions. Consequently, questions of when they occur, where they take place, and the rate of occurrence are all relevant to defining the scene.

The most difficult problem of our family observations is that the interactions between family members occur across a broad spectrum of time and place, but we have a very restricted venue of contact. We must be very careful of creating distortions when using the few time windows available. Similarly, ethnographers talk about those critical instances when something significant occurs to break the normal flow and reveal the underlying meanings. While those critical instances can sometimes be manufactured, more often, they are happenstance. High levels of interaction increase the likelihood of these critical instances occurring in the presence of the analyst.

Consider that one is studying the forms of argument that arise within classroom settings. If the intent is to study them as they naturally occur, then the analyst is going to have to be there when they take place. Some judicious choices based on the interaction history of the available classroom groups can obviously be made.

Coherence

We move now to consider the inner characteristics of the scene—the nature of the understandings which direct that scene. Not every scene is well defined; not every actor is well informed. Beginnings, endings, and disruptions are confusing for actor and analyst alike. Typically, they will be made sensible by the actors in retrospect, but the action itself will not be very meaningful to the participants at the time of its performance. A study that would focus only on these unprocessed moments needs to be carefully considered. There is real danger of the elevation of the objective view. On the other hand, the sense making that follows these moments is a very rich source of the underlying meanings to which we are directed.

The question of coherence is also raised with those forms of social action where the referent interacting unit is the public or society. Novices often want to start the examination of social action by looking at bus riding, or elevator behavior or dining out. While there are certainly discernible patterns of behavior in each of these, the assumption that all actors are conducting themselves from the same point of view is a large one. These settings have the additional problem that often there is little interaction among the individuals present. It is, of course, in the interaction that we gain insight into the collective meanings. Without it, what may be considered a norm may only be an average of what is observed.

Compactness

Organizations may be tightly knit or loosely coupled. Performances can be highly scripted or very improvisational. The underlying meanings, therefore, can be very compact or diffuse. Compact meanings are difficult to unpack. Much more of the action is significant, and subtle variations can have great meaning. Compact meanings require greater technical knowledge of the scene. Such meanings are the result of extended periods of socialization for the actors. They may have elaborate mechanisms of negotiation and maintenance. All of this makes greater demands on the competence of the analyst.

Intimacy

The intimacy of meaning refers to level of protection which is practiced by the actors. Intimacy may, first, be part of the scene itself. Friends and lovers may define their understandings as restricted to the two of them. The analyst may be refused admission to the entire scene. But also, most scenes have circumstances of the sacred and the profane. Sacred performances, such as client relations, contract negotiations, jury deliberations and the like, just don't get done in the presence of the third party. The naturalistic study of intimate scenes is very difficult. Extraordinary solutions are required to make these actions accesible. Generally, they require the researcher to be an insider, a true member by qualification and certification, rather than a permitted outsider. There is a considerable ethical burden in using the insider role for public purposes.

Emotional Range

Finally, scenes place limits on the acceptable range of emotion that can be expressed. The strategies of management and expression of emotion will obviously vary widely. From my family observations, it appears to me that the initial presence of the analyst has an important effect in redefining the acceptable emotional range. That redefinition appears to restrict the range.

It would appear that the emotional range of a situation can be very sensitive to the presence of the analyst unless the social action provides support for the public expression of emotion. In those situations where the scene is more intimate than public, the analyst may need to be an insider to gain full access.

Researcher Resources

The personal resources of the researcher have to play a significant role in selecting the scene. The scene must be accessible in terms of time and money. One's personal schedule must be able to met the required schedule of contacts.

Although there are few research equipment demands, questions of personal support during the period of research, the potential demands of membership in terms of appearances or activities, and travel may not be insignificant.

Equally important is that the scene must be of high interest for the analyst. Motivation has to be high to maintain the contact over the extended period required for this type of study. At the same time, the analyst must be able to distance himself or herself from the scene in order to conduct observation and analysis. One can become committed to the extent that the critical view is lost.

Evaluating the Research Potential of the Scene

Given sufficient time, energy, and other resources, any scene can be approached by the researcher. But in practical fact, choices have to be made to keep the burden of effort within reasonable bounds. In general, the following questions can be useful in evaluating the scene for research:

- What is the size of the population at the level of explanation to be attempted?
- How many different interactive units would have to be joined?
- How does the setting(s) provide for observation and participation?
- How many settings would be involved?
- When, how often, and for how long do the actors come together?
- What is the extent of involvement for the actors?
- What competencies are required for member understanding?
- What are the conditions of membership?
- Do the actors have sufficient history with one another?
- Is there an elaborate mechanism of socialization?
- Is an insider role required?
- Will the cycle of interaction mesh with the available time venue?
- Are there financial demands in dress codes, activities, and the like?
- Is the analyst's interest sufficient to maintain the research program yet not so great as to interfere with critical analysis?

The answer to these questions is usually not available to armchair analysis. Some time, perhaps considerable time, will have to be spent hanging around and talking to the people that are part of the scene. Even then, the answers will be tentative. Novice researchers would do well to consider the scene of an ongoing group that has a restricted scope of action and membership requirements—both implicit and explicit—that can be easily met.

DESIGNING A CONTRIBUTION TO THE DOMAIN OF THEORY

In designing the study, the analyst can anticipate the move from the documented story of the scene to a contribution to the domains of problem solving or theory development. This move is a delayed one, occurring after the analyst has accomplished a holistic understanding of the scene. The necessity of that delay, however, does not mean that many procedural decisions cannot be made in anticipation of the theoretical analysis to follow. In fact, the scene itself, the sites used, the methods of collection, and the form of the **ethnographic text** or research argument may all be decided on the basis of that analysis. To meet our interest in mass communication theory, we visit families who use television and other media; there are families that don't. If one is going to analyze conversational theory, then audio recordings are going to be very useful. Such decisions follow common sense. On the other hand, theory cannot legitimately drive the analysis of the scene. That analysis must be directed by the perspective of the actors. Theory arrives after the scene is understood.

Perhaps, I can show this relationship by returning to the Utah research team's long-time interest in the ways television and other media get accommodated in family life. Now, in that statement we see the two parts of the final contributory effort: the scene and the **theoretical domain**. The scene is, of course, family life. The theoretical domain is within the rubric of media use as particularly defined by the construct of accommodation. In our approach, our first responsibility is to grasp the scene.

When we enter the homes of our families, we cannot simply plop down in the beanbag next to the set and wait for the family members to come and view. Rather, we begin the process of coming to understand the family as a functioning unit of individuals in a relationship. It is only when we understand the unit that we can appreciate the elements within it. For example, to understand the viewing performance of a 14-year-old male as an enactment of status requires understanding the character of the relationships among family members, the other enactment opportunities available within the family setting, other performances of the enactment, and so on. Consequently, we cannot bring the analytical frame into play until we understand the scene.

Once we begin to feel comfortable with our understanding of the family, we can begin to consider how the member practices of media use can be interpreted from the perspective provided by the theoretical construct of accommodation. It is at this point that we begin to make the contribution to the theoretical domain of the discipline.

The contribution to the theoretical domain is the evaluation, explication, modification, and addition to the constructs of relevant theory on the basis of the success of that theory to illuminate the scene. This contribution occurs when the analyst who is conversant with these constructs examines them in light of the research text. It helps me to think of the analyst as standing between two semantic frames—systems of meaning (see Figure 10-2). The one is that of the scene; the other contains the constructs of relevant theory. The task of the analyst is to interpret one within the other, but both must first be understood independently.

This need for independence places the analyst squarely in the middle of competing demands when designing a study. On the one hand, the contribution to theory is based on the evaluation of the capacity of the theory to interpret the social action. For theory to be relevant to any part of the ethnographic text

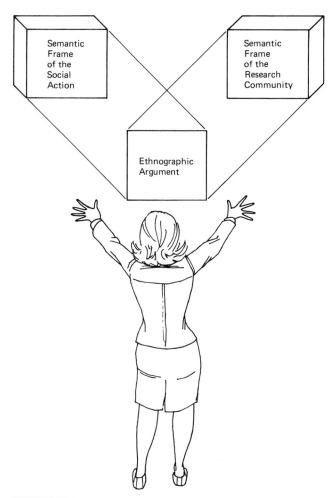

FIGURE 10-2
The researcher must attain a grasp of each system of meaning.

developed out of that social action, however, requires that the manner of creation of that text makes evidence available to the constructs of the theory. It is, therefore, necessary for the researcher to anticipate the theoretical analysis to follow in order that the research text be in a form amenable to that analysis.

On the other hand, the analyst cannot approach the scene with the terms of the theory as the resulting research text will be true to the terms but not to the action. The twin demands of creating an independent research text and providing for a contribution to theory are a dilemma. The analyst must anticipate but not define. The solution to the dilemma resides in the contemporary practice of the epoche which requires the analyst to deliberately expand the view taken beyond that provided by one's theory.

Dealing with the Separate Demands of Scene and Theory

From our analysis of the separate design requirements for analysis and theory, we can see that there are two crafts involved in making a contribution to our knowledge domain. There is the craft of taking in the scene—the development and preservation of a research text which is based on a holistic understanding of the situation. And there is the craft of the analysis of that text from the perspective of one competent in the discourse of a field of study.

The demands of these two crafts are quite different. Capturing a scene in participant observation is a far-ranging social performance; critical analysis is much more an intellectual exercise. Further, there are great differences within each. An analyst may be competent to join family scenes but not at all comfortable in industrial organizations, and competence in one area of theory does not suggest competence in another.

One way to overcome the limitations these varying demands impose on the single researcher is to work with someone who is competent in a different area of analysis. This was the relationship between Pacanowsky and myself in the writing of the "Cop Talk" article.

Pacanowsky had done the work of the research text. My work was the critical evaluation of the constructs of the uses and gratifications paradigm. In order for me to conduct that analysis, Pacanowsky had to prepare an episodic text which presented, in written, objective form, his lived experience as analyzed in the interpretations of media nicknames, value authentication, and descriptive referent. There is no way that I could have attacked the research text; it is Pacanowsky's experience. But once he had created the written text of his interpretation, I could begin the process of my critical analysis. Once I had created my written analysis, Pacanowsky could examine it in light of the research text to determine if it was true to his experience.

Relationship between Forms of Argument and Dialectical Analysis

In the previous chapter, I talked about the three forms of argument which characterize the qualitative research articles currently appearing in the communication journals—the narrative, inductive exemplar, and models and types. We can now consider the relationship between these forms of argument and the **dialectical analysis** they support.

The naked narrative—the ethnographic text without an interpretation within a theoretical notational scheme—makes its contribution by directing the reader's encounter with the other through the structure of the narrative. It leaves to the reader the task of examining the appropriate constructs of the field in the light of the narrative. Such insights that occur are held in the **private knowledge** of the reader and are not part of our public knowledge. The narrated story and its interpretation, however, is the explicit form which offers both the public encounter with the other and the dialectical analysis. It offers a complete contribution to public knowledge.

The inductive exemplar form of argument produces categories in the claims of the meaningful similarities discoverable in the episodes of the research text. The contribution can end here with the constructs tightly bound to the episodes they interpret. The inductive form of models and types would advance the claims to greater generality. In both forms, the contribution can be continued in a dialectic among the categories, models and types, their defining episodes, and the constructs of the field.

The deductive argument from models and types begins with the existing constructs and interprets the research text from that stance. There can be no dialectic because the elements to compose the dialectic are not independent as the text is already created out of the theoretical constructs.

Summary: Defining the Research Contribution

In this section, we have been concerned with the manner in which qualitative research offers its contribution to the discourse of the field. We have found that it does so in two ways: first, by offering an encounter with the other in the ethnographic text, and second, by interpreting that text in a dialectical analysis with some set of constructs of the discipline with which the analyst is conversant. In this dialectic, the reader comes to understand the ethnographic text as seen through these constructs and to understand the constructs as enacted in the text.

To make this contribution, the analyst must first approach a holistic understanding of the scene from the perspective of the actors in the development and preservation of the research text. That understanding is presented through the vehicle of extended or episodic narrative. In creating the complete form, the analyst details the formal properties of some construct set and considers those properties in the light of the ethnographic text and the ethnographic text in the light of those properties.

In practice, not every research work makes the complete contribution explicit. The interpretive dialectic may be missing if the theoretical constructs in play are not made explicit or if the ethnographic text is created from them.

AN EXAMPLE: ILLUSTRATING DESIGN

Let me offer an extended example of how these various design considerations come into play: Assume with me that we have spent about a year working to develop the research text on a small (15-member) organization that provides data processing services, keypunching, disk and tape files, computerized billing, and the like. The organization can be seen as composed of four working groups—administrative (the owner and the bookkeeper), client contact (the owner and two salespersons), programmers and computer operators (four persons), and a seven-person clerical staff which does the keyboarding, data handling, and preparation.

At the end of this year, we have quite a large repository of information. We have the recordings from each staff meeting (38 ninety-minute tapes); our field notes from 840 contact hours (3 hours per day for 280 days), about 4500 pages; copies of all of the memos and work orders; advertisements and other communication artifacts that we could save; the transcripts of interviews conducted with each of the members; photographs of each person's work station; maps of the working area detailing the objects of the organization, territories, boundaries, trails, use sites, and the like. We have notes on work schedules (in policy and in practice), job descriptions, job practices, work ways, working groups, interactive units, and friends and enemies. We know which people take cream in their coffee and their explanation for doing it.

We have our own experience of learning how to keyboard, process data, make sales calls, and of finally finding a "gofer" niche that would let us be part of the organization but still conduct our observation work.

There it sits before us—two boxes of notes and partial narratives, four boxes of artifacts, some 621 pages of transcribed interviews, a stack of cassettes, a photo album, and our memories.

And fortunately, there are some good ideas about how to proceed. We decide that for our first article, the concept of ritual would be useful as an interpretive tool and can, in turn, be brought to life by the episodes in our text. That decision is not just happenstance. The construct of ritual has been getting good play in the literature. And sometime during those observation we began to notice recurring performances which seemed to serve both to release the tensions of order and at the same time to reinforce it as proper. We now have a coda by which we can decide what is important and not important in our repository. We might first address ourselves to finding the notes and supporting materials of those performances and writing the episodic text of them. We would also search for references to them, comments about them, and evaluations of them in the whole research text. We would try to learn the meaning they hold for the actors, both as performers and as audience, in the record of what was said and done. In all of this, we would be seeking to understand the network of meaning that binds together the social action of these performances.

With that interpretive search well under way, we would begin an analysis of the formal properties of the construct of ritual by reviewing its use and development in the literature and considering it in our own analysis. The final written work would bring together the ethnographic text and the formal construct analysis into juxtaposition to find the points of contact—the interplay, facilitations, paradoxes, and contradictions.

This dialectic does not hypothesize ritual as an objective property of action to be validated in its discovery. Rather, it shows, on the one hand, the extent to which the concept of ritual will work the obdurate material of the research text into a meaningful form, and, on the other, it demonstrates the enacted meaning of ritual in the episodes of this situation. In the end, the reader has learned about both the rituals of the organization and the construct of ritual.

Now for our next article, I noticed that there was the distinct character of a clerical ghetto in this organization. Let's find out what content in conversation and organizational documents is used to construct this segregation. You go read about the ideology and metaphor of segregation; I'll start to work on the episodic texts.

SUMMARY

This chapter has considered the elements that go into the design of the research study. Qualitative research begins with an interest in the situated individual. The individual present in everyday life, enmeshed in the networks of shared, mutually negotiated, and maintained meanings. The object of study is these jointly held meanings which define social action. Generally, study is directed toward one of four aspects of the situated individual: (a) Focusing on the individual per se, it presents the individual as a biographical other, revealing the other self as a thinking, feeling, and acting individual. Or using the individual as an informant vis-à-vis social action, it has (b) concentrated on the content of those meanings, (c) their structure and function, or (d) the processes by which they are negotiated and maintained.

All research is directed by analytical metaphors. The fundamental metaphor of qualitative research is the narrative. In the narrative form, the flow of experience is punctuated to create an event. The narrative encodes the relationships among what is observable. These relationships tell the story of the scene. The creation of the written narrative moves the event from private to public knowledge.

The narrative can appear as embedded in other metaphors. The metaphor of the theater has a long history within symbolic interaction and dramaturgical theory. The metaphor of culture has appeared in the analysis of organizations.

In the design of this research, it is the scene that is the unifying concept and the starting place of study. The scene presents the situated individual. A scene is defined by the actors' understanding of the situation they are in not by objective characteristics. Selecting the scene of study is the way one begins research. In making that selection, the analyst evaluates the scene as a suitable research site. The criteria of evaluation are based on the relative difficulty of attaining a holistic understanding of the situation.

The contribution of a study begins with the presentation of the other in the written narrated story. This contribution is adequate, but incomplete as science. The contribution to the scientific discourse of a discipline is presented in the dialectic between the ethnographic text and the constructs of the discipline used to interpret that text. This dialectic provides a critical analysis of the ethnographic text in the light of the theoretical constructs and of the constructs in light of the text.

Actual examples of written research show a variety of presentational modes. Insightful writing is rarely formulaic. However, the reader should expect to learn both of the situated individual and of the constructs of the field.

EXERCISES

1 Describe an ongoing group scene that would be appropriate for you to study.
2 How does the "of-course-it's-true" response of committed membership interfere with critical analysis?
3 In the naturalistic side of our campaign studies, we are interested in how the campaign gets accommodated in everyday family life. Given what you know about naturalistic research, what are the explanatory responsibilities of this study?
4 How does a dialectical analysis differ from the verification of a hypothesis?
5 Is the consequence for theory the same in qualitative and quantitative research?
6 If the answer to question 3 is "no," then it might have something to do with reductionism. How would that argument proceed?

RELATED READINGS

Blasi, A. J., Dasilva, F. B. and Weigert, A. J. *Toward an interpretive sociology.* Washington, D.C.: University Press of America, 1978.

Douglas, J. D. (Ed.), *Introduction to the sociologies of everyday life,* Boston: Allyn and Bacon, 1980.

McCall, G. J. and Simmons, J. L. *Identities and interactions.* New York: The Free Press, 1978.

Morgan, G. (Ed.). *Beyond method: Strategies for social research.* Beverly Hills, CA: Sage Publications Inc., 1983.

Putnam, L. L. and Pacanowsky, M. E. (Eds.). *Communication and organizations: An interpretive approach.* Beverly Hills, CA: Sage Publications Inc., 1983.

Van Maanen, J. (Ed.). *Qualitative methodology.* Beverly Hills, CA: Sage Publications Inc., 1983.

CHAPTER 11

PARTICIPANT OBSERVATION: GETTING STARTED

SYNOPSIS

In this chapter, we will consider the **researcher as instrument**. The methods of participant observation are a set of strategies and tactics for managing access to and understanding of the network of meanings that define social action. This chapter picks up where Chapter 10 left off—the scene has been tentatively selected and a research focus vaguely defined. I make no pretense of giving *the* method of participant observation. Each researcher develops his or her own set of strategies and then responds improvisationally to the demands of the situation. À la Indiana Jones, we make it up as we go along. Consequently, what is presented is a discussion of the typical activities that start the process of participation and observation. Those activities are hanging around, gaining access, learning the ropes, experiencing member activities, and participating as a member. Along with an introductory discussion of the nature of participant observation, these are the headings of this chapter.

THE NATURE OF PARTICIPANT OBSERVATION

What does it mean to do **participant observation**? The participation that we are concerned with is a participation in the understandings held by the social actors. It is often gained by doing what the social actors do, but it is not the same thing. This participation is having a member's knowledge. It is knowing the right thing to do and the right time to do it. In its most developed form, it is the participation in the negotiation, maintenance, and evaluation of the network of meanings that define the right act and the right time for it. The observation that we are concerned with begins with the careful recognition of the details surrounding the objects and actions which constitute the scene. The primary activity, however, is the recognition of the meaningful significance of those objects and actions in those critical instances in which these meanings are displayed.

Participation and observation are both competitive and complementary efforts. They are competitive because they must be done separately. It is very difficult to cast the dispassionate, observational eye when struggling to improvise your next participant move. They are complementary because one supports the other. One uses the participant's understanding to observe the significance of things, and good observations can lead to better participation. Participant observation moves into the social action by alternating the emphasis on participation and observation. By moving back and forth between the two, the analyst can both understand the meanings of the members and make those meanings explicit.

Levels of Participation

Participation levels range from the interviewer to the insider positions. The interviewer tries to create a condition of revelation in which the meaning of things is exposed. Participation in the interview revolves around the interaction between the interviewer and informant as they attempt mutually understandable discourse. At this level, participation is a staged effort and observation is a product of a routine. At the other extreme, the insider has the "of-course-it's-true" knowledge of the member. For the insider, participation is effortless, observation difficult.

In levels between these two, the analyst tries to find some participant niche which will be recognized by the members as a legitimate position within the scene. Such a position will require the members and the analyst to negotiate their relationship. If negotiated well, the relationship will evoke interaction in instruction, correction, supervision, praise, blame, and other comment by members. It will bring the analyst face-to-face with the member's rules and values. It will provide an understanding of the metaphor and humor of the scene. In these interactions, the meaning of things would be revealed.

Participation is *not* analytically neutral. In some manner, the analyst must interact with a stake in the outcome. Written at this abstraction, it all seems so bloodless. What the analyst must do is to move from the stage of "Who's the creep that keeps hanging around?" to "Oh, here's that observer again" to "Hey, Jim, come over here and help me with this."

Levels of Observation

A quick look at the notion of observation might suggest a process in which the analyst watches while reality displays itself. Closer consideration shows observation to be a process of sense making. It is not a record of senseless detail but an understanding of actions and of meaningful objects. The notation "He moved his arm 6 inches to the right'' is not a good observation when "He reached for his coffee cup, but then thought better of it" tells the story.

Observation begins with watching, listening, touching—all the sensory activities at careful attention. It continues in the interpretation of what was seen, heard, etc., and ends with the careful record of what went on. Let's explore each of these three phases a bit:

Careful Attention   The watching and listening of observation has a different quality from the watching and listening of participation. In observation, what is seen and heard is held up for inspection. In participation, it is the context for our own action. Observation lacks the anticipation of a performance of one's own but has an interrogator's stance in which the analyst adopts an extended sensitivity, searching for the smallest clues about what is going on. Those significant elements are somehow preserved—in memory, in notes, on recordings. The careful detailing of the scene gathers the evidence necessary to demonstrate the significance of the action.

Good observation includes careful attention to one's own participation. Indeed, if the participation is going to have a meaningful contribution to the research effort, the analyst must systematically reflect, observe, and record the meaning of that participation.

Interpretation   Our observations are always a reconstruction because the meaning of the social action emerges in its performance. The analyst sees the clues to what is going on after they have happened. All observation involves interpretation; good observation bases that interpretation in the member's meanings. That things become objects and behaviors become actions according to the meanings held for them is the core proposition of research from this perspective. What is out there is the thing and the behavior; we can see the object and the action only in interpretation.

The Extended Record   Observation reaches closure in the creation of the field notes. Field notes are usually a narrative which begins at the beginning and works through to where the understanding of the action falls apart; the narrative notes that dissolution and then starts again at the next beginning. Despite their name, field notes are rarely written in the field, but in a place where the analyst can withdraw and contemplate what was attended to and the interpretations given to it.

Field notes provide a check on the other phases of observation. One quickly learns how much was missed and how weak the insightful interpretation is, when trying to make explicit in the written word what passed before. The note, however, is a record of what the analyst understands at a given point in time. My initial notes of a scene are usually filled with mere detail because lacking **member maturity**, I don't know enough to understand objects and actions. That immaturity is itself useful in later reflection. It gives me a reference point for what I have learned.

Just as one never takes enough pictures on vacation, one never writes enough field notes. It is a deficit which is always felt. Observations that don't make it into notes are soon lost. The work of careful attention and interpretation is wasted.

Participation and Observation: A Summary

The rubric of participant observation is a set of improvisational strategies for learning the significance of a member's knowledge. The participation that we are concerned with is in the network of meanings from which objects and actions emerge. Participation can range from the insider to the interviewing visitor. Whatever the level of participation, it must both involve a stake in the outcome and permit the critical observation of its product—the meanings of social action.

Observation can be seen in three phases: (1) listening, watching, touching, etc., in careful attention; (2) interpreting the significance for the members of what was seen, heard, etc.; (3) creating the extended record of what happened. Observation is not the passive notation of reality displayed before the analyst.

With this overview of participant-observation, we can move to a discussion of the strategies of how it gets done. Throughout this discussion, I will adopt the general stance that we are dealing with the open analysis of a group, organization, or institution with a recognized and recognizable membership from the analyst's native culture (wierdos are OK, but no exotics). Usually, I will avoid comment on aggregates (line standing, parade watching, etc.). Most communication studies involve memberships rather than aggregates, and it is my opinion that aggregates are much more difficult for the novice to study. We begin at a typical beginning.

HANGING AROUND[1]

Qualitative research has an emergent, negotiated nature. What the study can be about depends on the interpersonal competence of the researcher[2] and the choices made by the members as those choices get expressed within the research site. Except for the unexpected, there are no guarantees.

Once the analyst has selected two or three possible research sites, he or she begins to frequent them to discover the principal actors, characteristic methods, the individuals and their practices which control access, the likely match between researcher and members, the conditions of membership, whether a covert or overt research stance should be taken, and the capacity of the site to respond to the demands of the research. At this point, the researcher is "just hanging around" without committing him/herself to the scene or identifying him/herself with a research project. In this manner, most options are kept open.

---

[1]A word about the colorful headings: It is common practice both to emphasize the action (the participle form) and to use mundane language. A more officious heading might be "Preassessment of the Research Site."

[2]There is, perhaps, no clearer statement of the notion of the researcher as the instrument.

Hanging around is itself a negotiated status. Only in a very few of the most public sites can an individual show up day after day without engendering some comment. Any scene with a recognizable membership may, of course, require substantial negotiation just to come in and look around. A favored strategy of mine is the guest status. I become the guest of some members whom I have known previously or have gotten to agree to show me around. They provide my justification. I suggest more than one guide to get a broader perspective, to lighten the demands on an individual and to avoid getting unintentionally identified with whatever that individual might represent within the group.

In my own tactics of hanging around, I try to extend this period until I am able to describe the interactive unit of the study and have met and either conversed with or interviewed[3] all the members of it. I hope also to know where that interactive unit fits within a possible larger structure and, of course, the answers to the assessment questions presented in Chapter 9.

Hanging around is preparatory to writing the research prospectus. In hanging around, the analyst should gain enough information to adequately describe the parameters of the project to justify the taking of the risk. Each project is a risk because its precise nature or even its successful engagement cannot be predicted. The nature of the study will be successively changed as it gets negotiated throughout the study's lifespan. And as we have seen, the research focus probably won't be defined until after the majority of the encounter has been completed.

The threats to the successful engagement of a project are clear and deadly. The members may deny access to the project, cripple it with restrictions, or terminate it in midlife. The researcher may prove incompetent to the scene and be unable to sustain a level of participation. Or the scene itself may dissolve in financial, legal, or social collapse.

In quantitative research, those of us who sit on review boards for funding or other institutional approval (such as theses or dissertations) evaluate the methods and assume the individual can practice them. In qualitative research, we have to evaluate the stability of the scene and the likelihood that the individual can improvise the methods for its study. The evidence for that evaluation is the result of hanging around.

GAINING ACCESS

A successful field study requires the gaining and returning of the trust, confidence, and cooperation of, at least the majority of the members of the interactive unit. Gaining access, first involves an initial entry into the interactive unit for the marginal and ill-defined role of research, and, second involves the continuous cultivation of a research presence among the members. We will

---

[3]I have found the request for an interview a very successful technique to use when I have no contacts within the membership. It is a particularly useful way for initiating contact with families where other forms of hanging around are virtually impossible.

consider the problem of gaining access as divided into these two tasks and under the headings of "Getting Permission" and "Negotiating a Research Presence."

GAINING ACCESS: GETTING PERMISSION

Getting permission is the first step in any open research project. In this discussion, I'll report on the tactics which have been used to gain permission in families and friends, **loosely coupled memberships**, and organizations.

Getting Permission—Families and Friends

Friends and neighbors were an early source for our family studies.[4] (Using an inside contact is usually productive.) As we progressed (and began running out of friends with families), it became obvious that we were going to need a systematic method for generating volunteer families. Although the Utah rate of households with families is twice the national rate, we ensured our contact with family households by selecting names from elementary, middle (seventh and eighth grades), and high school directories. As our school districts use a feeder system (given elementary schools graduate their students to a specific middle school and so forth), it is possible to identify families with children across different school ages by comparing entries in the different directories. When a new family is needed, a pool of 10 families selected from these directories gets the following introductory letter which is mailed midweek:

> Dear Mr. and Mrs.   and family,
> The Communication Research Center at the University of Utah is conducting a ten-year study of family life. This study is being conducted in cooperation with other leading universities throughout the nation. Among other things this study focuses on the way children use media—television, radio, books and magazines—within their family settings.
> We want to ask your family to join this study. At the first of next week I will call you to set up an appointment to explain the study. Of course your participation is entirely up to you.
> If you have any questions, please call me at the Department of Communication 581-6888 during working hours or at my home 555-3344 at other times.
> Sincerely,
> Dr. James A. Anderson
> Professor

All ten families are called the following week. The telephone conversation is a brief explanation with an emphasis on the positive values of the study. It goes something like :

---

[4]Sampling bias is rarely an issue in qualitative research. There is no claim that there are core attributes which will describe all families. In fact the opposite claim, that each situation is unique, is made. The absence of the core attribute claim makes the notion of sampling bias meaningless. Unique events cannot be biased toward anything nor can they be of all the same kind which are the typical concerns of sampling bias.

What we try to do in this study is to spend some time with your family getting to know you, sharing a little bit of your family life. We're going to be interested in where television and newspapers and radio fit into that family life especially with your children, but with you too if that's all right. As we go along we'd like to share with you what we see and that's usually interesting for our families.

Right now, we want to talk with your family to see if the study would work for you. Would Tuesday at 7:00 be a good time?

Appointments are made only with the number of families that are needed. The remaining families are "cooled out" with an explanation that our quota is filled for now and a request to keep their name on the active file.

This strategy has worked well for us. We have always been able to get the one or two families needed from the pool and usually within the first five calls. It is an efficient method of identifying English-speaking, family households. It intends to be considerate of the individuals involved and provide a large enough pool that we can be persuasive without being desperate.

Other researchers have used other means to gain access to family and friends. Lull (1980) reports contacting his families through clubs, religious groups, nursery schools, and the like. His studies have used a relatively large number of families at a time. He reports his acceptance rate at 30 percent (p. 200).

Alexander and Newell (1981a) used requests before college classes as their primary means of getting volunteers for their study on friends. In a personal conversation with him, Alexander commented that each class contact usually resulted in one volunteer pair for the 8-week study. He found, however, that once the study was started, participants began to tell friends of the interesting and personally rewarding study in which they were involved. The word of mouth was apparently good enough that the researchers ended up turning people away.

The net of this discussion is that it is relatively easy to gain access to, at least, some families, friendship pairs, and couples. People who have volunteered for our studies have shown a surprising diversity. I have had experience with families of different classes—in tony districts and slums, different races, single-parent families, families on welfare, and even one family in which the breadwinner's occupation was clearly beyond the law.

My guess about why we succeed is based on Alexander's comments. Qualitative research involves a genuine interaction—an opportunity for individuals to see themselves in the eyes of another. It is a relationship which is to be free of cynicism, comparison, and evaluation and to provide valid description. It is something we can offer in exchange for participation. On the other hand, there have been individuals who would have nothing to do with our research. They represent the limits of research based on voluntary participation.

Getting Permission—Loosely Coupled Memberships

By loosely coupled memberships, I mean that broad range of organizations which permit a number of different ways for the individual to achieve membership. Many social or recreational memberships are loosely coupled. There are also loosely coupled occupational groups which make use of volunteers or ideological groups, such as the wilderness conservationists. Loosely coupled memberships have a freedom of entry and exit. An individual can enter by meeting requirements of interest and without invoking a long-term commitment.

If the analyst can meet the requirements of membership, a simple tactic is to join up and start taking notes. One's position as a chronicler can be openly established in conversation or in the newsletter (if available):

> Jim Anderson reports that he is writing a book on our Wednesday night bowling league. Nothing scandalous, just people being people, he says. Good luck to you, Jim.

By doing so, the analyst gains a tacit permission and establishes an ethical position in which the normal contracts of membership can be preserved.

No tactic is always successful. Members could take action against the analyst particularly if there are secrecy clauses in the bylaws of the organization. For the analyst, the prevailing attitude in these moves is a commitment to membership, a willingness to negotiate, an honorable manner, an openness of one's methods, and an understanding that one's final position simply precedes the next one. As Schatzman and Strauss (1973) point out: "Any restrictions initially accepted by the researcher should be regarded as renegotiable at later, more propitious times" (p. 29).

There are, of course, loosely coupled memberships that the analyst will be unable to join directly because of age, gender, competencies, and the like. In these organizaions, a new membership category will have to be negotiated. Roles such as tag-along, mascot, gofer, groupie, fan, agent, good-luck charm, auxiliary, associate, and just plain friend have all been used. A person in an enlarged membership role is not a stranger, but one who receives recognition, response, and even deference. Gaining tacit acceptance in such a role usually permits the deviant behavior required by the research, gives access to the members, and avoids forcing an official position with possible restrictions or involvement in power struggles.

Having established one's presence through one of these roles, it is, then, possible to negotiate the research aspect of that role with each individual member. Again, the benefit is that no official position has to be taken by the group leaders which could rebound to their detriment. Further, even with leadership approval, individual negotiation will have to be conducted by the analyst. Official approval is no guarantee of access. The costs are that the researcher's position is more tentative without sanction and that it is easy to exploit a member's ignorance of the research component.

There are, finally, those groups which will permit neither membership nor a tacit, enlarged membership role. In those groups, an officially sanctioned researcher status will have to be negotiated. As that negotiation involves the principal strategies with formal organizations, we will continue this discussion in the following section.

Formal Organizations

For our purposes, I am distinguishing loosely coupled memberships from formal organizations because the primary approach to gaining access is quite different between the two. The simple advice for loosely coupled organizations is to join and to use the looseness of the organization to negotiate an individual research status. It is unlikely that this strategy will be available for most formal organizations. Formal organizations generally have restrictive entry requirements and rigidly defined memberships; they expect a long-term commitment and require high levels of involvement from their members. Further, analysis of the organization itself is considered a proprietary right. In this setting, formal negotiations for entry as a researcher must be conducted. Some possible strategies follow:

Keep the Permission Line Short   If possible, negotiate entry only with the interactive unit of interest. For example, most school districts have policies regarding research in the classroom which require district or Board level approval. In many cases, actual practice dictates only the approval of the classroom teacher and, perhaps, the school principal. (This variance is discovered by hanging around.)

If the value of the research can be made apparent to the interactive unit, they may be able to justify the research within existing protocol. A classroom observation can become a unit on social science research; a study of a working group can become a seminar on "Quality Circles." The ethical problem is rendered moot if the purposes of the redefinition can be met—the kids do learn about social science, etc.

Violations of policy involve some level of risk for both the member and the analyst. These are risks which most members of organizational life regularly experience. Nevertheless, the researcher's first concern should be for the member and not for the study.

Develop Contacts   In my mind, developing contacts is the sine qua non of getting permission in formal organizations. One enters an organization as a stranger—a nuisance to be dealt with. The analyst can relieve this alienation by deliberately laying a plan of contacts with the gatekeepers of the firm. These contacts can be practiced through interviews, letters, sharing research reports, providing academic services such as informal seminars or literature reviews (even dropping an "FYI" article in the mail), taking classes on tours, social invitations, joining common activities and clubs—in fact all of the methods that any good salesperson would use.

The determining characteristic in all of this is good-natured persistence—the continued presentation of the value of the research for the organization and of the competence of the analyst. The researcher may still fail: A colleague of mine has tried for three years to get into a major retailing firm. He hasn't made it yet;

he has a very long approval line, but his contacts are growing. In themselves, they are an invaluable resource.

Get Sponsors   If it is possible to establish strong, qualified contacts during the initial scouting of the organization, those contacts may be willing to advance a proposal for the necessary permissions for the study. The proposal which the analyst will write can be, nonetheless, presented over the signature of a contact. The advantage is that refusal implies a cost to a fellow member of the organization rather than to an outsider. Of course, the standing of the contact can adversely affect the evaluation of the proposal.

Work All the Territory   Approval for entry can come from the top down or from the bottom up. It is folly to work only on upper management in developing contacts. A sponsor from below can be just as effective as a sponsor from above. Equally important, approval from above does not guarantee cooperation at the level the analyst will need it the most. It is most important to sell the project at the point of the study—the interactive unit. Finally, working all the territory gets one out of the "It's all right with me if it's all right with them" trap.

Develop Consensus on the Nature of the Project   Understanding the viewpoint of the other is an integral part of getting permission. In the early going of getting permission, the project should be in soft focus—something to talk about but not that much to react against. Although the analyst may initiate the project, research is a mutual effort. A study emerges from the encounter; it is not imposed by the analyst. Throughout the process of entry, the analyst must be attuned to the benefits attributed to and the objections raised against the project as it exists in the minds of the members. The project that comes into clearer focus is one which is the product of this interaction. It emphasizes the benefits possible, eliminates false expectations (such as major changes in productivity), and meets the objections.

Consensus can develop commitment to the project as personal effort has been expended in its construction. The project will likely need advocates not only at the point of decision but through its duration. Consensus building can produce those advocates.

Use Documentation Carefully   As the research project will always have an emergent quality, prior documentation such as proposals or work schedules and time lines can provide only the broad outlines of the study. There is, typically, pressure to "tell us exactly what you are going to do." In response to this pressure, the analyst can provide a description of objectives rather than methods. An objective for a work organization might be written as:

> To develop a multifaceted description of the methods by which members of the Megatrends Corporation support work activities, validate work practices, and find value in work performances.

This objective can be followed by an extensive discussion of what the multifaceted description would entail.

Any documentation should be written with the assumption that everyone in the organization will have access to the document. (It is good practice for the analyst to ensure that access.) Avoid supporting one interest group against another ("This study will identify problems in worker productivity"). Although the document (and the project) will most likely become identified with whatever group approves it, selling the project to one group to the neglect of another (or worse, its control or dominance) can result in later reprisals by the disenfranchised group.

In short, prior documentation is always a problem. At best, it provides the prospect of an interesting look at one's self. But, it can also be seen as threatening, describing an invasion of privacy, or a method of management control. It can be used against the project if it promises something not delivered or raises expectations of what it is not. A proposal can trap the analyst into work which appeared fruitful from the outside but is sterile in fact.

This section began with the advice to keep the approval lines as short as possible; it ends with the advice to keep the paper trail equally short. Assuming that the exchange of money is not involved, documentation rarely works to the researcher's advantage. Work from an oral history or a letter or two, if possible. If a proposal is required, use techniques of consensus building to develop the document. Check wording with contacts from various territories within the organization. Be specific with objectives and not methods. View the proposal as a strategy for gaining access not as a recipe for concocting a study. Be honest, but say no more than necessary; everything said can be held against the project. Finally, be particularly careful about describing what the project will deliver as its outcome. Loose talk about "exit interviews" almost always is read as evaluation and recommendations. Such expectations are an obstacle to the study.

Getting Permission: An Analytic Summary

This section has looked at the strategies for getting permission to conduct a research study within intimate, loosely coupled, and formally organized groups. This discussion did not provide a script for gaining entry. It came more from a retrospective analysis of things done wrong than the handbook of success. We have been looking at scenarios for improvisations.

Getting permission is a process which involves the group. In this process, the role of the researcher is legitimized and sanctioned. It provides space for that role and begins to define its terms. These terms will set the parameters for the nature of the participation permitted the analyst. In the best negotiation of getting permission, these terms will neither demand too much participation nor restrict one's performance.

Qualitative research always puts the personal resources of the researcher on the line. Getting permission means using what leverage there is and developing what is necessary in a manner that won't disrupt the cooperation needed for the study. Use friendship, make contacts, find sponsors, develop consensus, and negotiate everything. Then find some way to make it worthwhile to everybody. Entry is a matter of time and effort. No rejection is final. Even gatekeepers die.

Gaining entry is not some technical, rational operation which follows a Queensbury set of rules. It is well to keep in mind Johnson's (1975) criticism of the typical analysis of access. He writes:

> The traditional literature is replete with vague prescriptions about "being a nice guy," "being open," "being honest," "being a regular guy," and so forth. Using these prescriptions is implicitly considered to open the magic door to the setting so as to obtain valid and reliable data in field research. Cunning, deception, or the use of power are never reported by field researchers as elements of their own actions (p. 59).

This absence undoubtedly supports the proper image of research, but hardly provides an adequate description of what often needs to be done.

GAINING ACCESS: NEGOTIATING A RESEARCH PRESENCE

Getting permission will provide a pass for the front gate; it will not give you the hearts and minds of the members. The presence of the analyst has to be personally negotiated with each individual in the targeted interactive unit. That negotiation may be a simple introduction and explanation with base-touching follow-up. It can also involve extensive discussion and a set of specific rules for interaction.

The researcher's role is an odd one. People do not overtly conduct themselves the way an analyst must. The very process of research is alien as it makes significant what is common and ordinary. Members will have to make sense of why the analyst is taking notes on the way they do things or recording conversations where nothing lasting is intended. It is important that the researcher participate in that member sense making.

I am reminded of the 5-year-old member of one of my families who came up to me and said, "I'm not supposed to talk to you because you're doin' 'search.'" I commented that I couldn't do "'search" unless he did talk to me and offered to play a game of his choosing. While we got along fine, I was never able to find out why he thought he couldn't talk to me.

For some families, my presence is a continual violation of their norms of privacy. They are now constrained in dress and action. They are forced to accommodate my presence. Some members do so in anger and irritation. But each member will have to deal with me in some way. I gain entry to my families through the parents, but I have to negotiate who I am with each member. This negotiation is one of those check-list requirements of a good study. You should be able to find it in your field notes.

Finally, the negotiated research presence will determine what, from the lives of the members, is legitimate for the analyst to use and the manner in which it can be preserved. This negotiation will involve the entire frame—what goes in, what goes out, and how it gets saved. Typically, the adults in a family will let me sit in and record any conversation between friends (undoubtedly edited), but not every conversation between the couple. On the other hand, the children appear oblivious in any conversation between siblings, but not between friends.

Perspective Taking in Negotiation

When the interactive unit is composed of separate groups, it is not unusual to find the analyst adopting the perspective of one of those groups within these negotiations. The classroom is a good example. It is usually easy for the researcher to adopt the teacher's perspective. Most of us who do academic research also participate in that teaching role. It is difficult to negotiate a place among the students. This difficulty increases with the decreasing age of those students.

Adopting a perspective means that the analyst references his or her behavior within that group. Choices in dress, ways of speaking, and the like are directed by that group's alternatives. When sides are to be taken, the analyst finds solidarity within that group. Look again at the letter we send to families. The phrase, "Among other things, this study focuses on the way children use media," establishes an "us/them" connection with parents. In this case, it is a strategy to gain access, but it could also indicate a view of the family through parent's eyes.

Perspective taking is common in the study of organizations. As I noted in Chapter 2, the view of the manager most often appears. When the analyst takes a perspective, he or she typically negotiates a presence with the referenced members only. Nonreferenced members in the interactive unit are treated as objectified others. In organizational communication studies, we usually get inside the network of managers (or union leadership) but remain outside the network of workers. The meaning network of the workers is treated as an objectified element of the environment in which managers perform.

Perspective taking is a necessary device. It sets the limits of the view provided. To be valid, it must be appropriate to the explanatory purpose of the study. It would not be valid for me to adopt only the parental perspective if my intent was to explain the family. Parents are only one element in a family. (Others are children, siblings, the couple, cross-sex alliances, same-sex alliances, and the like.) Similarly, it would not be valid to adopt the manager's perspective if the intent was to explain the interaction between managers and workers.

Difficulties in Negotiating a Presence

The negotiations for a presence will not be equally successful. Covert rejection is not uncommon ("I'll just shut up when she's around") and overt rejection occurs. Rejection is part of the research experience to be written up like any other. Rejection (like acceptance) has to be defined and maintained. It involves strategy and tactics which are as much grist to the researcher's mill as any other. The analyst is much more likely, however, to find his or her own humanity in writing the episodes of rejection.

When the analyst is attempting an explanation of an interactive unit composed of separate groups, the difficulties are compounded by the view taken of the analyst. Neutrality is not a legitimate position in membership. ("He who is not with me is against me.") The analyst can end up being shunned by all groups.

The analyst can also be seen as taking sides. To begin with, gaining sanction for a study carries with it the onus of being identified with the sanctioning group. A study approved by management is a management study. It's no wonder the researcher may implicitly adopt the managerial position when presented with this reflected view. If conflict is present, the access granted to the analyst can be seen as a valuable asset which can be used by one of the parties.

One parent turned to me during an argument with her 10-year-old son over the use of the TV set and said, "You see how much he watches television. Don't you think he spends too much time in front of that set?" (Damn that letter!) My relationship with that 10-year-old was never the same. Not only because of his view of me, but also because I felt the guilt of being used against him.

In working with divided units, my own tactic (which obviously doesn't always work) is to make sure that two stories get told again and again. They go something like:

> Look, my problem is that I've got to stay on the straight and narrow here. What I'm trying to do is to tell your story to the people out there. To tell them what working for Megatrends is all about.

> Anyway, it's going to take me over a year to get this thing written up. You know I can't offer anything until that's done. I just don't know anything until its written.

Of course, analysts do take sides. The key is to make one's own position clear and not to transfer it to someone in the scene. One's perspective must be identified in the written work. I get angry at managerial exploitation and worker's intransigence, a teacher's lack of sensitivity and the students' apathy, and that nasty older sister who browbeats her little brother. That's all part of participation; my responsibility is to write it up.

Negotiating a Research Presence: An Analytic Summary

Getting permission involves the legitimization of the role of the researcher within the group. It is a sanctioning process by which space is provided for that role. Negotiating a research presence is much more a one-on-one activity. It specifies how the analyst will behave toward each member of the interactive unit. Who will be a sponsor, a friend, an informant; who will be unavailable, resistant, an enemy. What can be seen and listened to; what is permissible to record, photograph, preserve.

While they signal the beginning of a research project, both getting permission and negotiating a presence are continuous activities. Permission must be gained from every membership grouping. It can be lost and regained. The relationship with another is ever emergent as the history of the relationship is an integral part of it. Both permission and presence must be managed throughout the life of the study.

Permission and presence are not attributes but actions. As actions involving members, they are part of the explanatory responsibility of the study. How members manage the granting of permission and the negotiation of the researcher's presence is a required element of analysis.

EXERCISES

1 Briefly distinguish between participation and observation.
2 Why is observation not the passive notation of displayed reality?
3 Why is the research prospectus for a qualitative study difficult to write?
4 What is learned from hanging around?
5 Describe the strategy of perspective taking that is used in our letter to families.
6 It is a management principle that policies are for punishing people, not for providing a rule of practice. What are the implications of this principle for the consideration of an organization's policies concerning research?
7 Can you suggest some of the personal difficulties and stresses that might befall a researcher in the process of gaining access from your own entry experiences?
8 What would have been a good response to the parent's demand for an evaluation of the child's viewing? What do you think has to be and can be accomplished with your proposed response?
9 What is accomplished in the negotiation of a research presence?
10 How does perspective taking influence the negotiation of a research presence?
11 What does it mean that access and presence have to be managed throughout the study?

LEARNING THE ROPES

Learning the ropes is a deliberate attitude taken toward one's own knowledge and the responsibility of understanding the unique character of the unit of study. This attitude places in doubt one's own knowledge about how things work and assumes that the particular way these people sustain their membership is important. Good field researchers try to keep their ignorance in front of themselves. Stepping into an organization, a family, or any membership requires that the analyst be freed from preconceived notions of the structure, functions, and methods of such memberships.

The goal of learning the ropes is not the rapid integration of the analyst into the system, but to take advantage of the "new person" status for as long as possible. The "new person" status forces the membership to give an account of how things are done. That is, to suspend the taking for granted of common sense knowledge. This is a privileged period when questions, that would otherwise not be tolerated, can be asked.

Unfortunately, it comes at a time when the analyst is least able to understand the answers. The answers are, of course, given from the perspective of the member. Even though answers to a new person are far more detailed than ones given to a member, they still gloss the deep meanings on which those answers depend. This is a period, then, when a great deal of information is being displayed by members most of which is not meaningful to the analyst.

Consequently, the analyst, rather than struggling to understand or even to force one's own meaning on the action, should be attending to the literal qualities of the scene. This is a period when conversations should be preserved and set aside for later analysis; when maps of space and things (rather than areas and objects) should be made; when the actors should be identified and the settings with their props and decorations described in detail.

Documentation of the literal qualities of the scene should be done before the analyst understands as a member. A member's understanding is a particular interpretive reading, not a literal one. At a later time, it will be possible to compare the literal values of the scene with what is significant and insignificant to members.

There are other values to the busy work of detailed descriptions. This effort gives the ethnographer something potentially valuable to do during a period of personal confusion. They provide a connnection to the professional activities of research. They provide a temporary answer to the question, "What the hell am I doing here"

They are also very useful in forcing the analyst to take notice in scenes in which he or she is a familiar actor—such as my work in families or classrooms. Becker, quoted by Wax and Wax (1971), comments on the difficulty of observing the familiar classroom:

> [I]t is first and foremost a matter of it all being so familiar that it becomes impossible to single out events that occur in the classroom as things that have occurred, even when they happen right in front of you. I have not had the experience of observing in elementary and high school classrooms myself, but I have in college classrooms and it takes a tremendous effort of will and imagination to stop seeing only the things that are conventionally "there" to be seen (p. 10).

Doing detail work renders the familiar strange and makes the scene noticeable.

There are several practices which can be useful in doing the detail work of learning the ropes. Essentially, they provide ways for making initial contacts within an open research study. Tactics, such as the ones that follow, establish a research presence, begin a personal relationship, and provide opportunities of discovering what is permissible and impermissible inquiry. The practices are listed here in no particular order. As always, they are strategies—not methods— and must be considered for their appropriateness in specific applications.

Routines and Rhythms

Our interest is in people coming together for some purpose. They do so in regular routines and rhythms. In families, we see bedtimes, meal times, time for work, time for school, time for church, time to mow the grass, and the deeper, time to talk, time to fight, time to play, time to make love. Routines and rhythms provide the structure of everyday living. They express the priorities set and the pressures felt by the members.

The routines of an organization can inform the analyst what a workday is, what is a proper workload, and the significant activities within it. Personal routines within organizations can show the individual solutions to the constraints and freedoms (absence of structure and demands) which compose the scene.

Discovering routines means showing up too early and staying too late. Johnson (1975) writes of his first day in the field:

> I began my field research at the Lake side office today and arrived there about 15 minutes early, which was quite fortunate, because I became aware of one of the things which my inside informant forgot to tell me, namely, where to find a parking place. I arrived at the office sharply at eight o'clock, and, well I guess I should've known better . . . I was the only one there! (p. 62).

Routines also become apparent in coincidental activity records which in a sanctioned project can be developed with the simple tactic of dropping by an office and inquiring:

> "Do you mind if I ask you what you are doing now? [Pause for the answer.] What were you doing before you started this? [Pause again.] What you think you'll be doing next?"

As long as the analyst is not perceived as an accountability expert, conversations like these are innocuous openers and can demonstrate the interest of the researcher in each member.

Description of Actors

"You can't tell the players without a scorecard" (baseball dictum). Entering a large membership, it can be a good plan to begin a file on each of the members. That file can contain the usual personal biography and organizational references. Other useful material could be an interview with the individual just talking about him or herself, descriptions offered by others of that individual, detailed descriptions of personal territories, available artifacts (memos, doodles, whatever) produced by that individual, and the analyst's commentary on the relationship between them.

Individual files can certainly be considered threatening or an invasion of privacy. The social science principle that knowledge of patterns and motives can lead prediction and control is well ingrained in common sense. Care of and respect for the individual need to be shown.

Language

As noted, a precept of qualitative research is to provide description using the language of the actors. The analyst, then, needs to become familiar with the terms and usage of the membership. This familiarity has to be more than that of assimilation; it requires a lexicographic understanding that can be used as a tool of analysis.

To develop this understanding, it is useful to systematically identify vocabulary and forms of usage which are particular to the membership. Transcripts of naturally occurring conversations are an excellent source. In addition, the regular practice of the verbatim principle (Spradley, 1980) in which the actual language-in-use is preserved in observational and field notes will provide entries and encourage the skillful use of member language in description. It is not necessary to speak as a member (in fact, doing so may be wholly inappropriate); it is necessary to understand the meaning and metaphor of member language and to be able to present them to the readership community.

Maps and Tours

Arrangement of settings usually signify much more than the happenstance placement of objects. Arrangements (or proxemics), as they are interpreted by the members, can give a good indication of the relative importance of objects and their functions within the activities of the members. Further, architectural characteristics can be interpreted as significant (relative office size, number of windows, etc.). Finally, space provides the stages of performance. What gets done where involves the context of space and its interpretation.

One strategy in approaching these meanings is to draw literal maps of the space and arrangements within them. This is, again, a good activity for the initial contact period when things are strange and therefore notable and one's participation activity is limited. Approximate dimensions are generally sufficient, but the details of the scene are very important.

Drawing the map is but half the job. The remainder is the detailed verbal description which accompanies it. The impression of each area should be recorded. Include a description of wall treatment, floor covering, decorations, maintenance (dirt, dust, stains, etc.), and general condition.

The value of the map is that it takes advantage of the researcher's initial naïveté and will help the analyst, at a later time, to see what is important and unimportant in the eyes of the various members. That value will be lost if the analyst simply substitutes his or her own judgments of what is worth recording. The tedious drawing of detail is the best approach.

For example, a student's broken desk chair sat at the end of the hall in the communication building of a famous western university. The metal spine of the chair and one of its legs had been broken in two. The chair was scrap. Yet, it had been moldering in that corner for over a year. Two valuable bits of information were retrieved from noting the presence of that chair.

One came from the explanations that were given by the members. Some attributed it to janitorial incompetence, but others had well-elaborated stories of how the chair could not be moved except by a special crew from Surplus Properties. The chair, it was pointed out, still had its inventory tag, and, therefore, could not be disposed of even if completely valueless.

The other bit of information came from its length of tenure. The chair was obviously not seen as the business of faculty, students, or staff. When it finally disappeared, it was dispatched by a faculty member of whom it was said, "Oh yeah, but he'll do anything."

Beyond giving the route to the executive washroom, maps have a variety of purposes. By overlapping the observations of member activity, maps can be used to indicate territories, access rights, action areas, sanctuaries, notable changes, and the stages of individual performances.

One particular tactic in the application of maps is the use of tours. Once a map is drawn, individual members can be asked to give a tour of the area. What things are identified as objects of the environment, how they are identified and the significance attached to them should be recorded. The points of the tour can be indicated on the map to compare things noted and those not.

I have found tours very useful with families. They open up the private areas of the house for inspection. They give an opportunity to negotiate access to those private areas. ("I presume it's OK to come up here as long as the doors are open?") After the adults have shown me around, I ask each of the children separately to give me a tour. Each person describes the house in obvious and subtle differences.

Photographs

Photographs can be used in a manner similar to maps, snapshots of the actor in performance are a good addition to each personal file, and the activity of having members photograph what they think is important can be a useful analytic tool in interviewing.

In practice, photography cannot substitute for mapping. The problem, obviously, is that enclosed areas rarely offer an adequate vantage point from which to take the covering shot. Photographs can be a useful supplement, however, to show particular arrangements, decorations, color, and the like (the new color emulsions require only normal room light).

Because a photograph is a picture *of something,* it involves a purposeful judgment. That judgment is part of the information contained in the photograph (a fact we will use in the following paragraphs). When the analyst takes a photograph, the judgment must be recorded also. Notes taken on the photograph should indicate the date, time, and purpose. Those notes should be made when the picture is taken. When the photos are developed, it is often too late.

Photographs of actors in performance are a good notational system for characteristics of dress and deportment. In the throes of writing an episode, photographs can jog the memory and provide access to a richness of detail. (They do not substitute for observational note taking, but in fact, must be annotated themselves.) Photographs can also be shared with the members as a simple gift and as a basis of further interaction or interviews.

The purposeful judgment aspect of photography can be used to explore member meanings by having the members themselves take pictures of their scene. The photographs are then used as a basis for discussion about what the photographer was attempting to accomplish. (An objective content analysis would rarely be appropriate.) Because pictures do not always come out right and one's memory fades rapidly, an instant camera is best for this exercise.

Kinships

I will use this anthropological term to indicate the various memberships that one can have within an organization. Some of these will have a public quality such as functional work groups, certain assigned memberships and sanctioned constituencies; others will be submerged in the social action. The study of **kinships** and their relationships begins by learning the memberships which are claimed by the individual.

Kinships can be formed on age, race, gender, sodality, task, ideological, and similar grounds. Clearly, some of these can be contrary to organizational policy and publicly denied (such as a caucus based on gender). The identification of these kinships will require deep study. Many kinships, however, can be identified in the early going. The observer should be attentive to who works with whom, talk about social arrangements, conversations about sporting activities and so on. Organizations are a multifaceted reality. Kinships are one of the practices by which the many faces of that reality are maintained.

Review of Policy Statements

The last in this list of things to occupy the early weeks of a study is the attendance to the policy statements (if any) of the organization. Policy statements are the usually written statements which contain the official line. Again, the emphasis is on the comparison between the literal and the pragmatic. The finding of a literal contradiction between policy and action is of little value itself. What is of interest is whether that contradiction is recognized by the members, its significance to them, and how it is managed by them. It is the practices which surround the relationship between policy and action that is of interest; but to recognize them, the analyst must be knowledgeable of the policy itself.

Learning the Ropes: An Analytic Summary

In this section, we have considered some tactics to take advantage of the "new person" status granted to the entering researcher to establish the peculiar rights and privileges of a research presence and to generate activities which both use the researcher's entering naiveté and offer the security of something to do for that researcher when there may be little participation available.

The "new person" is ordinarily granted a period where competency expectations are relaxed and broad inquiry rights are granted. Unfortunately, for research purposes, it comes at a time when the analyst is least able to reflect on the information given. The recommendation here was to make literal preservations for later analysis.

Interviews, mapmaking, study of official documents, and similar activities can be used to establish the understanding of what having a resident researcher entails. Done well, of course, the more access to individuals and documents is gained in the early going, the more established the expectation of access becomes.

The naiveté of a stranger allows one to see notable objects and occurrences which the native simply takes for granted. Because the explication of the taken for granted is part of the analyst's explanatory responsibility, the analyst should capitalize on that entering naiveté by using activities which result in literal, highly detailed preservations of the scene. These preservations—notes, recordings, maps, photographs and their accompanying descriptive analysis—can then be used at a later date, to identify the understandings—member maturity—gained.

STRATEGIES FOR EXPERIENCING MEMBER ACTIVITIES

While first-hand knowledge of member activities is not a requirement of participation, it does have undeniable benefits. It clearly multiplies the layers of understanding which are available to the analyst. Many situations common to communication studies, however, have built-in impediments to obtaining first-hand knowledge. One does not step into the manager's shoes for a few hours to gain experience of that profession. Competency requirements, work rules, union rules, and concerns about job protection all militate against first-hand experience in working situations. Nevertheless, there are usually routes to first-hand experience in groups that have initially accepted the research project. The next several paragraphs suggest some strategies for gaining that experience.

I want to offer one caveat immediately. There is a considerable difference between the experience of an expert and that of a novice. Cognitive psychologists hold that expert knowledge of complex activities may take 10 years to develop. The frustration, fatigue, and confusion of the novice may be no part of the expert. Experience may be the worst teacher if the analyst is seeking to understand the expert.

The four sections that follow deal primarily with strategies to gain experience in the work situation, but they have clear implications for social memberships, too.

The Apprentice and the Mentor

Apprenticing is an excellent way of approximating first-hand knowledge of complex activities. It is a developing performance under the supervision of a mentor. Its negotiation often begins by finding someone who will tolerate the analyst hanging around and is willing to talk about the work being done. Apprenticing can develop out of a gofer or tag-along role. In labor and skilled craft activities, there is often some part of the job in which an extra hand is useful. One's entry might be earned at these points. It is belaboring the obvious to note that the analyst needs to be cognizant of one's ignorance, respectful of the member's knowledge, and be willing and prepared to do the work offered. It is also obvious that the analyst can be exploited, set up for failure, or exposed to very real dangers.

Apprenticing can also work in the corporate office. Again, it is a matter of attaching oneself to a manager and talking about the work. Over time, the manager can come to use the analyst as a sounding board and permit suggestions and recommendations. The analyst approaches the role of an administrative assistant.

Not everything is positive about apprenticing. It is very difficult to distance oneself in the involvement of learning. The research presence can simply disappear. The analyst can become identified with the mentor's factional memberships restricting access to other groups. The total research effort can be compromised as expectations change from those appropriate to a research role to those of the politically active with secrets to keep and tasks to accomplish.

Apprenticing can require a major commitment of time. It may mean putting the research on hold while first-hand knowledge is gained. It will mean developing strategies for maintaining or reintroducing a research presence. It involves a commitment to contribute as a member to the organization with all the potential ethical considerations of that commitment.

Playing

George Plimpton has spent a good part of his journalistic career playing at being something else. His book *Paper Lion* (1966) chronicles his efforts at being a quarterback in a single series of downs for the Detroit Lions football team. He was certainly not a real quarterback, but gained insight into what one was by the playing of one.

Playing, the temporary assumption of a role one is otherwise unqualified for, requires the permission of the membership. Because it is playing, qualification rules can be waived and an opportunity given which would otherwise not be available.

The difference between playing and apprenticing is that playing is clearly not a member role. Members recognize that the rules don't hold for the playing analyst. Where there is a substitution involved, no new position is negotiated. The typical understanding between the analyst and the member he or she is playing for is that the member remains in control and can retrieve the activity at any time.

Playing can give the analyst first-hand knowledge of the activity but not of the activity from a member's perspective. The analyst can walk away, generally suffers little consequence from a poor performance, and so on. Usually, it is a controlled, protected experience.

Playing finds another application in situations where the analyst is over qualified, such as many of the settings involving children. The analyst cannot be a 4-year-old, but can play the 4-year-old. It is a demanding role. My experience is that children are quick to comment when adult strength or height is used in violation of the playing rules.

Take a Course

Getting training prior to entry can develop a certain level of first hand knowledge of the skill components of a scene. Many technical courses are offered inexpensively within community education programs. While the training may not lead to competence, it does provide familiarity with terms, language in use, the tools of the trade, how good workmanship is defined, and so on.

The training does not relieve the analyst from learning all of this again at the research site. (There are generally enough differences between classroom and field practices to enforce that relearning.) It can, however, provide a leg up on understanding what's going on. It is certainly worthwhile to get a member's advice concerning the proposed course.

Use Past Experience or Present Involvement

The typical view of the different as exotic and the exotic as scientifically more important, can lead the analyst to ignore the wealth of first-hand knowledge available in past experience and present involvement. Starting as a camper almost 40 years ago, I have decades of experience as a participant in wilderness camping. Yet it was not until the summer of 1985, as a walk-along addition to a horse party in the mountainous wilds of Wyoming, that I saw the social processes by which an assemblage of greenhorns and tinhorns becomes a functioning group. I had been too busy thinking of campsites and firepits to recognize the social action. In this case, however, as a backpacker on a trail ride, I was just far enough away from the main action to see it.

Almost everyone reading this book has had several years of experience in classrooms. Nevertheless, few have thought about the social action by which a "class" comes into being, how members formulate rules, negotiate curriculum, workloads, evaluative principles, and the like. Almost all of us have expert knowledge, here, which could be used as a basis for scientific knowledge.

A warning, however: Scientific knowledge requires the analyst to take special steps to ensure the distance necessary to observe what the expert knows to be true. Often, the scientific document is developed after the researcher has left the scene or returns to it specifically for research purposes. First-hand knowledge does not guarantee (and may indeed impede) a useful contribution to science.

PARTICIPATING AS A MEMBER

The criterion of participation is generally taken to be that of a member. Membership, however, is not readily defined. For our purposes, membership is the degree to which members take account of and accommodate the researcher. Membership is the legitimacy which accrues to the analyst as an individual performing a role within the scene. That the role may be unique is less important than what is granted that role in terms of power, status, rights, and privileges. As with all social actions, membership is not an attribute conferred on an individual but a continuous process of enactment. Membership is not given or taken; it is a mutual exchange. The specific definition of membership is, therefore, dependent on the way it is enacted within the group. In the sections that follow, I comment, first, on a false but common definition of membership and then on the impediment of the attitude of **marginality**.

Member Participation and Performance

It is not uncommon to find membership described on a continuum ranging from the insider to the so-called, nonparticipating (actually only noninteracting) observer behind a one-way mirror. A continuum such as that suggests an activity-based definition of member participation. That is, if the analyst is not doing what the members are doing, then participation is reduced.

If, however, a family member thinks, "I live in a house that has a resident researcher; she can ask me anything and I can tell her anything," then a very high level of participation has been accomplished with no need of common activity. The researcher has been made a legitimate part of the scene with very useful access privileges by virtue of an enlarged definition of membership practiced by the family.

What I am doing here is building a distinction between member participation and performance. It is certainly possible that some memberships will not accommodate the presence of nonperforming roles. Nevertheless, when the membership grants the analyst broad, legitimate access, participation is inevitable. The sociological literature is replete with nonperforming analysts in street gangs, prostitution rings, organized crime, and so on. What is sought by these analysts is acceptance for their role as researchers. The members can accommodate and take account of that role within the scene. The analyst may not gain (or want) first-hand knowledge of any of the activities in which the members perform, but that analyst is necessarily part of the social action.

Member Participation and Marginality

The researcher's role is often reported as the marginal member—always looking in from the edges of the action. I find that a distracting metaphor. In the first place, it seems to suggest that there is a central action in which all "real" members are equally involved or equally aspire to be. It also suggests that the role of the researcher is not a true member role—that the definition of membership has not been changed by the presence of the analyst. To me, neither suggestion is valid. Social action involves layers of action. And generally, the greater the number of members, the greater the number of layers. What the central action is depends on the layer at which it is observed.

Second, memberships can contain commentator roles—the researcher, with a responsibility of presenting the group to those outside of it, may be one of them. In spite of our pretenses, the role of the researcher is not that difficult, not that special, and not that complex that it can't be readily understood and accommodated by a membership. The office of the researcher may be problematic in certain exotic settings and even with given individuals, but it is a sanctioned office. An open research posture has been negotiated in the most unlikely settings, such as Chambliss's (1975) 10-year study of organized crime in Seattle.

Rather than a response of the membership, then, the notion of marginal membership suggests a researcher's attitude about the people being studied. This attitude of marginality develops because the analyst's default position in the relationship between the analyst and the membership can be viewed as exploitative, with false superiority, devoid of passion and temporary. To view as a member and to be viewed as a member requires the analyst to manage the role of researcher to counter the effects of this initial state. I cannot give a bag of tricks in the discussion that follows but I can raise the issues.

Exploitative   The researcher's stance vis-à-vis the membership has a high potential for exploitation. The analyst is making a living by using the access granted by the membership. What return is given for this access or for the expert explanation offered by a member which was gained through his or her time and effort? Wax (1971) comments on what is given by members:

> The less anxious a fieldworker is, the better he works, and, as he becomes aware that he is doing good work, he becomes less anxious. Usually the essential factor in this transformation is the assistance and support—the reciprocal social response—given him by some of his hosts. It is in their company that he begins to do the kind of "participation and observation" that enables him to "understand" what is going on about him at his own speed and at his own level of competence. It is his hosts who will let him know when he behaves stupidly or offensively, and will reassure him when he thinks he has made some gross blunder. It is they who will help him meet the people who can assist him in his work, and it is they who will tell him when his life is in danger and when it is not (p. 20).

Wax (1971) has also commented on what the analyst offers in return:

> The gifts with which a field worker repays the efforts of his informants will, of course, vary with each investigational situation. Some will be simple gifts like relieving boredom or loneliness. Others will be on a more complicated psychological level, like giving an informant who thinks himself wronged an opportunity to express his grievances (p. 36).

These gifts may be enough. But a return should not be taken for granted. The justification of doing science is not enough. The researcher has a responsibility to provide his or her share in these human relationships. One aspect of managing the researcher's role, then, is to devise strategies for a legitimate reciprocal relationship.

False Superiority   The "us/them" character of ethnographic work and our own socialization as researchers—keepers of the truth—can lead to a sense of superiority about our social action as compared with those we study. Schatzman and Strauss (1973) give a flavor of this superiority when they suggest that it may be more difficult to manage hosts who "have had a course in research methodology" (p. 24). Closer to home, I have seen dissertation committees shaking their collective heads in wonder at how a group could live with the contradictions surfaced by the novice analyst. (How do they live with their own?)

Field research can be considered as the coming to see as normal what is now seen as different and, of course, recording the steps along the way. This understanding can never be achieved if there is a fundamental disrespect for what gets done.

Devoid of Passion   "Why should I? You don't care about us. When you leave, we'll never hear from you again." I was taken aback by that high school student's reply when I was questioning his sullen refusal to talk with me. I was taken aback because his answer was right on the mark. I didn't care about him. All I wanted was what he could give me.

There was no attachment, no affiliation, no bonding with this group of students. My lot was not pitched with theirs. There was never any thought that I would cash anything in to help them accomplish their ends. No wonder I could not achieve any sense of membership.

Observational distancing can turn people into subjects—objects of study. Membership requires passion. A stake in the outcomes that affect people. If the researcher is to achieve membership, what happens has to make a difference. The analyst cannot remain objective, detached from the scene.

Temporary   The boundaries of membership are permeable but resistant. Membership is gained not with a card but with commitment expressed over time. In the communication studies reported to date, the most common barrier to membership in organizations with extended histories is the well-defined, temporary nature of the field work. This temporary quality certainly has something to do with duration (a year is a minimum says Sanday, 1979), but it has more to do with the terminal nature of the relationship. Memberships have undefined endings. They may last no longer than field contacts, but their ending is not anticipated. The analyst who announces to herself and her members that she will be around for only 6 weeks or 6 months is unlikely to motivate commitment from herself or the membership.

Membership is reciprocal, respectful, passionate, and committed. It is not exploitative, superior, objective, or temporary. To achieve membership, the analyst needs to develop strategies to constrain the default quality of the latter four and to demonstrate the former. What those strategies are, of course, will depend on the scene one is entering.

Going Native

"Going native" is generally considered one of the impediments to doing good research. Going native implies a lack of proper perspective, distance, and objectivity. Warnings against it encourage the analyst to limit commitment to membership. Going native, however, has little to do with membership. Its status as a problem appears in field notes and in the ethnographic text when the analyst becomes an advocate for the membership rather than an interpreter. Going native limits one's ability to be analytically descriptive because of confusion over the purpose of the writing not because of membership.

Disengagement

In almost every research study, there will come the time when the researcher will have to leave the site and relinquish membership. Disengagement involves all the problems of breaking up. If one has been successful in accomplishing membership, a series of understandings or social contracts have been reached, a dependency has been established, a relationship formed. The first concern in disengagement has to be for the members—that the responsibilities accepted by the researcher can be reasonably shifted, that the emotive bonds developed can be accounted for, and that a new but continuing understanding of the relationship between members and researcher can be reached.

The problems of disengagement are lessened when the research is undertaken from an open stance. Given an overt research presence, the analyst can introduce the issue of disengagement directly into the social action: "I've got to be moving on in a few; any problems I ought to be working on?" In a hidden stance, disengagement can involve accusations of deception, disloyalty, and the like. It's tempting to just walk away, but better to take the heat and attempt reconciliation.

As I work openly in almost all of my studies, I find disengagement as much a relief as a problem. The open presence of a researcher places some burdens on the membership. The researcher has to be dealt with in a special way. When disengagement comes, there is one less element to account for. Nevertheless, I initiate an explicit strategy designed to force attention to the reasons why I am leaving and to what my leaving means to the relationships that have developed. I am particularly careful to talk at length with the children of my families.

The second concern of disengagement is the continuing need the researcher will have for the membership. The analyst *may wish* to return as a full-time member to expand the original scope of the study or to examine changes over time. The analyst *will need* to return as he or she moves to the writing of episodes to receive confirmation that the narratives written capture a good sense of the meaning of the social action described. Again, in an open presence that contract can be expressly developed. There is, then, good, selfish reasons for being careful of the membership when it comes time to leave.

On Participating as a Member: An Analytic Summary

This discussion first distinguished between participation and performance. The participation we are concerned with in participant observation is participation in the meaning world of the members. That participation occurs when the analyst is both taken account of and accommodated by the members. That participation is revealed in the interaction between the analyst and the membership. That interaction does not require the analyst to be performing the same activities as each member.

The impediments to membership inherent in the analyst/membership relationship were then considered. In the absence of contrary strategies, the analyst's stance in that relationship can default to being exploitative, falsely superior, devoid of passion, and temporary. Membership, on the other hand, is most likely to be reciprocal, respectful, passionate, and committed. To experience membership, one must approach these qualities.

SUMMARY

This chapter has led us through the first experiences in an extended encounter. From hanging around to participating as a member, the analyst may have spent a couple of weeks to several months. At the end of it, the analyst is part of the membership—albeit a special part. He or she has been granted rights of access, taken into account within the social action with legitimate demands accommodated including the right to gain first-hand knowledge. None of these rights and privileges is secure from attack or change. They all involve a continuous process of management.

What lies ahead in the next chapter is a discussion of the technical aspects of observation and the whole process of creating a contribution to the public knowledge of science.

EXERCISES

1 What is the natural attitude of the new person, and how does it interfere with scientific observation?
2 How does maintaining the "new person" status conflict with demands for member participation?
3 How will the literal detailing of learning the ropes be used in later analysis?
4 The image of child in the company of adults is often used to describe the researcher entering an organization. Consider that image: What rights and privileges are given; what access denied?
5 Catalogue your own experiences. To what social groups could they be an aid to membership?

6 Imagine that an analyst is just being introduced: "Dr. Wilson will be visiting with us for the next 6 weeks to see how we do things around here. I want you to give her your full cooperation." What does Dr. Wilson say in her opening remarks?

7 What should have Dr. Wilson done prior to the introductory ceremony?

RELATED READINGS

Adelman, C. *Uttering, muttering: Collecting, using and reporting talk for social and educational research.* London: Grant McIntyre, 1981.

Bowen, E. S. (Bohannan, L.). *Return to laughter.* Garden City, NY: The Natural History Library, Doubleday and Co., Inc., 1964.

Spradley, J. P. *Participant observation.* New York: Holt Rinehart and Winston, 1980.

Wax, R. H. *Doing fieldwork.* Chicago: The University of Chicago Press, 1971.

PARTICIPANT OBSERVATION: CREATING THE RESEARCH TEXT

RITUALS: AN EPISODE IN THE WILDERNESS

For the backpackers I walk with, the first night's meal is usually the best. It's real food for one thing. Steaks, corn for roasting, even salad and wine (decanted in a plastic sack) can be carried in on that first day. A trout or two might be added, but with the heavy pressure on the close-in lakes, it's usually just trout stories that are the fish course.

One sense of the ritual is to reward the effort of the first day which usually includes a long drive and then a strenuous change in elevation. First-day hikes are short but steep with the campsite a couple thousand feet above the parking lot. With a 50-pound pack, the vertical feet are much more important than the distance.

The ritual also marks the end of civilization. It gets rough and risky from that point on. The ritual reminds us of what's to come—repeating the truths of the experience in the stories that get told.

I was a bit surprised to find this ritual being unpacked along with the wall tents, folding chairs, and cots that were part of our base camp in the Green River Lakes, Wyoming campground. The justification was missing. There was little effort or risk involved in this drive-in camping.

"We always have steaks on the first night," Paul explained. "The first night has to be the best, then we don't mind the rest of the meals so much." Paul's comment indexed the freeze-dried delights that are the trail's usual fare. The rest of our meals, however, would be home cooked with fresh ingredients coming from the kitchen in Sue's camper.

Promising to "get some trout to go with those steaks," Paul and Bob went off to try their luck on the nearby Green River. Later, Paul would refer to Bob's catch as "the minnow." It was not served that evening; it was stories as usual.

With two bottles of cabernet selected from the case stored in the front seat of the camper's cab, the ritual was played out. The stories from past outings were recalled, lies were told, and plans were made for the morning hike which they would do on horseback and I on foot. We had all done this before around many campfires.

Sue told a "bear in camp" story that had Paul and herself at our very site. "The bear came out of those woods [pointing up the hill]. *I was scared to death." When I wondered if she wasn't completely safe in her camper, she told a story of an acquaintance killed when "the bear tore the door right off."*

I told my well-rehearsed story of being chased into a lake by a she-bear who had taken an interest in our food packs. It's a funny story that has a strong moral element about the costs of stupidity in the wilderness with, nonetheless, a happy ending.

Other stories followed one from another, and the lies were only mildly outrageous. After we had made our plans for the morning, another difference between packers and riders was discovered: They could stay up and party, but I had 16 miles and 3600 vertical feet to hike. I went to bed.

SYNOPSIS

In this chapter, we consider the moves from participating to observing to constructing the written research text. These moves include writing observation notes, conducting interviews, writing field notes, managing data, constructing episodes (such as the opening story), and making the research contribution. Not surprising, perhaps, these are the headings of this chapter.

OBSERVING

In Chapter 10, we learned that scientific observation involves careful attention, interpretation, and the creation of an extended record. Whether scientific or mundane, observing is the process by which we make explicit the experience in which we are participating. It marks the continuous flux of experience with reference points and carves it up into discrete events. It is the process by which we make sense of what is going on about us.

Standards for Scientific Observation

When we observe scientifically, we are held to certain standards of performance. Our observations are expected to be intentional, intensive, extensive, and documented.

By intentional, I mean that the analyst establishes observation as the context for his or her activities. It is what the analyst is about. The analyst participates to observe what is going on. Observation, then, is intentionally present in the activities of the analyst during the social action about which the analyst will report. The standard of intentionality is that the observation is deliberately conducted during the time frame of the social action. Although documentation may occur at a later time, observation is not reminiscence.

Intensive refers both to the expected level of effort and to the layers of action which the observation must penetrate. For example, having first-day stories to tell on a back-country trail validates the teller as a competent member. The teller has met adversity, struggled with it, and overcome. The teller can display strength, cunning, knowledge, and dependability in a crisis, so that the audience knows he or she is worth having and will not be a liability.

The game of "campfire stories" is equally important. Rightly done, campfire stories are not told at breakfast. They emphasize the wilderness at its most dangerous time—the night. They reinforce our notions of what can happen and the values of being prepared. Stories are expected to be embellished but not incredible. One can't be caught in an obvious lie. Sue's bear-in-camp story was accepted despite its setting of a well-developed campground where stock were regularly kept because it happened "years ago."[1] Its moral—the wilderness (even a civilized wilderness) is a dangerous place—was validated with her second story. None of us, however, expected a bear in camp. All of us were well instructed in the procedures, but no one made any effort to bear-proof food or garbage. All of this interpretation has to be observed inside the action.

Because an event continues to emerge over time and settings, scientific observation has to be extensive. The analyst has to hold the closing boundaries of the event open to make the connections with different times and places. I can make the claim that our first-day stories were used to validate the teller's competence because of references to the stories in later conversations. At one point, Bob started into a lengthy explanation on how to do a common task in trail work, but cut himself off with the phrase, "Well, you know how to do that from your own experience."

The event also has to be observed from the different perspectives of the assembled memberships. The four adults' Green River experience was different from that of the three children's; the backpacker's was different from the riders'.

Finally, it is expected that scientific observation will be well documented in notes, preservations, and artifacts. That documentation should be close to the observation and regularized in its performance.

What to Look For

What the analyst is trying to observe are those **critical instances** when the underlying meanings of the action are revealed. How are those instances recognized? Having good mentors from the membership works best. Otherwise, it is a bootstrap operation where the analyst has to know enough to learn more.

Critical instances are recognizable after the fact because they stand out from the routine. To see them, then, the analyst must become intimately familiar with the minutiae of the everyday. There are times and events which may be more fruitful than others, however. Firsts of any kind—first days, new persons, new equipment, even new hairstyles—in an established routine evoke comment and

---

[1] The actual truth of the story is irrelevant. If the story is not acceptable, its purpose is lost.

some accommodation. Celebrations and mournings help identify what and who are considered successes and failures. Stories and rituals are performances which present, metaphorically, the meaning of things. Any point of change can be revealing.

The analyst's ignorance and the member's response to it will be, perhaps, the most fruitful source of insight. When told you are wrong, even nicely, it is hard not to notice. Correction by a member offers a moment when it is legitimate to seek an explanation. It takes no small amount of discipline, however, to stand one's ground and reply to criticism, "Yes, that was stupid of me; what should I have done?"

There are a number of check-list approaches to observation, e.g., Bruyn (1966), Denzin (1978), and Lofland (1976). Spradley (1980) offers a 9-by-9 matrix of questions directing the observations of nine elements and their interactions: space, object, act, activity, event, time, actor, goal, and feeling. The check lists are useful reminders of things to look after, but for the novice and the expert they can become a universal template of interpretation. No check list will work for every scene.

Personally, I find the effort of field work overwhelming. There are so many things to attend to that at first nothing gets done. As is obvious from my advice in Chapter 11, I have to enter a scene slowly, in the beginning narrowly focusing on detail; then, with effort, I force a wider and wider view.

Taking Observation Notes

There are two separate and quite different processes of note taking in observation. The first process is in the taking of **observation notes**. These notes are made in the midst of the social action. The second process is the writing of the field notes which involves the creation of an extended narrative in a reflective examination of what went on. Field notes are written after (and directly after) the analyst has become disengaged from the social action. Observation notes should be regarded as markers which will guide the reconstruction of the experience in one's field notes.

The standard of observation is thorough documentation. Under fire, the practice of making observation notes is often scribbled messages on whatever is handy, tape recordings that were started too late, and the like. It certainly seems simple: The analyst should either write down verbatim or record everything significant.

Unfortunately, the analyst cannot predict and often not recognize until well after the fact when something significant will be said or done. Further, when in the process of participating in something significant, one cannot hold up the proceedings to get the wording right or the recorder on. Nevertheless, the analyst has to be committed to this activity. He or she has to stop and write it down.

The manner in which one deals with the subsequent problems of field notes directs the taking of observation notes. The general advice is that field notes should be written within hours of the field experience. If that advice is followed, then the observation notes can be short phrases—even single words—which will cue one's memory. What is written should be what is considered significant about the event. That might be the timing, phrasing, action, intonation, context, actors, and so forth.

Recordings which are being used as observation notes should be transcribed and annotated as to actors, context, and significance on the day they are made. If this work isn't done quickly, the recordings become objectified, disembodied conversations which are useful for understanding language-in-use, but not much help in reconstructing what happened. Recordings as observational notes present serious logistical problems which are discussed in a later section. The practice is not recommended.

As long as our research pursues everyday life in natural settings, there is no satisfactory solution to the standard of documentation. There are some rules of thumb which get passed along. Keep your observational notes close to the action. When something significant happens, take notes on it as soon as possible. The notes may be more important than what happens next. Keep the making of field notes close to the process of observation. The closer these two activities, the less demand on observational note taking. Finally, the documentation of social action involves the preservation of the significance of the action along with the evidence of that significance. The note taker must preserve both what was done and what was signified.

Observation: Final Thoughts

The proof of the observation is in the writing. The tasks of writing field notes and constructing episodes will demonstrate the worth of the strategies of observation. The field notes will indicate whether the analyst has captured sufficient detail, can re-create the perspectives represented in the scene, can interpret the layers of expression, can understand the broad significance of the action, and can find the evidence for these claims in the record of the encounter. The tasks of writing and observing are mutually correcting. The effort of good observation motivates a complete report. The demands of an adequate report motivate good observation. It helps to see them as twin tasks. It is essential to perform them that way.

INTERVIEWING

Interviewing holds a peculiar place among researchers. It is first of all a strategy for participation, but it is uncertain if the participation is within the parameters of the social action under study. It is a strategy for observation, but it is uncertain what is being observed. And it is a substitute for observation, but it is uncertain if the report can be used as a substitute. Despite these uncertainties, interviewing has widespread acceptance. This section starts with some brief comments on strategies and then considers the more interesting issues.

Strategies

Qualitative interviews are most often seen as conversations with informants. It is the competent member instructing the analyst on the ways of the world. In power relationship terms, the dominant figure is the member. It is, however, the analyst's agenda that gets accomplished.

Interviews are best used to build a stock of member explanations. They answer the basic question of how do members talk about the subject. The aim of the analyst's strategy is to evoke a lot of talk. The analyst is not looking for *the* answer but for discourse which on subsequent analysis may prove to be a repository of social meanings.

An interview such as this requires both a willing informant and an analyst knowledgeable enough to hear the points which are glossed and, therefore, merit further pursuit. Consequently, formal interviewing is usually best conducted well into the study. It is usually valuable to prepare an opening which both justifies the interview and sets the agenda, and a closing which will signal the end of the contract and permit leave taking. In the middle, a few questions can be prepared to tap the context of controversies or to direct a different look at the subject. Mostly, however, the analyst should follow the lines of discussion which are opened by the response.

For the analyst the interview is an improvisational performance requiring good skill. This is a time to use a recorder to preserve the response and to use the note pad as a device for listening carefully. As the informant replies, the analyst should be jotting down names, descriptive phrases, issues identified, and so on. Subsequent questions should come from these notes. Not everything noted will get treated in a reply. I cross off the ones introduced into the interview. The remaining are a collection for further inquiry. The notes provide an index to the tape and are a handy way of comparing interviews on the same subject with different informants.

The analyst is well advised to transcribe the interview as soon as possible. If you haven't done transcriptions, it is hard for me to write convincingly that what was heard in the interview will not be what is recorded on the tape. Conversationalists do a great deal of mutual filling in, verbally unannounced subject shifts occur, occult references are made. Those coupled with speech production errors, the typical oral grammar, variations in recording quality, background noises, talkovers, and the like guarantee that the analyst will be forced to make many decisions as to what was said and what was being talked about. The closer to the interview, the better these guesses are likely to be.

Finally, the interview is a field experience like any other. It requires the analyst to prepare observation and field notes. The conditions of the interview, what the informant was trying to accomplish in his or her performance, and what the analyst was attempting should all be noted.

Issues

Our mythical discerning reader has probably noticed that I have not dealt with the interview as a source of information about how things get done. That information can certainly be available in the responses given. It is, however, not likely to be adequate. The detail necessary for the analyst to understand even simple social actions is well beyond the normal contract struck when one agrees to an interview. The explanation is valuable for what it is—an explanation. When the researcher is knowledgeable of the action, the explanation can be analyzed for what gets presented as givens, what gets emphasized, public terminology, and forms of language—all of which can deepen the analyst's understanding.

The structured interview has also been left out as an interviewing strategy. Structured interviews are those in which each question has been prepared in advance with an occasional "probe here" improvisation. Structured interviews are themselves well-known social actions. They can be performed independent of the scene. They are not on our recommended list because, as an explanation, they are essentially an analyst performance rather than a member performance. That is, the structured interview forces conformance to the researcher's perspective.

I am not saying that one cannot ask specific questions of people. I am saying don't be naive about what is going on. A structured interview can be a good strategy for establishing a research presence or for behaving like a researcher. The replies can show the member's interpretation of the researcher's perspective. They are, however, neither a natural, member explanation nor an adequate description of social action.

Interviewing: The Round-up

An interview is an event with some formal standing in public life. What results, therefore, to some degree is the public performance of explanation—a member's interpretation of what is appropriate to the task of an interview. This is not a question of individuals attempting to deceive or in any way not responding honestly (although such can occur). It is the recognition that the explicit explanation of social action is not there for the asking. It has to be created. A member's knowledge is in the doing. That knowledge is not symbolically present in coherent explanation without an intentional effort to produce it. It would be unusual to find that somebody has done your work for you.

RECORDINGS AND TRANSCRIPTIONS

From time to time, I have made disparaging remarks about and even recommendations for the use of recordings. This love-hate relationship has developed over a number of attempts to use recording technology which seems so attractive and yet generates so many problems. First of all, let me repeat that we are focusing on the study of everyday life *in natural settings.* Many of the problems inherent in the preservation of adequate records can be eliminated or lessened through artificial settings or constraints on action. Those solutions, however, pursue simulations.

The attractions of recording technology are many. Miniaturization has created palm-sized audio recorders, and video recorders which are not much bigger. These recorders can be carried into any setting. Recorders appear to give the analyst the luxury of having the actual words spoken or the actual performance given available for analysis under the best of conditions—not when the researcher is scrambling about on site. Why take notes when you can have it all before you?

There are, however, five intractable conditions which are imposed upon the research process when recordings are used as the primary method of preserving the scene. I list them as follows:

• Recording devices must be tended to. It is one thing if the recordings are the icing, quite another if they are the whole cake. Video recorders require constant attention. I have yet to find a single shot setup that did the job. Audio recorders require regular attention. That clear, well-modulated dialogue that we hear on radio and that all-around view that we see on television comes from considerable technical effort—well beyond what can be supported in natural settings.

• The frame of the recording is different from the frame of the observer. Watching and listening involves a whole perceptual process, not just sound waves and light energy. The observer is making moment-by-moment decisions as to what is important, the recording devices make none. With audio, the researcher discovers this difference when a recorded conversation which was clearly heard by the observer, is completely obscured on the tape by background noise or competing talk. For example, an observer standing in the middle of an active classroom can easily track a single conversation among many. That same conversation on tape is just part of a babble of voices.

There are similar problems in the video frame. The field of human vision is just slightly less than 180 degrees. The field of vision of a normal camera lens is less than 60 degrees. Standing to the side of a classroom, the observer can take in the whole scene. The camera will be able to clearly reproduce the teacher and part of the first row. It is a significant loss.

• Recording adds the burden of some system of using the material recorded. That box full of audio- or videotapes has to be catalogued, the performances indexed, and the dialogue transcribed to gain full utilization of the resource. Efficient transcription requires specialized equipment (such as a word processor and a transcribing playback device). Even with good transcribing equipment, the task creates enormous time demands. An hour's tape takes an hour to listen to and 5 to 10 hours to carefully transcribe, depending on the number of speakers participating in the recorded conversation. There is an enormous amount of waste. Most of what is transcribed will never be used again.

• The use of recordings in analysis as the primary analytical resource generally leads to the objectification of behavior. The emphasis is placed on *the* words and *the* performance, rather than words and performances in context. As soon as the analyst steps out of the scene the context disappears, only the objectified images remain. The analyst can work to make the context present in his or her interpretation, but it is difficult to sustain that effort.

• Finally, there is an effect that I call the analytic breeder reactor. The typical approach to an event on a tape is to pick it apart, categorize the elements, find meaning in the pieces rather than the whole. This process breeds its own explanation. It becomes independent of the scene. The emphasis on the member's meanings is lost.

These five, then, are what I consider the intractable conditions of recordings. I find them sufficiently serious to warrant the application of recording technology only for specific purposes such as the literal detailing of linguistic analysis, the collection of conversational or performance fragments, or the preservation of interviews. I have considerable doubts as to their use as the primary means of documentation.

Managing Recorded Materials

In order to make the content of recorded materials accessible to the other research processes, the researcher has to provide—at minimum—an index of the content of each tape. Literal indexes of conversations on audio- or videotapes can be produced fairly quickly. The start of turns of talk a minute or so apart can be used as a table of contents. The first three or four words of the turn are usually enough to identify shifts in the conversation. With a videotape, a short description of the visual image shown at the same time should be provided.

An index to the social action preserved in the recording, of course, requires that the interpretation of the action be completed within the field-note process. (Social action is interpreted human behavior; it is not there for all to see.) Generally, an efficient way to index the evidence of the interpreted action is to include the tape location in the field note itself.

The Art of Transcribing Video Recordings

The analyst can make the greatest use of recorded materials when both the recording and its transcription are available. In this section, we consider the art of transcription of the visual image; in the next, we consider the recorded word. Traditional techniques of the transcription of visual images are usually based on a shot-by-shot or sequence-by-sequence basis. Shot-by-shot analysis looks at each camera view; a sequence-by-sequence analysis considers each coherent combination of shots. Either analysis produces a view of the content from the perspective of the director. This perspective is not appropriate for our purposes.

Our responsibility is to produce a view of the content from the perspective of the actors. The appropriate unit of analysis, then, is the action sequence the evidence for which has to be found in the performance of the actors.

Viewing the tape, the analyst must interpret the performances to determine when one action sequence ends and another begins. Clearly, this interpretation is greatly aided if the researcher was participating in the scene. The sequences are named with some dialogue from the actors and indexed by length and position on the tape. The transcription of the action sequence is the meaningful, detailed description of it. That description is of the same quality as that of a field note—it tells the story of what happened. It is a sense-making interpretation, not a listing of meaningless detail.

The Art of Transcribing Audio Recordings

The transcription of the recorded word also follows the rule that the sense of it is what counts. It is rarely necessary to attempt to re-create each sound, pause, and intonation. Such efforts are usually displays of false precision.[2] It is important to indicate anything made significant by the speaker or the audience, affected or intentional speech patterns or accent, deliberate pauses both vocalized and silent, notable emphasis, and the like.

Transcriptions, therefore, always involve judgment. Not only about things made significant, but also about what turns constitute a conversation; i.e., who is speaking to whom, what is being referenced in the turns and the very words themselves. Consequently, I believe that the transcription task must be done by the analyst or at least completely reviewed and corrected by the analyst. Let's look at some examples:

Picture a situation where students are seated two to a worktable. An instructor, wired for the recording, stands between two tables. Both sets of students are conversing about the task; the instructor interjects comments into both conversations. One solution to this problem is to treat each conversation separately doing only the turns applicable for one at a time. To accomplish this transcription requires a judgment on each turn of talk as to which conversation it belongs. To do this blind, without having been there and taken adequate notes, is an exercise in probability.

Everyday speech can get along very well without names or nouns, particularly if the persons or objects referenced are present. I have a number of tour tapes which are less useful for understanding members' meanings because they are full of statements like:

> Now this is very interesting. It was given to me by my great-grandmother who brought it all the way from Ireland.

It is, of course, obvious that the analyst should offer the name or ask about it in order to get it on the tape. Obvious, but it is not always accomplished.

---

[2]The exceptions to this comment are those studies which are specifically pursuing the analysis of these characteristics. In conversation analysis, the exact duration of a pause may be an important element in determining when a turn is considered ended by another.

With the exception of studio-quality recordings, a certain percentage of the words will be unintelligible on first listening. In our classroom tapes where we were focusing only on interactions directed to the teacher with the microphone, about 10 percent of the words were in question. Multiple conversations can easily raise this to 50 percent. It is useful to remember that every word involves a decision as to what was intended and produced. On some, the analyst is simply less sure. My rule is that if I hit on a word by the third pass, it gets transcribed without notation. If it takes more than three, I put the word in brackets. If I can't get it in six tries, I leave an underlined blank for the word. Occasionally, the word will become apparent in a later turn. I then fill in the blank, leaving the underline. These rules are easily followed with a word processor and transcriber; they are quite difficult with a tape recorder and a typewriter.

A transcription is never an exact copy. Moving across communication modalities, something is lost and something added. Tonality, volume, intonation, pitch, rhythm are all lost; written structure, layout, sequencing, punctuation, spelling are all added. The transcribing effort has to be kept in perspective; it is the sense of it that the analyst is trying to preserve and pass on.

WRITING FIELD NOTES

I was running in my usual manner with my head up, eyes focused on the clouds above, so I was probably about a hundred yards from him when I first saw him. He was riding a 27-inch, standard frame, silver 10-speed in the intersection inscribing a 30-foot circle between the four points of the curbs. The bicycle looked new, the seat and handlebars were at their lowest position, but he was ankling just right. He couldn't have had the bike for long, but he showed a remarkable mastery. As I ran those hundred yards, he made five circles guiding his bicycle past those 8-inch curbs with but a few inches to spare. His speed was constant; he kept the same pedaling pace throughout. No pauses. He was going fast. I judged his lean to be almost ten degrees. Any faster and I think he would have been forced out of the intersection. His body was held straight in an angle into the wind. It seemed an extension of the machine. I saw no sign of concentration or effort on his face. He seemed serene, enjoying the sensations of the rhythm and the forces acting upon him.

He must have been a 5th grader; he looked 10. It was 7 or 8 minutes after the elementary school got out; 20 minutes before the middle school (7th and 8th grades) dismissed.

About 10 yards out, our eyes met, passively. But when I picked up my pace so that I could pass through his circle without disturbing his rounds, I caught a faint smile. I felt a connection—he and I were doing the same thing, relieving the tensions of our day.

This extract is an exemplar field note based on 90 seconds or so of action. The note contains most of the things that ought to be there. It reports a good deal of detail, but more importantly the detail is significant to the understanding of the action. It describes the acts and their context. It considers the state of mind of the actor and the observer attributing feelings and motives. It presents the character of the interaction. And, finally, it provides an interpretation of the whole. Let's consider each of these a bit more.

Significant Detail

Every scene has an infinite amount of detail. It is just a matter of cutting it into smaller and smaller bits. My advice to the analyst entering a scene has been to be unstinting in the preservation of detail, even though an unending task. At the point or entry, the analyst does not have the knowledge to make the decisions as to what is important and what not. Hence, the advice to write extensively to avoid prejudging the scene. As the analyst becomes more familiar with the scene, the writing of detail can become more focused. Remember that with an infinite amount of detail available, one has to make choices. The detail which is chosen should be significant to the action as it is interpreted. The detail justifies the claim of the interpretation. One of the claims in the field note is that the kid rides with "remarkable mastery." What details support that claim? Those which describe the size of the bike, the stature of the kid, and the quality of the performance.

The claim is the insight the analyst has as a participant in the scene. I'm running along looking at this performance which is beautiful in its precision, and my thought is "that's remarkable." My training takes me into the performance to find the elements which makes sense out of that insight—to answer why it is remarkable. Those are the details which are significant to the action.

There are, of course, other times when the action will not make sense, not be coherent. In those cases detailing becomes a refuge from the confusion. It gives the analyst something to do and provides a repository of potential evidence should the action become meaningful upon reflection or with more experience.

Of the two types of detailing, the one motivated by an insight is considerably easier than the other of disjointed acts. The former comes with its own principles of organization. That organizing principle which is the insight itself can be used to check the detailing for intensive and extensive completeness. Where the coherence of the scene is not evident, the analyst has no structure on which to make decisions of inclusion and exclusion.

While there is obvious benefit in reaching an understanding, the analyst must be skeptical of any insight drawn. The analyst can marshal evidence for nearly any claim. Withholding judgment can be a meritorious act.

Acts and Context

Our example presents a fairly simple narrative. There are three sets of acts—my running, his bicycling, and our interactive glances. The context is one of a chance encounter in a public setting between two individuals engaged in private actions at a notable time of day. Let's examine the descriptions of acts and context in this note:

Description of Acts The description of my running is weak (so is my running). It is a typical failing. I already know my own behavior; why should I write it down (an argument from private knowledge), or worse, my own behavior is not important for an understanding of the scene (the invisible observer assumption). Promise to do better.

The description of the boy's acts is fair. I missed his hand placement which might have told me something more of his skills. What seems to be good in this description is the understanding of the relationship between the speed of travel, the inherent danger represented by the curbs, and the precision of the performance. I am not prepared to make a claim of a testing rite in this note; I have no justification for it (meritorious restraint of judgment), but it is something I would want to explore in future interactions.

The description of our interaction suffers because I have evidence only from my perspective. There was nothing in that scene, beyond the faintest smile, that gave me evidence of his. I could have generated some more. I could have stopped in the center of his circle and made some admiring remark. He might have just ridden away, but that is a response of some kind. More likely, I would have engaged him in a conversation, explored what he was doing, gotten confirmation that the bicycle was new and that he was an avid rider, and so on.

Of course, doing so would have destroyed a very fragile scene. Generally, I have no compunction about doing this, although it is an intrusion of research purposes into a naive scene and an obvious imposition on the actor. (Ah well, my being there is an intrusion, and he does get to talk to a real scientist in return.) In this case, it would have ended my own pleasure of watching the performance.

Description of Context   Context is the social and material reality in which the action occurs. The material reality is composed of the location and its character-istics, light, heat and other energy, the individuals, and the physical forces brought into play. The social reality is composed of place (public thoroughfare), time (after school and between work), actors and roles (runner and cyclist, man and boy, observer and performer), acts, action, expectations, understandings, values—nearly all the important things.

The elements of the material reality—such physical characteristics as, energy, friction, gravity, and so on—are always part of the scene, but not always part of the description. They are brought into the description when they are made significant by the actors. In this case, perhaps, the most significant element is the presence of the curbs. They are used to define a space and (maybe) to define a risk to be challenged. The rest of the physical reality is simply considered as permissive. That is, the physical conditions neither determine nor obstruct the action, but allow for its performance.

This treatment of material reality is in keeping with the principle that it is the meaning we have for the physical world that is the determining factor of human action. For example, the same game could be played without the curbs by selecting four spots on the road and piloting the bicycle as close and as fast as possible to those spots. The curbs make neither the space nor the criterion, but they provide for both.

The social elements of the context establish the interpretation of the action as private acts in a public setting. It is in that context that we can understand the meaning of the interaction as an act of deference or accommodation by the jogger for the cyclist. There is an inherent conflict when two performances of separate private acts begin to impinge upon one another. The conflict concerns the order of precedence. When I give way to the cyclist, I have granted him dominion over this public place.

My knowledge of this action's social context comes from membership in the larger public to which both the boy and I belong. With no history of interaction, we have no membership common beyond that. Because we lack the necessary interaction, as an analyst I am forced to surmise that *my* understanding of the social context is adequate to account for *his* behavior. It certainly is adequate to account for mine, but I have to presume that he, too, is a competent member. This presumption is not particularly doubtful. It is necessary, however, in order to use that social context as an analytic tool.

State of Mind

While the social context is of considerable help in understanding human action, it, too, permits a wide latitude of performance. Consider the cyclist's smile. His smile is enigmatic. I cannot determine if it is one of victory, one of thanks, one of acknowledgement, or one of surprise (that an adult has given way to a child). I cannot find the meaning of that smile in its enactment. I have to get to the understanding which directed it. What I or anyone else would do is irrelevant. What this note is clearly missing, then, is any evidence of the understanding held by that individual. In this case, that evidence is missing because it was not presented in the performance.

Unlike behaviorists who deliberately eschew evidence of cognitive states, the qualitative researcher uses feelings, motives, and other cognitive states as contributing elements in the interpretation of human action. The emphasis, however, is on the social meaning of these states rather than their physiology or idiosyncratic expression.

Let me give a few examples of these social components. There have been a spate of articles in women's magazines asserting that it is now "all right" for women to be ambitious, to be hard-driving go-getters in the marketplace. While such articles don't sanction behavior, they are good indicators of what's problematic. What are acceptable ways in which a woman executive can express her ambition? As one of my respondents, a female executive in a research division, put it:

> It is difficult to know how far you can go. Research is usually not a route to upper management, but it is a traditional entrée for women. How can you show that you want to get ahead, get out of research, move up, and still not scare the hell out of everybody around you?

Physiological states also have their social components. In Chapter 7, I reported to you a study in which we tested sexual behavior codes 30 minutes after an alcohol dosage approximately equivalent to three martinis. There was virtually no change in the performance of the respondents on the test. There was, nonetheless, considerable social action in the testing room. The respondents used the context of the alcohol and the testing situation to act out a number of sexually related performances.[3]

The point of these examples is that the conscious states of the individuals are an important element of the analysis. The researcher must be cognizant of the impact on social action of feelings, motives, and other mental states as well as such physiological states as pain, fatigue, and chemical influences.

Character of the Interaction

Interactions are the heart of any analysis. The analyst must be particularly careful to write adequate field notes on interactions observed and participated in. The test of adequacy begins with the verbatim principle which lays a heavy burden of detailing what was heard, seen, and performed. Equally important is the analysis of what the performance was intended to accomplish and some judgment of what actually got done. Unlike some forms of conversation analysis which examine an interaction as an objectified text, the analysis of interactions from our perspective requires us to see them as a lived experience within a given context performed by particular actors. Because our cyclist example gives us little interaction to work with, consider the following between a teacher (*T*) and a student (*S*):

T: OK, we're using oh eleven.
S: Oh eleven.
T: Oh.
S: Oh.
T: Oh.
S: Oh.
T: Not zero.
S: Oh.
T: Oh for October.
S: Oh.
T: Eleven.
S: Slash? Oh slash?
T: No, no. No slashes.
S: Just eleven.

[3]Becker (1953) has written on the social learning that is necessary to become a proficient user of marijuana.

This conversation is one of my favorites from the Anderson and Eastman (1983) study of conversations in an eighth-grade science class using computers to access an interactive encyclopedia resource. Whenever I read it, I am guaranteed a laugh because it is so nonsensical. The individuals who produced this conversation intended no humor at all. The analyst's job is to make this conversation sensible from the viewpoint of the actors. The analysis must show how this conversation could be treated as proper by the actors when, on the face of it, it is Abbott and Costello playing "Who's on first."

The field note on this conversation should record the significance of the content, any comment on the interaction, and the pertinent circumstances surrounding the conversation; it should also indicate the relevant interactive history and whatever was notable of its performance. The field note on this conversation reads as follows:

> It is the usual closing-time rush with maybe just a little bit more. Shields is supposed to have somebody helping him to check out materials. Nobody seems to be there. People are milling around the checkout counter. He keeps reminding them to sign the cards. There's a lot of walking and talking going on with the students as they put away materials and get ready to leave.
>
> Shields is going from carrel to carrel seeing where the student is in the closing procedure and then just pitching right in with help and advice. He wants to end the class smoothly and make sure that everyone gets something onto his or her disc.
>
> I'm standing behind Kevin, having left Mark's table. Kevin is sitting leaned back with his arms down at his sides, apparently waiting. He makes no effort to close out even though the time has been announced. Shields moves to his carrel, and Kevin puts his hands on the keyboard.
>
> Shields tells him the code for closing and they immediately get into this thing about "Oh" and zero. Shields corrects him several times before he finally gets it right.
>
> Afterwards, I talk to Kevin. He complains that they should be using something besides "Oh."

This note[4] is obviously typical and not perfect. From it, we get a good idea of what's going on from Shield's perspective. Confusion bordering on chaos is felt. Shields has two responsibilities which require him to be in two separate places. In spite of that pressure, Shields is able to stay with a student and patiently give advice to someone apparently unwilling to try or perhaps risk much.

We get hardly any feeling for the perspective of the student. In fact, this analyst never makes contact with the students. His participation is strictly with the teacher's side. His report of the subsequent conversation is hardly helpful. Kevin's complaint suggests that he may know a lot more than what he is showing. At least he knows that some other code should be used. The analyst's note, however, is so brief that it precludes any follow-up.

If we use the report-of-interaction-check-list of significance, history, comment, and circumstances of setting and performance, the note is strong on

---

[4]The note has been extracted from the field notes on the entire class period and slightly edited.

circumstances from the teacher perspective, fairly catches the significance, misses any history, and is incomplete on comment. All in all, give it a "C."

Providing an Interpretation

Qualitative interpretation occurs at a number of levels. In the interpretive work of the field note, the analyst develops a narrative from a particular viewpoint—the cyclist note is from the viewpoint of the observer-jogger, the classroom note from the viewpoint of the teacher. The narrative of it is the story, the manner in which the observed elements are brought together and connected to one another. In the classroom note, for example, we have the view of Kevin waiting, not just sitting but purposefully waiting, to avoid what might be considered the proper initiative. Shield's arrival is what Kevin has been waiting for, and the story progresses.

Kevin's action of "waiting" is an interpretation for which the description of his acts is evidence. Could there be other interpretations of his acts? Of course, he could be resting, dreaming, thinking, puzzling, resisting—any number of things. Presumably, however, from the perspective of the participant-observer, the evidence for those actions was not as strong. The interpretation represents the analyst's best guess following a considerable effort at discovery. The interpretation is not to be avoided. It is the payoff in understanding for all the work of research.

The field note's interpretation is generally the story of the actors. It focuses on making sense of their acts in narratives of action. It is conducted at a relatively low level of abstraction with time and sequence rather than topics or constructs being the organizing skeleton.

Final Thoughts on Field Notes

Field notes are the product of observation and participation at the research site and considered reflection in the office. They approach a variety of questions. First, they consider what happened today. Then, such questions as: "What did I learn today? What mistakes were made? How can I improve my observation? Participation? What should I be looking for? To whom should I be talking?" In short, they provide a narrative of the day's events and an analysis of the research activity itself.

Field notes mark the first of a series of moves from private to public knowledge. The other two moves, as we shall see, are the episodic narratives and the ethnographic argument. All three of these moves, if they are to be successful, must progress from the firm foundation of the intensive private knowledge gained in participation and observation. Figure 12-1 shows this relationship.

Field notes are notes to the analyst. They are written so the analyst can reenter the scene of the action and of the research at a later date. Because they

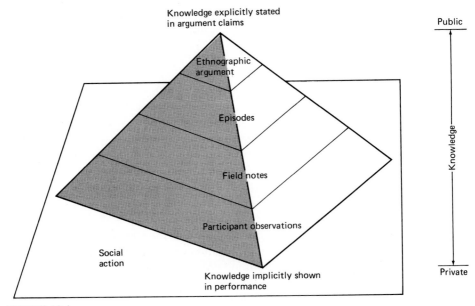

FIGURE 12-1
The structure supporting public knowledge in the study of social action.

are personal, the novice (and veteran) analyst often makes the mistake of writing in a cryptic shorthand, shortening the work of describing and elaborating by depending on personal knowledge to fill in the gaps. Unfortunately, it doesn't work that way. A year later when writing the research contribution, the notes simply make little sense. You can draw your own moral.

On the other hand, the field note is not an operational definition of the event. It is a first-level interpretation which is to be an aid for further analysis and interpretation. I expect a given note to contain my view *at a particular point in time* and to do so in sufficient detail that I can reconsider it. I may determine at a later analysis that what the note purports is not what happened. It is not a good interpretation. At a later date, I may be able to tell a better story.

The analyst in Kevin's classroom, for example, may finally make contact with Kevin and discover that he has quite a complex explanation for what is the student's responsibility in a classroom. "You have to let 'em show you how; otherwise, they expect you to do everything." Aha, clever Kevin.

Finally, a comment or two on the scope of the work of field notes. Writing field notes is of equal importance to participating and observing. Without the writing there is no research. It is a demanding task which takes time and energy. We may all work at different rhythms. I prefer 3- to 4-hour blocks of writing figuring to produce four to six pages an hour, sometimes less, rarely more. The amount of work depends on the complexity of the action and the number of layers I can address. The more maturity I have with a scene, the more work I can produce. As a minimum, I try to give one hour of writing for each hour of field work.

I also try to keep my writing current with my field work. That means that if I do an 8-hour stint in the field, I have at least 8 hours of writing to do before I go back into the field. This schedule doesn't always work out, and the quality of the writing suffers because of it. I simply lose things; I can't remember; they don't make sense; they're gone.

In short, the analyst will spend more time in reflecting and writing than in participating and observing if the participant observation is to be adequately utilized. When a study is overloaded with field time, it is very likely that much of that effort is being wasted. The study should be specifically designed to ensure the reflecting and writing necessary.

MANAGING NOTES AND MATERIALS

Qualitative research generates a library of data. An hour of observation will yield 10 to 12 pages of notes, a 30-minute interview runs between 12 to 15 pages, and a 50-minute interactive classroom session will be nearly 20 pages single-spaced. Special techniques have to be used to manage this amount of paper and to make the contents accessible to the analyst.

Managing Paper

A system that works is a multiple-file system. To use this system the analyst makes three to four copies of each set of materials. Multiple copies can be generated with carbon setups, duplicator masters, or access to a copy machine.

One copy is kept intact in an **archive file** that is organized by type of material (notes, interviews, artifacts) and day the material was collected or created. The remaining copies are coded and filed according to the purposes of the research. Common types of **coded files** are breakouts over events, principal actors, performances, settings, and roles. A separate storage file can be used for each breakout; a cardboard box with hanging folders works quite well.

Because this coding is specific to the content involved, I will give you just one example to show you what I mean. We set up a principal actor rule in dealing with the conversations from the eighth-grade science class. Separate files were kept for each of the two teachers in the setting.

Within that coding, the use of the videotext encyclopedia could be seen as a series of events which would begin with "Logging On," include "Finding a Search Term," and end with "Logging Off." The great bulk of the interactive conversations could be roughly coded and filed according to this scheme.

Another way of coding these same conversations was by topic, theme, or story. The confusion between the letter "O" and the numeral "0" continued to be a subject of conversation throughout the project. (It was coded as "The Story of 'O.'") There were several other stories that regularly appeared: The "Ballad of the Lines" attributed unforeseen troubles to the telephone connections;

"Somewhere in Ohio" was the story of the encyclopedia itself; and "We are on the Air" told the story that made sense of the research presence.

Each coding cuts the conversations in different ways, hence, the need for the multiple copies and to save one copy whole. Each detached conversation (cut apart from one another) is referenced by type of material and date in order that its place in the larger body can always be retrieved.

Microcomputer technology, particularly with the more advanced machines and software, is becoming a great aid to field studies. Whereas the paper chaser is limited to the number of physical copies on hand, the electronic wizard can multiply copies at will, split them electronically into various parts, and then code and file them on disk. The codes can be sorted by the machine and called up as needed. Of course, a power failure can do significant damage. I keep a hard copy archive.

Artifacts

Artifacts pose a particular problem in making their information usable. They first of all have to be adequately annotated at the time they are collected. That annotation should contain all the usual locating information and, equally important, some comment on the context and significance of the piece. I hate to think of the number of times I have looked at a memo or photograph or whatever, apparently captured with glee, but not annotated at the time. The piece which was so meaningful is now dead—objectified remains.

Artifacts or the notation of artifacts have to be moved into the coding system being developed. That is, they have to be made sensible in the same system that the analyst is using for notes and transcripts. If they sit away in a box in the closet, they'll be examined only on special occasions and underutilized.

Tapes

Tapes should be transcribed and the transcriptions coded. If they are merely indexed, the indexes can be coded. The special effort which is required to get to the recordings themselves will limit their use. If they are neither transcribed nor indexed, they are nearly worthless.

The Value of Files

Filing is not only a housekeeping chore. It is an integral part of the research. The coding should begin somewhere in the middle of the project when directions of the analysis begin to come clear. There are usually some dead ends, and always some new ideas appear. The coding cannot be thought of as a rigid taxonomy. It is a tool by which communalities within the data are explored. The coding procedures force the analyst to go through the material again and again to gain **intimate familiarity** with it. That familiarity itself is a significant benefit.

Well-kept systems of files are indicators of the respect the analyst has for the data and for the responsibility of coming to know the whole of it. Validity claims in qualitative research begin with the evidence of extensive contact with the membership. The value of "hundreds of hours" of participant observation is greatly diminished if not matched with hundreds of hours of reflection and writing which is then made available for analysis in some systematic manner.

EXERCISES

1 The intentionality of observation is often considered as the act that separates the analyst from the member. Discuss the nature of this separation first from the perspective of the member and then from that of the analyst.
2 Identify the critical instances in the "Green River" note.
3 What are the problems in using interviews as a substitute for observation?
4 Some people drop their "g's" when they speak. When would that be important to transcribe?
5 How does the focus on the cyclist's performance determine what details of the scene are significant?
6 How might the reporting of detail change if the focus was on the jogger's performance?
7 If abstraction in the field note is at the level of narrative, what is the role of theory in the writing of those notes?
8 How does "intimate familiarity" with notes and materials prepare the analyst for the next steps in research?

WRITING EPISODES

Writing episodes is a method of constructed analysis which initiates the move from the more private knowledge of field notes to the more public knowledge of an objectified text. Field notes cannot be readily exported. They are, after all, notes for the analyst's self-use. Episodes, on the other hand, are, usually, fully constructed narratives which contain not only the sequence of events and acts but also an extended interpretation of the action in context. Episodes are vignettes to which critical attention has been paid. They are the product of analysis and become available for public review.

Episodes as Constructions

An episode is an episode *of* something. It is constructed from some organizing abstraction and the field notes. The organizing abstraction or inductive construct is used to create a coherent entity of analysis. That inductive construct is not imported, but is the result of an insightful experience within the total research activity. (This all sounds like wimp-talk at this level of abstraction.)

What it means in practice is the repetitive reexamination of notes and artifacts and the extended reflection on one's participation until the major explanatory principles of the scene begin to emerge. These principles are inductive constructs, the contents of which are contained in the scene. At this point, the construct is little more than a name which identifies certain instances in the field notes and the analyst's experience. The "little more" is the promise that it will work to provide a coherent and compelling interpretation of those instances. If the application of the principle produces that coherent and compelling interpretation, then the argument for its value is made in that success. The successful episode shows the meaning of the construct and its utility for understanding the action of the members.

Let's see how it works. From a process of reexamination and reflection on the science class conversations, an idea of legitimized or sanctioned confusion has begun to emerge. It appears that there are certain performance areas in the use of the videotext where the responsibility for failure can be reassigned from the student and attributed to a point of confusion which is part of the system. Student error is commonly considered due to a lack of preparation. ("You made that mistake because you didn't read the manual.") Student error which involves the points of confusion, however, are assigned to the hardware, the software, the vendor, or even the teaching staff. The confusion between "O" and zero is one of those legitimized points. Consequently, when a student types an "O" for a zero or a zero for an "O," it is not the student's fault, even though that distinction is also contained in the manual.

What I have done is constructed a rough argument for an implicit distinction in the meaning structure of this science class. We can point to the evidence of this distinction in the practices of the members. The next question is whether it can be used to make greater sense of the member action.

My next step would be to reach for the "O" file. That file contains all the conversations in which "O" or zero was the topic. If it is a valid principle, the theoretical construct of legitimized confusion should be helpful in producing coherent and compelling interpretations of the conversations which have error assignment as an implicit or explicit theme. It should also be helpful in understanding other conversations which reference error, comment on student performance, and the like.

I don't have the space to present that analysis here, but one can see the edges of it by looking again at the field note accompanying my favorite conversation. Is the notion of legitimized confusion helpful in understanding Kevin's and the teacher's behavior? Does the analyst get a better sense of what the conversation is accomplishing (not just what is said)? Who has what responsibility in this scene? Is Kevin's waiting and the teacher's visitations consonant with shared notions about responsibility?

If the construct is not informative, the analyst must explore why. The incident selected may not be appropriate to the construct. That is, the incident may not be the content of an episode of legitimized confusion. If the principle never works, it is, of course, an empty construct and no analysis should result. More likely, because we rarely abandon our own insights, the interpretation will be forced, but the analysis developed will be weak and unconvincing.

At the end of the effort of episodic analysis, the researcher will have identified a number of principles which alone and in combination will interpret much of the social action of the scene. These principles are derived from the scene and are limited to the scene. That limitation may be very restrictive—identified with only those actors performing in that setting—or it may more broadly define the characteristics of many performances.

As an example, let me return to Stoll's analysis of the high school classroom. We pick the study up at the point where she has the transcripts of 30 classroom sessions. She split those transcripts into hundreds of "interactive conversations." Those conversations were then coded into a system of 55 categories based on their internal structure. The coding system was a procedure which brought her into intimate contact with all of the information. None of that system is part of her conclusion. It was rather like the scaffolding in a construction project, necessary for the building but not part of the finished structure.

Her episodic analysis of the conversations led her to identify four accomplishments typical of classroom talk: progression of the subject matter, control of the members, furthering relationships within the subject matter context, and accommodating members within those personal relationships.

Each of these four accomplishments is a way of interpreting classroom talk and each is used to interpret the conversations that occur within the classroom. Stoll (1983, p. 89) would claim, for example, that the following conversation shows the progression of content through the negotiation of contracts:

T: Then I will give you the option of taking the test after you have finished those chapters but it will mean a 10 percent reduction in the grade that you earn.
GS: Ohhh.
T: Now I'm not going to go below 10 percent reduction. So if you feel, hey I haven't completed those chapters and I better not take the test and I'd rather take a 10 percent reduction that's OK with me. It's up to you.
B1: That's OK with me. Heh Heh Heh.
T: [Softly] If you feel that you want to try and take the test and go ahead then that's OK, too.
B1: You vomit and get a worse grade than you would before.
S's: [inaudible mumbling].
GS: Can I go to my locker and get my notebook?
B2: If we take it now.
T: I'll give you a note.
B2: If we take it now and bomb out can we take it later?
T: Yes.

The interpretive principle appears valid. One can clearly see the content activities of this class progressing into defined practices in the negotiation of this explicit contract.

Stoll implies that her findings are not limited to the classrooms she visited. Her claim is that these four accomplishments will typically appear in classroom talk though (a) the manner in which they are achieved may differ, (b) not all will appear in every classroom, and (c) other accomplishments may also be achieved. It would have to be a very different classroom where none of the four accomplishments occur, although there are very different classrooms around.

Inductive Nature of Episodic Analysis

Episodic analysis is entirely inductive. That is, the analysis does not require the introduction of any constructs; the meaning of which is dependent on elements outside of the meaning structure of the members. For example, the episodic analysis of an ethnological study of an organization does not require nor necessarily benefit from such notions as myth or ritual. Both myth and ritual are concepts of particular theory which have meanings residing outside the member community. There may be episodes which are examples of myth and ritual, but the analyst does not need and, indeed, should not use these notions *to construct episodes*. If the analyst were to do so, the result would be the weak form of argument I have called "deductive models and types." We have seen this argument as one which develops no internal support. Let me hasten to remind you that a point of contact with external theory will be part of the study. It is simply premature at this state. The concepts of myth and ritual would be rightfully introduced in the dialectical analysis.

The properly constructed episode, however, sustains itself. The evidence for the interpreting principle or principles is found in the performance of the members. That interpreting principle is the creative discovery of the researcher. The utility of the discovery is shown in the greater sense which can then be made of those performances. (I do have a larger sense of what's happening when I see Kevin's conversation with the teacher as a use of sanctioned confusion.)

Accommodation of Information in Episodic Analysis

How many incidents make an episode? One and sometimes more. The character of the episode is in the compelling nature of its interpretation, not in the number of incidents which can be subsumed beneath it. An episode which provides a powerful interpretation of a single event makes a contribution comparable to one which has many exemplars. It is the thoroughness of the understanding gained of some human action that counts, not the number of times that action occurred during the tenure of the research.

Finally, episodic analysis may not make sense of all the information available. Our purpose is to interpret social action within a given context. Not all human behavior is social action, as we have seen. Further, the emergent, reciprocal nature of social action means that not all attempts will be successful; some are poorly formed, aborted, or blocked. Not all social action makes sense within the context the analyst has assumed. And, of course, some social action will be beyond the analyst's grasp. The leftovers are bothersome, especially if they are the greater part. They are, however, to be expected.

WRITING THE ETHNOGRAPHIC ARGUMENT

The analyst makes the final move to public knowledge in writing the ethnographic argument. As we have seen, this contribution can be explicitly drawn or presented implicitly in the narrative of the action. The structure and style of the qualitative contribution is still much under construction. Plummer (1983) comments:

> [I]n the field of qualitative research there is much less clarity, consensus and coherence about the way in which research should finally be presented. The data, theory and hypothesis do not simply announce themselves, but usually have to be artfully woven into a literate text. Some researchers, for sure, try to bash and order "the data" into a systematic technical report; but for many the underlying imagery for writing is derived from art not science. It is to the tools of the novelist, the poet and the artist that the social scientist should perhaps turn in the qualitative humanistic tradition (p. 106).

Whether implicitly or explicitly, in technical report or in artistic narrative, the contribution to be made will approach the three major forms of explanation possible for any science. That is, it will describe the characteristics, methods and practices, and/or causes and consequences of the object of study—social action. In addition, the inductive method of qualitative research permits the evaluation of a priori, theoretical constructs as interpretations of social life in a dialectical critique. Examples of each follow.

Characteristics

Stoll concludes her analysis of classroom interactions between teacher and student by identifying five characteristics of these interactions. She lists them as presentness, informalness, openness, valuableness, and teacherness. These characteristics typify the social action. Presentness, for example, describes the practices of participation. Students and teachers are responsible for what happens in the classroom when and only when they are themselves present. Missing a class eliminates the expectation of performance for the student and the teacher is not responsible for the action of the substitute.

The concept of "presentness" is derived from an examination of those interactions which involve absence. The characteristic itself is something seen by the analyst in the practices of the members. The notion shows itself as useful in considering conversations like the following (Stoll, 1983, p. 204):

T: Umm, you're having your vocabulary quiz. Those of you who were absent um Lisa [sigh] Let's see Mona was absent last time and um Penny you were absent last time. Did you find out about that? // No. Are you totally unprepared? I changed—I moved the date. Last time I moved it up one day. Uh, what about Lisa. Also totally unprepared to take the quiz or do you want to try it.

G1: I'll try it [giggle] I'm not promising a lot.

T: Well // will you do something by next time. I mean would it be worth it to ya to wait?

Methods and Practices

Alexander and Newell (1981a) investigated among other things the methods friendship pairs used to manage conflicts. In a section titled "Doing Friends," they write:

> Friends may use idiosyncratic words or phrases as a means to signal a personal need or to suggest what is needed relationally. For example, one friendship pair explains to the researcher that they don't 'argue' rather they "discuss." The signal they use for one another when a problem needs to be worked out between them is, "Let's go for a ride." They explain:

> *J:* We'll be together—either work it out or just say I hope you work it out. We'll say, "Let's go for a ride and get this thing worked out." We've never really been mad at each other.
>
> *D:* Not really mad.
>
> *Interviewer:* Never really argue?
>
> *D:* We've discussed. [to friend] I think I've been mad at you before, but it really hasn't made any difference" (p. 10).

The authors conclude this section with two other episodes demonstrating the use of key phrases to trigger activity which is intended to maintain or repair the friendship relationship. These episodes document examples of the methods and practices of this relationship form.

Causes and Consequences

There is clearly cause and consequence in social action. The explanation of cause and consequence takes on a somewhat different character in qualitative research. The causal explanations are valid only in the context of the social action explained. What is cause and what is consequence is defined with the meaning structure of the members rather than external forces—not that those forces are not real; they are simply not the focus of explanation. Because behavior has the potential for a variety of meanings, a given causal relationship between acts is dependent on a particular semiotic configuration.

Bryce gives us a good example of how the semiotic field in which a given activity is performed affects the relationships formed among acts. In her study, Bryce compares the televiewing performances of two families. One family is characterized by a monochronic definition of activity. Once an activity is selected, it is pursued in a singular focus. This singularity included watching television. As Bryce states, "Their children were encouraged, both explicitly and implicitly, not to engage in concurrent activities while viewing." She quotes the mother:

> I really feel that when they watch TV, I want to see them watch TV rather than just have the TV on as a companion, you know? (Bryce, in press).

In the other family, activities are overlaid in polychronic fashion. A single activity rarely occupies center stage. Televiewing particularly is seen as something done while doing something else. The meaning of television viewing is different for these two families. The uses one would have for television, the relationships it would have with other activities, and the potential consequences can be understood only within these separate meanings. The causal arguments for media effects, then, have to be constructed separately for each meaning configuration.

Critical Dialectic

We have previously considered the critical dialectic analysis of theoretical constructs in the final section of Chapter 9. This method of analysis seeks to find the worth of the constructs as devices which can interpret everyday life. Those constructs which show little utility are suspected of being devoid of any empirical component. They may explain what's possible, but apparently not what is.

Anderson (1983), for example, examined the likelihood of success for programs which taught television literacy. The question he addressed was whether the methods and practices which characterized television viewing would support the critical appraisal of its content. In examining his library of episodes of viewing in family settings, Anderson found that critical viewing did not occur in the homes that he visited and, furthermore, that critical viewing was antithetical to the ordinary uses people had for television. He concluded:

> This collection of ordinary viewing structures does not admit to the performance of the critical viewing skills espoused. . . . It is not to say that critical viewing cannot occur in these mundane cases of viewing; it is to say that it will not. We can speculate that the relationship among medium, content, and viewer is not fertile ground for the discipline of criticism (pp. 324-5).

His prognosis for such programs is that they will continue to show success in the classroom—critical viewing can be taught and well learned. They will, however, not have an impact where it is intended. What Anderson has done is to show that the concept of the critical evaluation of content, if it is to be applied in everyday life, has to be different from that which is presently being used to motivate programs of critical viewing.

While the example used here documents an apparent failure of the current configuration of the theoretical notions surrounding media literacy, it does not mean that all such analyses will be negative nor that the theoretical notions themselves cannot be reconfigured to show more explanatory utility. Scholars in media literacy are indeed working to improve their conceptualizations.

The Ethnographic Argument: Final Thoughts

Remember that the first responsibility of the analyst is to document the scene. Often what we see in publication is only the final section of the analysis and its conclusions. The narrative of the scene which underlies that analysis is missing. The missing narrative is an everyday fact of journal publication, but it does not justify the analyst failing to write that narrative. In whatever manner chosen, the story of the scene has to be told because it is only from that story that appropriate conclusions can be drawn. This final comment is a plea to resist the tendency to hold the narrative in private knowledge in that world of field notes, artifacts, and memories. Write it out.

EVALUATING QUALITATIVE RESEARCH

In this section, I want to shift the emphasis from the practitioner back to the reader and consider the principles under which one can evaluate a published piece. The principles defined here are those which appear to be the minimum requirements òf adequacy. Once these principles have been met, there remains such questions as the elegance of the argument and the strength of the contribution, the evaluation of which is particular to the work.

Of these general principles there are six: the explanatory purpose, the source of the information, evidence of a committed study, completeness, generalizeability, and the propriety of the argument. A discussion of each follows:

Explanatory Purpose

The purpose of qualitative research is to approach an understanding of social action from the perspective of the actors. This explanation must include an interpretation of the meanings these actions have for the actors. This interpretation must be found in the actors' social discourse. It is not an interpretation which the researcher as an "omniscient author" supplies. Let me exemplify this difference by quoting from a behavioral sequence presented by Reid and Frazer (1980):

(Larry, age 5, and Allie, age 2, are watching *Captain Kangaroo,* a regular for the children.)

> *Larry:* I like this. That's Captain . . . the one with the red hat.
> *Allie:* That one? [Points on screen to another character.]
> *Larry:* No. The one with the hat and the other one is Mr. Green Jeans (p. 70).

One would expect the ethnographers to use this bit of dialogue to describe the nature of the relationship between Larry and Allie and how they use television in symbolic action to define that relationship. Instead (Reid and Frazer, 1980, p. 70):

> Although the program was not explicitly educational, through their involvement with the show and characters and their actions toward them Larry and Allie created an educational drama. This suggests that children play at learning by "rehearsing" for educational roles.

Say what? The reader must ask: "What are the notions of 'educational drama,' 'play,' 'learning,' 'rehearsing,' and 'educational roles,' and how have they been defined in the social discourse of Larry and Allie?'' What is represented here is the analyst's perspective, not the actors. In fact, we hardly need Larry and Allie at all. This study would not appear to be directed toward the diagnosis and coherent interpretation of the meanings that social actions have for the actors (nor perhaps, intended to), which is the first principle of qualitative research.

Source of Information

The source of this coherent interpretation should be the researcher's participation in and observation of those meanings. We have spent a good deal of time considering what "participation" and "observation" mean. The relationship and distinction between "observation" and "participation" is important. I participate naturally in my own family, but I observe it only with special effort. It is relatively easy to observe someone else's family, but very difficult to participate in it. If I were to appeal to my own family's action as a warrant for some claim the reader should demand evidence of observation as a protection against **solipsism**. On the other hand, should I appeal to my observations of someone else's family, the reader needs to request evidence of participation as protection against **materialism**. Participation has been described as being accepted as a legitimate part of the scene with rights of access and interaction. Observation is the considered reflection on that scene and that participation. Consequently, the second evaluative principle is that the ethnographer demonstrate (a) participation through arguments which support his or her acceptance as part of the social context in which the actors perform, and (b) observation through a careful record of the scene of which he or she is a part.

Evidence of a Committed Study

The understanding of the meanings held by another requires an extensive effort. The strongest bit of evidence of a committed study is the time appropriated to the effort by the analyst. While absolute limits are impossible to specify, we are talking weeks and months, not hours and days. Our six-week history with each family barely qualifies. Commitment to a study is also evidenced in the work produced. How lengthy is the record? How many interviews were conducted? How many contacts made? Time in the field has to be profitably spent.

Completeness

The index of quality of the final product is the completeness of the accounting of the social actions. Sanday (1979) states:

> If, after having completed the ethnography, the observer can communicate the rules for proper and predictable conduct as judged by the people studied, he or she has produced a successful product (p. 529).

In short, the final appeal is to a criterion of utility (Does it work?), a criterion to which all studies should be responsible.

Nevertheless, it is an awkward one; should the reader not happen to have the particular group referenced in the study in his or her social aquarium (Social-arium, perhaps?), he or she is reduced to looking at the evidence in the presentation on which to hang one's credence. That evidence which I hold dear is the detail provided in the description of the scene, the use of the actors' social discourse to define the terms of the abstractions drawn, the number of layers of meaning in which the actions are interpreted, and the contribution to my understanding of human social action.

Generalizeability

Perhaps, surprisingly, generalizeability is an important issue in qualitative research. The conclusions of naturalistic studies are not limited to the particulars of the observations. The business of ethnographic studies is not to explain individuals one at a time. It is rather to explain the social action of the scene. The scene is an identifiable part of human life; the social action is the myriad of performances which give it meaning. The analyst has to make those generalizing steps from acts to action to social action within a scene.

Note that the discourse is still expansionistic. The analyst is not going to arrive at the description of a handful of attributes which accommodate all that is possible within the scene. The constraints of the scene are rather like the constraints imposed by the range of numbers between 1 and 2. The number line is everywhere dense. Consequently, there is an infinite set of numbers between 1 and 2, but there is no 3.0. The social action of the members of any scene is ever expanding within the limits of the scene.

Naturalistic studies being conducted now are searching for the meaning of such universals as parent, child, friend, colleague, classmate, stranger—all in a given time, setting, and context. Whatever the universals sought, the reader has to find their adequate description in the study.

Propriety of the Argument

The final evaluative principle is that author and reader alike must honor the perspective of the social construction. If an author happens to comment that the social act of signing one's name requires a pen, she should be able to expect that the reader will not jump to material determinism arguing that, of course, people can sign their name in pencil. Rather, the reader will accept that she means the ordinary, competent practice of signature is done with a pen—and even when done with pencil, it is done with the knowledge that it is not quite right.

On his side, the reader will rightfully expect that the author has entered into a genuine exploration of the member-held meanings which constitute the practiced selection of writing implement in the social action of signature. The claim, therefore, will not be simply the reflection of the analyst's a priori beliefs, but the product of a systematic effort in the coming to know another.

Without subjecting you to a review of the philosophic notion of the incommensurability of perspectives, criticism of this effort must be appropriate to its character as a personal encounter, documented by a careful record, which results in an interpretation of the social action which rises inductively to a coherent explanation of the scene. To criticize this effort for its lack of objectivity, random sampling, statistical measures of reliability, deductive logic, and the like is inane. Such criticism simply establishes the ignorance of the critic.

Evaluation: A Summary

As with all research, the success of a qualitative study is dependent on reaching the knowledgeable, skeptical reader with a compelling argument. The discerning reader will consider the naturalistic study from the criteria of purpose, informational source, commitment, completeness, generalizeability, and propriety of the argument. The skeptical reader will give none of these criteria away, demand an honest effort, and consider the weaknesses as well as the insights in reaching a judgment of value. That judgment of value is the bottom line of research. Ultimately, the research piece must be helpful in understanding the social world in which we live.

SUMMARY

This chapter has taken us through the steps of qualitative research beginning at the point where the researcher has become a participant in the scene and is starting to create the research text. We have examined the moves from the documentation of observation to the writing of field notes to the construction of episodes, and, finally, to the creation of the research contribution.

In all of these moves, the explanation of the meanings of social action from the perspective of the members has been our goal. The researcher is always reaching out to the other trying to make and maintain that contact.

In the last section of this chapter, we considered six general principles of evaluation which can be applied to naturalistic inquiry: purpose, source, commitment, completeness, generalizeability, and propriety. In considering the sum of these, the knowledgeable and skeptical reader is expected to make that ultimate judgment of value.

EXERCISES

1 Do a little "mental observation" of your own "home-life" situation. Can you discover an episode of something which captures a significant element of the social action within that setting? From your mental field notes, write that episode up.
2 Read and analyze Pacanowsky and Anderson's article "Cop Talk and Media Use,"

(*Journal of Broadcasting,* 1982, *26,* 741–756) or similar article (see the bibliography) using the evaluative criteria provided.

RELATED READINGS

Denzin, N. K. *The research act: A theoretical introduction to sociological methods* (2d. ed.). New York: McGraw-Hill, 1978.

Lindlof, T. (Ed.). *Natural audiences: Qualitative research of media uses and effects.* Norwood, NJ: Ablex Publishing Corporation, in press.

Lofland, J. *Doing social life.* New York: John Wiley and Sons, 1976.

Plummer, K. *Documents of life: An introduction to the problems and literature of a humanistic method.* London: George Allen and Unwin, 1983.

EPILOGUE

This chapter takes a look at the problem of ethics in research, cleans up a bit of unfinished business concerning the relationships among perspectives, and considers the future routes that research methods might take. It is a chapter full of personal opinion with an emphasis on the faults and failings of our research practices—we certainly must understand those, too. The criticism, however, comes from a loyal member. Best, perhaps, the chapter is mercifully short.

ETHICS

It is typical that the last chapter in a research text spend some time with the ethics of science. In the main, I have chosen to integrate comments on the ethics of a practice at the point of its introduction. There are, nevertheless, certain larger considerations which remain. To begin this discussion, I'm going to pull back a bit further from the ordinary view of ethics to consider two issues in the stance of science in society. Then, I will turn our attention to the safeguards due our respondents, the responsibility imposed by the implied contract of data, and the ethical presentation of claims. Here, a brief introduction to each:

• In Chapter 1, I argued that the role of science was to develop public knowledge for some human purpose. That statement imposes two ethical burdens on the practitioner: First, it establishes that science is in the public domain and that making the move toward publication of some kind is a necessary part of the practice. Failure to publish is more than a personal omission; it is also bad science. Second, the purposeful nature of science means that those purposes are open for comment and criticism. Decisions taken from certain purposeful stances can lead to excesses and errors. As I have said, the practice of science is not self-justifying.

• The pursuit of the purified attribute or the nature of the scene can make us neglectful of the individuals who wittingly or unwittingly are the subject of research. The researcher's use of subjects is easily exploitative as known by any student who has had an hour of paid instruction time summarily appropriated in the name of science.

• Once constructed, data impose significant responsibilities on the analyst for their safeguard and preservation. Quantitative measurements and the qualitative research text are the empirical connections which make science science, yet they are often incomplete, inconsistent, contradictory, or incoherent. The researcher is faced with preserving the very sources of problems.

• The end of all research is the argument that a contribution to public knowledge has been made. That argument justifies the effort and establishes its worth. That the contributing argument is the ultimate value of the research lays a trap for the analyst. That argument has to be fair, keeping evidence and claims in proper alignment.

A paragraph or two designed to illumine the issues, but not to offer solutions on each of these points, follows:

The Ethical Demand for Publication

Science makes demands on the commonweal. It uses public resources and seeks special access to individuals and their social action. Science requires society to suspend many of the rules which govern the concourse of individuals and to provide for its special needs. These demands are presented in an implied contract that offers repayment in knowledge gained. That knowledge is, of course, something more than the private knowledge of the analyst. Every study, therefore, requires a public record. This public record is not the publication of a journal article or the presentation of a convention paper. Those are only partial derivatives of the public record. The public record is the daily journal, the log, if you will, of the study. In it, the scientist records the events (both notable and ordinary), the decisions, the step-by-step procedures, all instrumentation, all the collected data, their analysis, and the concluding interpretation. It is a complete record, and it is in the public domain. One should be able to expect that the record will be maintained and that access to it will be granted.

In practice, not one in a thousand keeps a record like this. There are few research archives in our universities. One cannot study the life work of the majority of contemporary scientists. Research which does not make an appearance in the media is simply lost. And even those appearances are poor substitutes for what is needed. Further, many consider their work as proprietary to be safeguarded from inspection, possible criticism, or unauthorized use. The contract is often not kept.

The Critique of Purpose

Academics use research to play a number of games—padding the vita, finding the grant, getting tenure. Industrial scientists have their own set—building the empire, justifying board decisions, playing the wizard. In both sets, the central purpose is not the knowledge to be gained but some other accomplishment. That is, the criteria used are not for the best conduct of research but for winning the game. In building the vita, for example, long-term research is avoided, "hot" topics are sought, and a study which (with a minimum of rewriting) can hit more than one publication is a winner. In justifying the board, the industrial scientist (or consultant), consciously or not, designs research which will justify or verify decisions being supported by some faction of management.

There are those who argue, "Sure, we play those games, but we also conduct good research." The claim seems unlikely. At least, the research is not as good as it could be. The wrong best interests are being served. As with most ethical issues, the decisions are not cut and dried. The systems in which scientists operate give rise to the games, encourage our participation, and reward the winners. It can be asked if the human sciences are not particularly susceptible to game playing. Theory is so poorly developed that the social significance of research fndings is hard to discern. The hope of achieving something is hard to maintain. All the better to play the game.

Safeguarding Respondents

In the name of science, we expose even children to antisocial content, provide them the opportunities to be racist, sexist, and violent, deceive them as to what we are about, put potentially fragile relationships in jeopardy by subjecting them to soul-searching interrogation, ask members of organizations to expose their positions, and on and on. It is an incredible list.

We justify this exposure to risk by invoking the name of science. There is little question that some risk is entailed in any study of social import. The ethical principle involved is "informed consent," which means that the respondent has been made actively aware of the potential physical, psychological, and moral risks. It is not a mumbled statement, "Well, we'll show you some films and then have you fill out a questionnaire." Nor is it a decision by the researcher that no risks are involved—"Oh, everybody's seen a film like this sometime. This is just ordinary TV."

The Department of Health, Education and Welfare (now Health and Human Services) listed the following seven principles of informed consent (DHEW, 1975 as quoted by Chadwick et al., 1984, pp. 19–20).

1 An accurate description of the research procedures and its purposes must be presented in terms understandable to the potential subject.

2 A description of the risks or of any discomfort or injury reasonably expected must be disclosed.

3 A description of the benefits for the subject and the scientific discipline reasonably expected from the research must be noted.

4 Disclosure of any alternative procedures that might be advantageous to the subject must be made. This pertains to biomedical research where patients with specific medical problems are being treated with experimental procedures.

5 An offer to answer questions about any of the research procedures must be given.

6 The instruction that the subject is free to withdraw from the research at any time without prejudice must be fully explained.

7 If there is the possibility of physical injury, an explanation as to whether medical care and compensation are available must be presented.

Few studies in communication involve physical risks, but many involve psychological and other personal risks. Perhaps a risk analysis of an exemplar study would be helpful to see the pressures on the principle of informed consent. Presume that a researcher wishes to study the effects of stress on beginning relationships. The purpose of the study is to develop strategies which will help individuals dissipate stress in their relationships. But first, we have to know how stress is expressed within relationships which are susceptible to dissolution. A protocol is devised in which volunteers are provided the opportunity to interact with another—a covert research confederate—in an ostensible research task over a 6-week period. In the protocol, the individuals will be paid on their performance as a team. At the end of the 6 weeks, the experimenter confronts the confederate with accusations of mismanagement and malfeasance and delivers a general dressing down. The experimenter leaves the room. The criterion will be the recorded conversation that follows. Will the subject attempt to shoulder some of the burden, disassociate or distance, attack, or use some other strategy for dealing with the induced stress?

Let's examine the ethical tensions the researcher encounters in trying to meet the requirement of informed consent. The first problem concerns the question of the extent to which the success of the protocol is dependent upon the subject's belief in the deceptions of (a) a genuine interaction, (b) the confederate being a peer, (c) the nature of the evaluation, (d) the attack, and (e) the validity of the conversation that follows. All of these, of course, are lies either by commission or omission. It would appear that the deceptions are necessary to make this protocol work. If so, how does the subject give informed consent to participate in them, or rather, to be duped by them? Because natural relationships are the object of explanation, the researcher will certainly want the respondent to participate ingenuously.

The second problem is to anticipate the risks that the respondent might be exposed to. On the face of this example, I see no physical risks, but there are psychological and, perhaps, moral ones. The psychological risks involve the respondent's reaction to the attack, the revelation that the relationship is a sham, and that the commitment and effort that was expended on it was apparently wasted. The moral risk (a test of one's values) occurs in the criterion conversation. Will the respondent perform as his or her value structure would indicate? There may be other risks that I haven't seen. In informed consent, the respondents must have the opportunity to evaluate the potential for themselves —another certainly couldn't do it for them.

A common solution to these ethical tensions is the debriefing. Debriefing procedures are designed to help the respondent make the proper sense out of the study and deal with any conflicts or problems that arose. In this protocol, the researcher would presumably explain what the study was about, the necessity for the deceptions, minimize the attack, emphasize the value of the respondent's work, and deal with any guilt that may have arisen around that person's criterion response. But what of the person who complains, "You cheated me; you lied to me; you robbed me of my time." Or the one who simply thinks to himself, "I can't believe I did that."

Debriefing seems least useful an answer when the study anticipates a negative outcome. That is, any study which has as its criterion an antisocial act or proxy thereof. For example, if the researcher anticipates that long-term exposure to violent (*Chain-Saw-Massacre*-type) films results in increased rates of violent acts, then providing the conditions of that exposure may well be providing for actual antisocial acts. One cannot debrief during the time of exposure. Further, what evidence is there that the debriefing will neutralize the effect of the stimulus materials. Isn't the whole point of these studies that the dramatic visual images are more powerful than simply telling people what is right? If indeed the experimenter had an effective antidote, wouldn't it be more useful to society to be studying that? These are legitimate questions for which there are a variety of answers. Both the questions and the answers, however, should be an explicit part of every design.

All too often we treat our respondents as marks to be conned into participation and committees on human subjects as unfortunate bureaucratic hurdles. When we do, we evidence little concern for the personal consequences our research has for the people who volunteer.

The ethical tensions in a qualitative study are no less difficult. They do, in fact, involve all the tensions of everyday living. In addition, the research aspect of the relationships seems to add a few. Here are three:

1 I am personally opposed to infiltration and covert studies. To me, they are inherently invasive and exploitative. Further, the relationship between analyst and member is inherently flawed based on a deliberately deceptive contract. Another may argue that the analyst does no more than report on his or her own experience. Yet, what of the lies and covering stories that are common practice of getting started, conducting interviews, and collecting artifacts? As Bellah and his associates write: "We cannot deny the moral relationship between ourselves and those we are studying without being untrue to both" (1985, p. 303). The analyst seems particularly susceptible to an exploitative mind set when working with a group which is seen as less competent, out of step, different, or even antisocial as if "those people" don't deserve our care.

2 One of the more difficult problems is the circumstance when the analyst is faced with the choice of an active intervention or a passive observation. Perhaps the analyst finds a mistake in a report about to be issued from a manager's office. It is a major error, one that will surely draw a response. Does the analyst intervene? Protect that manager by pointing out the error? Or is observing the organization's response the greater value?

The American Anthropological Association's rather self-serving statement on this issue reads: "Researchers should maintain a level of integrity and helpfulness in the field so that by their behavior and example they will not jeopardize future research there" (Sommer and Sommer, 1980, p. 18). Into what practice would this translate?

3 The treatment of individual relationships that develop in the course of a study gives rise to another dilemma. To a certain extent, the researcher is a guest of all the members. Nevertheless, stronger relationships will develop with some rather than others. How are the demands of those relationships dealt with? What are the questions of fairness? For instance, the analyst has a special access to information which can be useful to and used by members. Demands are made by members both on that information and on that access. Should those favors be distributed with careful equity, for the researcher's greatest good, or as a member would? The answers will significantly negotiate the researcher's presence.

Respecting the Data

This section looks at the problems that are faced when measurement and observation are completed and analysis is about to begin. For qualitative and quantitative researcher alike, the first responsibility is to represent, fairly and accurately, the behavior and social action of another. For the quantitative researcher, this responsibility entails ensuring that the data upon which the conclusions are drawn are the direct result of the respondents. For the qualitative researcher, this responsibility means that the descriptions, quotations, and interpretations of the narrative are traceable to the experimental observation of the analyst. Both of these responsibilities raise ethical issues that we will consider in their turn.

Dealing with quantitative measurements, the dictum is simple: The data are inviolate. The practice, however, is full of gray-area decisions that must be made. There are the simple-appearing problems of incomplete questionnaires, improperly marked answers (e.g., a mark between two response positions), answers which are outside the range or are otherwise impossible, answers which are contradictory, and the rest.

Generally, these problems are approached with a set of a priori rules for their solution—improper markings will always be assigned the more central of the positions, contradictions resolved to the more reliable response item, and so forth. When the problem rate is relatively high, say, 20 percent of the data, the rules are not trivial. They form a potentially substantive bias and must be reported. The analyst cannot merely set the rule and forget it.

Another judgment problem often faced by the researcher is evidence that the respondent has not bought into the manipulation or is otherwise responding illegitimately (from the researcher's viewpoint). The analyst may overhear some chance remarks, may see evidence on the response forms, or may have an item testing for the success of the manipulation. The practice of discarding the data from respondents, when there is evidence—even compelling evidence—of inappropriate action, is problematic. For instance, I was using a response form of 50 bipolar adjectival scales. Three or four respondents in this freshman class had some fun with the form. One brought a diagonal from right to left; another worked an X by interlacing responses. In a class of 200 with an anonymous questionnaire, I couldn't ask them their intent.

Throw them out? In this case, I had a large enough sample and was confident enough in the effect I was measuring to leave them in. With a small sample and an effect that missed by a few hundredths, I would have very likely dismissed them with the typical line in the methods section, "Four questionnaires yielded unusable data." The data, of course, are not unusable; they are unwelcome.

Processing errors are a fact of life in a data collection of any size. Our campaign studies make use of 5000 data points on each respondent. It is unlikely that even one respondent's data set is error-free. The analyst has to institute controls to manage the error rate and to ensure that the errors that do occur do not systematically affect the findings.

Errors occur in the coding, keying, and computer reading of data. Coding and keying should be verified; that is, they should literally be done twice. Errors in the reading of data occur because improper instructions are given (reading the wrong data set), or because the computer algorithm is designed differently from what the user assumes (e.g., the algorithm may read blanks as zeros when the researcher is using blanks for missing data and zeros as a response). Computer-read errors are particularly vexing as they often produce results which are indistinguishable from those of the correct data set. A good rule is to hand calculate the mean or a frequency count for each data set. An analyst's good intentions or self-confidence are not enough.

The problems on the qualitative side are centered on the continuing effort to contain the interpolation of fiction within the descriptive interpretation of the narrative. Fictions occur when the descriptions are not documented in observation, when sentences presented as quotations were never said, when the action is filled out to make sense, when composite characters are introduced into the scene, and the like. The use of such fictions can be legitimate but only *when they are explicitly identified as such*. They are not legitimate when the reader has been led to expect an interpretation based on the empirical evidence.[1] Fictions are

---

[1]Note that I am being careful to distinguish the analyst's interpretation of experience from fictions which may be introduced into the narrative. An interpretation of socially constructed reality is not fictional although it is personal. The reader is cautioned not to apply objective reality constructs to this analysis.

very attractive when the analyst has arrived at an interpretation of the social action based on hundreds of incidents and is now faced with finding the compelling evidence to demonstrate the claim. People rarely say exactly the right thing or perform the quintessential act. The evidence is almost always muddied —spoiled by the wrong phrase or imperfect action. It is quite easy to honestly remember a conversation or a performance as better evidence than it was. The analyst's only protection is the quality of the research text and the consistent use of it.

One way to reduce the pressure is to abandon the expectation that creating the research argument is a simple task—that there will be clear evidence for every claim. The analyst has to build the evidence in the same way that it was presented—in many imperfect instances. For every claim, the researcher should plan to use several examples which taken as a whole verify that claim. Claims should not turn on a single word in a remembered conversation.

The most difficult of cases occur when the research text is inadequate. These cases include those moments in writing the narrative when some hitherto trivial incident is finally seen as the resplendent critical instance that it has always been. One moves to the research text to verify the memory only to find that there is nothing noted or what is noted is inappropriate. The ethical dilemma is set. It is often resolved with the introductory phrase, "Although my notes do not show it, . . ."

That solution is easy but not necessarily good. A better approach would be to return to the text to find evidence for the claim elsewhere. If the claim is a useful interpretation, then there should be other incidents which it explains. Failing that, the researcher must return to the scene.

I have already noted that not every analyst considers fictions to be a problem in interpretive research. Presenting exemplar dialogue that is typical (but not actual), actions and characters that are composites, or stories that are more coherent than performed are considered legitimate extensions of the interpretation. There is no question, in my mind, that such writing can make a valuable contribution to our discourse on the human condition. There is also no question that to present it as if it were empirical science is unethical.

Qualifying the Claims

This last section on ethics considers the inherent argumentative character of research. Whether quantitative or qualitative, the final task of the researcher is to present a convincing argument that the evidence does indeed support the conclusions. In no case do the facts read themselves. And in most cases, the facts themselves are trivial; it is what those facts signify that is the contribution.

The tension in this task is to be insightful rather than pedestrian while staying within the range of evidence that can be meager and flawed. We can see the tension by examining the task of the argument construction. The analyst is first called upon to display that evidence for what it is—to point out its flaws and defects (perfect studies occur only in textbooks). Then, the analyst is called upon to provide a substantive contribution to public knowledge. If the write-up spends too much time on the flaws and defects, then the enthusiasm for the conclusions is lost. If the conclusions are emphasized, then the evidence can be glorified. Because the conclusions justify the presentation, few authors err in the first direction. Much of our literature teeters on the edge of the conclusion justifying the evidence. Some take the dive.

Examples of questionable arguments are common. In quantitative research, typical practices include:

- Treating volunteer convenience samples as if they were randomly selected
- Claiming validity in measurement with no empirical evidence
- Using a synthetic protocol as if it were valid in natural settings
- Treating nonsignificant findings as if they were substantive by either claiming that indeed the two events are the same or that the effect was close enough to significance
- Ignoring measurement demand
- Treating post-hoc tests as if they were hypothesized
- Adapting one's theory to one's findings and presenting the match as a confirmation

In qualitative research, examples include:

- Claiming observation from reminiscence
- Claiming participation from presence
- Reporting manipulated performances as if spontaneous
- Using a priori constructs as if inductive
- Editing the evidence of episodes to fit the claim
- Claiming a coherent inductive construct from incoherent evidence
- Writing a better story than what was observed

In general, these ethical difficulties can be resolved by strengthening the quality of evidence. If you want more potent conclusions, "do better research" is a good principle. Commit the time and resources; avoid the expedient. Of course, the time to make those commitments is in the design of the study, not as the pressure to publish mounts. Once the analyst has decided to use college freshmen as proxies for expert personnel managers or determined that four weeks of observation in a working group is sufficient, it is too late.

Summary on Ethics

Ethics concerns our relationships with ourselves, with the individuals we study, with our colleagues with whom we work, with the community of scientists to which we belong, and with society as a whole. The questions of ethics revolve around the nature of those relationships as open, honest, reciprocal, fair, responsible. The tension in ethics is that these various relationships are often in conflict. An open, reciprocal relationship with one group does not always result in a responsible one with another. Because there are no simple answers, ethical conduct has to be a regularized concern—part of every check list of methods.

EXERCISES

Evaluate the ethical conduct of the following:

1 A researcher, wanting to survey the rate of alcoholism in an urban area for the local public health officials, plants a story in the newspaper indicating that a public health survey will be taken. The survey form collects extensive family and individual health histories. Buried within are the crucial alcoholism questions. In the analysis and report, only these questions are used.

2 A researcher exposes friendship pairs to stress by inducing frustration in a task completion test. The criterion is the appearance of helping or competitive behaviors. The pairs had been told that "they would work together to complete a difficult task."

3 An ethnographer studying a failing "quality circle" is asked by management to construct a questionnaire based on information gathered in the participation to "help improve the productivity of this group."

4 An ethnographer studying a family is told by the wife that she fears that her husband might "discipline" her for not getting an errand run on time. The ethnographer leaves—as scheduled—before the husband gets home.

THE MOVE TOWARD SYNTHESIS

The unfinished business is left over from Chapter 3 where the possibility of a middle ground between the quantitative and qualitative research approaches was raised. The exploration of this middle ground has been deferred until now. Throughout this text, we have considered the two perspectives as if they were coherent opposites. Certainly, they can be reconstructed in analysis as such, but in practice, they are not always coherent or even opposite. Further, they are not the only players on the field. Morgan and Smircich (1980), in their analysis of the debate, laid out a continuum marked by six separate communities with differing ontological, epistemological, and metaphorical assumptions, all claiming some right to the title of science. In addition to those who would claim membership in science, there are others who construct empirically based arguments who reject membership preferring to be called social researchers or critical theorists. It is indeed a most confusing and yet exciting time.

This section is motivated by (a) the continuing discussions about the nature of science and (b) the growing number of calls for research using multiple methods (see Faules, 1982, or Jicks, 1979). As to the first, if it is the nature of science to be singular, then the current state of community crisis is a condition which must be resolved. If, indeed, one perspective must be right and the others wrong, our attentions should be directed primarily to discovering which is which. On the other hand, the calls for multiple methods seem to suggest that there really isn't any problem because the perspectives have the same epistemology. Consequently, the differences between perspectives are political rather than essential and can be negotiated.

In the paragraphs that follow, we consider the nature of the calls for unity, the arguments for separatism, and one vision of what would be required for a genuine synthesis.

Motivations toward Unity

It doesn't take too cynical an eye to see most motivations toward unity as simple power management. One ensures the survival of one's community by managing the opposition. Calls for unification that begin with, "You know there really aren't any differences in what we do," or "You people just work the inductive side of science and we work the deductive side," are essentially coopting moves. Such moves minimize (trivialize) the differences between communities so that one can still claim the other.

Generally, claims of no differences focus on methods and procedures. It is pointed out that ethnomethodologists use questionnaires and even perform field experiments. Behaviorists do observation studies; what's the difference? This "small world" argument begins with the claims that method is ideologically neutral and that the evidence from method is material. In short, an experiment is an experiment, and its evidence is there for all to see. Such claims are, of course, self-fulfilling and self-serving.

More altruistic motives for unity are based on the belief that science is progressive—moving toward a true epistemology. Conflicting scientific communities, so the argument goes, can only impede this progression. It is, therefore, in everyone's best interests to reduce or ignore their differences and emphasize the similarities. The similarities between communities may be very shallow, but with a commitment to unity, unity in fact will follow.

Science is, after all, more important than any given group. If science appears in disarray, it will not be able to maintain its sociopolitical status.

Arguments for Separatism

New communities in science develop when old ones have not been successful or can no longer serve particular purposes. These purposes may be as base as the outs versus the ins, or they may reflect the larger issues of societal expectations for science. Let's take a look at this latter point. Society as it expresses itself through government funding, congressional hearings, citizen panels, and the like has an extensive shopping list of purposes for the human sciences:

Do something about violence in society (without redistributing power).
Do something about poverty (without redistributing resources).
Fix education (cheaply).
Improve the democratic process in campaigns and government (but be careful who wins).

Both the statements and the parenthetical disclaimers are important. The combinations establish the criteria for successful science. (Because the distribution of power is a given, studies on the effects of violent content in the media become more attractive.) The combinations may also present intractable problems. (What if the solution to violence in society is the redistribution of power?) Critics of the establishment in science say: "You haven't done the job; you have failed to deliver what you promised. Where are the solutions?"

When the established science fails its societal purpose, it opens the door for competing approaches. The argument for encouraging the growth of separate communities is based on the benefits of competition: Science has to compete in the marketplace like any other human endeavor. Competition is healthy. It weeds out the unproductive. But as the economics scholar knows, there are forces in every marketplace—including the marketplace of ideas—that move to reduce competition. There must be systems of governance which force an open, competitive market. Science alone cannot govern its own marketplace. Funding agents, universities, editorial boards, and other societal institutions must take affirmative steps to ensure the development and presentation of alternatives.

The argument for competition is based on the belief that the problems that society presents to the human sciences are not intractable, that solutions are within human ability, and that no particular community of science has shown itself successful in addressing these solutions.

But, separatism is also a powerful movement in the human sciences in its own right because the differences between the perspectives are substantial. It is not possible to combine them without doing damage to the metatheoretical underpinnings of one or the other. As we noted in Chapter 3, the two perspectives have different notions on the nature of reality, of humans and their society, of the meaning of things, of the purposes of science, of the significance of the methods of science, and of the nature of its contribution to human knowledge. A progression from those different standpoints can have no common ending. It is only a superficial view that sees no difference.

Toward a Genuine Attempt at Synthesis

If one were to make a genuine attempt at synthesis, what would need to be done? I would suggest that first, the opposing perspective would have to be seen as thesis and antithesis. That is, that they are ontologically and epistemologically competitive systems of thought—both of which cannot be true and that, most likely, neither is completely true. It would be, therefore, necessary to move from both perspectives to arrive at a valid synthesis.

What concepts would one need to be synthesized? Clearly, the notion of reality would be a place to begin. Perhaps following Watzslavick (1976) and Toulmin (1974) among others, we need to think of reality as a multitiered concept with the inescapable material reality of the individual as the first, most general, level, followed by several levels of socially constituted reality beginning with grand culture and working up the particular to the negotiated meanings of an individual's personal reality concepts. A given explanation could be limited horizontally to a single tier or could plunge vertically through several tiers.

"Meaning" is another obvious candidate. A synthesis would have to arrive at a new formulation of the constructed versus delivered debate, and to find ways for dealing with context. How one formulates meaning has telling implications for protocol design and measurement in research.

The dominant model of the individual as the sum of a set of objectified attributes cannot accommodate the model of the individual as an expression in time and place. The concept of the individual would have to be redefined. That redefinition would also have to establish the role of the individual in scientific explanation. Are individuals important for science only for what they hold in common with others, or are they to be approached in their full uniqueness?

Finally, in this list of starting places, is the purpose of scientific explanation. Are we to continue an emphasis on prediction and its sister control? If so, laws and contingent rules obviously cannot both be the end goal. Laws and rules are formulated on different conceptualizations of social reality. A rule is not a "little law." It is not a weak universal. It describes, rather, a disposition of action that sets the boundaries of improvisation.

Using rules has an additional problem for science seeking prediction. Rules explanations are essentially backward looking—they are contained in the past performances of the social unit. These performances are themselves based on an ongoing semiotic. Rules document where a social unit has been. They are not very useful in predicting where it will go given some radical change in the governing semiotic system. As MacIntyre argues,

> . . . the elaboration of a radically new concept cannot be predicted, for a necessary part of the prediction is the present elaboration of the very concept whose discovery or invention was to take place only in the future. The notion of the prediction of radical conceptual innovation is itself conceptually incoherent (1984, p. 93)

Rules, therefore, are a reasonable goal in a predictive epistemology only if one adopts the assumption of orderly transitions within gradual change. Certainly, in some finite time span with some social arrangements, the assumption is valid, but the clock is running on any rules-based prediction. None of this argues that we should abandon prediction and control as a goal. It does say that we will have to come to some better notion of the character of those kinds of explanation.

Finally, both law and rules theory are inadequate formulations for dealing with explanation of the situated individual. Explanation from rules like that from laws is inherently reductionistic. Explanation from the situated individual is inherently expansionistic. It would appear to eschew the formats of prediction and control and find a more comfortable fit in the story. Reductionistic explanation is not useful in preserving the individual, and expansionistic explanation is not adequate for aggregate analysis. A synthesis, as I will argue again in the "futures" section, will have to address the epistemological contribution of science.

Implications

The current debate in the human sciences covers the entire topic. There is no convention of science that is not open to question. It is not possible to maintain a business-as-usual attitude with intellectual honesty. On the other hand, some set of conventions has to be assembled by the practitioner to engage in research. One can do that with the fervor of a true believer or situationally with a pragmatist's view. The work has to find a community of acceptance. So, too, must the worker.

At the same time, there has to be a recognition of the viability of other beliefs. The intellectual life of science requires us to keep a skeptical eye even on science itself. Given the tenacity that intellectual communities have demonstrated in history, it is not reasonable to expect an early resolution for our present embarrassment. This text should contribute to, not solve, the problem of multiple perspectives. Any synthesis derived, even an incredibly successful one, will simply be one more point of view which can be taken.

A CRITICAL LOOK INTO THE FUTURE

In the 20 years that I have been permitted to make my living in research, there have been substantial changes in the questions that can be asked and the methods that can be used in the conduct of science. I would expect a similar era of change in the next 20. This section, then, takes a brief look at current practice to gratuitously offer some suggestions as to where change might do the most good. The analysis is presented separately for the two perspectives.

Possible Beneficial Changes in Quantitative Research

The arrival of the high-speed computer has significantly marked the past 30 years of quantitative research. It has increased the sophistication of our statistical analytical tools, decreased the sophistication needed to use them, greatly shortened the amount of time required to conduct research, and virtually eliminated any contact between the data and the researcher. It has been a mixed blessing.

One result has been a heavy emphasis on more complex analyses. There is an excitement about being part of the introduction of a new technique. Path analysis, cluster analysis, and certainly multidimensional scaling have all generated part of that excitement. It will be interesting to see if that excitement continues as access to sophisticated statistical routines becomes even more widespread with the adoption of the home computer. All routines can be programmed for these computers, although there are presently limitations in the size of the data matrix that can be used. (Even that problem can be solved with a mainframe telephone interconnect.)

It is quite possible that such common access will take the shine off mere technique. Nonetheless, current developments in statistics will probably return us to the computer centers. "Brute force" routines are being developed which eliminate the need for parametric assumptions by simultaneously considering a large number of models. Only the larger computers make such routines cost effective. Being the first on the block to have the magic decoder ring will undoubtedly continue its attraction.

Ignoring that seduction, however, the new routines do promise release from parametric pretense. This freedom has important implications for protocol design and measurement development by permitting us to consider each underlying assumption.

As with any activity, emphasis on one part leads to neglect of others. The emphasis on computer technology and statistical routines has led to a neglect of protocol design and measurement. It is my judgment that quantitative research has suffered from this neglect. Protocol design and measurement establish the quality of the data to be analyzed. Our analytical routines far exceed our ability to deliver data of sufficient quality to analyze. We have achieved significance without much signification. Possible improvements in design and measurement are discussed in the next few paragraphs.

Interest in the demand characteristics of protocols has been a part of the criticism of research from the first. In the practice of research, nevertheless, the adoption of verification procedures to demonstrate general laws has tended to eliminate this concern from design. That is, the press to demonstrate that a hypothesis works under the best of conditions has been confused with evidence that the hypothesis will, therefore, always work.

As we have seen, verification procedures use optimal contexts. Because those contexts are optimal rather than sufficient, the analyst is limited to statements of what *can* happen rather than what *will* happen in mundane contexts. When the intent of the analyst is to comment on social action in the natural world, that limitation is fatal. We could greatly enlarge the perspective of design by adopting the notion that a hypothesis, if true, is true for certain conditions and that it is equally important to know under what contexts a hypothesis is unsuccessful.

There is not much new in this recommendation. Scientists presently qualify their hypothesis, on occasion, through the use of control variables. What would be different (perhaps, not new) would be the attitude that because any hypothesis can be made to fail and because the natural world presents the contexts of failure as well as those of success, the test of the hypothesis is incomplete until we begin to understand the conditions and relative proportions of both success and failure.

This attention to protocol would require two important shifts in current practice:

• First, research would have to become more programatic. The researcher and the working system would have to support a long term commitment to an area of study.
• Second, a great deal more effort would have to be spent in understanding and describing the protocol itself. We now take for granted or render transparent most of the conditions under which data are collected. They would have to be made explicit.

Measurement is, without question, the area where we show the most uneven quality of work. The critical analysis of claims based on the careful reading of questionnaires is often embarrassing. Items are naive, simplistic, and artificial. Reliability coefficients, when given, are used unthinkingly like seals of approval. Scales are just as likely to be reliable because of their imprecision as their validity. Little work gets done in studying conceptual validity and virtually none in external validity. Much of our practice appears as if measurement was merely a way to generate numbers for the good stuff of analysis.

Stout criticism, but when the practice of research is taken as a whole and not just examined from the prestigious journals, it is well justified. Measurement has been trivialized by the doctrine of operationalism. That doctrine, we remember, holds that theoretical concepts are defined *only* in measurement. While this notion has been advanced as the most perfect empirical connection, it also tends to eliminate concerns for conceptual validity and mundane realism. Little harm would be done if the conclusions drawn were expressed in the terms of the measurement items. But, of course, they are not. The conclusions are expressed in the terms in which we express our concerns about ourselves and our society.

Simply said, without much more complaint, measurement is our weakest link. Our current practices are inconsistent and the theory which directs them is inadequate—full of unjustified assumptions and unrealistic claims. Now, all of this means that there are still many opportunities for significant contributions to be made.

Areas of Growth in Qualitative Research

Qualitative research faces a significant struggle to become successful in the scientific study of communication. I believe there are three elements necessary for this success:

- First, there has to develop a reasonable consensus of what the practice of qualitative research will be within our community.
- Second, there has to be an adequate instructional base in our graduate and undergraduate programs.
- Third, publication outlets and presentational forms will have to be developed.

There is the added difficulty that these three elements are interdependent and will have to develop concurrently.

Stabilized practices of any human activity develop codes of good workmanship. Communication scholars are in the process of developing those codes for the practice of qualitative research. While it is true that qualitative research has a long history elsewhere, it is uncertain what form it will take in communication. At this point, it is difficult to distinguish the shoddy from the substantial. We simply do not know enough about human communication performances to determine when they have been well documented. There are, however, certain conflicting demands becoming clear that will have to be balanced in order to achieve quality in this research.

Time in the field is certainly the focus of one of them. The system of academic research in communication has not shown itself likely to support the novice researcher over the months and years that many claim a single qualitative study requires. Adding two years to a graduate student's program of study will be difficult to accomplish, particularly when viewed in comparison with quantitative colleagues. There will be heavy pressure to accept less.

We can presently see a response developing to this pressure in the practice of team participation. This practice rotates members of a research team through observation at a research site. The research text is developed in consensus among the team members. Lengthy observation can be accomplished in this manner in substantially smaller time frames and with much less demand on any individual. There are serious difficulties with this practice which are generally ignored. They raise questions of expertise, commitment, participative membership, consensus judgments, group interpretation, authorial responsibility, and the like. Until these questions are answered, this practice is susceptible to the charge of expedience at the expense of interpretative validity.

Across all practices, the quality of the research text is extremely vulnerable. At present, there is no collegial review of even the public components of that text. This is parallel to the problem of data in quantitative research, which are supposed to be part of a public record but often are not. In both cases, it is impossible to know whether the data have been wholly or partially fabricated. The fact that the research text contains the private knowledge of one's own experiences would seem to facilitate abuses. Beyond deliberate deceit, however, the lack of access and review encourages the idiosyncratic performance of practices about which there is supposed to be communal agreement. There is too heavy a dependence on trust and not enough opportunity for mutual correction.

Finally, in this preliminary list, we show a great deal of uncertainty as to what is the explanatory target and epistemological purpose of this research. In this text, we have specified the object of our explanation as the situated individual in the performance of social action. Not all agree. Further, the model for this explanatory object is unclear. How shall the situated individual be conceived? Does the quantification model of the individual as the sum of its attributes apply? What model is appropriate for the concept of socially constructed meanings? What is the character of social action?

The epistemological purpose of qualitative research in communication is equally muddied. We still need to develop a clear consensus of what this research is all about, which is not to say that there are not many opinions. We need to be able to identify explanatory adequacy to understand how this explanation contributes to our knowledge—to answer the questions: "Is this good?" "And so what?"

The answers to these questions—and there are answers—requires a literate audience. To make qualitative alternatives to communication research viable alternatives will require the presentation of these approaches in our undergraduate and graduate programs. This presentation will best be accomplished when qualitative researchers have a significant body of literature. (The continuing presentation of what might be done grows wearisome.) It is obvious that these two statements represent the conflict that qualitative researchers face in making their presence known in the teaching of empirical science. Teachers and students alike use the word "empirical" as synonymous with "quantitative." Qualitative research will have to force its appearance. Much of this early stuff has been and will be immature, but the perspective will win its place if it is persistent. Qualitative research carries a certain appeal as a maverick perspective in what has been historically a maverick discipline.

Lastly, qualitative research needs to develop its own forms of argument and its own publication outlets. Again, these are better developed in other disciplines than in communication. In the development of things, the publication outlets will probably have to precede the argumentative forms. As long as the qualitative study has to compete for space with the quantitative, the argument form will tend to mimic the deductive format. In a more sequestered location, qualitative scholars will be able to test and compare different forms to develop more successful ones.

A FINAL THOUGHT

My crystal ball is always cloudy, but I am personally excited about the future. I see it filled with challenge, conflict, change, and growth for both perspectives and such new ones as may develop (it will be a wonderful era for critics). We are reaching the maturity to be able to question what we do and to be able to face the consequences of the answers. For the established scholar, this era presents the opportunity to legitimately consider those doubts and nagging questions. But, I think it will be a period particularly adapted to the young scholar—full of enthusiasm and opportunity.

RELATED READINGS

Bellah, R. N., Madsen, R., Sullivan, W. M., Swindler, A. and Tipton, S. M. *Habits of the heart*. Berkeley CA: University of California Press, 1985.

Dubin, R. *Theory building* (2d ed.). New York: The Free Press, 1978.

Dufour, B. (Ed.). *New movements in the social sciences and humanities*. London: Maurice Temple Smith, Ltd., 1982.

Hindess, B. *Philosophy and methodology in the social sciences*. Hassocks, Sussex (U.K.): The Harvester Press, 1977.

GLOSSARY

This glossary contains the terms that are highlighted in the text.

absolute (true) zero   A value representing the total absence of some property.

absurdists   Theorists who reject the position of a rational world.

accuracy   The goodness of fit between one entity and its representation or reproduction.

act   A discernible element of an action also the initiating step in an interaction.

action   Considered atomistically, it is a discrete, interpreted behavior composed of elemental acts. Considered holistically, action is the shared, covering understanding of what is being done within a scene.

aggregate   A collection of elements. In communication studies, a sample of individuals who do not interact with one another.

algorithm   A computation or the rule (formula) for computation.

alpha level   The probability of Type I errors in a decision protocol.

analysis of variance   A statistical analysis which tests for the reduction of the variance of the criterion measure when that measure is distributed across a categorizing variable.

analytical metaphor   An interpretive device by which we come to know one thing through our knowledge of another. Examples of analytical metaphors are the narrative, theater, and culture.

antecedent conditions   The set of conditions identified in a dependent relationship which results in or leads to some consequent or outcome.

arbitrary zero   A value representing a segment of an interval number line. Does not represent the absence of some property.

archive file   The repository of the complete and ordered set of field notes.

argument   Any human discourse which contains a claim. The term "argument" is used to emphasize the perspective that any explanation is always open to doubt.

artifact   The product of action. The understanding of an object or concept as an outcome of some action.

associational validity   The argument for the validity of one measure because it correlates with another measure of the same trait.

atomistic   The view that an object or concept is fragmentable into independently understandable parts.

attribute   A meaningful (interpreted) property or characteristic of an individual person or phenomenon.

authorial stance   The viewpoint of the analyst taken in the narrative (invisible narrator, character in the scene, etc.)

authoritative   Accepted by the community.

axiom   An irreducible statement which is accepted not argued. The foundation of an evidentiary argument.

beta   The probability of Type II errors in a particular decision protocol.

beta weight   The regression coefficient indicating the amount of change in one independent variable given a unit of change in the dependent variable.

bipolar adjectival scales   A response form that has opposing adjectives (such as good/bad) separated by several intervals; e.g.: Hot: : : : : : : :Cold. Also known as "semantic differential scales."

bivariate data sets   Data sets in which each element has two observations.

canonical correlation   A statistical analysis which generates an index of the strength of the relationship between two sets of variables.

categorical aggregate   A collection of elements based on some characteristic held by all.

category   A boundary definition which separates elements into members and nonmembers.

cause   The phenomenon used to explain the appearance, characteristics, or performance of another.

causes and consequences   The explanation of causes and consequences is one of the primary purposes of science.

census   The collection of data from all elements in a population.

central limit theorem   A proposition of statistics which describes the tendency of characteristics to congregate around a central value.

characteristics   The description of characteristics is one of the primary forms of scientific explanation.

class   A category.

classification   The identification of elements as members of categories.

cluster analysis   A statistical analysis of the proximity structure of a set of measurements testing which traits bunch together in some space.

cluster sampling   Sampling which uses preexisting groups as the sampling element and then selects all or specific members from the groups.

coded file   A file of field notes and other evidence related to an episodic category. The empirical evidence of the category.

coefficient of determination   The square of a correlation coefficient giving the proportion of variance shared between the two variables.

combination designs   Experimental protocols which provide within group and between group controls.

common core   The universal nature of an attribute.

communicants   The participants in a communication act.

composite characteristics   The characteristics of an aggregate which arise from the collection of individuals assembled.

composite variable   A variable which is itself composed of two or more distinguishable variables.

concepts   The terms of a theory. Interpretations of reality.

conceptual validity   The argument that a measure represents its intended theoretical concept.

conditional relationship   A form of dependency in which one phenomenon reliably predicts the appearance of another.

confidence interval   The range of values in which the population parameter is presumed to have a given rate of appearance.

consequent   A phenomenon seen as the result of another.

constitutive interpretation of experience   The manner in which one creates an understanding of the social action in its interpretation.

construct validity   The argument for the conceptual validity of a measure when the measure performs as predicted across different individuals.

constructed settings   The environmental conditions within a protocol which have been devised or manipulated by the researcher.

constructed composite variables   Variables such as factor analytic dimensions which are generated through a structural analysis.

construction of meaning   A sense-making process. In communication, it is a phrase used to direct the focus on the producer or receiver of content as the source of meaning.

constructionist   A theorist who argues that meaning is produced in the interaction between content and consciousness both at the point of production of content and at the point of its reception.

constructs   Strings of argumentation which interpret reality.

contamination   Any unforeseen circumstance which negates the fair test of a hypothesis or invalidates a protocol.

content analysis   A form of analysis which identifies and classifies the characteristics of written, visual, and/or oral texts.

context   The physical and semiotic environment of social action.

contingency table   A tabular format which displays the values of variables in column/row combinations. The value in the cell is contingent on particular column/row combination.

contingent reality   The reality of the here and now—everyday life.

contingent understanding   A phrase used to describe a sense-making process which is contextually bound. For some theorists, all understanding is contingent.

control   A form of explanation which permits the manipulation of the characteristics of some phenomenon. In experimental research, control refers to the efforts to limit the effect of phenomena not included in the hypothesized relationship.

controls   Elements of the protocol which eliminate the influence of phenomena.

convenience sample   A sample used because of its availability; not randomly selected.

core dimension   The central property of a composite variable.

correlation coefficient   An index of the strength (and with linear coefficients, the direction) of the relationship between two variables.

covariation   The degree to which relative change in one variable is matched with relative change in another.

covering laws   A form of explanation that aims at an absolute description. That is, one that will hold for all cases within the scope of the law. The traditional goal of scientific explanation.

criterion measure   The measure upon which the test of the hypothesis hangs; the dependent variable.

criterion of utility   An evaluative principle that holds that the product of research should have some instrumental value.

critical instance   An event within a scene of social action in which some part of the underlying meaning structure is revealed.

critical reader   A member of the scientific community able to evaluate claims presented.

cross break   Examining a bivariate data set by displaying the values of one variable congregated under each of the values of the other. A contingency table.

cultural relativism   The position that truth (or valid argument) is relative to the culture in which it appears.

data   Most generally any information derived from observations—usually expressed in quantified terms.

decomposition   The method of investigation of complex entities by examining the component elements.

deduction   An epistemological method which moves from general propositions to the specific. The method which characterizes quantitative research.

dependency   A relationship in which the characteristics of one phenomenon is understood as the result of another.

dependent variable   The variable whose value is explained by the values of other variables; the consequence; the variable to be predicted.

dialectical analysis   The process of using one set of constructs to engage another. In qualitative research, it is using the ethnographic text to develop a better statement of the theoretical domain.

dimension sampling   A form of stratified sampling in which the research starts with a set of exclusive and exhaustive categories and then selects elements from each.

discriminant analysis   A statistical analysis which predicts membership in discrete groups according to the members' performance on other measures.

distribution curve   The relationship between the values in a number set and their frequency of occurrence. The graphic presentation of that relationship.

dyad   A pair of individuals usually considered as in a mutually dependent relationship.

effect   A phenomenon described as a consequence.

effects   A term ordinarily used to describe media studies which focus on the consequences of exposure to content.

empathic understanding (verstehen)   The special knowledge of human behavior given by our own experience as humans.

empirical   Having to do with experience. Not to be confused with quantitative (having to do with numbers). Empirical science is a form of explanatory discourse which bases its arguments on what can be experienced.

empiricism   The ideological belief in the primacy of empirical arguments.

empiricist   As a noun, it refers to one who holds to the doctrine that human experience is the source of valid scientific explanation. As an adjective, it refers to an excessive reliance on the concept of experience.

enactment   The term used to describe the doing of some category of social action. (Friendship pairs enact friendship.)

episode   The written description of a significant event in the social action.

epistemology   The study of the growth of knowledge. Also used to describe questions and explanations relating to cause and consequence.

epoche   In modern qualitative usage, it is the explicit referencing of one's own ideology before the analysis of another's.

equivalent units   The interpretation of continuous experience as divisible into discrete events which have common characteristics.

ethnographic text   The scientific argument in qualitative research.

ethnological   See "ethnology."

ethnology   A name generally applied to those studies which focus on individuals in action in everyday life.

ethnomethodology   A branch of ethnology which seeks to explain social action by studying the methods and practices of the members. Associated with the work of Harold Garfinkel.

existentialist   Of the theoretical position that human existence is understood in the experiencing of it.

expansionism   The belief that scientific explanation about any social action phenomenon and its relationships is ever-expanding because the nature of any such phenomenon is always in process.

expected value   A theoretic value derived analytically that is the most likely answer to an unknown. Examples: the mean is the best guess for any number in a set of interval values; given four choices, the expected probability of any one is .25 and so on.

experimental design   The conventions of experimental protocols.

experimental protocol   A research design characterized by control and manipulation and aimed at explanations of cause and consequence. All of the conditions surrounding the findings from an experiment.

explanation   Discourse which interprets experience. There are many forms of explanation. The forms of scientific explanation are directed toward characteristics, methods and practices, and causes and consequences.

external validity   The claim that a finding generalizes beyond the protocol.

face validity   The argument for conceptual validity from the content of the measurement. (It looks right.)

facilitation   A form of dependency explanation in which one phenomenon is seen as aiding (increasing the likelihood of) the appearance of another.

fact   An interpreted experience accepted as true.

factor analysis   A structural analysis which reveals core dimensions which underlie a set of elemental variables.

fair test   A test whose outcome is reasonably in doubt and reasonably explained by the alternatives offered.

falsification   The method of hypothesis testing in which conditions are sought in which the hypothesis will fail a fair test.

field experiments   Experimental protocols which make use of natural settings.

field notes   The extended, written record of participation in social action.

frequency distribution   The number of occurrences for each value in a number set (i.e., the number of 1's, 2's, 3's, etc.).

functional equivalence of meaning   A theoretical position which holds that content delivers meaning which if not exactly equal is sufficiently comparable to be considered equal.

gap   The members of a population lost when a sampling frame does not include them.

group   A collection of individuals which may or may not involve membership.

holistic   Of a unity. Generally references the view that social action must be understood in the whole of it, not atomistically.

human sciences   The name given to a group of scientific disciplines whose purpose is the explanation of human behavior. Also called "social sciences".

hypothesis   A testable statement expressing a relationship between phenomena.

ideal type   The model of a type of social actor (teacher, student, politician, etc.).

independent groups design   An experimental protocol in which the different treatments are assigned to separate groups of respondents.

independent variable   The variable used to predict another; the cause; the variable whose value is set by the experimenter.

index   A variable which points to the appearance of another.

indexing   Refers to a relationship in which the appearance of one phenomenon gives reason to look for another.

individual differences   The component of a human characteristic attributed in the given explanation to its expression in the individual.

induction   An epistemological method which moves from the specific to the general. The method which characterizes qualitative research.

inductive category   A descriptive generalization or abstraction which covers at least one specific instance. A form of argument in qualitative research in which the inductive categories are the claims.

inferential statistics   Statistical analyses which use sample characteristics to estimate population characteristics or those which use the expected distribution of a statistic in a decision rule.

informed consent   The ethical standard governing the voluntary participation of individuals as respondents in a research study.

instrumentalism   The position that scientific arguments are validated when the purpose for which they were developed is fulfilled.

in-tab-sample   The sample of observations available for analysis.

intellectual traditions   The texts, methods, and practices regarded as privileged by a scholarly community.

interact   A unit of action composed of an act and a react; e.g., two connected turns of talk.

interactionist   Of the theoretical position that human social behavior is known in the relationships between individuals.

internal validity   The claim of the validity of a measure because it performs according to the hypothesis.

intersubjective agreement   The use of the agreement among common observers to define reality.

intersubjectivity of meaning   The doctrine that meaning is constructed and maintained jointly by the members.

interval scale   A set of exclusive and exhaustive categories ordered in equal units of distance along some dimension.

intimate familiarity   The state of intellectual grasp the analyst attempts to achieve of the field notes before pursuing episodic analysis.

invented settings   Environmental conditions designed by the researcher for the purposes of the study.

isomorphism   Refers to the capacity of a measure to represent or reproduce in its own form that which it measures.

judgment sampling   The sampling procedure in which elements are deliberately selected to represent some population characteristic.

kinships   The notion of special relationships within memberships that are generally recognized and respected.

law   A statement describing a relationship between phenomena which has universal application within its scope.

level of generality   The degree to which a statement can be validly applied to different conditions.

level of significance   The alpha level.

levels of measurement   The nominal, ordinal, interval, and ratio scales of quantification of observations.

lifeworld (lebenswelt)   Everyday life. The privileged site of research in qualitative studies.

likert-type statements   A measurement form composed of a declarative statement and a response scale; e.g.:
"I look forward to taking more research classes."
Agree Strongly   Agree   Neutral   Disagree   Disagree Strongly

linear function   The mathematical expression of a relationship between two sets of numbers which can be described by a straight line.

linear regression   A form of statistical analysis which produces a straight-line model of the relationship between two sets of numbers.

linear relationship   A relationship between two sets of numbers which can be described by a straight line.

linearity   The property of a relationship to show a straight-line change.

longitudinal research   Generally any research conducted over time and sets of observations.

loosely coupled memberships   A contracted relationship which has restricted scope for the members.

manipulation   A characteristic of experimental protocols in which the values of the antecedent conditions are established by the researcher.

Markov analysis   A structural analysis which determines the contingent relationships within a set of events. For example, given a set of five events and given any first event, Markov analysis will determine each likelihood of the following single event being a 1, 2, 3, 4, and 5, and then the probability of each two-event combination (1/1's, 1/2's), and so on.

marginality   A type of membership where the individual is permitted to make few contributions or exercise power or influence.

material determinism   The doctrine that the world is best understood in lawlike relationships between material phenomena.

materialism   The doctrine that the significant explanatory influences in the universe (including human behavior) are in physical acts.

material reality   The physical universe.

mean   A descriptive statement about a set of numbers. The expected value of a normally distributed population. The arithmetic average.

measurement   The process by which observations are defined, conducted, and given numerical values.

measurement demand   The influence on an individual's behavior induced by the measurement procedure itself.

measurement error   The failure of the measurement procedure to represent the entity measured.

median   A descriptive statement about a set of numbers; the point at which 50 percent of an ordered set are below and 50 percent above.

member maturity References a level of participation in which the individual has a practicing understanding of a member's stock of knowledge.

membership The practice of a social contract defining a relationship between or among individuals.

membership-as-process The view of a membership as an ongoing practice.

membership-as-sum-of-members The view of a membership as the composite of its members.

memberships Individuals bound in a mutually defined membership.

methodological ideology Any position which holds that a particular set of scientific practices is more valid than any other.

methodologist An individual who studies the methods of science and their relationship to knowledge.

methods and practices The actions used by members to create their social world. The explanation of methods and practices is one of the purposes of science.

mode A descriptive statement about a set of numbers; the most frequently appearing value.

multidimensional scaling A structural analysis which determines the relative distance between one judgment and all others.

multiple analysis of variance A statistical analysis which tests the reduction of variance within a composite variable extracted from two or more criterion measures when that variable is distributed into categories by another variable set.

multiple regression A statistical analysis which develops a straight line model of the relationship between an independent variable set and a single dependent variable.

multistage sampling A sampling procedure in which the element is first selected in a set of larger categories. For example, first selecting cities, then neighborhoods, then city blocks, then addresses, and, finally, the individual.

multivariate analysis Any form of statistical analysis in which three or more observations are taken on each unit of analysis.

multivariate data sets Any data set which contains three or more observations on each unit of analysis.

mundane contexts Settings which occur in everyday life.

mundane realism A criterion or characteristic applied to research protocols which compares the protocol to the conditions of everyday life.

natural setting A setting occurring without intervention by the researcher.

naturalistic A name given to qualitative research, particularly that which uses participant observation in natural settings as its method.

naturally occurring action Action which would occur without the research protocol.

nominal scale A set of exclusive and exhaustive categories within a single dimension.

nonlinear relationships Relationships which are best described by other than a straight line (e.g., $Y = X^2$ is a parabola).

normal curve The graph of a normal density distribution; the familiar bell-shaped curve.

normal density distribution A mathematical model used to describe certain populations of numbers. It is symmetrical about the mean; the mean, median, and mode are the same value; and every possible value has some frequency of occurrence.

null hypothesis The hypothesis of no relationship—that an obtained effect is the result of sampling error.

objective reality The notion of a common reality available for all based on the assumption that there is a "natural connection" between existence outside the human consciousness and our interpretation of that existence. It is the source of the criterion of objectivity.

observation notes   Notes taken at the research site to aid in the reconstruction of the social action in field notes.

ontology   The study of existence. In science, it is used to refer to questions and explanations concerning the characteristics of things.

operational definition   The definition of a concept by means of the methods used to measure it.

operationalism   The doctrine that concepts have no meaning other than their operational definition.

ordinal scale   A set of exclusive and exhaustive categories that are ordered in increasing value along some dimension.

outcome   The consequent in a conditional relationship.

outcomes   The term ordinarily used to describe media studies which focus on the accommodation (integration) of content in mundane activities.

panel study   Survey protocol which uses the same respondents over time and measurements.

paradigm   The ideology and methods in which acceptable research is conducted.

parametric measure   Any statistic which depends on some assumption about the population characteristic of which it is an estimate.

partialed variable   A composite variable, within a set of "independent" variables in a multivariate analysis, whose shared information is statistically assigned to another variable in the set.

partialing   The statistical method by which correlated variables are decomposed into independent variables (see "partialed variable").

participant observation   The central method of qualitative research by which the analyst seeks to make explicit the commonly held meanings of the social action in which he or she participates.

partitioning   The method of decomposing the variance of one set of measures by distributing that measure across the values of another in the hopes that some of the variability will be explained by the partitioning variable.

periodicity   In sampling lists, the property of certain characteristics to be predictably distributed throughout the list (e.g., all eighth graders listed in a single group in a list of students).

perspective taking   The view the analyst takes to approach the social action.

perspectives in research   The differing points of view which can be adopted within a paradigm which direct the conduct of research.

phenomenological sociology   Primarily a field of social criticism rather than empirical research concerned with explicating the world of conscious experience.

phenomenology   A philosophy of science derived from the writings of Edmund Husserl. The study, both scientific and critical, of human life from this perspective. Such studies are characterized by an emphasis on everyday life and inductive analysis.

phenomenon (phenomena)   Any part of experience which can be identified—separated from the whole. An element of the world.

physical sciences   The name given to a group of scientific disciplines which includes physics, chemistry, and similar studies.

population   The totality of any definable group of elements.

population parameter   Any characteristic of a population.

population element   Any member of a population.

population estimate An estimate of a population parameter (characteristic) based on information taken from a sample of that population.

positivism The belief that the system of empirical science can achieve knowledge which is independent or transcendent of the observer and the particulars observed. That is, science can achieve a positive knowledge of phenomena and their relationships within some scope of time and place.

postulates of research The underlying assumptions about the world which permit the conduct of research from a given perspective within a given paradigm.

praxiology The study of performance. In science it refers to questions and explanations relating to methods and practices.

pre/post design Experimental protocols in which the criterion measure is given before and after the treatment (manipulation).

precision The distinguishing capacity of a measure.

prediction A form of explanation in which the appearance of one phenomenon is related to the prior appearance of another. It is not foretelling.

private knowledge The multilevel understanding gained from experience. Cannot be directly exchanged with another.

probability samples Any sample which rests on the random selection of elements.

process The conduct of an interpretable action which has both a definable beginning and definable outcomes.

prolificacy of meaning The notion that meaning is not constant, but is enlarged with every experience. Each contact generates some new meaning.

promiscuity of meaning The concept that a given event participates in meaning construction for all, although not all will have the same meaning.

proximities A set of distance measures used in multidimensional scaling.

public knowledge Authoritative discourse. The meaningful documents of a community.

qualitative The descriptor applied to a research paradigm which emphasizes inductive, interpretive methods applied to the everyday world which is seen as subjective and socially created. Characterized by the metaphor of the narrative.

quantification The process of assigning numbers to observations.

quantification theory The argument that any individual person or phenomenon is the sum of its elemental parts. Motivates the study of the individual in an atomistic (part-by-part) method.

quantitative The descriptor applied to a research paradigm which emphasizes deductive, objective methods applied to observations of a material reality. Characterized by the metaphor of quantification.

quota sampling A method of nonprobability sampling in which categories of elements must have a certain number of units.

random event An event which is without pattern and requires its own individual explanation.

range The spread of values between and including the smallest and largest in a set.

rank A position on an ordinal scale.

rate The occurrence of a phenomenon in a set of phenomena or over time.

rate of sampling error The frequency of nonrepresentative samples within all possible samples of the same size for a given definition of error.

ratio scale An exclusive and exhaustive set of categories ordered in equal quantities.

rationalistic The name given to quantitative research particularly that which involves hypothesis testing.

reality constructs   The system of beliefs which give meaning to the world around us.

reductionism   Any explanatory move which offers the same explanation for more than one phenomenon. The belief that the universe is explained by a finite set of statements.

region of acceptance   That portion of the distribution curve marked off by alpha in which obtained values in a hypothesis test call for the acceptance of the null hypothesis.

region of rejection   That portion of the distribution curve marked off by alpha in which obtained values in a hypothesis test call for the rejection of the null hypothesis.

regression coefficient   A weight representing the amount of change in its associated variable given a unit of change in the dependent variable. The beta weight.

regularities   Repeated patterns which permit explanation.

reification   The treatment of a concept as a material entity.

reliability   The capacity of a measure to reproduce a set of observations of a stable universe. A rationalistic criterion of good observation based on the repeatable description of an objective phenomenon.

representativeness   The property of a sample having the same characteristics in the same proportion as the population.

research hypothesis   The alternate to the null hypothesis. The statement of a relationship one wishes to verify.

research narrative   The "story" of the social action. It is empirical, not fictional.

research protocol   The assumptions and methods which surround the production of a particular research finding.

research text   The extended record, including the analyst's own experiences, field notes, artifacts etc., of participation in a social action scene.

researcher as instrument   The notion that the individual analyst is the interpretive device in the analysis of social action.

rule   In rationalistic research, a conditional statement describing the relationship between phenomena in terms of rates or probabilities. In naturalistic research, a statement of the conventions of the social action under study.

sample   A subset of a population.

sample variance (s^2)   A measure of dispersion of a set of numbers drawn from a population.

sampling   The method of selecting the elements of a subset of a population.

sampling bias   The systematic exclusion of population members due to the procedures of sampling.

sampling distribution   The set of all samples of a given size which can be drawn from a population.

sampling error   The deviations of sample characteristics from population characteristics introduced by the selection of a subset.

sampling frame   The list or set of procedures which identifies the elements for selection into a sample.

sampling unit   The type of element to be selected in a sample.

scale   A term used to reference the appearance or disappearance of notable phenomena because of the size of the universe studied.

scientific community   Individuals who identify themselves with and are recognized as participating in the human activity of science. They include scientists, technicians, critics, editors, publishers, teachers, and students. Together, they establish the operating content, methods, and standards of science.

scientism   The doctrine that science is the only true epistemological method.

self-evident reasoning   Fallacious reasoning whose conclusions are a restatement of the initial premises.

semiotic frame   The socially negotiated and maintained reality of meaning in which objects and actions are interpreted.

semiotic system   The set of interrelated meanings that govern the particular scene of social action.

sense making   Any interpretive process in which meaning is developed.

simple random sample   A probability sample in which every member of the population has an equal chance of being selected.

situated individual   The individual in time and place and embedded in a context.

social action   The meaningful, correlated performances of social actors within a scene.

social construction of reality   The doctrine that the significant influences of social action are contained in the semiotic system developed over time and maintained by the social actors.

sociological unit   The point of contact with human behavior whether at the level of the individual, group, society, culture, etc.

solipsism   An explanation based on the private knowledge of the individual with no external evidence.

standard deviation   A measure of dispersion which is commonly used in models of populations.

standard error of the mean (SE$_X$)   The standard deviation of a set of means.

statistical analysis   The investigation of numerical data sets for their characteristics; the use of mathematical models as decision rules.

stochastic   Probabilistic.

story   Authoritative, narrative discourse directed toward the explanatory goal of understanding. Most often used by the cosmological and ethnological sciences.

stratified random samples   A probability sample in which every member has a known chance of being selected. Population is first divided into categories (strata) and then random sampling is conducted within the strata.

subsequents   Phenomena which follow in time the appearance of others (precedents or antecedents).

sums of squares   A measure of dispersion—the numerator of the variance.

survey protocols   Research designs which collect data on the characteristics of phenomena.

symbolic interaction   A theoretical perspective directed toward the explanation of social action. It emphasizes the study of interactional discourse which contains the meaning of the member's social world.

synthetic actions   Actions which depend on the research protocol for their performance.

systematic observation   Observation conducted in accordance with a set of rules.

test of significance   A decision-making procedure in which the probability of sampling error is used as the basis for choosing between a hypothesis of no relationship and its alternate (see "alpha level," "null hypothesis," and "research hypothesis").

the scientific method   A name generally applied to the deductive method of hypothesis testing. In scientism, it refers to a set of practices (considered fictional by others) which purifies human knowledge from error.

theoretical domain   The realm of explanatory discourse, both oral and written, which describes the nature and relations of some set of phenomena.

theory An extended explanation of the relationships among phenomena which incorporates concepts, constructs, and empirical observations.

theory sampling A form of deliberate selection of elements until all different kinds of elements have been identified.

total variance A term used in the partitioning of variance or analysis of variance to describe the undecomposed variability of a set of numbers.

treatment effect An outcome understood as the consequence of a manipulation in an experiment.

Type I error Rejection of the null hypothesis when it is true.

Type II error Rejection of the research hypothesis when it is true.

unbiased estimate A population estimate whose method of determination does not introduce a deviation from the population characteristic. Other circumstances may introduce errors, however.

understanding A form of scientific explanation which attempts a holistic interpretation of the explanatory object.

univariate data set A data set with one observation per unit of analysis.

uses and gratifications A functionalist perspective found primarily in mass communication studies which explains communication behavior according to some purpose or reward to be achieved by the individual.

validity The truth-value of a claim.

valid story A research narrative which provides an interpretation of the social action from the member's viewpoint.

variables Phenomena used in a research protocol.

variance A measure of dispersion of values within a set of numbers.

verification The method of hypothesis testing in which conditions are sought in order that a hypothesis will pass a fair test.

volatility The characteristic of rapid change relative to measurement.

warrant An ideological statement which justifies claim and/or evidence.

BIBLIOGRAPHY

Adelman, C. *Uttering, muttering: Collecting, using and reporting talk for social and educational research.* London: Grant McIntyre, 1981.

Adler, P. and Adler, P. A. Symbolic interaction. In J. D. Douglas (Ed.), *Introduction to the sociologies of everyday life,* Boston: Allyn and Bacon, 1980, 20–61.

Agar, M. H. Whatever happened to cognitive anthropology: A partial review. *Human Organization,* 1982, *41,* 82–85.

Alexander, D. C. and Newell, S. E. Negotiating the role of friend. Paper presented at the *SCA/AFA Summer Conference on Argumentation,* Alta, UT, 1981a.

Alexander, D. C. and Newell, S. E. The intensive interview as a means of discovering the talk of friends. Paper presented at the *Western Speech Communication Association* convention, San Jose, CA, 1981b.

Allen, E. W. Journalism as applied social science. *Journalism Bulletin,* 1927, *4,* 1–8.

Allen, E. W. Research in Journalism. *Journalism Quarterly,* 1930, *7,* 40–54.

Anderson, J. A. An analysis of the methodologies used in media credibility studies. Paper presented at the *International Communication Association* convention, Phoenix, 1971.

Anderson, J. A. Research as argument: The experimental form. Paper presented at the *Speech Communication Association* convention, New York City, 1979.

Anderson, J. A. Teaching qualitative methods. Paper presented at the *Association for Education in Journalism and Mass Communication* convention, Athens, OH, 1982.

Anderson, J. A. Television literacy and the critical viewer. In J. Bryant and D. R. Anderson (Eds.), *Children's understanding of television.* New York: Academic Press, 1983, 297–330.

Anderson, J. A. Forms of argument in naturalistic inquiry in communication. Paper presented at the *International Communication Association* convention, San Francisco, 1984.

Anderson, J. A. and Avery, R. K. An analysis of changes in voter perceptions of candidates' positions. *Communication Monographs,* 1978, *45,* 354–361.

Anderson, J. A. and Avery, R. K. The influence of cognitive styles on voter perceptions of presidential candidates. Paper presented at the *International Communication Association* convention, Dallas, 1983.

Anderson, J. A., Avery, R. K., Burnett-Pettus, A., Dipaolo-Congalton, J. and Eastman, S. T. Voter rationales for candidate preferences: An analysis of conversational data. Paper presented at the *Speech Communication Association* convention, Denver, 1985.

Anderson, J. A., Avery, R. K., Burnett-Pettus, A., Dipaolo-Congalton, J. and Eastman, S. T. Ideology and history in campaign conventions. Paper presented at the *International Communication Association* convention, Chicago, 1986.

Anderson, J. A. and Eastman, S. T. Conversations occurring during the use of videotext resources in writing eighth grade science themes. Paper presented at the *Speech Communication Association,* convention Washington, 1983.

Anderson, J. A., Meyer, T. P. and Hexamer, A. An examination of the assumptions underlying telecommunications social policies treating children as a specialized audience. In M. Burgoon (Ed.), *Communication Yearbook 5.* New Brunswick, NJ: Transaction Books, 1982, 369–384.

Anderson, J. A. and Ploghoft, M. Receivership skills: The television experience. In D. Nimmo (Ed.), *Communication Yearbook 4.* New Brunswick, NJ: Transaction Books, 1980, 293–308.

Applegate, J. L. The impact of construct system development on communication and impression formation in persuasive contexts. *Communication Monographs,* 1982, *49,* 277–289.

Arnett, R. C. Toward a phenomenological dialogue. *The Western Journal of Speech Communication,* 1981, *41,* 201–212.

Arnold, D. O. *The sociology of subcultures.* Berkeley, CA: Glendessary Press, 1970.

Arntson, P. Testing Basil Bernstein's sociolinguistic theories. *Human Communication Research,* 1982, *9,* 33–48.

Askham, J. Telling stories. *Sociological Review,* 1982, *30,* 555–573.

Babbie, E. *The practice of social research* (2d ed.) Belmont, CA: Wadsworth Publishing Company, 1979.

Babbie, E. *The practice of social research* (3d ed). Belmont, CA: Wadsworth Publishing Company, Inc, 1983.

Bailey, K. D. *Methods of social research.* New York: The Free Press, 1982.

Bakhtin, M. M. *The dialogic imagination.* Edited by M. Holoquist and translated by C. Emerson and M. Holoquist, Austin, TX: The University of Texas Press, 1981.

Balswick, J. and Peek, C. The inexpressive male: A tragedy of American society. *Family Coordinator,* 1971, *20,* 363–368.

Barwise, T. P., Ehrenberg, A. S. C. and Goodhardt, G. J. Glued to the box?: Patterns of TV repeat-viewing. *Journal of Communication,* 1982, *32,* 22–29.

Baxter, L. A. Relationship Disengagement: An examination of the reversal hypothesis. *Western Journal of Speech Communication,* 1983, *47,* 85–98.

Beach, W. A. and Japp, P. Storifying as time traveling: The knowledgeable use of temporally structured discourse. In R. Bostrom (Ed.), *Communication Yearbook 7,* Beverly Hills, CA: Sage Publications, Inc., 1983, 867–888.

Becker, H. S. Becoming a marihuana user. *American Journal of Sociology,* 1953, *59,* 41–58.

Becker, H. S. Problems of inference and proof in participant observation. *American Sociological Review,* 1958, *23,* 652–660.

Behling, O. The case for the natural science model for research in organizational behavior and organizational theory. *Academy of Management Review,* 1980, *5,* 483–490.

Bell, C. and Newby, H. (Eds.) *Doing sociological research.* London: George Allen and Unwin, 1977.

Bellah, R. N., Madsen, R. Sullivan, W. M., Swindler, A. and Tipton, S. M. *Habits of the heart.* Berkeley, CA: University of California Press, 1985.

Benson, T. W. Another shooting in cowtown. *Quarterly Journal of Speech,* 1981, *67,* 347–406.

Berger, C. R. The covering law perspective as a theoretical basis for the study of human communication. *Communication Quarterly,* 1977, *25,* 7–18.

Berger, P. L. and Luckmann, T. *The social construction of reality.* New York: Doubleday, 1967.

Berkowitz, L. and Donnerstein, E. External validity is more than skin deep: Some answers to criticisms of laboratory experiments. *American Psychologist, 1982, 37,* 245–257.

Bhagat, R. S. and McQuaid, S. J. Role of subjective culture in organizations: A review and directions for future research. *Journal of Applied Psychology Monograph,* 1982, *67,* 653–684.

Blalock, H. M. *Theory construction: From verbal to mathematical formulations.* Englewood Cliffs, NJ: Prentice-Hall, 1969.

Blasi, A. J., Dasilva, F. B. and Weigert, A. J. *Toward an interpretive sociology.* Washington: University Press of America, 1978.

Blumer, H. *Symbolic interactionism.* Englewood Cliffs, NJ: Prentice-Hall, 1969.

Bogdan, R. and Taylor, S. J. *Introduction to qualitative research methods.* New York: John Wiley and Sons, Inc., 1975.

Boje, D. M., Fedor, D. B. and Rowland, K. M. Myth making: A qualitative step in OD interventions. *The Journal of Applied Behavioral Science,* 1982, *18,* 17–28.

Bolton, T. Perceptual factors that influence the adoption of videotex technology: Results of the Channel 2000 field test. *Journal of Broadcasting,* 1983, *27,* 141–153.

Bormann, E. G., Kroll, B. S., Watters, K. and McFarland, D. Rhetorical vision of committed voters: Fantasy theme analysis of a large sample survey. *Critical Studies in Mass Communication.* 1984, *1,* 286–310.

Bostrom, R. N. and White, N. D. Does drinking weaken resistance? *Journal of Communication,* 1979, *29,* 73–80.

Bowen, E. S. (Bohannan, L.). *Return to laughter.* Garden City, NY: The Natural History Library, Doubleday and Co., Inc., 1964.

Bowers, J. W. and Bradac, J. J. Issues in communication theory: A metatheoretical analysis. In M. Burgoon (Ed.), *Communication Yearbook 5,* New Brunswick, NJ: Transaction Press, 1982.

Bowers, J. W. and Courtright, J. A. *Communication research methods.* Glenview, IL: Scott, Foresman and Co., 1984.

Brewer, M. B. and Collins, B. E. (Eds.). *Scientific inquiry and the social sciences.* San Francisco: Jossey-Bass Publishers, 1981.

Brissett, D. and Edgley, C. (Eds.). *Life as theater.* Chicago: Aldine, 1974.

Brockriede, W. Arguing about human understanding. *Communication Monographs,* 1982, *49,* 137–147.

Brockriede, W. Constructs, experience and argument. *The Quarterly Journal of Speech,* 1985, *71,* 151–163.

Brown, R. H. *A Poetic for sociology.* Cambridge: Cambridge University Press, 1977.

Browning, L. D. A grounded organizational communication theory derived from qualitative data. *Communication Monographs,* 1978, *45,* 93–109.

Bruyn, S. T. *The human perspective in sociology.* Englewood Cliffs, NJ: Prentice-Hall, Inc., 1966.

Bryce, J. W. Family time and television use. In T. Lindlof (Ed.) *Natural audiences: Qualitative research of media uses and effects.* Norwood, NJ: Ablex Publishing Corporation, in press.

Bulmer, M. (Ed.). *Social research ethics.* London: The Macmillian Press, Ltd., 1982.

Burgatta, E. F. and Bohrnstedt, G. W. Level of measurement: Once over again. *Sociological Methods and Research,* 1980, *9.* 147–160.

Burgoon, J. K. and Aho, L. Three field experiments of the effects of violations of conversational distance. *Communication Monographs,* 1982, *49,* 71–88.

Burke, K. *The grammar of motives.* Englewood Cliffs, NJ: Prentice-Hall, 1945.

Burns, E. *Theatricality: A study of convention in the theatre and in social life.* New York: Harper Torchbooks, 1972.

Campbell, D. T. and Stanley, J. C. *Experimental and quasi-experimental designs for research.* Boston: Houghton Mifflin, 1963.

Carey, J. W. Graduate education in mass communication. *Communication Education,* 1979, *28,* 282–293.

Chadwick, B. A. Bahr, H. M. and Albrecht, S. L. *Social science research methods.* Englewood Cliffs, NJ: Prentice-Hall, Inc., 1984.

Chambliss, W. On the paucity of original research on organized crime. *American Sociologist,* 1975, *10,* 36–39.

Clifford, J. On ethnographic authority. *Representations,* 1983, *1,* 118–146.

Clifford, J. and Marcus, G. (Eds.). *Writing culture.* Berkeley, CA: University of California Press, 1986.

Cochran, W. G. *Sampling techniques* (3d ed.). New York: John Wiley and Sons, Inc., 1977.

Cook, T. D. and Campbell, D. T. *Quasi-experimental design and analysis issues for field settings.* Chicago: Rand Mcnally, 1979.

Cook, T. D. and Reichardt, C. S. *Qualitative and quantitative methods in evaluation research.* Beverly Hills, CA: Sage Publications, Inc., 1979.

Cooley, W. W. and Lohnes, P. R. *Multivariate procedures for the behavioral sciences.* New York: John Wiley and Sons, Inc., 1962.

Cooley, W. W. and Lohnes, P. R. *Multivariate data analysis.* New York: John Wiley and Sons, Inc., 1971.

Comisky, P. and Bryant, J. Factors involved in generating suspense. *Human Communication Research,* 1982, *9,* 49–58.

Congalton, D. The relational uses of television in the sibling network. Unpublished Ph.D. dissertation, University of Utah, forthcoming.

Copi, I. M. *Introduction to logic.* New York: Macmillan Publishing Co., Inc., 1982.

Craig, R. T. Galilean rhetoric and practical theory. *Communication Monographs,* 1983, *50,* 395–412.

Cushman, D. P. The rules perspective as a theoretical basis for the study of human communication. *Communication Quarterly,* 1977, *25,* 30–45.

Cushman, D. P. and Whiting, G. C. An approach to communication theory: Toward a consensus on rules. *Journal of Communication,* 1972, *22,* 217–238.

Dance, F. E. X., Speech communication as a liberal arts discipline, *Communication Education,* 1980, *29,* 328–331.

Daniels, T. D. and Whitman, R. F. The effects of message introduction, message structure, and verbal organizing ability upon learning of message information. *Human Communication Research*, 1981, *7*, 147–160.

Delia, J. G. Constructivism and the study of human communication. *Quarterly Journal of Speech*, 1977, *63*, 66–83.

Delia, J. G. and Grossberg, L. Interpretation and evidence. *Western Journal of Speech Communication*, 1977, *41*, 32–42.

Deming, W. E. *Sample design and business research*. New York: John Wiley and Sons, Inc., 1960.

Denzin, N. K. *The research act*. Chicago: Aldine Publishing Company, 1970.

Denzin, N. K. *The research act: A theoretical introduction to sociological methods* (2d ed.). New York: McGraw-Hill, 1978.

Denzin, N. K. Interpretive interactionism. In, G. Morgan (Ed.), *Beyond method*. Beverly Hills, CA: Sage Publications, Inc., 1983, 129–146.

Department of Health, Education and Welfare. *The institutional guide to DHEW policy on protection of human subjects*. Washington: U. S. Government Printing Office, 1971.

Department of Health, Education and Welfare. Protection of human subjects—technical amendments. *Federal Register*, 1975, *40*, 11845—11858.

Dervin, B., Jacobson, T. L. and Nilan, M. S. Measuring Aspects of information seeking: A test of a quantitative/quantitative methodology. In M. Burgoon (Ed.), *Communication Yearbook 6*, Beverly Hills, CA: Sage Publications Inc., 1982, 419–444.

Diesing, P. *Patterns of discovery in the social sciences*. Chicago: Aldine, 1971.

Dillman, D. A. *Mail and telephone surveys: The total design method*. New York: John Wiley and Sons, Inc., 1978.

Dominick, J. R. and Fletcher, J. E. *Broadcasting research methods*. Boston: Allyn and Bacon, 1985.

Donohue, W. A., Diez, M. E. and Stahle, R. B. New directions in negotiation research. In R. Bostrom (Ed.), *Communication Yearbook 7*. Beverly Hills, CA: Sage Publications Inc., 1983, 249–279.

Dooley, D. *Social research methods*. Englewood Cliffs, NJ: Prentice-Hall, Inc., 1984.

Douglas, J. D. *Investigative social research*. Beverly Hills, CA: Sage Publications, Inc., 1976.

Douglas, J. D. (Ed.) *Introduction to the sociologies of everyday life*. Boston: Allyn and Bacon, 1980.

Douglas, J. D. and Johnson, J. M. (Eds.). *Existential sociology*. Cambridge (U.K.): Cambridge University Press, 1977.

Douglas, J. D., Rasmussen, P. K. and Flanagan, C. A. *The nude beach*. Beverly Hills, CA: Sage Publications, Inc., 1977.

Downs, C. W. and Larimer, M. W. The status of organizational communication in speech departments. *The Speech Teacher*, 1974, *23*, 325–329.

Dubin, R. *Theory building* (2d ed.). New York: The Free Press, 1978.

Dufour, B. (Ed.). *New movements in the social sciences and humanities*. London: Maurice Temple Smith, Ltd., 1982.

Duncan, H. D. *Communication and the social order*. New York: Bedminster, 1962.

Duncan, O. D. *Introduction to structural equation models*. New York: Academic Press, 1975.

Duncan, O. D. *Notes on social measurement*. New York: Russell Sage Foundation, 1984.

Eastman, S. T. Videotex in middle school: Accommodating computers and printouts in learning information processing skills. Paper presented at the *International Communication Association* convention, San Francisco, 1984.

Eastman, S. T. and Agostino, D. E. Commanding the computer: Student's uses and understandings of videotex technology. Paper presented at the *Speech Communication Association* convention, Washington, 1984.

Espinosa, P. The audience in the text: Ethnographic observations of a Hollywood story conference. *Media, Culture and Society*, 1982, *4*, 77–86.

Ewbank, Sr., H. L., Baird, A. C., Brigance, W. N. Parrish, W. M. and Weaver, A. T. What is speech? A symposium. *The Quarterly Journal of Speech*, 1955, *41*, 145–153.

Faules, D. The use of multi-methods in the organizational setting. *Western Journal of Speech Communication*, 1982, *46*, 150–161.

Fedler, F., Counts, T. and Hightower, P. Changes in wording of cutlines fail to reduce photographs' offensiveness. *Journalism Quarterly*, 1982, *59*, 633–637.

Feyerabend, P. *Against method.* London: Verso, 1978.

Filstead, W. J. *Qualitative methodology: Firsthand involvement with the social world.* Chicago: Markham Publishing Company, 1970.

Fisher, B. A. *Perspectives on human communication.* New York: Macmillan Publishing Co., Inc., 1978.

Fisher, B. A. and Drecksel, G. L. A cyclical model of developing relationships: A study of relational control interaction. *Communication Monographs*, 1983, *50*, 66–78.

Fitzpatrick, M. A. and Indvik, J. The instrumental and expressive domains of marital communication. *Human Communication Research*, 1982, *8*, 195–213.

Fontana A. Toward a complex universe: Existential sociology. In J. D. Douglas (Ed.), *Introduction to the sociologies of everyday life*, Boston: Allyn and Bacon, 1980, 62–81.

Frazer, C. F. The social character of children's television viewing. *Communication Research*, 1981, *8*, 307–322.

Frentz, T. S. Falsification procedures for behavioral research in communication. *The Southern Speech Communication Journal*, 1983, *48*, 269–282.

Gale, G. *Theory of science.* New York: McGraw-Hill Book Company, 1979.

Gantz, W. The diffusion of news about the attempted Reagan assassination. *Journal of Communication*, 1983, *33*, 56–66.

Garfinkel, H. *Studies in ethnomethodology.* Englewood Cliffs, NJ: Prentice-Hall, 1967.

Geertz, C. *The interpretation of cultures.* New York: Basic Books, 1973.

Geertz, C. Blurred genres: The refiguration of social thought. *The American Scholar*, 1980, *49*, 166–178.

Georges, R. A. and Jones, M. O. *People studying people.* Berkeley, CA: University of California Press, 1980.

Giddens, A. *Central problems in social theory: Action, structure and contradiction in social analysis.* Berkeley, CA: University of California Press, 1979.

Giorgi, A. *Psychology as a human science: A phenomenologically based approach.* New York: Harper and Row, 1970.

Glaser, B. and Strauss, A. L. *The discovery of grounded theory.* Chicago: Aldine Publishing Company, 1967.

Glass, G. V., McGaw, B. and Smith, M. L. *Meta-analysis in social research.* Beverly Hills, CA: Sage Publications, Inc., 1981.

Glazer, M. *The research adventure: Promise and problems of field work.* New York: Random House, 1972.

Glymour, C. *Theory and evidence.* Princeton, NJ: Princeton University Press, 1980.

Goffman, E. *The presentation of self in everyday life.* Garden City, NY: Doubleday Anchor, 1959.

Gottman, J. M. Emotional responsiveness in marital conversations. *Journal of Communication,* 1982, *32,* 108–120.

Greenberg, B. S. and Atkin, C. F. The portrayal of driving on television, 1975–1980. *Journal of Communication,* 1983, *33,* 44–55.

Gronbeck, B. E. Dramaturgical theory and criticism: The state of the art (or science?). *The Western Journal of Speech Communication,* 1980, *44,* 315–330.

Grossberg, L. Does communication theory need intersubjectivity? Toward an immanent philosophy of interpersonal relations. In M. Burgoon (Ed.), *Communication Yearbook 6.* Beverly Hills, CA: Sage Publications, Inc., 1982.

Grossberg, L. The ideology of communication. *Man and World,* 1982, *15,* 83–101.

Guba, E. G. The search for truth: Naturalistic inquiry as an option. Paper presented at the *International Reading Association* convention, Chicago, 1982.

Guba, E. G. Criteria for assessing the trustworthiness of naturalistic inquiries. *Educational Communication and Technology Journal,* 1981, *29,* 75–92.

Guba, E. G. and Lincoln, Y. S. Epistemological and methodological bases of naturalistic inquiry. *Educational Communication and Technology Journal,* 1982, *30,* 233–252.

Hall, E. *Beyond culture.* Garden City, NY: Anchor Books, 1976.

Hall, P. M. Structuring symbolic interaction: Communication and power. In D. Nimmo (Ed.), *Communication Yearbook 4.* New Brunswick, NJ: Transaction Books, 1980, 49–60.

Hammersley, M. and Atkinson, P. *Ethnography: Principles in practice.* London: Tavistock Publications, 1983.

Hanna, J. F. Two ideals of scientific theorizing. In M. Burgoon (Ed.), *Communication Yearbook 5.* New Brunswick, NJ: Transaction Books, 1981, 29–47.

Hanushek, E. A. and Jackson, J. E. *Statistical methods for social scientists.* New York: Academic Press, 1977.

Harre, R. and Secord, P. F. *The explanation of social behavior.* Oxford (U.K.): Blackwell, 1972.

Harrington, E. W. The role of speech in liberal education. *The Quarterly Journal of Speech,* 1955, *41,* 219–223.

Harris, L. and Cronen, V. E. A rules-based model for the analysis and evaluation of organizational communication. *Communication Quarterly,* 1979, *27,* 12–28.

Haslett, B. Preschoolers' communicative strategies in gaining compliance from peers: A developmental study. *Quarterly Journal of Speech.* 1983, *69,* 84–99.

Hawes, L. C. *Pragmatics of Analoguing.* Reading, MA: Addison-Wesley, 1975.

Hawes, L. C. Toward a hermaneutic phenomenology of communication. *Communication Quarterly,* 1977, *25,* 30–41.

Hays, W. L. *Statistics for the social sciences.* New York: Holt, Rinehart and Winston, Inc., 1973.

Hefferline, R. F. Communication theory: I. Integrator of the arts and sciences. *The Quarterly Journal of Speech,* 1955, *41,* 223–233.

Helmer, O. *Looking forward: A guide to futures research.* Beverly Hills, CA: Sage Publications, Inc., 1983.

Henkel, R. E. *Tests of significance.* Beverly Hills, CA: Sage Publications, Inc., 1976.

Hiemstra, G. You say you want a revolution? "Information technology" in organizations. In R. Bostrom (Ed.), *Communication Yearbook 7,* Beverly Hills, CA: 1983, 802–827.

Higgenbotham, L. Practice vs. Ph.D. *Journalism Bulletin,* 1924, *1,* 10–12.

Hildebrand, D. K., Laing, J. D. and Rosenthal, H. *Analysis of ordinal data.* Beverly Hills, CA: Sage Publications, Inc., 1977.

Hindess, B. *Philosophy and methodology in the social sciences.* Hassocks, Sussex (U.K.): The Harvester Press, 1977.

Hirokawa, R. Y. Group communication and problem-solving effectiveness: An investigation of group phases. *Human Communication Research,* 1983, *9,* 291–305.

Hocking, J. E. Sports and spectators: Intra-audience effects. *Journal of Communication,* 1982, *32,* 100–108.

Hofstetter, C. R. and Strand, P. J. Mass media and political issue perceptions. *Journal of Broadcasting,* 1983, *27,* 345–358.

Hollstein, M. C. Personal letter, January 26, 1985.

Hopper, R., Knapp, M. L. and Scott, L. Couples' personal idioms: Exploring intimate talk. *Journal of Communication,* 1981, *31,* 23–33.

Huberman, A. M. and Miles, M. B. Drawing valid meaning from qualitative data: Some techniques of data reduction and display. Paper presented at the *American Educational Research Association* convention, 1982.

Huck, S. W. and Sandler, H. M. *Rival hypotheses: Alternative interpretations of data based conclusions.* New York: Harper and Row, 1979.

Husserl, E. *Ideas.* London: George Allen and Unwin, 1931.

Husserl, E. *Cartesian meditation.* The Hague: Martinus Nijhoff, 1970.

Husserl, E. *The Paris lectures.* The Hague: Martinus Nijhoff, 1970.

Huston, T. L. Conceptual and methodological issues in studying close relationships. *Journal of Marriage and the Family,* 1982, *43,* 901–925.

Hyde, Grant. M. Taking stock after 24 years. *Journalism Quarterly,* 1929, *6,* 8–12.

Jacobs, S. and Jackson, S. Strategy and structure in conversational influence attempts. *Communication Monographs,* 1983, *50,* 285–304.

James, L. R., Mulaik, S. A. and Brett, J. M. *Casual Analysis: Assumptions, models and data.* Beverly Hills, CA: Sage Publications, Inc., 1982.

James, N. C. and McCain, T. A. Television games preschool children play: Patterns, themes and uses. *Journal of Broadcasting,* 1982, *26,* 783–800.

Janson, C. Some problems of longitudinal research in the social sciences. In F. Schulsinger, S. A. Mednick and J. Knop (Eds.), *Longitudinal research: Methods and uses in behavioral science.* Boston: Martinus Nijhoff, 1981, 19–55.

Jicks, T. O. Mixing qualitative and quantitative methods: Triangulation in action. *Administrative Science Quarterly,* 1979, *24,* 602–611.

Johnson, E. M. The utilization of the social sciences. *Journalism Bulletin,* 1927, *4,* 30–35.

Johnson, E. M. What of the future of instruction in journalism? *Journalism Quarterly,* 1930, *7,* 31–39.

Johnson, J. M. *Doing field research.* New York: The Free Press, 1975.

Kanter, R. M. *Men and women of the corporation.* New York: Basic Books, 1977.

Kaplan, A. *The conduct of inquiry.* San Francisco: Chandler Publishing Co., 1964.

Kapp, J. E. and Barnett, G. A. Predicting organizational effectiveness from communication activities: A multiple indicator model. *Human Communication Research,* 1983, *9,* 239–254.

Keat, R. and Urry, J. *Social theory as science.* London: Routledge and Kegan Paul, 1982.

Kelso, J. A. Science and the rhetoric of reality. *Central States Speech Journal,* 1980, *31,* 17–29.

Kerlinger, F. N. *Foundations of behavioral research* (2d ed.). New York: Holt, Rinehart and Winston, Inc., 1973.

Kerlinger, F. N. *Behavioral research: A conceptual approach.* New York: Holt, Rinehart and Winston, Inc., 1979.

Kerlinger, F. N. and Pedhazur, E. J. *Multiple regression in behavioral research.* New York: Holt, Rinehart and Winston, Inc., 1973.

Kidder, L. H. Qualitative research and quasi-experimental frameworks. In M. B. Brewer and B. E. Collins (Eds.), *Scientific inquiry and the social sciences.* San Francisco: Jossey-Bass Publishers, 1981.

Kirk, R. E. *Experimental design: Procedures for the behavioral sciences* (2d ed.). Monterey, CA: Brooks Cole Publishing Co., 1982.

Koch, S. Psychology and emerging conceptions of knowledge as unitary. In T. W. Wann (Ed.), *Behaviorism and phenomenology.* Chicago: The University of Chicago Press, 1964.

Koch, S. and Deetz, S. Metaphor analysis of social reality in organizations. *Journal of Applied Communication Research,* 1981, *9,* 1–15.

Kreps, G. L. Using Interpretive research: The development of a socialization program at RCA. In L. L. Putnam and M. E. Pacanowsky, (Eds.), *Communication and organizations: An interpretive approach,* Beverly Hills CA: Sage Publications, Inc., 1983, 243–246.

Krippendorff, K. Values, modes and domains of inquiry into communication. *Journal of Communication,* 1969, *19,* 105–133.

Krippendorff, K. An epistemological foundation for communication. *Journal of Communication,* 1984, *34,* 21–36.

Krippendorff, K. On the ethics of constructing communication. Paper presented at the *International Communication Association* convention, Honolulu, HI, 1985.

Krueger, D. L. Marital decision making: A language-action analysis. *Quarterly Journal of Speech,* 1982, *68,* 273–287.

Kuhn, T. S. *The structure of scientific revolutions* (2d ed.). Chicago: The University of Chicago Press, 1970.

L. W. M. Anniversaries recall history. *Journalism Bulletin,* 1924, *1,* 28.

Lakatos, I. Falsification and the methodology of scientific research programmes. In Lakatos, I. and Musgrave, A. (Eds.), *Criticism and the growth of knowledge.* Cambridge (U.K.): Cambridge University Press, 1970, 91–195.

Lakoff, G. and Johnson, M. *Metaphors we live by.* Chicago: The University of Chicago Press, 1980.

Leahey, T. H. *A history of psychology.* Englewood Cliffs, NJ: Prentice-Hall, Inc., 1980.

Leedy, P. D. *How to read research and understand it.* New York: Macmillan Publishing Co., 1981.

Leiter, K. *A primer of ethnomethodology.* New York: Oxford University Press, 1980.

Lemish, D. The rules of viewing television in public places. *Journal of Broadcasting,* 1982, *26,* 757–782.

Lester, M. and Hadden S. C. Ethnomethodology and grounded theory methodology. *Urban Life,* 1980, *9,* 3–33.

Lindlof, T. (Ed.) *Natural audiences: Qualitative research of media uses and effects.* Norwood, NJ: Ablex Publishing Corporation, in press.

Loether, H. J. and McTavish, D. G. *Descriptive and inferential statistics: An introduction.* Boston: Allyn and Bacon, 1980.

Lofland, J. *Analyzing social settings*. Belmont, CA: Wadsworth Publishing Company, Inc., 1971.

Lofland, J. *Doing social life*. New York: John Wiley and Sons, Inc., 1976.

Lovejoy, E. P. *Statistics for math haters*. New York: Harper and Row, 1975.

Lull, J. The social uses of television. *Human Communication Research,* 1980, *6,* 197–209.

Lull, J. The rules of mass communication. Paper presented at the *International Communication Association* convention, Minneapolis, 1981.

Lull, J. A rules approach to the study of television and society. *Human Communication Research,* 1982a, *9,* 3–16.

Lull, J. How families select television programs: A mass observational study. *Journal of Broadcasting,* 1982b, *26,* 801–812.

Lustig, M. W. and King, S. W. The effect of communication apprehension and situation on communication strategy choices. *Human Communication Research,* 1980, *7,* 74–82.

Luxon, N. N., Sutton, A. A., Brinton, J. E. and Westley, B. The integration of journalism and the social sciences. *Journalism Quarterly,* 1955, *32,* 463–475.

Lyman, S. M. and Scott, M. B. *The drama of social reality*. New York: Oxford University Press, 1975.

Mandelbaum, M. Social facts. In Ryan, A. (Ed.), *The philosophy of social explanation*. London: Oxford University Press, 1973, 105–118.

MacIntyre, A. *After virtue* (2d ed.), Notre Dame, IN: University of Notre Dame Press, 1984.

Marlier, J. T. What is speech communication, anyway? *Communication Education,* 1980, *29,* 324–327.

McCall, G. J. and Simmons, J. L. (Eds.). *Issues in participant observation*. Reading, MA: Addison-Wesley Publishing Co., 1969.

McCall, G. J. and Simmons, J. L. *Identities and interactions*. New York: The Free Press, 1978.

McHugh, P. *Defining the situation*. Indianapolis: The Bobbs-Merrill Company, Inc., 1968.

McLaughlin, M. L., Cody, M. J. and Rosenstein, N. E. Account sequences in conversations between strangers. *Communication Monographs,* 1983, *50,* 102–125.

McNemar, Q. *Psychological statistics* (4th ed.). New York: John Wiley and Sons, Inc., 1969.

Mead, G. H. *Mind, self and society*. Chicago: The University of Chicago Press, 1934.

Meltzer, B. N., Petras, J. W. and Reynolds, L. T. *Symbolic interactionism: Genesis, varieties and criticism*. London: Routledge and Kegan Paul, 1975.

Mettetal, B. Fantasy, gossip and self-disclosure: Children's conversations with friends. In R. Bostrom (Ed.), *Communication Yearbook 7*. Beverly Hills CA: Sage Publications, Inc., 1983, 717–736.

Meyer, T. P. The effects of viewing justified and unjustified fictional versus real film violence on aggressive behavior. Unpublished Ph.D. dissertation, Ohio University, 1970.

Meyer, T. P., Traudt, P. J. and Anderson, J. A. Non-traditional mass communication research methods. In D. Nimmo (Ed.), *Communication Yearbook 3*. New Brunswick, NJ: Transaction Books, 1980. 261–276.

Miles, M. B. Qualitative data as an attractive nuisance: The problem of analysis. *Administrative Science Quarterly,* 1979, *24,* 590–601.

Miller, D. C. *Handbook of research design and social measurement* (3d ed.). New York: D. McKay, 1977.

Miller, G. R. Taking stock of a discipline. *Journal of Communication,* 1983, *33,* 31–41.

Mintzberg, H. *The nature of managerial work.* New York: Harper and Row, 1973.

Mioulis, G. and Michener, R. D. *An introduction to sampling.* Dubuque, IA: Kendall Hunt Publishing Co., 1976.

Mitchell, W. T. C. (Ed.). *On narrative.* Chicago: The University of Chicago Press, 1981.

Mitroff, I. I. and Kilmann, R. H. *Methodological approaches to social science.* San Francisco: Jossey-Bass Publishers, 1982.

Mitroff, I. I. and Mason, R. O. *Creating a dialectical social science.* Boston: D. Reidel Publishing Company, 1981.

Montgomery, B. M. Trait, interactionist and behavior assessment variables in open communication. *Communication Research,* 1980, *7,* 479–494.

Morgan, G. Paradigms, metaphors and puzzle solving in organizational theory. *Administrative Science Quarterly,* 1980, *25,* 605–622.

Morgan, G. (Ed.). *Beyond method: Strategies for social research.* Beverly Hills, CA: Sage Publications, Inc., 1983.

Morgan, G. and Smircich, L. The case for qualitative research. *Academy of Management Review,* 1980, *5,* 491–500.

Morris, G. H. and Hopper, R. Remediation and legislation in everyday talk: How communicators achieve consensus. *Quarterly Journal of Speech,* 1980, *66,* 266–274.

Morris, M. B. *An excursion into creative sociology.* New York: Columbia University Press, 1977.

Mueller, J. H., Schuessler, K. F. and Costner, H. L. *Statistical reasoning in sociology* (3d ed.). Boston: Houghton Mifflin Co., 1977.

Murphy, L. W. Schools of journalism, past and future. *Journalism Quarterly,* 1938, *15,* 35–43.

Nicholson, M. *The scientific analysis of social behavior: A defence of empiricism in social science.* New York: St. Martin's Press, 1983.

Nisbett, R. and Ross, L. *Human Inference.* Englewood Cliffs, NJ: Prentice-Hall, 1980.

Nunnally, J. C. *Psychometric theory* (2d ed.). New York: McGraw-Hill Book Co., 1978.

O'Donnell-Trujillo, N. E. Managerial work as communicative performance. Unpublished Ph.D. dissertation, University of Utah, 1983.

O'Keefe, D. J. Logical empiricism and the study of human communication. *Speech Monographs,* 1975, *42,* 169–183.

O'Keefe, D. J., Nash, K. and Liu, J. The perceived utility of advertising, *Journalism Quarterly,* 1981, *58,* 534–542.

O'Neill, J. M. The national association. *Quarterly Journal of Public Speaking,* 1915, *1,* 51–58.

O'Neill, J. M. The professional outlook. *Quarterly Journal of Public Speaking,* 1916, *2,* 52–63.

O'Reilly, III, C. A. and Anderson, J. C. Trust and the communication of performance appraisal information: The effect of feedback on performance and job satisfaction. *Human Communication Research,* 1980, *6,* 290–298.

Pacanowsky, M. E. A small-town cop: Communication in, out and about a crisis. In L. L. Putnam and M. E. Pacanowsky, (Eds.), *Communication and organizations: An interpretive approach.* Beverly Hills, CA: Sage Publications, Inc., 1983 261–282.

Pacanowsky, M. An idosyncratic compilation of the 27 do's and don't's of organizational culture research. Paper presented at the *Speech Communication Association* convention, Chicago, 1984.

Pacanowsky, M. E. and Anderson, J. A. Cop talk and media use. *Journal of Broadcasting,* 1982, *26,* 741–756.

Pacanowsky, M. E. and O'Donnell-Trujillo, N. Organizational communication as cultural performance. *Communication Monographs,* 1983, *50,* 126–147.

Palmgreen, P. Uses and gratifications: A theoretical perspective. In R. Bostrom (Ed.), *Communication Yearbook 8.* Beverly Hills, CA: Sage Publications, Inc., 1984, 20–55.

Palmgreen, P. and Rayburn, II, J. D. Gratifications sought and media exposure. *Communication Research,* 1982, *9,* 561–580.

Patton, M. Q. *Qualitative evaluation methods.* Beverly Hills, CA: Sage Publications, Inc., 1980.

Paulson, S. F. Speech communication and the survival of academic disciplines. *Communication Education,* 1980, *29,* 319–323.

Pearce, W. B. Consensual rules in interpersonal communication: A reply to Cushman and Whiting. *Journal of Communication,* 1973, *23,* 160–168.

Pearce, W. B. Metatheorétical concerns in communication. *Communication Quarterly,* 1977, *25,* 3–6.

Pelto, P. J. and Pelto, G. H. *Anthropological research: The structure of inquiry* (2d ed.). Cambridge (U.K.): Cambridge University Press, 1978.

Perloff, R. M. Journalism Research: A 20-year perspective. *Journalism Quarterly,* 1976, *53,* 123–126.

Peter, J. P. and Olson, J. C. Is science marketing? *Journal of Marketing,* 1983, *47,* 111–125.

Pettigrew, A. M. On studying organizational cultures. In J. Van Maanen (Ed.), *Qualitative methodology.* Beverly Hills, CA: Sage Publications, Inc., 1983, 87–104.

Pettigrew, L. S. Organization communication and the S. O. B. theory of management. *The Western Journal of Speech Communication,* 1982, *46,* 179–191.

Philipsen, G. Speaking "like a man" in Teamsterville: Cultural patterns in role enactment in an urban neighborhood. *Quarterly Journal of Speech,* 1975, *61,* 13–22.

Phillips, A. F. Computer conferences: Success or failure. In R. Bostrom (Ed.), *Communication Yearbook 7.* Beverly Hills, CA: Sage Publications, Inc., 1983, 837–856.

Pingree, S. Children's cognitive processes in constructing social reality. *Journalism Quarterly,* 1983, *60,* 415–422.

Plimpton, G. *Paper lion.* New York: Harper and Row, 1966.

Plummer, K. *Documents of life: An introduction to the problems and literature of a humanistic method.* London: George Allen and Unwin, 1983.

Poole, M. S., McPhee, R. D. and Seibold, D. R. A comparison of normative and interactional explanations of group decision-making: Social decision schemes versus valence distributions. *Communication Monographs,* 1982, *49,* 1–19.

Popper, K. R. *The logic of scientific discovery.* London: Hutchinson, 1959.

Putnam, L. L. The interpretive perspective: An alternative to functionalism. In Putnam, L. L. and Pacanowsky, M. (Eds.), *Communication and organizations: An interpretive approach.* Beverly Hills, CA: Sage Publications, 1983, 31–54.

Putnam, L. L. and Pacanowsky, M. E. (Eds.) *Communication and organizations: An interpretive approach.* Beverly Hills, CA: Sage Publications, Inc., 1983.

Putnam, L. L. and Sorenson, R. L. Equivocal messages in organizations. *Human Communication Research,* 1982, *8,* 114–132.

Rahskopf, H. G. Speech at mid-century. *The Quarterly Journal of Speech,* 1951, *37,* 147–152.

Raj, D. *The design of sample surveys.* New York: McGraw-Hill Book Company, 1972.

Rawlins, W. K. Friendship as a communicative achievement: A theory and an interpretive analysis of verbal reports. Unpublished Ph.D. dissertation, Temple University, 1981.

Rawlins, W. K. Negotiating close friendship: The dialectic of conjunctive freedoms. *Human Communication Research,* 1983, *9,* 255–266.

Reardon, K. K. Conversational deviance: A structural model. *Human Communication Research,* 1982, *9,* 59–74.

Reid, L. N. and Frazer, C. F. Television at play. *Journal of Communication,* 1980, *30,* 66–73.

Reynolds, H. T. *Analysis of nominal data.* Beverly Hills, CA: Sage Publications, Inc., 1977.

Reynolds, P. D. *Ethical dilemmas and social science research.* San Francisco: Jossey-Bass Publishers, 1979.

Reynolds, P. D. *Ethics and social science research.* Englewood Cliffs, NJ: Prentice-Hall, 1982.

Richmond, V. P., Davis, L. M., Saylor, K. and McCroskey, J. C. Power strategies in organizations: Communication techniques and messages. *Human Communication Research,* 1984, *11,* 85–108.

Rieke, R. D. and Sillars, M. O. Argumentation and the decision making process (2d ed.). Glenview, IL: Scott Foresman and Co., 1984.

Rogers, E. M. The empirical and critical schools of communication research. In M. Burgoon (Ed.), *Communication Yearbook 5.* New Brunswick, NJ: Transaction Books, 1981, 125–143.

Rosengren, K. E. Communication research: One paradigm, or four? *Journal of Communication,* 1983, *33,* 185–207.

Rosenthal, R. *Experimenter effects in behavioral research.* New York: Irvington Press, 1976.

Rosenthal, R. The "file drawer problem" and tolerance for null results. *Psychological Bulletin,* 1978, *85,* 185–193.

Rosenthal, R. and Rosnow, R. L. (Eds.). *Artifact in behavioral research.* New York: Academic Press, 1969.

Rowland, Jr., W. D. *The politics of TV violence: Policy uses of communication research.* Beverly Hills, CA: Sage Publications, Inc., 1983.

Runyon, R. P. and Haber, A. *Fundamentals of behavioral statistics* (4th Ed.) Reading, MA: Addison-Wesley Publishing Co., 1980.

Sammons, J. L. *Literary sociology and practical criticism.* Bloomington, IN: Indiana University Press, 1977.

Sanday, P. R. The ethnographic paradigm(s). *Administrative Science Quarterly,* 1979, *24,* 527–538.

Schatzman, L. and Strauss, A. L. *Field research.* Englewood Cliffs, NJ: Prentice-Hall Inc., 1973.

Scheflen, A. *How behavior means.* Garden City, NY: Anchor Books, 1974.

Schramm, W. Education for journalism: Vocational, general or professional? *Journalism Quarterly,* 1947, *24,* 9–18.

Schramm, W. Twenty years of journalism research. *Public Opinion Quarterly,* 1957, *21,* 91–107.

Schutz, A. *The phenomenology of the social world.* Translated by G. Walsh and F. Lehnert. Evanston, IL: Northwestern University Press, 1967.

Schwartz, H. and Jacobs, J. *Qualitative sociology: A method to the madness.* New York: The Free Press, 1979.

Searle, J. R. *Speech acts.* Cambridge (U.K.): Cambridge University Press, 1969.

Secord, P. (Ed.). *Explaining human behavior.* Beverly Hills, CA: Sage Publications, Inc., 1982.

Shaffir, W. B., Stebbins, R. A. and Turowetz, A. (Eds.). *Fieldwork experience: Qualitative approaches to social research.* New York: St. Martin's Press, 1980.

Shweder, R. A. and LeVine, R. A. (Eds.). *Culture theory: Essays on mind, self and emotion.* Cambridge (U.K.): Cambridge University Press, 1984.

Siegel, S. *Nonparametric Statistics.* New York: McGraw-Hill, 1956.

Simon, C. T. Speech as science. *The Quarterly Journal of Speech,* 1951, *37,* 281–293.

Smart, M. N. Two responsibilities of journalism schools. *Journalism Quarterly,* 1955, *32,* 349–352.

Smircich, L. Concepts of culture and organizational analysis. *Administrative Science Quarterly,* 1983, *28,* 339–358.

Smith, D. K. Origin and development of departments of speech. In K. R. Wallace (Ed.), *A history of speech education in America.* New York: Appleton-Century-Crofts, Inc., 1954, 447–470.

Snedecor, G. W. and Cochran, W. G. *Statistical methods* (6th Ed.). Ames, IA: The Iowa State University Press, 1967.

Sommer, R. and Sommer, B. B. *A practical guide to behavioral research.* New York: Oxford University Press, 1980.

Spradley, J. P. *Participant observation.* New York: Holt, Rinehart and Winston, 1980.

Stern, P. C. *Evaluating social science research.* New York: Oxford University Press, 1979.

Stevens, S. S. Mathematics, measurement and psychophysics. In S. S. Stevens (Ed.), *Handbook of experimental psychology.* New York: John Wiley and Sons, Inc., 1951.

Stoll, E. L. A naturalistic study of talk in the classroom. Unpublished Ph.D. Dissertation, University of Utah, 1983.

Stovall, J. G. Foreign policy issue coverage in the 1980 presidential campaign. *Journalism Quarterly,* 1982, *59,* 531–540.

Strine, M. S. and Pacanowsky, M. E. How to read interpretive accounts of organizational life: Narrative bases of textual authority. *The Southern Speech Communication Journal,* 1985, *50,* 283–297.

Sudman, S. *Applied sampling.* New York: Academic Press, 1976.

Sudman, S. and Bradburn, N. M. *Asking questions: A practical guide to questionnaire design.* San Francisco: Jossey-Bass Publishers, 1982.

Suppe, F. (Ed.). *The structure of scientific theories.* Urbana: University of Illinois Press, 1977.

Susman, G. I. and Evered, R. D. An assessment of the scientific merits of action research. *Administrative Science Quarterly,* 1978, *23,* 582–601.

Sutton, A. A. *Education for journalism in the United States.* Evanston, IL: Northwestern University Press, 1945.

Tan, A. S. and Scruggs, K. J. Does exposure to comic book violence lead to aggression in children? *Journalism Quarterly,* 1980, *57,* 579–583.

Tardy, C. H., Gaughan, B. J., Hemphill, M. R. and Crockett. N. Media agendas and political participation. *Journalism Quarterly,* 1981, *58,* 624–627.

Taylor, K. P., Buchanan, R. W., Pryor, B. and Strawn, D. U. How do jurors reach a verdict? *Journal of Communication,* 1981, *31,* 37–42.

Thayer, L. On "doing" research and "explaining" things. *Journal of Communication,* 1983, *33,* 80–91.

Thomas, D. *Naturalism and social science: A post-empirical philosophy of social science.* Cambridge (U.K.): Cambridge University Press, 1979.

Thompson, L. and Walker, A. J. The dyad as the unit of analysis: Conceptual and methodological issues. *Journal of Marriage and the Family,* 1982, *44,* 889–900.

Toulmin, S. E. Rules and their relevance for understanding human behavior. In T. Mischel (Ed.), *Understanding other persons.* Totowa, NJ: Rowman and Littlefield, 1974, 185–215.

Tunstall, J. The British press in the age of television. In, Whitney, D. C., Wartella, E. and Windahl, S. (Eds.), *Mass Communication Review Yearbook,* Vol. 3. Beverly Hills, CA: Sage Publications, Inc., 1982, 463–480.

Ubell, E. Sex in America today. *Parade* magazine, October 28, 1984, 11–13.

Van de Geer, J. P. *Introduction to multivariate analysis for the social sciences.* San Francisco: W. H. Freeman and Company, 1971.

Van Maanen, J. Observations on the making of policemen. *Human Organization,* 1973, *32,* 407–417.

Van Maanen, J. (Ed.). *Qualitative methodology.* Beverly Hills, CA: Sage Publications, Inc., 1983.

Van Maanen, J., Dabbs, Jr., J. M. and Faulkner, R. R. *Varieties of qualitative research.* Beverly Hills, CA: Sage Publications, Inc., 1982.

Walker, H. M. *Studies in the history of statistical method with special reference to certain educational problems.* Baltimore: The Williams and Wilkins Co., 1929.

Wann, T. W. (Ed.) *Behaviorism and phenomenology.* Chicago: The University of Chicago Press, 1964.

Watzslavick, P. *How real is real?* New York: Random House, 1976.

Wax, M. L. and Wax, R. Great tradition, little tradition and formal education. In M. L. Wax, S. Diamond, and F. O. Gearing (Eds.), *Anthropological perspectives on education.* New York: Basic Books, Inc., 1971, 3–18.

Wax, R. H. *Doing fieldwork.* Chicago: The University of Chicago Press, 1971.

Weaver, D. H. and Grey, R. G. Journalism and mass communication research in the United States. In G. C. Wilhoit and H. de Bock, *Mass Communication Review Yearbook,* Vol. 1. Beverly Hills, CA: Sage Publications, Inc., 1980 124–151.

Webb, E. J., Campbell, D. T., Schwartz, R. D. and Sechrest, L. *Unobtrusive measures: Nonreactive research in the social sciences.* Chicago: Rand McNally, 1966.

Weber, L. J. and Fleming, D. B. Media use and student knowledge of current events. *Journalism Quarterly,* 1983, *60,* 356–358.

Weber, M. *The methodology of the social sciences.* Translated and edited by E. A. Shils and H. A. Finch. Glencoe, IL: The Free Press, 1949.

Webster, J. G. and Wakshlag, J. J. The impact of group viewing on patterns of television program choice. *Journal of Broadcasting,* 1982, *26,* 445–455.

Webster, S. Dialogue and fiction in ethnography. *Dialectical Anthropology,* 1982, *7,* 91–114.

Webster's new world dictionary of the American language, college edition. Cleveland: The World Publishing Co., 1960.

Willbrand, M. L. and Rieke, R. D. Reason giving in children's supplicatory compliance gaining. *Communication Monographs,* 1986, *53,* 47–60.

Willemsen, E. W. *Understanding statistical reasoning.* San Francisco: W. H. Freeman and Co., 1974.

Willey, M. M. Quantitative methods and research in journalism. *Journalism Quarterly,* 1935, *12,* 255–265.

Williams, B. *A sampler on sampling.* New York: John Wiley and Sons, Inc., 1978.

Wimmer, R. D. and Dominick, J. R. *Mass media research.* Belmont, CA: Wadsworth Publishing Co., 1983.

Winans, J. A. The need for research. *Quarterly Journal of Public Speaking,* 1915, *1,* 17–23.

Winch, P. *The idea of a social science.* London: Routledge and Kegan Paul, 1958.

Woelfel, J., Cody, M. J., Gillham, J. and Holmes, R. A. Basic premises of multidimensional attitude change theory: An experimental analysis. *Human Communication Research,* 1980, *6,* 153–167.

Wolf, M. A., Meyer, T. P. and White, C. A rules-based study of television's role in the construction of social reality. *Journal of Broadcasting,* 1982, *26,* 813–829.

Woolbert, C. H. The organization of departments of speech in universities. *Quarterly Journal of Public Speaking,* 1916, *2,* 64–77.

Woolbert, C. H. Suggestions as to methods in research. *Quarterly Journal of Public Speaking,* 1917, *3,* 12–26.

Wright, R. L. D. *Understanding statistics.* New York: Harcourt Brace Jovanovich, Inc., 1976.

Zahn, C. J. A reexamination of conversational repair. *Communication Monographs,* 1984, *51,* 56–66.

Ziff, H. M. The journalist's body of knowledge. In American Newspaper Publishers Association, *Proceedings: Education for newspaper journalists in the seventies and beyond.* Washington: ANPA Foundation, 1973, 73–86.

Zillmann, D. and Bryant, J. Pornography, sexual callousness and the trivialization of rape. *Journal of Communication,* 1982, *32,* 10–21.

Ziman, J. M. *Public knowledge.* Cambridge (U.K.): Cambridge University Press, 1968.

Ziman, J. M. *Reliable knowledge: An exploration of the grounds for belief in science.* Cambridge (U.K.): Cambridge University Press, 1978.

Zuckerman, D. M., Singer, D. G. and Singer, J. L. Television viewing, children's reading and related classroom behavior. *Journal of Communication,* 1980, *30,* 166–174.

INDEX

INDEX